Written in Blood

Ethnic Identity and the
Struggle for Human Harmony

Written in Blood

*Ethnic Identity and the
Struggle for Human Harmony*

Stephen Worchel

University of Southern Maine

WORTH PUBLISHERS

Written in Blood: Ethnic Identity and the Struggle for Human Harmony

Printed in the United States of America.
Library of Congress Catalog Card Number: 98-86528

ISBN: 1-57259-648-1

Printing: 1 2 3 4 5—02 01 00 99 98

Executive Editor: Catherine Woods
Project Director: Timothy Prairie
Development Editor: Jennifer E. Sutherland
Design Director: Jennie R. Nichols
Cover Design: Lissi Sigillo
Interior Design: Ruttle, Shaw & Wetherill, Inc.
Production and Composition: Ruttle, Shaw & Wetherill, Inc.
Printing and Binding: R. R. Donnelly & Sons

WORTH PUBLISHERS
33 Irving Place
New York, New York 10003

http://www.worthpublishers.com

To three people who matter to me:
Phil, Libby, and Dawna

Contents

CHAPTER 4

Looking Inward: The Dynamics of Groups and Interpersonal Relations   86

CHAPTER 6

CHAPTER 7

CHAPTER 8

Whose Woods Are These? Expanding the Responsibility for Reducing Conflict   211

CHAPTER 9

Preface

I am not sure of the exact age at which I discovered that I was different from most people in my neighborhood, but I do remember the incident as if it were yesterday. My best friend told me that his mother had forbidden him to play with me because I was Jewish. He then told me his mother had said that "we" had killed Jesus, and he innocently asked me why we had done that. I wasn't sure who the "we" was, and I certainly couldn't figure why we would want to kill Jesus. Despite the admonishment, we remained steadfast friends and the incident never came up again. But it set the stage for me to view my world in a different way. Slowly Austin, Texas, became a town not of people, but of groups. There were Mexicans, blacks, Chinese, Irish, Jews, Catholics, and Protestants. There were neighborhoods where Jews could not live, restaurants where blacks could not eat, and schools that excluded Mexicans. People were hated or hired, excluded or embraced because of the groups to which they belonged. And of all the groupings that guided social interaction, ethnicity was a top contender. The quirk of the grand social lottery that placed people in ethnic groups also shaped the road map of social relations.

The world has undergone dramatic change in the nearly fifty years since my friend asked me why we had killed Jesus. I can travel around the world in the time it took me to traverse Texas. The computer is my window to the world, allowing me to compute the most complex statistical problems in seconds and to contact my colleagues around the world at my whim. Diseases that would have killed or crippled tens of thousands of people now hardly merit mention in a dictionary. So much has changed in so many areas of life. But at the same time, so little has changed in the way people relate (or do not relate) to one another. The world is still divided into groups, and people still respond to each other on the basis of group membership.

It is ironic that although humans have learned to create life within the confines of a test tube, they have not developed the means to ensure that the results of their creation will not discriminate against or destroy each other on the basis of group identity. Almost any group identity can serve as the basis for conflict and violence. But the most destructive and enduring conflict often revolves around groups into which people are born and will forever remain members, the ethnic group. Ethnic conflict can reach such horrible proportions that it merits a special descriptive term, *genocide*. Nearly every corner of our world has played host to genocide during the last decade.

Although each individual is stamped with an ethnicity at birth, ethnic violence is only the final destination of an unfolding journey that involves individual psychology and group behavior. It begins with the individual adopting an ethnic identity. Individuals with a common identity must perceive themselves as belonging to a common group. The group must then develop a structure, identify friend and foe, and be excited to act.

The process is complex, but it is not outside the grasp of our understanding. Theories and research in fields such as psychology, political science, and sociology shed light on the conditions behind each step of the journey. These theories show us that those who travel down the path toward ethnic conflict and genocide do not begin the journey with evil intentions. Instead, the basic human quest for personal meaning and value and the seemingly innocent goals of groups for survival and identity form the foundation for ethnic violence. As depressing as the story of ethnic conflict can be, the theories that explain its development also instruct us on ways that ethnic conflict can be avoided or controlled.

The aim of this book is to examine the basis for ethnic identity and ethnic conflict. Theories and research in several areas of social science are used to explain why ethnic identity and ethnic conflict are so comfortably linked. However, a central thesis of this book is that ethnic conflict is not necessarily the by-product of ethnic identity. Harmony between ethnic groups and between people of different ethnic identities can be achieved. But just as there is no single cause of ethnic conflict, there is no simple step that can be taken to ensure ethnic harmony. Progress toward developing positive relationships involves a combination of efforts aimed at the individual, the group, and the system in which groups exist. There is no one-time fix. The potential for ethnic violence will forever be with us, so continual vigilance and effort are required to achieve and preserve ethnic harmony.

This volume is not intended to be an exhaustive survey of theory and research related to ethnic identity and intergroup conflict. Rather, I have attempted to draw selectively from the literature to illustrate how the work in social science can give us insight into the personal and group issues related to ethnicity. I have also drawn on my own experiences, both in the laboratory and in my own life, to illustrate and give perspective to many of the points I have made. For obvious reasons, I have altered slightly the details of some examples to protect the identities of those involved.

Although I take full responsibility for the ideas and content of this book, I am indebted to several people who have shaped my thoughts and helped me with this book. It is difficult to remember all the people who have influenced my thinking on this topic over the years. As a student, I was deeply influenced by several professors including Muzafer and Carolyn Sherif, Carl Rogers, Elliot Aronson, Jack Brehm, John Selby, Ned Jones, and Darwyn Linder. More recently, many of my colleagues have given me ideas on several issues related to this volume. Thanks to Daniel Bar-Tal, George Goethals, Sabino Ayerstaran, John Turner, Penny Oakes, William Graziano, J. Francisco Morales, Joel Cooper, Abe Ashkenasi, Kay Deaux, Radmila Prislin, Arnie Vedletz, Dave Thomas, Januz Reykowski, Anne Maass, and Dora Capoza. In the same vein, several of my students have played a tremendous role in helping me develop my ideas. Among this group are Bill Webb, Jon Iuzzini, Frankie Wong, Hank Rothgerber, Carla Goar, and Manuela Ivaldi. With regard to the present manuscript, I had an incredibly supportive cast. The insightful reviews and encouraging comments of David Hamilton, John Dovidio, Jeff Greenberg, and Charles Stangor were most appreciated. Bill Webb, John Iuzzini, Hank Rothgerber, and Carla Gore have also reviewed the manuscript and given me excellent guidance. The support I've received from Worth Publishers could not have been better. All of you were great. Catherine Woods invited me into the fold, kept me on track, and showed great confidence in the project from the beginning. Tim Prairie used a wonderful sense of humor, incredible patience, and a genuine willingness to help keep the process going and to make me feel that I had the Worth team behind me. Jennifer Sutherland was an ideal developmental editor, combining gentleness with firmness. She kept me from butchering the English language, corrected my revisionist view of history, and managed to make the editing process truly enjoyable. Thanks, too, to Peg Markow who guided the book through production. Several people pitched in to give me the clerical help necessary to complete the book. Thanks to Sharmon Toner, Kim Cozzi, Jennifer Ford, and Val Thurmon. Finally, the people closest to me made this project possible and they made it worthwhile. My kids Leah, Jessica, Hannah, and Elise allowed us to build our lives around "the book" and refrained from the temptation to destroy my carefully crafted piles of manuscript. Dawna Coutant not only supplied me with the love and constant support necessary to complete the book, but she was my intellectual soulmate throughout the process. She allowed me to "steal" her ideas, guided me to pertinent literature, and supplied valuable insight. Last, but not least, I want to thank my parents for their support, their caring, and their encouragement. I have the great fortune of having parents who not only support my efforts, but who also guide and challenge my thinking. What more could an author of a book on ethnic identity ask for, but an English instructor and a psychology professor as parents!

Stephen Worchel
Yarmouth, Maine
July, 1998

CHAPTER 1

SEARCHING FOR THE SELF

Setting the Stage for Intergroup Conflict

I have always been fascinated by cemeteries. When I was a kid, my ultimate high—and an undisputed demonstration of courage—came from spending the night in the company of the cold marble testaments and the spirits that resided in the small cemetery on the hill near my home. As a college student, I spent a summer wandering through cemeteries in Europe, spellbound by the tales told on ornate monuments slumbering beneath lonely church spires. And as an older adult, I continue to examine cemeteries with the critical eye of the real estate investor searching for the perfect final home.

My long association with the gardens of rest has had a profound influence on my perspective of death and life. My initial attraction to cemeteries, morbid as it seemed, was based on a fascination with the process of dying and with the dead themselves, contained within the rock walls of these often green, peaceful acres. Given that my experience with the dead was confined to cemeteries, a certain comfort was provided by the walls or fences surrounding cemeteries. These walls held death a prisoner and seemed to keep it isolated from the daily life that was busily being attended to in the world outside the walls.

But several years ago, my perspective changed dramatically. No longer do cemeteries talk to me about the dead who inhabit carefully manicured plots. Now they speak more to me about the lives and thoughts of those living mortals who have been left to carry on. The occasion of my dramatic and complete conversion was an interaction with a plot salesman who accompanied me through a cemetery in Virginia. As we walked over the grounds, he indulged in a running monologue designed to convince me that this was not a bad place to reside, and that I should buy a family plot now, while choice sites were still available.

Before taking me on what was, to him, a spiritual tour of the death gardens, the salesman quizzed me thoroughly about my family background. I had a strange feeling that I was being considered for membership into one of England's finest clubs. But later I learned that the aim was to identify the ideal location for my remains. After carefully examining my religious practices, this earnest fellow began winding his way down my family tree. "What kind of name is Worchel? Where were your grandparents from? Where were their parents from? Did they live in southern Romania or in the area now known as Latvia?" On and on went the questions; deeper and deeper into the family closet we went, rattling bones that had long slumbered undisturbed. The salesman's frustration and irritability grew as he realized how remiss my parents had been in not schooling me about my twelfth-century ancestors. Slowly, a deep feeling of depression accompanied by near-panic began to overtake me; I was on the verge of being rejected as an applicant for a cemetery plot. My lineage, my very identity, was uncertain, and as a result, my barren bones would be unfit to consort with those of more certain lineage, who presently inhabited the hallowed grounds.

My discomfort goaded me to ask why my past was relevant. The salesman was dismayed, and in an effort to forestall an unpleasant outburst of disbelief, he asked me to accompany him on a tour of the grounds. To my untrained eyes, the cemetery looked like a neatly constructed city. Death seemed to be the ultimate equalizer, although I did notice considerable variability in the size and shape of the monuments that had been erected to memorialize the deceased loved ones. My naive notion was quickly dispelled by my more experienced tour guide. "We take great care," he said, "to ensure that people are with their own in their eternal slumber. In death you can reach the supreme goal that is denied to you in life, the goal for which we all strive—to associate only with those who are most like us and most able to understand us. It is through these similar others that we gain strength, inner peace, and indeed a sense of acceptance and identity."

I quickly looked up, thinking that my solemn guide had finally shown a sense of humor in this morbid joke. But he was deadly serious. And through the sincerity of his very deeply held conviction, I began to take a different, more careful, look at the central question he was raising about identity and belonging.

The Holy Grail of Life:
Personal Value, Meaning, Order

Walking among the markers of death, which reach out of the ground like cold fingers grasping for the sky, gives one pause and makes one consider the meaning of life. What was it that each of the inhabitants of the "Pleasant Gardens" cemetery had sought when they still had their feet firmly planted on the ground rather than in the ground? What was I seeking? What did my guide and the other inhabitants of my planet seek?

This question has spawned the species we commonly call philosophers, has given them an exalted role in society, and has placed them on a pedestal. Philosophers live with one eye turned searchingly toward the sky and the other turned inward to the soul, but the most fertile ground for answering the ultimate question about the meaning of life may be in the markers of death behind the cemetery walls. For learning what people achieve in death may be key to unlock what they strive for in life.

Scanning manicured cemetery lawns lays bare a falsehood—the belief that we are all equal in death. There is inequality in death, just as there is in life. The markers of people's final homes range from imposing granite castles to simple carved stones. Modesty is not a characteristic one finds in a cemetery. Rather, death seems to be only another step in our striving for *importance and recognition of personal value*. I don't know of any study on the subject, but walking through the silence, I wondered how the size of the tombstone related to the position that the remembered soul had held in society. I suspect that many a citizen scorned in life balanced the scales by erecting an imposing monument to his or her death. This speculation aside, the pattern of peaks and valleys carved by the tombstones illustrates that the quest for importance and recognition is one of the endless journeys of life (and death).

A second lesson is found in the inscriptions carefully etched in marble and granite. "Here lies Jim Pritchard, who spent his life in service to God." "Sylvia Louise Jankovich: A wife, a mother, a friend." "William W. Webb . . . hated order and convention." "Barry J. Wilson devoted his life to peace and the search for truth." Each poignant, presumably everlasting message gives *meaning* to the life of the deceased. The humanistic psychologist Abraham Maslow (1971) suggests that the highest state of being is reaching our potential, becoming self-actualized. Many people have interpreted this state as one in which we use our skills (whether mental or physical) to their greatest potential. But a more careful reading of Maslow suggests that the highest level of self-actualization may be finding meaning in our lives. Indeed, one of his most engaging works is entitled "The Need to Know and the Fear of Knowing" (Maslow, 1963).

Another goal of life is captured not in the messages on the cold stones in the cemetery but in their placement. Life outside the cemetery walls is hectic, unpredictable, and chaotic. But inside the walls, there is perfect *order*. The grass is maintained at a uniform height; the boundaries of each plot are clearly delineated. The purity of "neighborhoods" is jealously maintained by screening potential residents to ensure a good fit. The slumbering souls are the epitome of good neighbors, even without the good fences mentioned in Robert Frost's famous poem. (A farmer in the poem observes, "Good fences make good neighbors.") Life has few right angles, few absolute rules of behavior, and few clear schedules. Even the weather refuses to be completely predictable, often showering on our picnic in July or melting the snow during our skiing vacation in January. Birth is merely a license to search for order and predictability. But order eludes most of us, except for the mentally ill, throughout our lives. As death approaches, many of us retreat to retirement villages, which often resemble cemeteries of the living with predictable schedules, planned gridwork, and comforting routine. But only in death do we find real order and predictability.

Distilling human existence into a search for importance, meaning, and order offers some insight into the complexities of human behavior. The first and most important step toward attaining these three goals is the development of a self-identity. Roy Baumeister (1986) suggests that self-identity serves as a road map for reaching the answers to three questions: "How shall I relate to others? What shall I strive to become? How will I make the basic decisions needed to guide my life?" (p. 247). It is self-identity, then, that moves us through our journey toward defining our importance, finding meaning in our lives, and establishing order in our personal universe. Because of the role played by self-identity, we spend our lives dealing with our inquisitive soul, which constantly asks us "Who am I?" Within this question we combine our need to know and our fear of knowing. Much of the energy of our lives—indeed, even our dreams—is spent in developing a sense of self, a self-identity, and in fighting our fear of what this identity will tell us about ourselves.

Knowing our destination provides some comfort, but only temporarily. The horizon is quickly clouded with the daunting question of how we reach that destination. How do we develop our self-identity? What events shape and mold it?

Self-Identity: The Importance of Groups

How do we determine who we are, or, for that matter, any of our other characteristics? Let's start with a relatively simple and basic characteristic: beauty. Are you beautiful or handsome? Answering this simple question reveals one of the greatest human curses: our eyes are turned outward. What a terribly cruel limitation! We can see others; we can watch them laugh and cry; we can observe how they act when they are overcome with joy or when they are in the mood for lovemaking. We can see their beauty and their ugliness. But no matter how hard we try, we cannot see ourselves. At the very best we can see only a reflection of ourselves. Indeed, this might explain why we find it so hard to pass by a mirror without gazing at ourselves, or why humans gather like bees to a flowering bush when they have the opportunity to have their faces captured on a video camera.

But silver mirrors are not the only pools that reflect our image. We don't need a mirror to inform us if we are beautiful, intelligent, witty, or friendly, or if we have thousands of other characteristics. We learn how we stand on these dimensions by the way others treat us. Charles Cooley (1902) coined the term "looking-glass self" to capture the fact that we develop a self-image by the ways others treat us. In some cases the image is relatively direct and clear. We're beautiful because others tell us we're beautiful and seek our company. Counting the number of friends we have tells us whether or not we are friendly or popular. An interesting demonstration of how this reflected appraisal affects our self-image was in a study in which schoolchildren were (1) told that others viewed them as neat and tidy, or (2) told that they should be neat and tidy, or (3) told nothing about tidiness. Those children who were told that *others saw them as neat* reported that they viewed themselves as neat; and when observed during the day, they were less likely to litter the school grounds than children in the other two groups (Miller, Brickman, & Bolen, 1975).

Thus others may inform us of many of our traits. But in order to determine some of our other dimensions, we must engage in the more covert process of social comparison (Festinger, 1954), which involves comparing our behavior or standing with that of others. I can count my money to find that I have $100,000 in the bank. But to determine if I am rich, I must compare my bank account with other people's accounts. I'm rich if I find that most other people have only $10,000; but I'm poor if most others have $1 million. A neighborhood in which I once lived was hounded by

One of the most important questions facing each of us concerns our identity. An intriguing issue is the role that ethnicity will play in defining that identity and how decisions about our ethnicity will affect our relationships with others. (Tony Freedman/PhotoEdit)

a rhythmic sound, a "thud-thud-thud-thud" that pierced the relative quiet every day between 4 and 6 P.M. After several weeks of being driven nearly mad by this noise, I investigated the source and found a freckled-faced boy hitting a tennis ball against a wall in his backyard. After watching his hypnotic action for nearly an hour, I decided to become better acquainted with the source of the "thud-thud-thud." I told him that I was impressed with his ability and politely asked him if he was a good tennis player. He shrugged his shoulders and told me that he wouldn't know how good he was until he played Billy Cooper, who, it turned out, was a hotshot player from the adjacent neighborhood.

Leon Festinger argued that we learn about ourselves and develop a self-concept by comparing ourselves with others. We don't make random comparisons; rather, we compare ourselves with others who are similar to us. The freckled-faced tennis player could not determine much about his game by playing a novice. He needed Billy Cooper, who was similar to him in age and experience, to make this comparison. Taken a step further, the process of social comparison may explain why we humans are such social animals. We need others to see our own reflection, to learn about ourselves, to develop our self-image. Further, our reflection is most clearly mirrored by other people who are similar to us, so it is to relatively similar others that we are most attracted. Maybe the reason "birds of a feather flock together" is that each is searching for his or her identity. Indeed, the concern for social comparison may be behind one of the more common human motives: competition. Individuals and groups may eagerly seek competitive exercises to determine how righteous, strong, or worthy they are. My own research found that a group preferred competition with other groups when it had a clear sense of who belonged to it or when its identity was threatened (Worchel, Coutant-Sassic, & Grossman, 1992). As much as we cry for peace and harmony, we secretly yearn at times for competition, to define important characteristics of our group. Peace and harmony tell us little about ourselves or our groups.

Although our reflections in the social mirror give us some sense of place and identity, this is not the whole story. Ask yourself again the question, "Who am I?" Your answer probably includes a number of personal traits such as friendliness, good looks, and happiness. But there is another side that defines who you are—your social identity. This social identity includes reference to groups: "I am a Baptist," "I'm a student at the University of Kentucky," "I'm a Kiwi" (a New Zealander), "I'm the oldest son in the Chung family." The fact that the groups to which we belong help define our identity guides many of our social behaviors and perceptions.

First, we are generally attracted to the best groups that will have us as members. Just as we carefully choose dance partners on the basis of their ability to dance, we choose our groups on the basis of their ability to enhance our identity. You may decide to accept a job, even at a lower salary, with I.B.M. rather than a smaller upstart company because being an employee of I.B.M. reflects positively on you. You may strive to join a prestigious social club because such an association will raise your esteem. Likewise, you will avoid "bad" groups, and you will leave a group when its reputation suffers. Interestingly, a group uses its reputation like currency; an attractive group does not need to directly compensate members as highly as a less attractive group. As noted above, you may not earn as much working for a prestigious company as you will working for an upstart. I once interviewed for a faculty position at an Ivy League university that proudly offered me 20% *less* salary than I was currently making but reminded me how impressive it would be to list this school on my résumé. I might go hungry, but at least others would be impressed that I was starving in good company! The elevation of members' self-identity is part of the compensation package.

Henri Tajfel and John Turner (1986) suggest that once we are part of an in-group, we attempt to enhance its position compared with relevant out-groups of which we are not members. It is this seemingly innocent motivation to enhance our group's image and ultimately our own self-image that sows the seeds of intergroup conflict and discrimination. In a series of intriguing experiments, Tajfel and Turner found that individuals awarded more points or higher pay to members of their own group—even members they have never met—than to people in out-groups. Even more revealing was the finding that individuals chose to increase the relative distance between in-group and out-group even when that choice caused their own group to suffer on an absolute basis. That is, I would be more likely to give my own group $20 and your group $5 than to give my group $50 and your group $45. My research (Rothgerber & Worchel, 1997) has found that the level of discrimination increases in direct proportion to the value of the rewards involved in discrimination.

The more important the dimension for comparison, the more likely people are to discriminate against out-groups. By advantaging our own group relative to other groups, we enhance our own identity.

In many cases, these actions are relatively harmless. I have often marveled at a common practice in the United States: alumni who are well past their prime giving vast sums of money to the athletic departments of universities they once attended. Why would anyone send thousands or millions of dollars to support a football team? These alumni were never members of the team, and most never set foot on the playing field. The answer is quickly found during the football season, when these alumni strut around like roosters, sporting their school colors and informing all those around them how wonderful and powerful their university is. During the season, these aging alumni renew their association with their university, and the team's victory is their victory. As the score mounts up, one can almost see the identities of these faithful supporters take wing and soar. They are the winners, if only by association.

Although this ritual is harmless, even humorous, the situation becomes more somber when we replace the football team with one's country, one's religion, one's ethnic group. In these cases, the attempt to elevate one's group over others is played out in the job market, on the social or educational stage, or on the battlefield. As an employer, I am motivated to hire someone of "my own kind" (in terms of race, religion, or nationality) rather than "other people." Helping "my own kind" helps me. Taking away property, materials, esteem, or life from "other people" enhances the relative position of my group, and consequently makes me look better for being a member of such a strong and powerful group. The desire to build our own esteem, then, is one of the major motivating forces behind prejudice, discrimination, and even war. I will examine this process in more depth in later chapters.

Not All Groups Are Created Equal

Although we might argue that each group to which we belong represents one brick in the wall of our identity, it is clear that some groups play a larger role than others. Indeed, some of the groups to which we belong *are* more important than other groups. We might be able to gauge the importance of our membership in each group by how much inducement it would take to get us to leave that group. Several factors affect the importance of groups. First, there is considerable individual difference in the value given to specific groups. You might consider your church or family central to your identity, while others place the highest value on their work group, neighborhood, or political party. Indeed, two people could belong to the same groups but have different social identities because of the different importance they place on the groups.

A second factor is external events that cause us to focus on or value some groups at a specific time. My identity as a Texan generally lies dormant in the far reaches of my self-concept. However, I was recently dining with a group of friends who began extolling the virtues of living in New York. On and on they went, heaping praise on the Empire State. As I listened, I could almost hear the rumble of slumbering state pride shaking off cobwebs and demanding recognition. At some point in the conversation, I could no longer control my urge to claim proper recognition for Texas. For the next half hour I loudly paraded every positive trait of my state before these shocked New Yorkers. Even my accent took on an extra Texas twang. And for the remainder of the night, I was the most Texan of Texans. I wasn't a human, a male, a father, or even an American. I was a Texan! Thus, external situations such as a personal crisis, an attack on our group, or even the context in which we find ourselves can affect the salience of specific groups that make up our identity. With regard to the context, compare a situation in which you are the only man among a group of women with a situation in which a gathering involves a more equal mixture of the sexes. Chances are that your identity as a man will be more salient in the former case than in the latter. Indeed, a friend confided that she paid little attention to the fact that she was a woman in the workplace until she became a chief executive, a rank typically populated by men. Being a member of a novel or unique group in a particular situation can give that group a more prominent place in our identity (Taylor & Fiske, 1975).

Also related to the issue of context is the finding that our group identities assume increased salience when we are faced with situations that are personally ambiguous or threatening (Ross, 1995). A major tenet of terror management theory is that people rush to the bosom of the group when faced with impending crisis such as death or loss of a job (Greenberg et al., 1990). It is no accident that many Germans embraced the Nazi party during a period of economic insecurity. Cult leaders like David Koresh of the Branch Davidians found willing disciples among the elderly, the poor, and the alienated—people facing an uncertain present and a threatening future. For example, Banton (1997) traces the relationship between the Tutsi and the Hutus in Rwanda and Burundi, showing that there have been long periods of peace between the two tribes, punctuated by flashes of ethnic violence. The periods of violence, Banton argues, have been preceded by social change that led to increased salience of ethnic identity: "The recent history of Rwanda and Burundi shows that ethnic consciousness did not create the conflict, but, to the contrary, the conflict has done much to increase the ethnic consciousness" (p. 76).

A third factor that affects the prominence of a group in the crown of our identity is how easily we can enter or exit the group. In the Western world, we have become accustomed to changing groups as easily as we change our shoes. When a group is no longer to our liking or ceases to serve our purposes, we leave it and seek other groups. We readily change our job, our neighborhood or state of residence, even our spouse. We surf through most groups as we surf the Internet. But there are some groups that are difficult, in some cases impossible, to change, and these become the bedrock of our identity.

In searching for candidates to form the foundation of our social identity, we have some rather stringent criteria. Remember that these groups need to provide us with a relatively safe and secure sense of being, a shield that both defines and protects us. As such, these groups need be large and powerful, capable of defending and rewarding. The ideal candidate groups must have ways to heighten their salience by constantly reminding us that we are members. We'd also like these groups to be enduring so that our sense of self is stable and grounded, for, as Glenn Chafetz (1996) reminds us, "The self-schema, which is the cognitive basis for identity, is the most highly resistant (to change) of all schemas" (p. 8). When we cast our net over our social horizons, we capture three groups that seem to fit these requirements: our nation, our religious group, and our ethnic group. On the positive side, these groups are large, powerful, and enduring. Each of them has become a master at developing symbols (flags, costumes, songs, medallions, physical characteristics) to maintain the salience of the group and ensure that we never forget that we belong. But interestingly, these groups share another, more dubious characteristic: throughout human history, with few exceptions, this unholy trio has been at the root of war and violent destruction. Because of their prominent place in our identities and in our conflicts, let's examine each of these groups in turn.

Nationality: The Color of Our Passport

My home is about 3 miles from my office. To get to my office, I pass a public school, a shopping mall, a hospital, and of course a cemetery. Except for the absence of a baseball diamond, my trip to the office is a journey past the icons of American civilization. In fact, these institutions represent the spectrum of life from birth to death. Despite their different functions and their different appearance, they all have one thing in common: a huge United States flag flies proudly over each. Indeed, I wonder whether there was some contest among them to see who could display the largest flag. (If so, the school won easily.) The important point is that I am reminded four times on my way to work that I am an American (actually a citizen of the United States), and anyone visiting any of these institutions is similarly reminded of his or her nationality.

Patriotism, the love of and devotion to one's country, is the stock in trade of politicians. In the United States, children begin each school day by pledging allegiance to their country. Adults stand at attention as they sing the national anthem and watch the stars and stripes being raised at sporting events. Burning the national symbol, or an irreverent delivery of the national anthem, quickly arouses passionate anger. Few scenes stir the heart like that of a slow, solemn procession following a horse-drawn cart carrying the remains of a national dignitary to a final resting place, flags fluttering at half-mast and the coffin gently covered with the nation's flag.

Indeed, our nationality resides deep within our hearts, but does it have a place in our souls? What is the nation that occupies such a central place in our lives? Boiled down to its bare essentials, a nation is a geopolitical entity defined by identifiable boundaries, a relatively permanent population, and a common political system (Holsti, 1992). We are citizens of a particular country: this fact is clearly stated on our passports. As defined, the nation clearly holds a prominent place when we describe who we are. Some of the most pitied individuals are those who find themselves stateless, people without a country.

But before you plant your personal identity too deep in the soil of your nation, consider what is said, and not said, in the definition of *nation*. Noticeably absent are

We may change our citizenship and take an oath of allegiance to another country, but our ethnic identity remains forever rooted. (AP/Wide World Photos)

words such as *constant* or *enduring*. Indeed, Kleiboer (1994) suggests that our system of sovereign nation-states is a relatively new event, dating back no further than the Peace of Westphalia in 1648, which ended the Thirty Years' War. This makes the nation and the concept of citizenship a relative babe in the history of the human family. Nations and nationalities can come and go and change their complexion. The boundaries of many nations might remind you of the figure of a dieter who alternates between starvation and binge eating. National boundaries do change, often radically, and then the individuals and groups making up the country change accordingly. Compare a world map of today with one from 10 years ago. Gone (or seriously disfigured) are East and West Germany, Czechoslovakia, Yugoslavia, and the U.S.S.R. In their place are new countries: (unified) Germany, the Czech Republic, Slovakia, Serbia, Croatia, Latvia, Estonia, and a dozen others.

The relatively short history of the United States is a case in point, but not an unusual one. Just over 200 years ago, the nation consisted of 13 states huddled along the eastern coast of the North American continent. Like a starved shark the United States quickly began to gobble up land and people. Some residents of Mexico one day found themselves residents of the United States the next, even though they had never changed location. Proud warriors of the Sioux nation found themselves the despised dependents of the United States as the country's boundaries expanded.

Indeed, the Sioux even found that they were initially not even citizens in the nation that had consumed their lands (Brown, 1971). A more recent example of this kind of switcheroo was highlighted in an interesting interaction with a Yugoslav colleague in 1992. At breakfast, he announced, "Last night, while I slept, I changed my identity. I was a Yugoslav, and I woke up a citizen of Serbia. Who knows what I'll be by lunchtime?" He made light of this change, but there was a certain sadness and confusion in his tone. The point is that our nationality can be changed through no action of our own as nations change boundaries.

What is the logic, the rationale, or the reason behind nations? Michael Billig (1995) argues they are an anomaly in a world striving for social order:

> There is something decidedly odd about the nation state system. Nations come in all shapes and sizes. They include entities such as the Republic of China, with its population of 100 million, as well as Tuvalu with its 10,000 citizens. . . . one cannot find a set of "objective" geographical principles which, if expressed in a computer program, would produce the present crop of jealously guarded national boundaries. . . . Nor does the hodgepodge reflect some underlying logic of language or religion. There are monoglot states, and there are polyglot states. . . . Sometimes different religious groups have nationalistic struggles, such as in Northern Ireland, and sometimes the groups do not, as in Scotland. Sometimes language is a symbol of nationalistic aspirations, as in Quebec. Sometimes it is not. (p. 23)

In other words, countries often make little sense. It is hard to find the glue that binds people of a nation together. In many nations, people do not speak a common language, do not pray to the same god, do not share a physical appearance, and do not trace their history to the same roots. And when this common bond is missing, citizens must constantly remind each other that they belong to a common nation. Fences, walls, and armed guards mark the boundaries of nations—in some cases, keeping people in, but in other cases keeping intruders out. Flags, portraits, and statues of present and past patriots are interspersed through public squares and buildings, holidays are invented to emphasize nationhood, and the mass media bombard citizens with messages reminding them of their common bond.

You can change your citizenship with relative ease by moving to another country and swearing allegiance to it. In this sense, nationality is not a skin that encases our bodies. Rather, it is clothing that adorns our bodies. We can choose to change that clothing, albeit with some difficulty. Or events outside our control can change that clothing for us. A new law could remove our citizenship. Therefore, while our nationality may be invited into our personal identity, it is a bit too fickle to serve as the bedrock of that identity.

Religion: Ideas and Ideals

If we cannot rely on nationality as the core element of our identity, can we turn to religion? Indeed, religion is a basic component of many people's self-identity. Not only does it involve a complex set of ideas, ideals, and practices, but its subject is the essence of creation and being. Religion seeks to define why we exist and how we should exist. It attempts to deal with the three basic goals of life: importance, meaning, and order. But if religion is a prominent strand in the fabric of being, is it the linchpin or only a small ornament of our identity?

Religion pays little mind to national boundaries. We are born into a religion, and many forces conspire to have us remain in the religion of our birth. Although nature does not adorn us with the markings of religion, humans have developed elaborate signs and symbols that proclaim their religious beliefs. Their homes, their places of worship, their physical adornments, and even their tattoos may display these signs and symbols, so that no one can mistake their identity. As if this were not sufficient, many religions boast of a supreme being that is capable of seeing into the depths of people's souls, ensuring that people will "keep the faith" even in their private thoughts.

Religion is another element of the bedrock of identity. But like nationality, religion alone is not sufficient to serve as the core of individual identity. This is because, like nationality, religion lacks certain aspects of stability and constancy that are needed to serve as the seat of personal identity.

Religious identity is not necessarily enduring or deeply rooted. People may fabricate their beliefs, being publicly pious but privately wicked and unfaithful. This, then, creates the necessity of a God who is unimpressed with public behavior that is not solidly bolstered by a true heart and soul. People may change their religious beliefs and practices. I have a friend who in the last 20 years has been Methodist, Lutheran, Baptist, Buddhist, Jewish, and Roman Catholic. As he moves from place to place, he adopts the religion of his locale so he "won't feel left out" of the community. Church doctrines—such as those of the Catholics and Mormons—may change and evolve to meet current social, political, and economic realities. So being a Catholic at one point in time or in one location may require very different behavior than being Catholic in another era or location. Jews still debate whether true Jewry is the Orthodox practice or whether those who have climbed out on the more modern Conservative and Reformed branches should be accepted into the sanctuary. Religion, then, may be little more than a pebble, tossed by the tides of time and place, and hardly capable of supplying enduring order and meaning to our self-identity.

And we can add to this stew the perplexing question of what exactly defines a religious group—its beliefs or its rituals? I had the interesting experience of attending services at two churches on the same Sunday. The only points in common between the two churches seemed to be the name Baptist over the entryway and the number of times Jesus Christ was referred to during the service. One congregation consisted solely of African-Americans; the other was all-white. The atmosphere during the service at one church was electric, punctuated by singing, individual displays of emotion, excitement, and spirit. The service at the other church was orderly, controlled, and somber. This is not an isolated example. For instance, Italy, Ireland, Spain, Mexico, and Puerto Rico are Catholic countries. But if you were to compare the beliefs and the practices of Catholics in these countries, you might well wonder how they could all claim the same faith.

And although we might cheer and support the success of proselytizers and missionaries in attracting converts to our religion, it must also give us pause. For if true conversion can be enticed by silver-tongued orators, by instruments of torture, or by offers of social, political, or economic assistance, then these same tools in the hands of a rival religious group can undo the conversion and lead to the adopting of yet another religion. How secure and enduring, then, are our religion and our religious group, and should we hitch the wagon of our identity to this undisciplined team?

The aim of this discussion is not to create a world of atheists or to invite my own destruction at the hand of fundamentalists. Rather, the point is to show that the face of religion has blemishes that caution against building one's identity on it. Although religions profess to have deep insight into issues of meaning, order, and the value of the person, religious beliefs and practices and the nature of religious groups are constantly buffeted by the winds of time, convenience, and changes in current human conditions. As a result, rather than supply meaning , order, and value to individuals, religions must constantly turn to individuals to give them meaning, order, value, and ultimately identity. It is, therefore, precarious to use religion as *the* lodgepole of personal identity.

Ethnicity: The Wellspring of Human Identity

Nations are imperfect candidates to form the basis of human identity because their own identity is subject to change and the logic of their boundaries is murky. Religion also has problems claiming the role as the preeminent foundation of individual identity because its permeable boundaries allow people to enlist and defect with relative ease. Rivers of blood, ruined cities, and piles of rubble are symbols of the importance of religion and nations in human interaction. But because of imperfections (from the perspective of human identity), an examination of national and religious behavior does not completely satisfy our desire to understand human relations and conflicts. Rather, I suggest, there is a third candidate that is more deserving of the starring role on the historical stage of human identity and conflict. That candidate contains elements of both national and religious identity, but its grasp on the individual is more enduring. It captures the individual at the moment of conception; some would argue that it invades the very blood that gives life. It is not a group that anyone can choose to join or leave, no matter how rich, powerful, or charming he or she is. The group is as old as humankind itself. That group is our ethnic group.

Despite the common use of the term *ethnicity* or *ethnic group*, there is actually quite a bit of confusion about what is meant by it. For example, the United States Census of 1980 asked people to indicate their ethnic group by checking "one box." Respondents were given the following choices: White, Black, Hispanic, Japanese, Chinese, Filipino, Korean, Vietnamese, American Indian, Asian Indian, Hawaiian, Guamanian, Samoan, Eskimo, Aleut, and Other (Spickard, 1992). This is a curious set of choices, to say the least. For example, if you are of Greek decent, do you check "White" or "Other"? If you identify yourself with one of the Indian populations of southern Mexico, do you check "Hispanic" or "Other"? This list of "ethnic groups," in fact, includes racial groups, nationalities, and cultural groups as well as ethnic groups. The confusion is also evident in laws. The British Race Relations Act of 1976, which prohibits discrimination on "racial grounds," defines racial grounds as "colour, race, nationality, or ethnic or national origin" (Banton, 1997). Once again, we have racial, national, and ethnic groups lumped under a single heading. Because of the common confusion, let's explore some of the concepts often limited to ethnicity before arriving at a definition of ethnicity itself. (I have already discussed nationality, which denotes citizenship in a recognized nation.)

CULTURE: LEARNED TRADITIONS AND LIFESTYLES.   I entered the field of psychology with the zeal of a pioneer ready to discover new territory; my lofty aims were to develop new theories of human behavior and to conduct penetrating research on human relationships. But when I review my life as a social scientist, I must admit that I have spent more time tilling already plowed fields than clearing new ground. One of my more time-consuming activities has been developing definitions of concepts that the vast majority of the public already seems to understand. The currency of science is precision, so no scientists worth their salt would accept the description of "air" as "the invisible stuff that surrounds us." As scientists, we must determine the characteristics of "the invisible stuff," including its weight, density, temperature, and so on. A similar picture arises when we examine the concept of "culture." Most of us toss this concept around very casually, giving little thought to what is actually meant but simply assuming that everyone knows what we mean. We jump lightly from discussing "pop culture" to "work culture," to "Mexican culture."

But social scientists cannot accept this cavalier approach. They must have precision so that there can be no misunderstanding about the target in their sights. As a result, nearly every discussion of culture begins with a carefully crafted definition. Each definition varies slightly, but each is aimed at clarity and precision. Harris (1983), for example, defines culture as

> the learned, socially acquired traditions and life-styles of the members of a society, including their patterned, repetitive ways of thinking, feeling, and acting. (p. 5)

Many anthropological descriptions emphasize the importance of "shared meaning systems" as an intrinsic part of culture. Joan Metge of New Zealand, an anthropologist, refers to culture as

> a system of symbols and meanings, in terms of which a particular group of people make sense of their worlds, communicate with each other, and plan and live their lives. (1990, p. 6)

The American anthropologist Robert LeVine (1984) emphasizes the collective meanings inherent in culture:

> A recurrent experience of ethnographers is that they are dealing with shared supra-individual phenomena, that culture represents a consensus on a wide variety of meanings among members of an interacting community approximating that of the consensus on language among members of a speech community. (p. 68)

Harry Triandis (1994) casts a wider net:

> Culture is a set of human-made objects and subjective elements that in the past have increased the probability of survival and resulted in satisfaction for the participants in an ecological niche, and thus became shared among those who could communicate with each other because they had a common language and they lived at the same time and place. (p. 22)

Finally, in one of the more modern definitions, Hofstede (1991) pronounces that "culture is the software of the mind."

All these definitions of culture share several features. There is no reference to biological characteristics such as skin color or "race," or to biological ancestry. This is because "culture" involves *learned* patterns of behaviors; anyone so inclined can adopt a culture. Culture is a moving target, changing shape and content as environmental demands change. It is neither rigidly enduring nor socially exclusive (including some people while excluding others). It does not bind us securely into a clearly defined group, past or present.

RACE.   The term *race* has generally been used to categorize people on the basis of physical appearance and sometimes other biological characteristics. In recent years most social scientists have ceased using the term as a way of categorizing human groups because it is seen as having no scientific validity (Phinney, 1996). Indeed, biologists have found more differences within "racial groups" than between them (Zuckerman, 1985). Therefore, it makes little scientific sense to classify people by their race. However, racial categorization is often used. For example, some countries still ask for information about people's "race" or "blood" when collecting census statistics. Police sometimes include a "race" label in descriptions of people to convey information about physical appearance (e.g., Caucasian, black).

Racial or "blood" labels, in their common usage, can best be characterized as mythical or folk taxonomies (Littlefield, Lieberman, & Reynolds, 1982). We cannot deny their everyday use, or the fact that many people identify others by outstanding physical characteristics such as hair texture or skin color. These physical features often form the basis for developing stereotypes of groups. But as a source of personal identity, "race" is suspect. Not only do we have wide variation on physical dimensions within so-called racial groups, but given the narrow focus on physical attributes, race carries no information about other important human dimensions such as religion, language, or culture. Therefore, race (e.g., physical features) may be a prominent dimension for developing personal identity, but it is severely handicapped by its limited focus and scientific imprecision.

ETHNIC GROUP: THE LONG LINE BACKWARD.   Your citizenship depends primarily on where you live. Your religion focuses on shared beliefs and attitudes. Your culture encompasses learned values and behaviors. And your race suggests shared biological characteristics. Ethnic groups involve all these qualities to varying degrees, and others as well. There have been many attempts to define ethnicity, each a bit different from the others (Barth, 1969; Phinney, 1992; Smith, 1986). Rather than review each, let's focus on their common points.

Members of an ethnic group have a shared lineage that they trace back to an ancestral group. In other words, they view themselves as having common roots. This often is expressed in terms of some magic ingredient "in the blood." You've got "Khmer blood" or you come from "Welsh stock." Our ethnicity is carried in our genes, our basic building blocks. Therefore, the center lane in the ethnic highway is biology, which ties one not only to the past but also to present members of the ethnic group. When we develop our family tree, we may adorn it with the stories of princes or robber barons, but the trunk of the tree is the genetic link we share with these heroes and rogues.

Do not make light of the seductive lure of this biological siren. Sociobiologists argue that a major force in life is perpetuation of one's genes (Wilson, 1978). If we follow the implications of this view, we can trace a controversial path. We are attracted to a mate because the offspring of our union will carry our genes into the future. But we do not mate indiscriminately. To do so not only would violate social etiquette but might create biological confusion and even chaos. Therefore, we may choose partners who are genetically compatible (Silverman, 1987)—partners who, from a biological standpoint, will honor and care for our genetic contribution. And who could be more biologically compatible than someone from our own ethnic-genetic line?

But the ancestral bridge of ethnic identity is not composed only of blood and genes. There is also the bond of a common history. Belonging to the same ethnic group implies that our ancestors fought together, worked together, played together, and prayed together. Ethnic groups share a collective memory that lurks just below the surface, awaiting a single spark to kindle the memory and unite the group (Dress, 1994). For example, the Maori people of New Zealand believe that their ancestors arrived there in seven canoes, and each Maori makes his or her claim to the right to address public meetings by tracing an ancestral line to one of the original canoes. The history of an ethnic group sensitizes it to threats that have endangered the group in the past; indeed, the group often develops rituals to remind current members of these threats. Therefore, a cry by an Arab leader to wipe out the Jews in Israel fires their memories of Hitler and brings a unified and swift response—"Never again!" A racial slur or a publicized incident of brutality ignites African-Americans' collective memories of discrimination and mistreatment, dating back to the period of slavery, and instigates collective action. Such shared memories and the desire not to forget the past often produce an interesting anomaly. Members of an ethnic group may refer to, even joke about, past insults and tragedies; but this territory is off-limits to anyone outside the group. For example, an African-American may call one of his or her fellows a "nigger" without exciting a violent response, but someone who is not African-American treads on dangerous ground if he or she utters the "N" word.

Worchel and Rothgerber (1997) point out that shared memories often identify and stereotype an ethnic group's "natural" enemies (other groups). A century from now, Jews will harbor a distrust of Germans, African-Americans will not have forgotten that white Americans enslaved their ancestors, and Bosnian Muslims will be wary of Serbs. It is these collective memories, not biological ties, that identify the "natural" enemies of an ethnic group and are often responsible for recurrent violence. And it is these collective memories that frustrate efforts to develop enduring solutions to ethnic conflicts. These memories, therefore, unite people within the group and exclude outsiders.

The bond formed by a common ancestry can be seen in the greeting Australian Aboriginal people exchange when they meet for the first time. It is usual to define their relationship by identifying a shared network or links through kin or relatives and friends (Von Sturmer, 1981, p. 13):

MAREEBA MAN:	Where you from?
MICKEY:	I'm Edward River man. Where you from?
MAREEBA MAN:	I'm Lama Lama man. . . . Do you know X?
MICKEY:	No. Do you know Y?
MAREEBA MAN:	No. Do you know Z?
MICKEY:	Yes. She's my aunty.
MAREEBA MAN:	That old lady's my granny. I must call you daddy.
MICKEY:	I must call you boy. You give me cigarette.

Network links may be established through descent (genealogies), marriage, knowledge about important events or places, or membership in specific groups or organizations. Recency and regularity of contact at cultural events may also be regarded as important in making a claim to membership in an ethnic group. Clearly, there will be variation among individuals and groups in terms of what criteria are regarded as legitimate in establishing this.

In addition to these bonds, the embrace of ethnicity includes many other historically based links. An ethnic group generally has a "homeland," a place that nurtured it. Human groups may have an insatiable desire to control increasingly large amounts of land and space. The control of property represents power or importance. But the distant drumbeat of our ethnicity makes one piece of property more important than any other; that area is the ancient homeland of our ethnic group. It is this land that we believe we have an inalienable right to control. A Jew may be willing to cede certain parts of the state of Israel to the Arabs, but to barter away Jerusalem or certain other areas is unthinkable. In a sense, the modern-day Jew doesn't "own" Jerusalem; he or she is merely the guardian of the city. The ultimate affront to an ethnic group is when their homeland is seized by "foreigners." In light of this, it is not difficult to understand the deep bitterness of Native Americans who were herded off their homelands and transplanted to other areas. The bitterness intensified when they witnessed the invaders showing no respect for these lands but instead carving them up, gouging mines into their hearts, burning off the vegetation that clothed the land, and soiling the rivers that nourished it.

Crucial aspects of the common ancestry of an ethnic group are its unique language, its characteristic culture or approach to life, and often its religion, although the proselytizing efforts of some modern religions have inserted "foreign" beliefs into unfamiliar ethnic territory. These common threads make up the tapestry that is

Ethnic violence is often the most destructive confrontation known to humankind. Possibly because people cannot change their ethnicity, genocide becomes the ultimate aim of many ethnic conflicts. (Eric Girard/Gamma Liaison International)

the ethnic group: a people with a sense of solidarity, a sense that they belong together, a sense of having been together in the past, and a sense of shared destiny. In the true sense of ethnicity, solidarity and a shared density do not involve the luxury of choice; they are, instead, preordained by nature.

Our ethnicity is not a matter of choice as is the case with religion or learning as in the case of culture. We're initiated into our ethnic group at the moment of conception, and (with a possible exception that we will discuss later) we are eternally condemned to it. We cannot relinquish our membership, and we cannot apply for membership in another ethnic group. I remember a childhood friend (I'll call him David to protect his privacy) who was enamored of the Apache Indians. He read everything he could about the Apache, adopted early Apache dress, and even learned the Apache language. He spent summers living on the open plains of his family's 5,000-acre ranch, just as the Apache had done nearly 100 years before. He cultivated friends at a nearby Apache reservation. But despite his greatest efforts, he could never *become Apache;* the closest he ever came was to be identified as *"like an Apache."* The irony of the story was that he married an Apache woman and their son Sam was accepted as an Apache. But Sam had little interest in his Apache heritage. He moved to New York and became an insurance executive. Still, no matter how far he traveled or how indifferent he was to his heritage, Sam was viewed by his friends and the Apache nation as being Apache.

I am suggesting that our ethnicity is unique in comparison with our member- ship in any other type of group. It is unique because it touches so many aspects of human existence, including biology, religion, culture, communication, and personal history. It is unique because we become permanent members of this group and never need fear excommunication. It is unique because membership is not a matter of per- sonal or group choice. Because of these characteristics, ethnic identity becomes the bedrock of our personal identity, and as such it plays a major role in human rela- tions, especially war and conflict.

Ethnic Conflict: The Bloodiest Human Confrontation

My discussion to place ethnicity at the core of human identity may seem surprising. We humans belong to many groups and are identified by these groups—our nation, our city, our work group, our social groups, our religion, and so on. But to determine which group is most central to our identity we need merely examine how people re- spond when any of these dimensions is threatened. If we consider the grandest of human conflicts, war, we find that this most noble endeavor of collective action in- volves three types of groups: nations, religious groups, and ethnic groups.

In itself, this is not especially surprising, because these groups are often the largest ones (except for our sex) that make up our self-identity. A call to arms by any of these groups is quickly answered by a gathering of people ready to take up weapons against the evil out-group. Often, the warriors know little about the out- group except that it has been deemed a threat to the in-group. Although those who rush to arms are cloaked in the mantle of serving (or saving) the group, I think that deeper probing would find that the private drumbeat in each soldier's head is to save his or her identity. For by elevating the power and dominance of our own group, we enhance their own identity.

The nature of war varies depending on the nature of the conflict. Throughout history, many of the most cruel and bloody wars have involved ethnic conflict. These wars are rarely confined to the battlefield. The very old and the very young are often slaughtered with frightening savagery. Rape and degradation of women and young girls are commonplace. So violent and so complete is the destruction in these wars that the term *genocide* has been coined to describe the horror. Genocide is the use of deliberate, systematic measures (killing, bodily or mental injury, unlivable condi- tions, the prevention of birth) to bring about the extermination of a group. In order to understand why genocide is so often associated with ethnic wars, we need sim- ply remember our discussion of the three major groups (countries, religions, ethnic groups) commonly involved in wars. In conflicts between countries, each side tries to expand its influence by capturing territory or resources from the other, by imposing its political system, by moving the policies of its adversary in a desired direction. From a single nation's standpoint, the successful resolution of conflict is measured in territorial gains, acquisition of resources, and political influence. The losers are often forced to *change* their nationality and pledge their support to the victor.

The aims of combatants in religious conflicts range from merely seeking to cast doubt on the validity of another religion to discrediting the symbols or holy places of that religion, to seeking to impose their religious beliefs and practices on members of another religion. Success in such conflicts may be achieved by capturing or discrediting a symbol, destroying or capturing a religious site, and, especially, by forcibly converting others to one's faith. Although the complete destruction of the other group is always a possible outcome, their conversion is often more satisfying because it increases the size and power of the victorious religion. As a young athlete, I recall a Christian organization coming to speak to our team, seeking to enroll us as members. With great pride, the group presented us with a recognized athlete who had converted from Judaism to Christianity. This athlete held an exalted position in the group because of his conversion. (It is hard to imagine a group presenting a member who had "converted" from being Asian to being Anglo.)

When conflict revolves around ethnic issues, however, the options for a "successful" conclusion and validation are often more limited. This is because the kinds of gains that often satiate the participants in national and religious conflicts—such as territory, political power, or conversion—have less currency and importance in interethnic conflict. The victors may capture territory or change the beliefs of the vanquished. But no matter how hard they try, they cannot change the ethnicity of the losers. Certainly they can pollute the strain; this is the goal of rape. They can destroy the external symbols of the ethnic group and banish it from its homeland. But in the veins of the banished, the blood of their ethnic group remains. The ethnic group remains, possibly dormant, waiting for an opportunity to arise and reclaim its place in the world. Thus, true, ultimate victory in an ethnic war results only when the opposing ethnic group—every member of it—has been destroyed. Nations can be eliminated by changing boundaries; religions can be obliterated by changing beliefs and practices. But ethnic groups can be extinguished only by destroying their vessels, the people of the group. We can conceive of a scenario whereby one state became so powerful that the world became its boundaries and all people became its citizens. Likewise, one religion may conquer the world. But it is inconceivable that one ethnic group could encompass all people, unless a significant proportion of the world's population were destroyed and the remaining single ethnic group inhabited the entire lonely planet. As a result, although genocide occurs in national and religious conflicts, it is most common in ethnic conflicts (Banton, 1997).

Herein lies one possible explanation for the wanton violence and seemingly senseless destruction that characterize many ethnic wars. And herein lies a pressingly important reason for understanding ethnicity and developing means that encourage the peaceful coexistence of ethnic groups.

Ethnic Identity and Conflict: Something Old but Always New

There is a great joy in learning about the activities of our ancient ancestors. Few of us can resist the temptation of taking a peek at history books. We cannot help being intrigued with the way our early relatives built their ships, constructed their villages, and secured their food. Their efforts to adapt to hostile environments are a source of pride. But lessons in ethnic identity are not reserved for students of history.

Although the roots of our ethnic origins reach deep into our past, ethnic identity is a topic of our present and our future. In fact, the challenge of coping with our ethnic differences is one of the most modern social issues we face. Countries such as the United States are experiencing rapid increases in the number and size of many ethnic groups (Table 1.1). Our newspapers are filled with accounts of people's struggle with ethnic identity and ethnic conflict. Indeed it is difficult to find a single location in our modern world where individuals are not being mistreated or destroyed because of their ethnicity. Ethnic conflict rages in the Balkans, Israel, the former Soviet Union, Northern Ireland, Central Africa, and Sri Lanka, to name just a few places.

TABLE 1.1 Population in the United States by Race/Ethnicity, 1980–1990

Race/ethnicity	U.S. population, total		Increase, 1980 to 1990	
	1990	1980	Number	Percent
Total U.S. Population	248,709,873	226,545,805	22,164,068	9.8
Asian/Pacific Islander American	7,273,662	3,726,440	3,547,222	95.2
Chinese	1,645,472	812,178	833,294	102.6
Filipino	1,406,770	781,894	624,876	79.9
Japanese	847,562	716,331	131,231	18.3
Asian Indian	815,447	387,223	428,224	110.6
Korean	798,849	357,393	441,456	123.5
Vietnamese	614,547	245,025	369,522	150.8
Cambodian	147,411	16,044	131,367	818.8
Hmong	90,082	5,204	84,878	1,631.0
Laotian	149,014	47,683	101,331	212.5
Thai	91,275	45,279	45,996	101.6
Hawaiian	211,014	172,346	38,668	22.4
Guamanian	62,964	39,520	23,444	59.3
Samoan	49,345	30,695	18,650	60.8
Other Asian/Pacific Islander	343,910	69,625	274,285	393.9
White, non-Hispanic	188,128,296	180,602,838	7,525,458	4.2
African American	29,986,060	26,482,349	3,503,711	13.2
Native American Indian, Eskimo	1,959,234	1,534,336	424,898	27.7
Hispanic	21,113,528	13,935,827	7,177,701	51.5
Other Race, non-Hispanic	249,093	264,015	(14,922)	–5.7

Industrialized nations such as Australia, New Zealand, United States, Canada, Mexico, China, Spain, Belgium, the Netherlands, and Brazil struggle to keep the lid on ethnic tensions and sadly count the cost of periodic outbreaks of ethnic violence. Ethnic hatred and discrimination are the rule of today rather than the exception.

There is also a very individual side to the story of ethnic identity that is written in personal searches for meaning and place. As modern humankind is being blessed with new technology to increase travel and communication between people, to conquer disease, to grow more and better foods, and to save labor, one might think that individuals would become less interested in and less concerned with their ethnic history. Why bother looking back when so much energy is required to keep up with the present? But this is not the case. Indeed, as our world becomes increasingly modern and complex, the tide of human interest seems to be turning toward ethnic identity. This tendency is understandable when we consider that one by-product of modernization is social confusion. Industrialization has reduced the need for multiple offspring, not only changing the nature of the family but directly calling into question the need for the family. As individuals become geographic nomads, roaming the earth in search of personal fortune, they are forced to move in and out of work groups, social groups, neighborhoods, and religious groups. Codes of behavior, the rights and wrongs in social relationships, change as rapidly as new car models off the assembly line. As confusion invades every part of our existence, the cry for order and predictability arises deep within our souls. And the most likely port in which to find this order is in ethnic identity, the most enduring bastion of human existence.

Despite all the imperfections built into the human machine, the supreme creator did endow humans with one gift: our eyes turn outward. Hence, we are quick to identify blemishes in others and slow to perceive our own foibles. As a result, we may see this march toward ethnic identity on the part of others, but not in ourselves. Several American social scientists have commented that ethnicity is "not a salient or important part" of the identities of Americans of European background (Phinney, 1996; Waters, 1990). This may be true to some degree. These groups are powerful, and indiscriminate breeding has blurred ethnic lines to the point that "White" is often the default category applied them as a whole. But, even with this disclaimer, I suggest that ethnic identity is alive and growing, even among European Americans. Witness the fact that one of the most widely read books of the last 30 years was Alex Haley's *Roots* (1976), which supposedly was an account of the author's ethnic history. One hundred thirty million people in the United States and millions others throughout the world watched the television dramatization of this book. Ethnic-based organizations such as the Italian Women's Society in the United States report healthy membership roles. And my own students flock to volunteer for class projects that involve exploring their ethnic heritage. I feel comfortable predicting that the importance of ethnic identity (and the frequency of ethnic conflict) will increase in the United States as science and technology chip away at the other bricks that make up individual identity.

Taking a more global look, the number of people seeking to establish their ethnic identity has exploded. Membership in genealogical societies is growing at a tremendous pace. For example, in New Zealand, which has instituted a national

Family History Month, the Genealogical Society reported that its membership increased fivefold during the 1980s (Wong, 1993). The American Indian population in the United States has surged in the last decade, owing "not to any acceleration in birth rates, but to increasing numbers of people asserting an ethnic identity as Indian" (Beal, 1996). Interestingly, this increase in the Native American population has been most pronounced in the southern United States, where prejudice against minorities is historically high. It is not uncommon to read stories of recognized figures who have "come out of the closet" to claim their ethnic identity and contribute to their ethnic group's heritage. The wife of the well-known writer John Kueubuhl (who wrote scripts for such popular television series as *Gunsmoke, Mission Impossible,* and *Hawaii Five-O*) came home one day to find her husband burning his scripts. He told her that it was time to go home to Samoa and to devote the remainder of his life to "coming to terms with his identity as a Samoan after half a lifetime spent as a stranger in a strange land" (Calder, 1993). Kueubuhl spent the remainder of his life writing plays about Samoa for Samoan actors. Business has not missed the opportunity to capitalize on the renewed interest in ethnic identity. The *Wall Street Journal* recently carried a feature story on the millions of dollars being poured into "ethnic advertising."

The issue of ethnic identity, then, is not about our past. The rising tide of ethnic identity is as modern as it is old. This fact adds both importance and urgency to understanding the lure of ethnic identification and its implications for interactions between people and groups.

An Admission of an Omission: Gender Groups

With all my discussion of the groups that form the basis of our identities, there is no way I could sneak out of this chapter without examining gender. Indeed, grouping by sex has all the characteristics that make ethnic groups so central to our identity. We are dispatched into one of these groups shortly after conception. We cannot choose to leave our sex group, save for the skill of a surgeon cutting and sewing his or her way through a sex-change operation. Thus, our sex group is clear, enduring, large, and powerful. It is at the foundation of our social identity, possibly even more fundamental than our ethnic identity.

But in history few, if any, wars are fought between men and women. (Some would argue, though, that sex issues have been at the basis of all wars, or that a "battle" between the sexes has existed since Adam and Eve were so rudely expelled from the garden of Eden.) This finding seems to call into question the reasoning I give for the central role of ethnicity in human conflict. However, I would answer this criticism by pointing out that classification based on sex is different from any other type. Men and women are uniquely complementary; under normal conditions, neither can perpetuate itself without the other. Men and women are biologically bound to cooperate, at least for some intermittent periods. Their existence is based on interdependence unlike that of any other human grouping or category. A nation, an ethnic group, or a religion can perpetuate itself without the existence of other nations, ethnic groups, or religious groups. But with present technology there can be no more males without the existence of females, and no more females without the contribution of males.

It is, therefore, this unique interdependence that allows our sex group to sit on the throne of our social identity without launching armies bent on the destruction of the out-group. Although this is not the place, it is interesting to contemplate how technological advances in cloning might affect the relationship between men and women. However, I will resist the temptation to wander down this intriguing path, choosing instead to focus on the topic of ethnic groups that are at the root of present-day violence and conflict.

Weaving the Net of Ethnic Confrontation

As part of this introduction, it should be of some help to provide a road map for the remainder of this book. I begin with the premise that our search for identity leads us to rush to the open arms of groups, the most basic of which is our ethnic group. Although nature stamps us with our ethnicity at birth, some of us have a choice as to whether or not we will reveal this stamp, though for others it is a mark that is immediately visible to all. Identifying with a group awakens a series of processes both within ourselves and within the group that propel us into conflict with others who are not members of it. Groups, I argue, are not content only to protect us. Rather, alliance with a group involves signing an unwritten pact that will change us and transform us into soldiers ready to march to the drumbeat of intergroup conflict.

The next few chapters will explore how identification with an ethnic group begins our metamorphosis from seeker to soldier. Whether wittingly or unwittingly, groups mold and shape our thoughts and behavior. They encourage us to move toward extremes; they excite us to act or react without careful consideration or planning; and our embrace of a group invites us to simplify our social world, viewing it in terms of categories and stereotypes. These forces prime the cannon, but it is the tendency for groups, more so than individuals, to engage in competition and conflict that aims the cannon toward ethnic confrontation and violence. I will establish my case by reaching into the literature of the social sciences—works identifying the forces that orchestrate the march toward conflict, hatred, and discrimination.

However, I will not end on this distressing note. Although human nature may start our journey toward conflict, violence is not inevitable. Like my humanistic colleagues, I believe that humans do have the freedom to chart their course. There are steps that can be taken, and have been taken, to reduce the likelihood of ethnic confrontation, including efforts that focus on the individual, the group, and the larger community of groups. The prevention of conflict requires constant vigilance and diligence. No single strategy will exercise the threat of ethnic violence and eliminate it for all time.

My goal is to develop an understanding of why ethnicity plays such a central role in human conflict, and to examine the steps that can be taken to harness the potentially destructive forces that rigid identification with ethnic groups threatens to unleash. With this promise of a silver lining, let's first explore the process of ethnic identity and the foundations of group conflict and hatred.

R E A D I N G   1 . 1

New England Tribes Look for Identity*

PAUL EDWARD PARKER

Probably more so than Navajo, Sioux or Apache, the Indian tribe best known in New England is the Mashantucket Pequots of Ledyard, Conn.

Their gargantuan Foxwoods Casino—generally regarded as the largest and most successful in the world—has become both a blinding light and a shining beacon.

New Englanders have become so blinded by Foxwoods, federal officials say privately, that, when a native group proclaims itself an Indian tribe, the unavoidable question that follows is: are you going to build a casino?

But the success at Foxwoods has also become a beacon of pride to those of Indian heritage, who long felt forced to hide their heritage, which carried a stigma in modern-day America.

"It was always something that was inside of us, but it was never allowed to come out," said Michael Markley, first councilman of the recently reestablished Seaconke Wampanoag tribe. "On the street in the town of Seekonk we always knew who we were; it was just something you didn't talk about."

Before Foxwoods, being an Indian was not exactly a glamorous station in life. "When you thought what an Indian was, you thought about an impoverished people that lived off the federal dollar," Markley said.

But the cards, dice, and slot machines—and the hundreds of millions of dollars they bring in every year at the Pequot casino—has changed all that.

"It gave acceptance to the outside society that we could be more than just an impoverished people," Markley said. "You saw a people that stood up for themselves."

And so Indian tribes, that have long been underground in this area, are happy to come out into the sun. Hence, the Seaconke Wampanoags reestablishing their tribal identity.

"If this was 10 years ago, they'd say what are you talking about? Why would you want to be that?" Markley said.

From a list of 103 founding members last October, the tribe now counts about 150, with "a long list" of others applying for membership. But to achieve full status, people must trace their ancestry to the branch of the Wampanoag Nation that called the

---

*Source: *The Bryan-College Station Eagle,* May 25, 1997, p. A24.

Seaconke Plain home, Markley said. That area, a broad expanse of rolling plain surrounded by dense woodland, stretched from Attleboro to Swansea, bounded on the east by Anawan Rock and on the west by the river now called Blackstone and Seekonk.

And the unavoidable question: do the Seaconke Wampanoags want to run a casino? Markley said the tribe has not thought that far ahead yet.

The first step on the road to a casino would be federal recognition, a process that the Seaconke Wampanoags have not decided to pursue.

Federal recognition is key because only tribes with that status are eligible to conduct gambling under the federal Indian Gambling Regulatory Act of 1988.

But federal recognition, acknowledgment of the tribe as a sovereign government, is not easily attained. In all, 554 tribes have that status, according to Thomas W. Sweeney, spokesman for the federal Bureau of Indian Affairs. But the vast majority of those 554 tribes achieved recognition before the 1950s, when the process was different.

Federal recognition was suspended from the 1950s until 1978, when the job was handed over to the bureau's Branch of Acknowledgment and Research.

Since 1978, 185 groups have petitioned for recognition. Twelve have been approved, Sweeney said. Four of those are in this area: the Narragansetts in Rhode Island, the Aquinnah Wampanoags in Massachusetts and the Mashantucket Pequots and the Mohegans in Connecticut.

The Chaubunagungamaug Nipmucs, near Worcester, Mass., is the only tribe from the region among six groups now in the final stages of the recognition process. They are third in line for a "proposed finding," Sweeney said. The head of the bureau issues a proposed yes or no to recognition, which is followed by a six-month comment period before a final decision is made.

Descendant Digs to Flesh Out Tale of "First" Black Family in America*

HELEN O'NEILL

HAMPTON, Va. – For 30 years Thelma Williams has spent more time with Anthony and Isabella and their child, William, than she has with many of her living relatives.

She sneaks out to libraries to be with them. She searches for them in court records. She smiles at their ghosts as she drives past the old forts and plantations that shaped their lives: Fort Monroe, where they were sold to an English sea captain; Jamestown where William was baptized; Blue Bird Gap Farm where their slave descendants may have lived.

---

*Source: Portland Press Herald, February 9, 1998, p. 2A.

"Girl, you are living in the past," her husband chides as his 54-year-old wife, a retired nurse, sets off on yet another genealogical journey.

The shortage of documents doesn't deter her. With stubborn faith in the stories that have been handed down through the generations, Thelma weaves the tale of her family's past.

It's a 375-year-old epic of love and adventure, hardship and endurance, slavery and freedom and redemption.

It's the story of Anthony and Isabella and their son, William Tucker, the first black child born in America.

Twists in the Family Tree

Today, miles away, there lives another William Tucker. Thelma's cousin is a 52-year-old New York City police officer who works a lot of overtime and talks about returning to Virginia when he retires. He plans to go back to where he came from, back to the town where his famous ancestor was born.

In the 3½ centuries that span the lives of these two William Tuckers lies the history of the black family experience in America, one Thelma has painstakingly traced, through documents and stories, through peace and revolution, through the vine-covered graves in the 300-year-old family cemetery that lies hidden down an old dirt road in Hampton.

Thelma believes the first William Tucker is buried here, although she doesn't have "100 percent proof."

She doesn't have 100 percent proof of many of the twists in the Tucker family tree, and some of what she does have she won't reveal. She's saving her best genealogical gems for her book.

What she does have is a head full of history, cases full of manuscripts and a rich trove of family lore. Her passion and conviction have won her a certain fame and following in her home state, where her family has been formally honored as direct descendants of the first William Tucker.

"They sailed across the high seas and landed here," Thelma says, standing by the shore at the tip of Fort Monroe and staring across the Chesapeake Bay. "This is where it all began."

Story Passed Down

Thelma first heard the story from her grandmother, who passed it on from her grandparents, who learned from their grandparents before them.

It tells of a young African couple, brought to the colony on a Dutch man-of-war and sold to a kindly sea captain who bestowed his name upon their son. The couple, Anthony and Isabella, worked in the tobacco fields and cypress groves of the captain's plantation. Their son married a mixed-race woman and had a family of his own.

More than three centuries after their arrival, the black Tucker family have stamped their soul upon this town. Teachers and tailors, pharmacists and musicians. They boast that they are everywhere except in jail.

"It's important that people know we didn't just fall out of the sky," Thelma says. "We have roots here that go back more than 350 years."

But like a million other families, they run into problems trying to trace those early roots. Where exactly did Anthony and Isabella come from? Were they slaves or indentured servants? Were they captured by pirates? Were they among the famous "20 and odd Negroes" that planter John Rolfe describes as arriving in a Dutch ship around 1619?

The first references to Anthony and Isabella appear in a list of the living and the dead after the Indian massacre of colonists in 1622. They are mentioned again in the 1624–25 census—along with 40 barrels of corn, four pistols and three swine—as part of the household of Captain William Tucker: "Antoney Negro and Isabell Negro and William theire child baptised."

Why was the baby baptized and given his master's name, a practice that later became common for slaves? Does it suggest that Anthony and Isabella were, in fact, among the first slaves? Could it mean Captain Tucker himself fathered the child?

No one knows for sure.

Every Birth Celebrated

Thelma argues that the birth of a child, any child, in a population ravaged by hunger, disease, and attack, was cause for celebration. After all, the colony was only 17 years old, a harsh-living place of rough wattle homes and flimsy palisades, where winters were known as "The Starving Time." Planters had little to fend off the elements but their wits and gunpowder. Women had just arrived. Family life, black and white, was just beginning.

In fact, there is little evidence that the baptized baby received Tucker's surname: that seems to have been more or less assumed by historians. If a birth certificate did exist, it was probably destroyed, like so many other records, in one of the Jamestown fires.

Questions about Anthony and Isabella's voyage are complicated by questions about their status. Slavery didn't exist as an organized labor system in the early 1600s, and Thelma sides with historians who argue that it developed, along with racism, as the need for cheap labor grew. Laws legitimizing slavery appeared in the 1660s.

"We came as indentured servants, but for Africans that was really just a notch above slavery," Thelma says. "We were on the first slave ship to come to America."

No one can argue because no one really knows.

Part of the difficulty is simply sorting out names. There were plenty of Anthonys and Williams carving slices of the colony for themselves, including Anthony Johnson, a free black planter and slave owner who built a thriving plantation in Northampton. Johnson's life is well known because, by a quirk of history, many Northampton documents survived.

The problem is that the records don't always make clear which Anthony they refer to. The same is true of the Tuckers.

Wars Obliterated Records

What is known is that the captain became one of Virginia's biggest landowners, amassing thousands of acres in and around Hampton. He left it to his children, including a son named William.

Establishing genealogical connections is further complicated by the fact that so many records were destroyed during the Revolution and the Civil War.

But there are other ways to make connections, ways not always readily available, or acceptable, to professional geneaologists.

Stories. Memories. Songs. Layers of family tradition passed from one generation to the next; well-worn anecdotes that stitch together the threads of the past.

But "the oral tradition is always very tricky," says Thomas Davidson, senior curator at the Jamestown museum and fort. "Different family stories start to sound the same, And who really knows?"

There is one place where Thelma knows for sure: The cemetery marked "Tucker Cemetery, 300 years."

She pulls out a property deed from 1896 that describes the "old colored burial ground," a two-acre plot her ancestors bought for $100.

Thelma's mother is buried here, and her grandparents and their parents, too. Their names are engraved on fading headstones: Mary Elizabeth Tucker, James William Tucker, Alexander Samuel Tucker.

But it is the sunken, unmarked graves that have the strongest pull. Who rests beneath the crumbling soil?

Anthony? Isabella? William?

READING 1 . 3

In Search of Our Roots*

The vigorous grasp for identity and place by Maoris has triggered a similar resurgence among Pakehas to search for their roots.

"The Maori renaissance does prompt you to think about your own place in society," says Anne Bromell, author of books on researching family history and a former president of the Society of Genealogists.

The trend shows up in membership of the society. At the beginning of the 80s membership stood at about 1500. At present it hovers at 7000 and continues to grow.

Every week genealogists gather all over the country in small groups to share information and offer support in what often becomes a never-ending task.

Subjects discussed illustrate how genealogy sifts through the minutiae of historical record: 19th century Auckland hotels, Stuart taxation, Freemasonry orders, history and records.

Great stirs run through the subculture of geneaology at the prospect of events that pass unnoticed by the rest of the community. The year 1991 was important because, under the 100-year rule, information collected for the 1891 British census entered the public domain, releasing a torrent of records.

Bromell's own curiosity was piqued by a 1979 visit to England. She spent time with relatives in Gloucestershire, including an 80-year-old aunt.

She returned to Auckland and began to trace a series of steps similar to many,

*Source: NZ (New Zealand) Herald, February 24, 1993, p. 3 (section 2).

checking with public libraries, joining the society and beginning the documentation through public records of her forebears.

The dry detail of birth, marriage and death registries, land deeds, business directories and sometimes yellowed newspaper clippings are the basic tools with which genealogists construct a life. Sometimes a well-kept diary or family Bible can flesh out the past.

"Every family story has a grain of truth," she says. The trick is teasing out the grain. Family propriety, nostalgia and the natural errors that creep into a story told many times can mask the reality.

A chainman becomes a surveyor, a corporal a sergeant-major. Illegitimacy once had a stigma and can result in dead-ends if births were not properly recorded because of public embarrassment.

The genealogist's burden is to "check, check and check again," says Bromell.

One huge resource are the family history centres of the Church of Jesus Christ of Latter-Day Saints. Church members believe the family is an internal relationship and that relatives can be "sealed" into the family unit after death.

There is a strong obligation for church members to do this, and to aid them the church has an ongoing project to copy as many public records as it can on to microfilm.

Asked about ethical considerations, Len Argent, who manages the church's microfilm ordering service, says: "We always ask permission before we copy anything and if it is denied, of course, we don't copy it."

New Zealand has 25 family history centres, with six in Auckland. Through them church members and members of the public can search through microfilm indexes of public registries, church records, cemetery records, to locate relatives.

Argent has no idea how many billions of names have been recorded by the Genealogy Society of Utah, a part of the church, based in Salt Lake City.

"The archives in Salt Lake City have more than 1.8 million reels of film and that number is growing all the time."

In this country Argent has accumulated 50,000 reels of microfilm of records pertinent to New Zealanders.

The church, says Argent, has always tried to acknowledge the broader genealogical interest in the records. Use of the centres is free save for a donation and administration charges.

And partly to cater for that wider demand, the church's ancestral file is a computer database which indexes genealogical research already conducted. A search here would save time.

"We're encouraging genealogical societies to include their indexes on the file."

The mania for records preservation seems a genealogical trait. Keith Vautier, of the society's computer group, has 50 members throughout the country transcribing the 1851 census of Cornwall.

The aim is to create a computer index of the census to speed research. Vautier estimates that 356,000 people will feature. After two years, the end is in sight.

The local society undertook the project because its sister Cornwall organisation did not have the resources.

The Cornwall case is no exception. Bromell has been given permission to microfilm early New Zealand electoral rolls. Starting at 1853 and up to 1925, only one copy of each roll remains. So far Bromell has preserved the rolls up to 1943.

It would be impossible to let streams of researchers handle the fragile rolls. And as Bromell remarks, "What if there was a fire? This part of our history would be lost."

Once hooked, genealogists often keep up their pursuit for life.

"Not everybody wants to whack a golf ball about," says Bromell. "It's a good pursuit for anyone who wants to exercise their mind."

One sensitive patch for a genealogist is Maori whakapapa. There have been cases of members with Maori ancestry striking problems.

The reason is pragmatic, though possibly painful for those denied. The ability to recite whakapapa is recognised by the Maori Land Court as evidence for a successful claim.

To protect tribal lands, the passing on of whakapapa depends on kaumatua and kula recognising a person as part of the tribe. So whakapapa is more than genealogy, it is the oral link to turangawaewae.

And whakapapa, says ethnologist David Simmons, is not restricted to the human line. Whakapapa also list the line of creation, through animals and fish to the gods. Maoris claim direct descent from their gods.

For Pakeha genealogists, the stakes are perhaps not so high. Though, as with Maori whakapapa, knowledge of family history links someone into a continuity.

Says Bromell: "How can you tell what sort of person you are unless you know where you have come from?"

CHAPTER 2

FROM THE LOST AND FOUND

Factors That Influence Ethnic Identity

The United States has a long history of confusion about ethnic groups. Its Constitution deals with the protection of the nation and the freedom of religious practice but is silent about ethnic groups. In fact, the country embraced the myth of a national melting pot, which boils and blends peoples until they become one, albeit mongrel, ethnic group—"American." But in practice, Americans have steadfastly maintained their ethnic identities and have targeted certain ethnic groups for hatred, discrimination, and violence. Indeed, the United States has a record of ethnic genocide, practiced with enviable precision, for instance, on the Native Americans who greeted early settlers and pioneers. But unlike some countries, which have directed their discrimination against only a few groups over generations, "Americans" have been a fickle people, frequently changing the main target of their discrimination: Japanese, African-Americans, Chinese, Jews, Irish, Poles, and Mexicans.

But this is not the only source of the confusion surrounding ethnic relations in the United States. For just as an ethnic group seems to become clearly enmeshed in the role of victim, the country seems to tire of mistreating it, and policy suddenly shifts. The victim becomes the object of solicitude and is declared a "protected" group, accorded special rights, property, and privileges. And although certain groups have been excluded from neighborhoods, businesses, and schools, members of these groups have not been excluded from the bedroom. As a result, the United States has become a nation of mongrels, people of multiethnic strains. But Americans have always been slow to acknowledge their indiscretions, so the habit of random breeding has been overlooked, and the confused offspring have been forced to "choose one" (ethnic group identity) when applying for jobs, responding to the national census, or dealing with other situations where some group or organization wishes to peer into one's private ethnic heritage.

It is within this context that Sam M. Davis (I've changed his name and some of the details of his case, for obvious reasons) applied to graduate school. Sam was asked to indicate his ethnicity ("check one box") on the application. Imagine the delight of the admissions committee when they read the application and learned that Sam was an African-American with excellent undergraduate grades and high scores on standardized tests. Sam was accepted and awarded a large fellowship. However, problems began when Sam arrived on campus. He didn't look African-American;

his skin was rather fair, and his eyes were deep-blue. Still, no faculty member was willing to challenge the rules of political correctness and confront Sam about his ethnicity. Life became more interesting, though, when Sam applied for a fellowship designated for Hispanic-Americans. On this application, Sam emphasized his middle name, Martinez, and responded "yes" to the question inquiring if the applicant was Hispanic.

Then all hell broke loose when Sam began to date the daughter of one of the faculty members from another department. During a casual discussion, Sam mentioned that he was French—in fact, that he had been born in France. The faculty member, a member of the Hispanic fellowship committee, began an investigation, which resembled an inquisition. Sam was ordered to appear before a board and asked pointblank, "What are you?" The board members thought they had uncovered a master charlatan, one who had no scruples or reverence for the academic goal of diversity. However, what they had actually found was a thoughtful, ethical individual, who admitted only to being troubled by the system.

Sam's initial response to the demand for identification was that he was everything he had listed. His maternal grandmother was African-American, and his maternal grandfather was Hispanic. His father and his father's parents were French. In high school he had strongly identified with the African-American students and worked hard to be accepted by them. He considered himself an African-American and had marked that box when forced to "choose one" on the graduate school's application form. Then, during his first months in graduate school, two profound events had occurred: Sam was rejected by other African-American students, who politely refused him admission into their organization (because they were not sure he was African-American), and his grandfather had died. These situations had led him to reflect on his identity. When the opportunity came to apply for the fellowship, he felt it would honor his grandfather to win the award. Indeed, he pointed out that he could not have accepted funds from the award because he was already on a full fellowship. Finally, he disclosed his French identity because his girlfriend was awed by his ability in French class. His reference to his French identity was an effort at humility, an effort to explain his aptitude for the language.

The ironic conclusion to this incident was that the inquisitors were, and I think still are, as confused as ever about Sam's "identity." Though they seemed to concede that Sam had never been dishonest, they still wanted to know "What is he?" The chair of his department puzzled aloud, "How should I list him when describing the composition of our graduate students—as Black, Hispanic, or White?" The consensus was that the chair could choose any one (but only one) of those categories!

100% Gold or Dime-Store Ethnicity: Ethnic Purity and Ethnic Mixing

Sam Davis's situation is one many of us face when confronting our ethnicity. His ethnic heritage was a tangled web with contributions from several ethnic groups. The United States has long been populated by a multitude of ethnic groups, and many ethnic groups may lurk in the biological closet of any individual. People in the United States are accustomed to this state of being, but we should not be so ethnocentric as to believe that all the world's people are mongrels. In fact, countries differ widely in the number of ethnic groups that reside within their boundaries and the ethnic "purity" of their citizenry. As we will see later, these variables are very important in any effort to explain ethnic relations within a nation and between nations.

Although it is difficult to estimate the number of people who are ethnically "purebred," we can get some indication by examining the populations of different countries. Kurian (1991) rated countries on their degree of ethnic homogeneity. Of the 135 countries in the sample, 35 were rated as 90% or more ethnically homogeneous. North and South Korea, South Yemen, and Portugal were the most homogeneous; Kenya, South Africa, and Tanzania were the least homogeneous. The United States fell squarely in the middle. Canada and Malaysia were low on ethnic homogeneity. New Zealand and Australia were on the high side. But even in those countries that are represented by several ethnic groups, many of the groups have strong customs demanding that members marry only within the group. These rules are especially common in collective cultures that emphasize the importance of the group over the individual (Triandis, 1994).

In the United States ethnic mixing is the rule rather than the exception, although some "mixtures" are more socially acceptable than others. Few eyebrows are raised by the combination of German and Irish strains, for example, but some people still find the melding of black and white or Asian and Anglo difficult to accommodate. One indication of the degree of mixing in the United States is a national study conducted by the University of Michigan in which a sample of voters were asked to list their ethnic ancestry. The results indicated that over 36% of the respondents reported more than one ancestry for each of their parents (see Smith, 1980).

These statistics may be mere trivia to most of us, unless we wish to establish a category of purebred humans analogous to the American Kennel Club's pure breeds of dogs. But at another level they have important implications. On one hand, they indicate that the common practice of requiring people to characterize themselves by choosing only one ethnic distinction forces many people to ignore part of their identity. As indicated in Reading 2-1, many individuals are finding this an unacceptable situation. The act of choosing one identity implies rejecting others.

One investigator has argued that inquiries about ethnic identity should allow individuals to claim all applicable categories (Gaertner, 1996). Rather than ask respondents to choose a label, the request could be to indicate all groups that apply. For example, we might give people the following options:

Please describe your ethnicity as you view yourself.

	Yes	No
I am:		
Korean		
African-American		
Native American		
German		
Irish		

	Yes	No
I am:		
Jewish		
Italian		
Malay		
and so on . . .		

This approach would not only allow individuals to present themselves in a manner consistent with their self-image but also provide more reliable information about the ethnic composition of a nation. An indirect result of this approach would be to make nations more aware of the ethnic diversity that characterizes their people. In fact, plans for the U.S. Census of 2000 include expanding ethnic options and allowing respondents to indicate multiple categories. Some colleges have also added these expanded options to their applications.

A second point suggested by the data on ethnic mixing is that when forced to choose a single category of ethnic identity, many people have a high degree of choice. In Chapter 1, I argued that ethnic identity is the bedrock of personal identity because people cannot choose their ethnic group or choose to leave it. Lest I be accused of misleading the reader, I should clarify this statement in light of our present discussion.

Individuals who are a product of a history of ethnic pure breeding have little, if any, choice about their ethnic identity. Their only latitude involves the degree to which their ethnicity is a salient component of their personal identity. On the other hand, those of us who are the product of more careless breeding have a choice of ethnic identities *within defined limits*. Sam Davis, for example, could choose to be African-American, Hispanic, or French. But he could not make a claim to being German, Chinese, or Malayan. He could be a pretender to these other ethnic groups, but he would always run the risk of discovery by others or the pangs of his own conscience. We are all like the Jews in the Nazi concentration camps in that the tattoo of our ethnicity is stamped permanently on us.

Therefore, within well-defined boundaries, we have some latitude in our decisions about our ethnic identity. For some, the choice involves how closely to identify with their ethnic group. For others, the choice concerns which of their ethnic memberships to claim. Although these are very circumscribed domains, the modicum of choice creates a fascinating psychology of the individual and human relations. Jean Phinney (1992) has addressed this issue most directly by constructing a measure designed to examine ethnic identity. Her questionnaire asks respondents to indicate, "I consider myself to be _____," and to answer questions about their degree of commitment to this group. How much do they follow the traditions and customs of their ethnic group? Do they belong to ethnic-based organizations? Have they tried to learn about the history and traditions of their ethnic group? This scale yields a picture of the individual's ethnic identity and the degree to which it is salient or affects behavior, or both. As a result, ethnicity is taken out of the biological closet and included in the behavioral realm.

But what factors determine when our ethnic identity becomes salient to us (and affects our behavior)? How, granted the opportunity by nature and fate, do we choose which ethnic identity to adopt? It is to these issues that I will now turn.

Parents often go to great lengths to ensure that their children do not forget their ethnic foundations. (R. Hutchings/PhotoEdit)

Strings of the Puppet:
Shaping One's Ethnic Identity

AS THE TWIG IS BENT, SO GROWS THE TREE.   Several years ago, my eldest daughter became close friends with a delightful Chinese girl, Ting Li. Ting Li was cute as a button, and her sparkling brown eyes could charm the spots off a leopard. Ting Li loved everything that was American—rock music, baseball, and hot dogs. But her Chinese identity was evident far beyond her physical characteristics. She was never without a necklace that bore Chinese symbols; her parents adorned her school notebook with pictures of China; and the interior of her rambling home could have come right from Beijing, with its carved furniture, ancestral worship shrine in a prominent corner of the living room, and chopsticks on the dinner table. Her family also observed all the traditional Chinese holidays.

Ting Li's situation is not unusual. Parents or grandparents often go to great lengths to ensure that children know their ethnic identity. The lessons may come in the form of preserving a language, celebrating ethnic holidays, hearing ethnic folktales, and making pilgrimages to an ancestral homeland. When the opportunity exists, parents may choose to send their children to ethnically distinct schools, where they are formally schooled in their ethnic heritage. And let's not forget the position of the church or synagogue, which has been referred to as the most segregated institution in the United States. I was recently given a tour of Boston by a friend. As we passed through the various districts, my friend, a devout Catholic, pointed out various palaces of worship. It was clear that these were all Catholic churches, so he gave me the shorthand description of each. "That's the Irish church. That's the Korean church. That one is Italian." Each ethnic group had its own church where parents could ensure that their children worshipped with their own kind and in their own language. The clear message in such childhood lessons is, "You are Chinese (Greek, Tamil, Polish), and don't ever forget it." These lessons (and the ethnic identity associated with them) are stamped on the relatively blank slate of the child's mind, never to be erased. Breaking ethnic tradition is grounds for punishment and a cause of guilt. A student in one of my classes reported that although she had "left the Catholic church" several years ago, she was afraid to inform her Italian grandmother because "being Catholic was part of being Italian." The issue was not so much religion as ethnic identity. The ethnic training that many children receive at home makes certain that the initial brick placed in the wall of identity will bear the mark of the ethnic group. Obviously not everyone receives early lessons in ethnic identity, but even in an ethnically diverse nation such as the United States, many people receive this training.

Our parents chart our ethnic course through the genes they pass on to us and the training they give us. But interestingly, if we ultimately choose our ethnicity from a unique menu of options, the influence of our fathers is more likely to dominate our choice than that of our mothers. Smith (1981; see Waters, 1990) examined the choice of ethnic identity by a sample of people whose parents were of different ethnic groups. Of those who chose an ethnicity represented by at least one of their parents, 58% selected the father's ethnic identity while 42% selected the mother's. Preference for the father's ethnic group could have resulted from the early training these subjects had received at home or the fact that they bore the paternal surname, or both.

BUT YOU LOOK JEWISH: THE IMPACT OF PHYSICAL TRAITS.   Although our parents start us on our journey toward our ethnic identity, there are several other influences that determine our ultimate destination. The whispering at the first meeting of the graduate admissions committee centered on Sam Davis. Was Sam really African-American, or had the committee been the butt of an elaborate prank? One faculty member put in words what was on everyone's mind: "He doesn't look African-American to me." Clearly, our physical characteristics are used by ourselves and others to place us in neat ethnic boxes.

In his theory of self-categorization John Turner (1987) argued that we constantly impose categories on our social world. Without categorization to organize it, our world would be too complex; we would have to respond anew to each event or individual. It is through the development of categories that we locate and define ourselves within our social landscape. We will examine this point further in Chapter 3, but here it is enough to point out that we do develop categories into which we place others and ourselves. A number of factors determine which classification will be applied at a specific time. One factor involves how accessible or salient a certain category is at the moment. For example, if you are involved in a conversation about religion, your world will be composed of different religious groups. If you have just been rejected from a job because of your ethnicity, your world will be constructed around ethnic groups. Once we carve our social universe into groups and categories, we place people (including ourselves) into those groups on the basis of their degree of "fit" (Oakes, 1983). One of the most common features we use in this categorization is physical characteristics. For many groups, we have a stereotype (a mental image; see Chapter 3) that includes their physical characteristics. We know what a typical woman or man looks like, and we use these standards to sort people into gender groups. We also "know" what a typical German (Pole, Jew, African-American, and so on) looks like. For example, a Jew has a large nose, an African-American has dark skin and kinky hair, a German has blue eyes and blond hair. Mary Waters (1990) found that most people she interviewed felt they could determine the ethnicity of others by their physical appearance. One respondent said, "Sure, I can tell other Irish. I can tell by their features usually. Mainly—well, in the Philadelphia area anyway—they are mainly big people. I imagine that was a selective something when they came over, they wanted a gardener or a chauffeur, or a horseman. They wanted a big guy that was imposing. . . . And their heads aren't the same as Germans or Polish. I can usually tell them apart because they have different shaped heads. Matter of fact, I can tell Sicilians from other Italians, too" (p. 80).

But nature seems intent on frustrating our quest for order and simplicity. Although some ethnic groups have relatively distinct physical features, many do not. And to this unholy mess, we must add the fact that the offspring of an interethnic liaison may not resemble either ethnic group. Still, humans are inventive creatures, not to be stymied by facts or data. Despite evidence to the contrary, many of us hold steadfastly to the position that there are distinct physical differences between people of different ethnic groups. This wonderfully human quality of making sense out of nonsense is evident in Waters's respondent, who was describing how he could distinguish Irish people: ". . . Now I'm surprised when I go to high school reunions and things that there are mainly Irish people that go and there are so many short people, because I figure I am short (and Irish). . . . I was only five foot ten and, well, I was short. . . . But some of those people are only five foot six or so. So I guess it all depends where you are from, but normally Irish people are big, or else they are really small. There doesn't seem to be any in between" (1990, p. 80).

The point is that many of us have images of the physical characteristics of people of certain ethnic groups; in the language of the cognitive psychologist, our schema of an ethnic group includes a physical prototype of that group (Fiske & Taylor, 1984). These images are important because we use them not only to place others into ethnic categories but also to choose our ethnic identity. In fact, Waters argues that our physical resemblance to a stereotyped standard influences the degree of choice we have in deciding on our ethnic identity. The more we physically resemble a commonly held physical image of an ethnic group, the more likely we are to identify with that group and the more likely others will be to identify us with that group. In other words, the more we physically resemble this standard, the less chance we have to decide our ethnicity; our appearance has made the choice for us.

We can make an interesting speculation by combining self-categorization theory with Waters's hypothesis regarding physical characteristics and ethnic identity. It seems likely that for people who strongly resemble the stereotyped physical attributes of an ethnic group, ethnic categories will be salient and accessible. That is, these people will be very likely to categorize their social world along ethnic lines, and they will be constantly aware of their ethnic identity. On the other hand, ethnic categories will be less salient for people who bear little physical resemblance to the stereotype of a specific ethnic group. These people will be less likely, without further provocation, to use the carving knife of ethnic groupings. In other words, their physical characteristics will be less likely to remind them of their ethnic identity and less likely to predispose them to view others along these lines. I must caution that I know of no specific evidence to support this position, but it does have theoretical grounding. The important point to remember is that our physical characteristics can affect our choice of our own ethnic identity and the identity we assign to others.

WE HAVE DECIDED THAT YOU ARE . . . : THE INFLUENCE OF EXTERNAL SOURCES.   Nature plays a part in deciding our ethnic identity by nominating our parents and stamping us with distinct physical characteristics. But nature is not the only factor that directs our choice of ethnicity. We live in a social world, in which others tell us whether we are moral, beautiful, intelligent, and successful. These people also inform us what our ethnicity is and is not. Even if we are somewhat uncertain about our ethnicity, other people are not. They often determine "what we are" on the basis of the scantiest information—the shape of our head, the color of our skin, the origin of our surname—and they leap without hesitation and place us in an ethnic category.

In fact, in many places and at many times the criteria for determining ethnic identity were written into law. For example, Virginia Code 1-14 declared, "Every person in whom there is ascertainable any Negro blood shall be deemed and taken to be a colored person, and every person not a colored person having one-fourth or more of American Indian blood shall be deemed an American Indian; except that members of Indian tribes existing in this Commonwealth having one-fourth or more Indian blood and less than one-sixteenth of Negro blood shall be deemed tribal Indians." This concern about "blood" was carried to an extreme when Louisiana required that a white patient be notified if a black person's blood was "all that could be found for transfusion and that he be given an opportunity to refuse it" (Sickels, 1972). Therefore, if anyone had difficulty determining his or her ethnicity, the law could help!

Even though this ethnic game is often based on faulty assumptions or incomplete information, it might prove relatively harmless if it did not influence other people's behavior toward us and their insistence that we play along with them and accept their conclusion. Indeed, Sam Davis, our ethnically perplexing graduate

Violence sparked by the acquittal of four police officers for beating Rodney King in Los Angeles was often aimed at Korean shopkeepers. Perceived threats to one's ethnic group can spawn actions aimed at other ethnic groups. (AP/Wide World Photos)

student, mused, "People have told me so often that I am not African-American that I am beginning to believe it myself." In many cases, we take on the ethnicity that others tell us is ours; we dance to their tune.

The more distinctive our physical features or names, the more others usurp any choice we might have in determining our ethnic identity. I'll never forget the time when one of my colleagues, who had a passion for genealogy and astrology, decided that I was Sioux Indian. She made this determination because she thought I resembled a painting of a Sioux warrior she had seen. No matter what angle I took, I could not see the slightest resemblance, but this made little difference to her. It also didn't matter that I could trace all my roots to Eastern Europe. She dismissed my protests, suggesting that I was missing some wanton branch in my family tree. (As she became more adamant, I was waiting for her to determine that a band of Sioux had once roamed the Polish plains!) She finally grew so angry at my refusal to go along that she delivered the lowest of blows: "You must really be prejudiced against Indians to be so determined to hide your heritage!" Needless to say, our communication ceased for some time after this remark. But I found myself paying special attention to photographs of Sioux people, and I became more intimately acquainted with my mirror as I searched for a resemblance. Indeed, it is difficult to deny the influence others have on determining our ethnic identities.

EVERYONE LOVES A WINNER.   The intensity of our ethnic identity and our decision to emphasize one aspect of our ethnicity over another is influenced by the power and prestige of various ethnic groups. Many Jews who had only tacitly recognized their Jewishness came "out of the ethnic closet" when Israel won the Six-Day War in 1967. They wore symbols announcing their Jewish identity and sent funds to help rebuild the homeland, Israel. Many African-Americans, some who had gone to great lengths to "pass" as members of other ethnic groups, reclaimed their African-American identity when they witnessed the courage of Martin Luther King, Jr., and the success of the civil rights movement in the 1960s. Black became beautiful, and there was a renewed interest in studying African and African-American history as Blacks began to take an equal seat at the table of United States ethnic groups. It was in this climate that Alex Haley's *Roots* was published in 1976. In the book, Haley traced his family origin back to Kunta Kinte, a black man stolen from Africa and enslaved in the United States. The story became a symbol of the struggle of African-Americans to rise above oppression and carve out a place in the United States. The success of our ethnic group enhances our desire to be identified with it.

But success is not the only factor that influences the salience of an ethnic group. In some cases, a threat to a group can ignite ethnic identity. Increased efforts by Saddam Hussein to destroy the Kurds in Iraq in 1991 sparked demonstrations by Kurds in the United States, demanding that the United States stop the genocide. Many of us pay quiet attention to the plight of our ethnic brethren throughout the world, and events that ignite recognition in one part of the world can create ethnic passion elsewhere. An Indian friend recently put on the trappings of Indian culture when he read about increased discrimination against Indians in the island of Fiji. Publicity about the treatment of Indians in Fiji led him to become more aware of his Indian ethnicity.

Finally, we must confront the self-serving side of ethnic identity. In many countries—such as Australia, New Zealand, and the United States—ethnic groups that were once the target of cruel discrimination have become a "protected class." Programs such as affirmative action have sought to level a historically uneven playing field by making opportunities available in education and employment to members of certain groups. Members of indigenous groups have gone to court to reclaim territory that they feel was unjustly taken from their ancestors. For example, in June 1993 a tribe of Aborigines claimed ownership of the property in Canberra on which the Australian High Court and Parliament House sit. The case was strengthened by the Mabo case, a year earlier, in which the High Court upheld the Aborigines' title to land if the tribe could prove a continuous connection with it. These situations create opportunities and, in some cases, wealth for individuals who can show membership in a protected ethnic group. As a result, many ethnic groups are besieged by individuals claiming membership. Following a series of financial successes a Kickapoo tribe administrator in Texas stated in disgust, "People drive up all the time and talk to us about how their grandmother was a Kickapoo. Seems like everybody's grandmother is a Kickapoo Indian."

Another external event that often fans the fires of ethnic identity is the immigration of significant numbers of people from a particular ethnic group. Johnson (1974) found that ethnic identity is high among immigrant groups. But these immigrants can also awaken the long-slumbering ethnic identity of people already living in the new homeland. A Chinese student whose family had lived in the United States for three generations reported feeling greater identification with his Chinese origins following the increased immigration of Chinese to the United States in the 1990s. Interestingly, he mused that his newly ignited identity was a mixed blessing: "I had become comfortable viewing myself as American, but with the increase in the numbers of Chinese in my community, I had to cope with my identity of being Chinese and American."

Indeed, almost any event that affects our ethnic group can lead us to emphasize our identity with it. The exception, at least at the public level, occurs when the ethnic group perpetrates some despicable act. For example, many German-Americans were loath to admit their ancestry after learning of the atrocities of the Nazis during World War II. Indeed, there was a noticeable increase in applications by German-Americans to change their surnames shortly after the war (Winawer-Steiner & Wetzel, 1982). Politics, then, plays an important role in determining when our ethnicity will be salient and—when we have a choice—which of our ethnic groups we will emphasize. Political correctness is alive and well in our construction of our ethnic identity.

JOINING AND STAYING: A QUESTION OF ECONOMICS.   Now that we have broached the topic of selfishness in the choice of ethnic identity, let's push it a bit further. For those of us with many branches of our ethnic tree, the question of identity involves two decisions—which identity to emphasize in the first place, and whether we will retain that identity or try another one. Sam, our student with many identities, demonstrated that many people can change ethnic identities—*within prescribed limits*. But while there are many factors pushing toward one identity, there are at least as many forces encouraging us to retain that identity. The reaction of the faculty to Sam's chameleon act indicates the pressures we receive from others to maintain consistency. Likewise, a host of theorists in social psychology argue that there are internal dynamics deep within the psyche driving us toward consistency and discouraging changes in our self-identity (Festinger, 1957; Abelson et al., 1968). But our identities do change, and we do, at times, "negotiate" our membership with groups.

John Thibaut and Harold Kelley (1959) argued that aside from concerns about whether a group will have us as a member, our decision about whether to claim and retain membership in a group involves analyzing both our options and our satisfaction with the group. Taking a "social exchange" perspective, Thibaut and Kelley suggested that we review our relationships with people and our decision to incorporate a specific group membership within our identity from an economic standpoint.

All relationships boil down to costs and rewards. What are we giving (time, effort, expertise, materials, and so on) and what are we receiving from the union (status, security, material rewards)? On the basis of our entire past experience with groups, we form a "comparison level" that tells us what we should receive from the cost-outcome formula. The comparison level is roughly what we feel we de-serve or ought to receive from group membership. If our net outcome from group membership is above our comparison level, we will be attracted to and satisfied with the group. The higher the outcome is above the comparison level, the more satisfied we will be. When the outcome falls below our comparison level, we will be dissatisfied.

Our level of satisfaction will determine how many complaints or how much praise we direct toward our group. Yet we do find people remaining in groups they seem to hate and leaving unions that are satisfying. Thibaut and Kelley caution that the comparison level influences only our satisfaction with unions, not whether we stay or leave them. In order to determine whether we will join (or stay in) a group we set up a *comparison level for alternatives* (CL_{alt}; Figure 2.1). The CL_{alt} is based on the level of outcome we feel is available from the best alternative group. In deciding whether to join (or stay in) a group, then, we look at what we can get from other groups. We will joint a group or stay in it so long as our outcome from that group is above the outcome we can get from our best alternative. We will defect, or not join the group in the first place, if we feel that our net outcome from another union will be better.

This wonderfully simple but unflattering analysis holds the key to many of our deepest questions. As you can see from Figure 2.1, a person will remain in dissatis-fying union when his or her net income is below the comparison level but above the CL_{alt}. Obviously this person is not likely to be a productive or loyal member, and he or she will be engaged in a constant search for alternatives. Likewise, we will leave a group that is satisfying (above comparison level) when our net outcome is thought to be below our CL_{alt}. A state of bliss results when our net outcome from a group is above both our comparison level and the comparison level for alternatives.

In terms of ethnic identity, this approach suggests that we compare the cost of stressing a particular ethnic identification (the possibility of suffering discrimina-tion) with the benefits (security, a sense of pride, friendship) derived from declaring our membership in the ethnic category. In other words, there is an instrumental di-mension in ethnic identification (De Vos & Romanucci-Ross, 1995). Being truly in-strumental, we also examine our alternatives. Indeed, this desire to know our alter-natives may be one of the motivations that lead some people to do research on their ancestry. The results of this analysis affect the identity we adopt, our satisfaction with it, and the likelihood that we will retain it.

A PORT IN A STORM.   It seems that nothing drives us to latch on to our identity more than a crisis. The crisis may be shared, impelling hordes of people to scurry into the relative safety of their ethnic identity. For example, Kenneth Gergen (1991) discusses the influence of our postmodern period on our search for identity. He ar-gues that our present world is confusing. The rules of behavior are unclear. We are bombarded with information. Change at every level of our lives lurks around every corner. The pace of life is fast and getting faster. We've not only lost order and pre-dictability but also lost a sense of self. Chaos is frightening, and our fear drives us to seek order. Others have echoed this theme. Bauman (1992), for example, suggests

FIGURE 2.1 Social Exchange of Group Membership

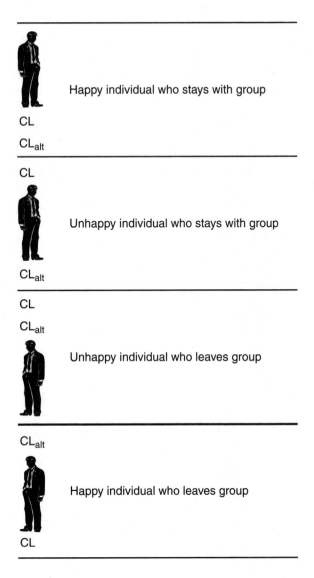

CL

Happy individual who stays with group

CL

CL_{alt}

CL

Unhappy individual who stays with group

CL_{alt}

CL

CL_{alt}

Unhappy individual who leaves group

CL_{alt}

Happy individual who leaves group

CL

that we are like nomads wandering between unconnected places, searching for a sense of purpose and belonging.

As I have suggested, one cognitive step we can take to establish order in our world is to clean up our own identity house. And one way to organize our identity is to grasp our ethnic identity firmly. Knowing from where we came informs us where we might be going. The security of our ethnic identity gives comforting structure to our very being and instructs us in how we should relate to others. Our ethnic identity tells us who is friend and who is foe, who "we" are and who "they" are. This view predicts that ethnic identity will become increasingly important as we are faced with more choices and opportunities and fewer rules to guide us. On this point, I must disagree with De Vos and Romanucci-Ross (1995), who characterize ethnic identity as "past-oriented" and national citizenship as "present-oriented." Ethnic identity is firmly set in the present. Not only do existing personal and group situations affect the desire for ethnic identification, but our ethnic identity serves as a road map to guide us through the cluttered social terrain we face.

The crisis that can lead us to increase the salience of our ethnic identity can also be a personal event. Each of us faces personal crises in life—the death of a loved one, divorce, loss of a job, or recognition of our own impending death. As Greenberg, Pyszcynski, and Solomon (1986) argue, these personal crises make people aware of their vulnerability and mortality. In order to combat these feelings, people are driven to bolster their self-esteem, to feel that they are valued in their world. One way to accomplish this is to nestle deep in the bosom of a group, to feel the comfort and protection that comes from a sense of belonging. In a series of interesting experiments, these investigators found that when people were forced to face their mortality (think about their own death), they raised the importance of the groups to which they belonged and depreciated out-groups. Along similar lines, Ethier and Deaux (1990; 1994) suggest that strong ties with one's ethnic group can act as a buffer against a perceived threat. In their examination of Hispanic students entering Ivy League universities, these investigators found that students who identified more strongly with their ethnic group tended to report less threat and insecurity in a predominantly Anglo (i.e., white) environment.

These studies illustrate how personal crises, especially those involving threats to our security, can increase our motivation to identify with our ethnic group. When our own situation is precarious, our group becomes a more salient part of our identity, and we become willing to sacrifice to enhance the position and security of our groups.

I once asked my students whether they were aware of their "family tree," in other words, their ethnic history. About half the class said yes. Next I asked them who gathered and maintained the family geneology. The majority said it was their grandparents. Interestingly, several others indicated that a parent who had gone through a recent divorce was the source. Why did old people and recently divorced people turn their energy toward a family tree at this crucial time? Because, according to my hypothesis, personal crisis leads us to seek our identity and align ourselves with our ethnic groups—the reality of death in the case of a grandparent, and the loss of family in the case of a divorced parent. Along these same lines, Waters (1990) reported young people between the ages of 15 and 24 were most likely to simplify their ethnic identity by identifying with only one or two of their possible ancestries. She makes the observation that in the United States this is the age when young adults typically separate from their homes. Becoming an outcast from one important group leads us to grasp for membership in another important group. Acknowledging that adolescence is a central period in the formation of identity, Phinney (1992) developed her ethnic identity scale using a sample of high school students ranging in age from 14 to 19 years.

In a fascinating book, the Maori author Witi Ihimaera (1973) describes the experience of a young man who had forsaken his Maori identity and moved to

Wellington, New Zealand, to live a modern life. When the young man's father died, he returned home to attend the funeral. Confronting the place of his birth and the death of his father reawakened his Maori identity and led him to return to his roots. Similarly, when Sam Davis's grandfather died, Sam began to focus more on his Hispanic identity. It was this death that motivated him to apply for membership in the Hispanic community.

Given my background as a psychologist, I am tempted to explain the collective rise and fall of ethnic identity solely on the basis of crises faced by individuals. Obviously, this professional ethnocentrism would be inappropriate. However, we can till one part of the ethnic field with an emphasis on personal crises. Because we all experience personal crises at some points in our lives, there are always walking wounded to tend the home fires of an ethnic group, ensuring that it will be waiting to shelter the masses should the situation dictate collective action. Individuals move in and out of the tent of ethnic identity as their own situation dictates, each helping preserve the ethnic group while residing under that tent. Our ethnic identity, then, lies like a dog sleeping by the hearth, waiting to spring up when a personal or collective crisis confronts us.

SOME OTHER CONTRIBUTORS TO ETHNIC IDENTITY.   Several other factors also conspire to influence our ethnic identification. As I have stated, ethnic identity is generally strongest among minority groups and recent immigrants. Being relatively alone against the majority invites minorities to recognize their ethnic components. I will explore one possible reason for this in a later section, but suffice it to say here that humans seem driven by two competing desires. One is the desire to be safe, motivating us to emphasize the most powerful ethnic identity to which we can lay claim. The other is the desire to be unique, to stand out from the crowd. We can emphasize our uniqueness by parading an ethnic identity that eludes most others. Special attention is given to the last of the Mohicans.

But the influx of immigrants does more than just reawaken the ethnic identity of their relatives. It also excites the majority group to reassess its own ethnicity. The interlopers are perceived with alarm, and a call to unite often arises in the majority. The new immigrants are viewed as a threat to the values that define the majority ethnic group. It is no accident that the loudest calls to designate English as the official language of the United States come from the states (Texas, California, Florida) experiencing the greatest influx of Hispanic and Asian immigrants. The neo-Nazi movement in Germany was given a boost when Germany increased immigration quotas for Turks and people from the former Yugoslavia. In the 1980s a violent confrontation involving Texas shrimpers ignited along the Gulf Coast. A number of Vietnamese immigrants had come to the coastal region and begun shrimping. The resident shrimpers united, burning the boats of immigrants, cutting their nets, and attacking them. The ethnic tone of the violence was summed up by one shrimper who stated, "These are American waters, and we don't want these damned foreigners fishing in them." The statement was ironic because many of the Vietnamese were American citizens, and the American spokesman had fought alongside Vietnamese during the Vietnam War. But the growing population of Vietnamese along the coast aroused ethnic identity and conflict. Several investigators (Tajfel, 1980; Worchel et al., 1992) have made the point that *we can most easily define our own group when other groups (out-groups) are present.* In fact, competition with these out-groups is sought in the service of drawing a clear line in the social sands between "us" and "them" (Worchel, Coutant-Sassic, & Wong, 1993).

The French philosopher Jean-Paul Sartre wrote, "If the Jew did not exist, the anti-Semite would invent him" (p. 13). The underlying message is that for some people ethnic identity and discrimination against out-groups is a central part of their personality. This view had been reflected 15 years earlier, when a group of investigators at the University of California at Berkeley examined the qualities of people who expressed the highest levels of prejudice. Adorno and his colleagues (1950) identified a common personality type in many prejudiced individuals, the authoritarian personality structure. The researchers developed a scale (the F or fascist scale) to measure this type. They found that high-F people displayed the following characteristics:

1. Conventional behavior—rigidly adopting middle-class values and feeling anxious that others would violate these
2. Authoritarian submission—a strong need to abide by the moral authority of the in-group
3. Preoccupation with power and toughness
4. Exaggerated concern with the sexual behavior of others

Overall, high-F people showed a strong desire for order, predictability, and correctness in their world. Although there is considerable debate about the relationship of this personality to prejudice, the research raised the possibility that certain features of our personality may influence our desire to identify with an ethnic group and even to have an impact on that group. Psychologists have identified hundreds of personality types or dimensions. Many of these revolve around the need for structure, or anxiety regarding a lack of structure. Further research along these lines might find that certain personality characteristics influence the salience of our ethnic identity.

Finally, I should mention the self-image. I still have a clear picture of a college friend, Gary Wenzel, who fancied himself a free spirit. He delighted in breaking every social convention. He lived in a dilapidated Volkswagen van, smoked every type of illicit plant he could find, boasted of his sexual prowess, and wore the most outrageous clothing. (I think Gary is a New York corporate lawyer today, but that is beside the point!) One of Gary's favorite pronouncements was that he was "one of the few true Gypsies in the United States." And he had his family tree, neatly etched in an old Bible, to prove his claim. If one examined the tree, there, on one obscure branch, was an ancestor who was a Romanian Gypsy. It was this branch that Gary grasped, because it fit his persona. We may, then, choose an ethnic identity that complements a self-image or an image we wish to project. Rooting that image in our ancestral line gives it a certain legitimacy and permanence. It places us in the position of recognizing and living up to our destiny. Hopefully others will overlook the healthy sprinkling of whimsy we have added to the stew.

Our Ethnic Identity:
Bringing It All Together

In Chapter 1, I made the case for ethnic groups as among the most important bricks in our wall of personal identity, because we are born into these groups and cannot leave them. Much of the discussion in the present chapter seems to call that conclusion into question. Indeed, it seems that we do have some choice about our ethnic identity, and a choice about when this identity becomes salient and which ethnic group we will identify with most strongly. How can we reconcile these seemingly opposed positions?

Reviewing the position outlined in this chapter, the answer is that the contributions of our ancestors (our biological lineage) define the parameters of our choice. For those who are ethnically purebred, having ancestors of only one ethnic group, there is no choice about the nature of their ethnic identity. If your ancestral closet is populated only with Maori people, you will be Maori. You cannot decide to be Malay or Polish. Your only choice is how strongly you wish to emphasize your Maori identity. But as we have seen, this choice may be largely usurped by others who decide to emphasize your Maori identity.

On the other hand, if your ancestral closet contains the ghosts of people from different ethnic groups, you may have a wider choice. If you find Germans, Swedes, and American Indians in that closet, you have some choice about which ethnicity to emphasize. But the choice is still limited by your heritage. These limits are certainly more rigid than those placed on you if you focus on religion and find Jews, Muslims, and Protestants in your ancestral closet. In this case you are free to ignore their beliefs and become a Buddhist. Who would argue that embracing Buddhism does not give you the right to proclaim that you are a Buddhist? But many would question your "right" to lay claim to being German, Spanish, or Czech simply because you decided to celebrate the holidays of that group and follow its customs.

Therefore, in the final analysis, our ethnicity is influenced by many events, both internal and external (Figure 2.2). The foundation of our ethnicity is set in stone at conception, but we have some latitude about how we will build on that foundation.

The Enduring Crisis:
To Belong or to Be Unique

I've painted a picture of humans as social animals, searching for groups and incorporating these groups into their personal identity. The insatiable need for security and social order directs this desire to belong to groups. But in addition to our desire for inclusion, we also have a craving to be unique, special, and independent. We want to be valued as individuals, and we want to recognize ourselves as standing out from others. Marilyn Brewer (1991) argues that we seek a balance between our need for belonging and our need for differentiation. When a situation is over-weighted in one direction, we scurry to the opposing need.

This quest for balance has some interesting implications for ethnic identity. Being a member of the dominant ethnic group provides protection and security, but at the

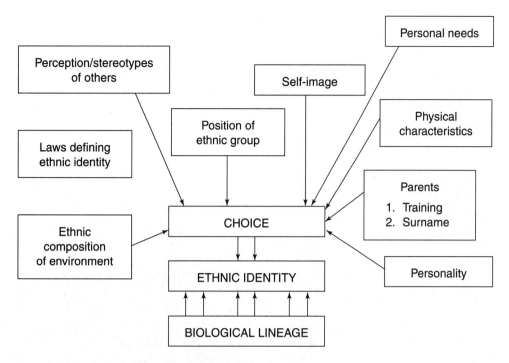

FIGURE 2.2 Hands That Craft Ethnic Identity

same time it marks us as one of "the many"—it detracts from our uniqueness. As a result, we may vacillate between emphasizing our identity in a large, powerful ethnic group and advertising our uniqueness by claiming our birthright—membership in a small, unusual, and often powerless ethnic group. It is this latter tendency that helps keep alive minority ethnic groups and helps explain their periodic rise in popularity. From an individual's standpoint, threats to your security may motivate you to affiliate with the most prominent ethnic group in the ancestral closet. However, a threat to your uniqueness may send you scurrying to grasp the branch of the most unusual ethnic group on the family tree. Similarly, when your security is threatened, you may proclaim that you are a "typical" member of your ethnic group. But when you are concerned about your personal uniqueness, you will try to differentiate yourself and emphasize your uniqueness within the group. You might, for example, revel in the fact that you are the descendant of a great Navaho chief or an English bandit, or you might emphasize your right to wear an ethnic coat of many colors, claiming membership in several ethnic groups. There are times when my heart yearns for the comfort of considering myself a "typical" Pole; at other times, I think that being characterized as "typical" anything is a supreme insult.

So our actions are ruled by two opposing forces: the need to belong to groups and incorporate them in our identity, and the need for independence and uniqueness (see Figure 2.3). This clash of forces is especially strong in cultures that stress individualism (Triandis, 1994), such as the United States, England, and Germany. These cultures stress personal independence and identity. Group membership is often temporary,

Uniqueness

To be different, unique,
and independent

Inclusion

To belong to groups
and be part of collective

FIGURE 2.3   Dilemma of Human Identity

and groups themselves have considerable latitude to eject members. People often move from group to group, as bees fly from flower to flower. The salience of their group identity (including ethnic group identity) waxes and wanes. Uniqueness in these cultures is relatively easy to establish, but it is bought at a considerable price. The comfort and security offered by permanent membership in a group is sacrificed. As a result, individuals often yearn for secure membership in an enduring group. This creates fertile soil for the rise and fall of ethnic identity and violent ethnic conflicts.

The situation in collective cultures such as those found in Asia and Latin America is somewhat different. Collective cultures stress the importance of groups and the interdependence between individuals within these groups. Personal identity is based on the role one has within a group, not on unique personal characteristics. Group membership is generally permanent, and one's place within the group is always available (Kim, 1994). Boundaries between the in-group and out-groups are clearly drawn and unyielding. There are established rules and norms for dealings between members of different groups. These norms result in two patterns of relations between ethnic groups. In some cases, they reduce both the intensity and the frequency of interethnic conflict, as evidenced by Hong Kong (Bond, 1987) and Malaysia (Provencher, 1987). In other cases, such as the Solomon Islands (Kuschel, 1987), these norms institutionalize conflict, maintaining it as a relatively consistent, stable level. There is not the dramatic rise and fall often seen in more individualistic cultures. The struggle in collective cultures is frequently at the individual level, where people strive for personal uniqueness within the context of their group identity.

From the Individual to the Group

Although my focus has been on how and when *individuals* incorporate ethnic identity into the psyche, my ultimate aim is to examine ethnic conflict, which is conflict between ethnic *groups*. To accomplish this aim, it is important to consider how individual identity is transformed into collective action. I will deal with this issue directly in the next few chapters. I will argue that our ethnic identity influences the groups we will join and the leaders we will follow. Our identity helps define our friends and our enemies, and the determination of friend and foe is often based on group membership. In other words, our ethnic identity is not simply a label that sits passively on our shoulders. Rather, it takes an active role in guiding us toward some people and against others. Once we accept membership in a group, there are specific dynamics of that unit that mold our actions to ensure that we march in unison with our soul mates. Therefore, although the early steps toward ethnic identity are taken in our private domains, the latter part of the journey—the part that results in ethnic conflict—occurs within the collective.

R E A D I N G   2 . 1

Multiracial Americans Rally to Add New Racial Category to Census*

WASHINGTON—Carrying signs that read "I'm proud to be me" and "I'll choose my category," a group of multiracial Americans held a rally Saturday to press the government to introduce a multiracial category for the 2000 census.

"To be proud of both your ancestries you need something like that. It's not anything we should be ashamed of," said Gwen Loftus. Loftus, an African-American married to a white man, had a "Yes, I'm her mother" sign on her daughter's stroller.

Multiracial groups have been lobbying the federal government for a change in racial categories that appear on official and unofficial forms.

Speakers at the rally, attended by about 200 people, complained that they were not treated equally.

"We stand for the struggle to gain acceptance for being honest about racial tolerance, racial acceptance, racial integration," said B.J. Winchester, president of the Unity Multiracial Social Group of Jacksonville, Fla.

Couples in interracial marriages complain that their mixed-race children have no appropriate category to check off on many forms. They usually choose the "other" classification, if it exists, one that they feel does not identify the children accurately.

Henry Robertson, who has a Japanese mother and a white father, said he supported the proposed change because it would solve the dilemma he has every time he is confronted with a form.

"I've had to fill out forms where they demand that you check the group you mostly identify with. . . . I just check whatever I feel like that day," said Robertson, 25, a computer programmer. "If some days I feel white I check white. Other days, if I feel Asian I check Asian."

Others say a new category would eliminate the hurt they sometimes feel when forced to make the choice.

Dawn Loftus, 16, said when her class had to fill out a form for a test, she complained to the teacher that the form did not have an "other" category on it.

"She said you just consider yourself as black," said Dawn, one of Gwen Loftus' three daughters. "I was confused about it. . . . I didn't want to deny my father."

---

*Source: The Bryan-College Station Eagle, July 21, 1996, p. A14.

Steve White, a teacher and one of the speakers, had this advice for parents:

"When your child gets one of those dreaded forms, go to the principal and ask, which part of my child should I deny? What kind of a lie are you asking me to tell our government?"

What Kind of American Are You?*

ARLENE LEVINSON, ASSOCIATED PRESS

WASHINGTON—Filed in an office near the White House, handy for presidential perusal, is one man's solution to the nagging need of the World's Greatest Democracy to sort people by race.

John Beresford, a retiree in Alexandria, Va., proposed a numbered skin-color chart: Forget "black" or "white." You could just pick the number nearest your skin tone.

When the Office of Management and Budget announced a few years ago it was rethinking its race and ethnic labels for Americans under a sweeping rule called Directive No. 15, Beresford's "Skin-Color Gradient Chart" was one of the more dazzling suggestions from hundreds of citizens eager to help.

It also was among the easiest ideas to discard, along with "Ameurofian," concocted for people of American Native, European plus West African descent, and "Western European" and "Eastern European" to differentiate the great mass of whites.

Meanwhile, at the suburban headquarters of the U.S. Census Bureau in Suitland, Md., social scientists and volunteer advisers helping prepare questions for the next national nose count on April 1, 2000, wrestled with conundrums like this one: "American Indian" or "Indian (Amer.)"?

Their aim: to deter those with a heritage in the India of curry and Gandhi from checking that box as if they were Sioux or Cherokee.

For most of this decade—largely unseen and on a democratic scale without precedent—the two agencies have enlisted help in and out of government to find up-to-date words for that awkward, yet persistent question: What kind of American are you?

How the various kinds cluster across the land helps weigh the fairness of bank loans and school assignments, of employment and pay. The labels aid scientists tracking diseases that plague certain groups, and drug companies selling the cures. They're used to ensure voting rights are upheld, and to attract federal, local, and private aid for historical victims of bias.

George Washington was president barely a year when the first census was taken in August 1790. Its only purpose, then as now and fixed in the Constitution, was to ap-

---

*Source: The Bryan-College Station Eagle, September 28, 1997, p. A6.

portion U.S. House seats. But the first census counted "free white" males and females, any other free persons, and slaves.

The 1850 census was the first to ask census takers to record race, under a "color" heading. But it was the civil rights movement of the 1960s that paved the way for today's acute attention to race.

Today, there are racial-minority advisers galore offering guidance. Plus top researchers from government, universities and private enterprise, demographers and anthropologists, civil rights lawyers and marketing experts. The National Academy of Sciences was enlisted. The public trooped into hearings from Boston to Honolulu. Congress heard testimony. Add the nameless good sports who submitted to test surveys and participation soars upwards of 250,000 Americans.

The Census Bureau and the OMB have different missions. The bureau, as part of the Commerce Department, counts people. The OMB is the higher authority, dictating federal standards, including names for things and people. The basic categories OMB decrees get used by all federal agencies. But they pop up far beyond, from birth records to death certificates, at school enrollment time, and on job applications.

The OMB expects to issue its final decision on the basic racial and ethnic categories by mid-October, which should give the Census Bureau time to make any changes before its spring 1998 dress rehearsal.

But many note that race is a social invention. They wish the labels would go away, and are impatient for that day to arrive.

Among the hundreds of letters that poured in when the government's quest began was this plea from Joanne Specht of San Jose, Calif.

"I do not encourage people to forget their heritage but these demands to be called a Black-American or Asian-American, etc., are deunifying America," she wrote. "Why can't we all be called just American?"

Specht signed herself: "American—freckled."

R E A D I N G S   2 . 3

"New" Indians Give Rise to Tribal Ire*

PAT BEALL

Across the South, American Indian populations are surging—due not to any acceleration in birth rates, but to increasing numbers of people asserting an ethnic identity that established Indian communities view with skepticism and even alarm.

According to the U.S. Census Bureau, the number of people who identify themselves as Native American is growing at a much faster pace in the South, from Texas to Florida, than in the nation as a whole. From 1980 to 1990, the number of such peo-

---

*Source: The Wall Street Journal, October 30, 1996, p. T1.

ple increased 71% in Dallas and more than 80% in Miami, Tampa and Atlanta. Many of these newly declared Indians belong to new tribes seeking government recognition; more than half of the 215 Cherokee tribes unrecognized by Washington are in Alabama, Florida, Georgia, North Carolina, Tennessee and Texas.

Previously undeclared Indians say they are claiming publicly a heritage that fear of discrimination long forced them to hide. "Growing up, I was told I was Cherokee, but not to tell anyone," says June Hegstrom, a representative to the Georgia State Assembly and a member of a recently state-recognized Cherokee tribe. "You have to understand, there were laws that made it illegal to be a Cherokee in Georgia. If you were of any Indian descent, you certainly didn't advertise it."

Motives Questioned

But many Indians who belong to federally recognized tribes of long standing consider the newcomers opportunists hoping to cash in on Indian-owned casino gambling operations and other perquisites of tribal sovereignty. They also fear the potential for increased competition among Indians for ethnic entitlements, including federal job-training and education benefits, for which federal spending is already shrinking.

The danger, they say, is that rising numbers of people who are Native American in name only will ultimately sap established tribes' political clout and dilute tribal culture. Says Richard Allen, research and policy analyst of the Cherokee Nation in Tahlequah, Okla.: "We are not flattered."

Consider the Kickapoo. Until August this year, members of the tiny Kickapoo Traditional Tribe of Texas attracted little attention where they live near remote Eagle Pass, speaking their ancient language and sheltering in cardboard huts under highway bridges. But then the Kickapoo opened their first and only casino, a 16,000-square-foot pink stucco attraction dubbed the Lucky Eagle. Now, says tribe administrator Robert De La Garza, Kickapoo membership carries cachet.

"People drive up all the time and talk to us about how their grandmother was a Kickapoo," he says. "Seems like everybody's grandmother is a Kickapoo Indian." Mr. De La Garza says his tribe will help investigate the bloodline of anyone who thinks he is a Kickapoo. He doubts there will be many who are, however, because Kickapoo have rarely married outside the tribe, which now numbers only 500 members.

In some states—notably, Georgia and North Carolina—newly proclaimed groups of Indians are gaining recognition from state lawmakers, thus qualifying for certain benefits without undergoing federal application procedures that can take a decade. In 1993, the Georgia Assembly recognized three new groups—two Cherokee and one Muscogee—even though some other tribes question their authenticity.

Fashion Statements

Nadine Horne, a Mohawk Indian and founder of the Recognized First Nations Advocacy Group in Augusta, Ga., says some members of the recently recognized tribes "were wearing Arapaho beads mixed with Mohawk or Seneca beads. It was like a bad John Wayne movie where they dress up the white actors to look like Indians."

Indeed, she and other members of federally recognized tribes question the ability of lawmakers to determine who is and isn't an Indian. "It's as though a state was telling Peru who is and is not a Peruvian," Ms. Horne says.

In Florida, the Governor's Commission on Indian Affairs has received unconfirmed reports of self-proclaimed Cherokees soliciting tribal-joining fees from individuals who hope to enjoy a share of Indian benefits. The agency says recognized Cherokee tribes in the state don't require joining fees from legitimate members.

Joe A. Quetone, the Florida commission's executive director, says these scammers focus on elderly people, telling them that if they join the tribe, the tribe will provide medical care, housing and the like free of charge and they won't have to pay taxes. "That doesn't even happen on the reservations," Mr. Quetone says. "Believe me, I'm a Kiowah Indian and I don't have a free house and I pay local, state and federal taxes."

Certainly, compared with the federal process, state recognition can be easily had. The Lower Muscogee Creek Tribe of Georgia sought federal recognition for 22 years before being turned down in 1981 by the U.S. Department of the Interior's Bureau of Indian Affairs, which determined that only about two of every 10 members of the group actually had a traceable Indian ancestor. The Georgia Assembly recognized the Muscogees along with the two new Cherokee tribes in a single measure in 1993.

Authentic or not, tribes with a state's seal of approval do qualify for cash, even when federal recognition isn't forthcoming. Federal money for education and job training has been awarded to the state-recognized Indians in North Carolina and Georgia. Economic-development programs for Indian-owned businesses are available to North Carolina's five state-recognized tribes, as well as that state's single federally recognized tribe. Further, some tribes in Georgia and North Carolina say they plan to use their state recognition to argue for federal recognition, which bestows the right to open casinos.

The "S" Word

That scenario chills members of federally recognized tribes. "There are people who can scalp a heck of a lot of money off this," says Ms. Horne of the Recognized First Nations Advocacy Group.

Deborah Craytor, an attorney with the Atlanta office of Holland & Knight who is representing several Indians from federally recognized tribes in the Southeast, says her clients "want to figure out a way to stop" Georgia from sanctioning more tribes. Earlier this year, she filed a lawsuit against the state in federal court in Atlanta seeking to stop the state from recognizing more tribes, but she withdrew the suit after a U.S. Supreme Court ruling recently limited the rights of tribes to sue state governments.

(Last year, the Georgia Assembly did turn down the three state-recognized tribes' request to create so-called Indian Housing Agencies that would be eligible for funds from the federal Department of Housing and Urban Development, partly because federally recognized tribes opposed the request.)

Dexter Lehtinen, a Miami attorney representing the federally recognized Miccosukee Tribe of Indians of Florida, is opposing attempts by other tribes in Florida to gain state recognition. "The real danger with all these new tribes," he says, "is that opponents of Indians will point to them and begin to say there are too many tribes able to exercise these rights, and so the doctrines of sovereign immunity and Indian control over their land should be abolished."

CHAPTER 3

I SEE WHAT I KNOW

Group Perceptions and Stereotypes

They say that one sign of advancing age is a tendency to glorify the past. If this is the case, I have surely entered old age. Life today seems so complicated and confused. I have great compassion for my daughters, who are faced with so many choices, who have so many decisions to make, and who must find order in a chaotic world. I contrast this situation with my early life, the good old days, when the world was orderly and simple. But even as I look back with fondness, I can detect a certain sinister character lurking in the background of this simplicity.

I grew up in a quiet middle-class neighborhood in Austin, Texas. There was amazingly little difference between the families in my neighborhood. Each earned a comfortable, but not large, income. The boys played football and baseball, and the girls seemed to be occupied with more domestic activities. Fathers held jobs outside the home, and mothers were homemakers. Similarity of behavior was not the only attribute that characterized the families. All the families were white. All the students in my school were white. The members of my football and baseball teams were white. I had almost no direct contact with anyone from a different ethnic group.

But despite my sheltered existence, I "knew" all about black people. Blacks lived in another section of town and went to different schools. "They" were poor, "they" weren't very smart, "they" were lazy, choosing to spend their time fighting or engaging in scandalous sexual activities rather than working or studying. Those folks were dangerous, and I was best advised to keep away from them and their neighborhoods. All my friends knew that this was what "they" were like. I had an equally clear impression of Hispanics. I could even give a detailed description of my country's archenemies, the Russians and the Chinese, although I'd never met even one member of these groups.

Everyone and everything had its place, and life was comfortable until I took a trip on the train with my father to Seattle, Washington. This was an exciting adventure for a 9-year-old boy. I was prepared to see new country and new sights—mountains, the Grand Canyon, the desert, and the Pacific Ocean. You don't find these things in Austin, Texas. But I was not prepared for the situation I faced just outside Los Angeles. A black man boarded the train and took a place in our compartment. As it turned out, he was a student and a star running back on the football team, traveling to the University of Washington for football practice.

I carefully inspected him from a vantage point behind my father. This guy was clean, strong, and handsome, and he was going to college—interesting, but confusing, given my clear picture of black people. I remember the panic I felt when my father left the compartment, leaving me alone with this man. What do you say to a black person? Was I safe? The man smiled at me and asked where I was going. When I sheepishly replied, he began telling me about places to see in the Seattle area. Then the conversation turned to the topic closest to my heart, football. He told me about his team, showed me some of his awards and newspaper clippings, and tossed me a football he had in his suitcase. I was in heaven, albeit a somewhat strange one, all the way to Seattle. This guy was great! I don't think I looked outside the train car the whole way to Seattle. When he departed, he gave me a small football medal, and I hugged him.

The incident left me in a state of confusion for many years thereafter. I didn't have the same image of blacks that my friends had. I felt I had a black friend, and my view of blacks was moving toward the positive side. I couldn't "get into" the racial jokes my friends made, and I even admonished them when they used derogatory racial names. As a result, I began to feel like an outcast from my own group; I felt left out. They all "knew" what blacks were like, but after my experience on the train, I wasn't sure I knew any longer.

I Know, Therefore I Act: Bias in Social Perceptions

I've always believed that I'm a reasonable fellow. I carefully consider what is going on in my world and respond in an appropriate fashion. I deal with obvious facts, reality, when explaining my behavior and the behavior of others. I'm not blinded by bias, mine or other people's. All this sounds good, but is this really how I behave? Are my judgments and actions guided by the objective reality of the outside world or by the subjective reality of my mind? Recent research in social cognition casts doubt on my laudatory view of myself and suggests that my actions are guided by "psychologic" (the logic of the mind) more often than by unbiased scientific logic. We make predictable "mistakes" when drawing inferences about ourselves and others. And these "mistakes" can influence our perceptions of our own ethnic groups and other groups.

For example, Jones and Nisbett (1971) found that we tend to believe that whereas we respond to our environment, other people's behavior is dictated by their internal traits. For example, when I spank my child, it is because she has done something naughty. But when I observe another father spank his kid, I am likely to conclude that he is an aggressive person. Likewise, when I discriminate against someone from another group, by denying him or her a job, for example, I believe that I am doing it because the person is undeserving (e.g., unqualified, unskilled, or untrustworthy). However, if others discriminate, I perceive them as doing so because they are unkind and unthinking. The tendency to attribute underlying dispositions to others on

We tend to see our own acts as being elicited by the environment but the acts of others as resulting from their internal dispositions. In the eyes of the participants, violence is justified by the acts of the opponent. (Reuters/David Silverman/Archive Photos)

the basis of their observable behavior is especially strong when their actions affect us (hedonic relevance) and are interpreted as being aimed at us (personalism).

Consider the implications of these processes for relationships between ethnic groups. If you or possibly someone from your group treats others badly, you put aside your misgivings by concluding that the target elicited (deserved) the actions. But if someone from your group, especially if that someone is you, is on the receiving end of harsh treatment, you are likely to conclude that the actor's behavior resulted from his or her traits or disposition, that the person was malevolent. As we shall see, this is only a short step from assigning the trait to the actor's entire group. What a wonderful system! It endows us (and ours) with Teflon and drapes others with flypaper.

There are a number of explanations for this difference between actor and observer. First, we know our own history; we know that we don't always act the same way. However, we have limited information about the past behavior of others, so it is easy to believe that they often act in ways we have observed. A second possibility implicates nature, which constructed us with our eyes pointing outward. When I observe the behavior of others, my attention is focused on them. They are the most salient features in my field of vision, and therefore I am likely to attribute the cause of their actions to their dispositions. However, when I act, my eyes are directed outward, away from my actions. So I readily view my actions as responding to the demands of the situation and attribute their cause to the environment. A third explanation for this bias is that we have a general tendency to think more positively of ourselves and our group than of others (Sande, Goethals, & Radloff, 1988). It is rather flattering to view our actions (especially negative ones such as failure or aggression) as resulting from situational demands. We have less need to see others in these terms, so we are comfortable attributing their actions to their traits.

It is easy to see how this bias can justify hatred and discrimination. We hate others because we are responding appropriately to their negative behaviors. They hate us because they are aggressive and mean-spirited. We, or our group, did nothing to invite this behavior. Hence we feel little reluctance in assigning traits and characteristics (stereotypes) to others and their groups (Jones & Davis, 1965).

The bias that creeps into our social perceptions almost inevitably guides our behavior as well. It is very important to realize that our responses to events and people are guided by our appraisal or interpretation, and not by the event itself (Lazarus, 1993). For example, if you give me a slap on the back I will respond aggressively if I interpret your action as aimed at hurting me. But I will respond to the same slap with gratitude if I believe that you intended to kill a wasp that had landed on me. Since I can't know your intentions and the slap on the back is the same in both cases, it is my appraisal that determines my response. Similarly, two people may confront the same situation but respond differently if they interpret it differently.

A number of factors can affect our interpretations of behaviors. One of the more interesting elements is our *expectations;* we often interpret situations to fit them (Snyder & Swann, 1978). To see how this works, consider the following example. On one of my early trips to Poland, I was warned by several people that Poles were untrustworthy and that there had been several reports of assaults on and robbery of tourists in Poland. I arrived in Krakow late one evening only to find that there were no vacancies in the hotels. As I stood outside a hotel wondering what to do, a young man approached and asked if he could help. Before thinking, I told him my predicament, and he offered to let me have a room in his family's home for the night. But by this time, my mind was in full gear. I remembered the warnings I had received before my trip. This overture of friendship must be a ruse; the man was only trying to get me alone so he could steal my belongings. I abruptly declined the invitation, priding myself on my wisdom, and proceeded to spend one of the most uncomfortable nights of my life camped in the Krakow train station. The next morning, I met an Israeli friend, who recounted that he had had a similar encounter the night before. But since no one had warned him about the evil intentions of Poles, he did not interpret the offer as having a sinister intent; he viewed it as a gesture of friendship. So he had spent a restful and socially rewarding night in the home of a Polish family!

The implications of this "expectancy effect" for ethnic relations should be obvious. Our expectancies about members of an ethnic group shape our interpretations of their behaviors and our responses to them. An overture of friendship can be interpreted as evil if we expect evil. And we interpret something as wicked once we respond to our interpretation. Notice also that because our actions are based on our interpretations, our behavior often ensures that our expectations remain frozen in our minds. I responded to the Polish man's friendly offer by withdrawing, and my response enabled me to retain my view of Poles as dangerous and untrustworthy.

Getting What We Expect

Our expectations affect how we appraise and interpret actions. But our expectations also play another interesting role in our relationships. In order to illustrate this role, let's consider a classic study by Rosenthal and Jacobson (1968). The experimenters told teachers at an elementary school that certain of their students could be expected to show dramatic spurts in academic achievement during the year. Supposedly, this prediction was based on scores on a reliable achievement test. Actually there was no such test. One-third of the students, chosen at *random*, were simply presented to the teachers as "spurters." At the end of the school year, the experimenters measured the IQ of all the students. As can be seen in Figure 3.1, the children who had been randomly designated "spurters" showed marked improvement in comparison with the other students.

How do we explain this difference? The investigators argued that the teachers' expectations about the students' potential unwittingly affected their own behavior,

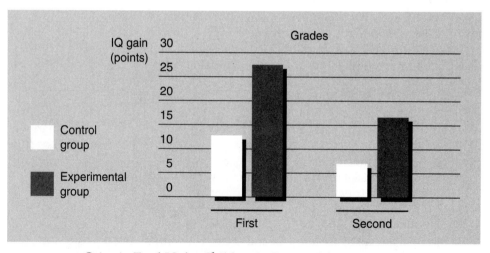

FIGURE 3-1   Gains in Total IQ for Children in First and Second Grades.
Source: Rosenthal and Jacobson (1968).

so that they encouraged the behavior they expected from the students. In other words, a *self-fulfilling prophecy* was involved. Although the teachers reported that they acted no differently toward the two groups of students, there were in fact small differences that accounted for the effects. The teachers smiled at the "spurters" more often and provided a warmer environment for them than for the other students. They gave the spurters more detailed feedback about what they should and should not do. The spurters were given more opportunities to answer questions and perform in class. These small, generally unconscious differences in the teachers' behaviors motivated the spurters to do better. Hence, the spurters achieved in line with the teachers' expectations.

Just as our expectations may lead us to behave in a way that elicits the responses from others that we expect, the resultant behavior may then reinforce our initial expectation. Research has also shown that our expectations are influenced by our experience in previous situations (Webb & Worchel, 1993). If I expect African-Americans to be aggressive, I may wittingly or unwittingly act in a cool, withdrawn manner. If my behavior elicits an aggressive response from the African-American with whom I am in contact, I may use that response to reinforce my opinion of African-Americans as aggressive.

At a group level, we find the expectancy effect creating ethnic conflict and war through the image of a "diabolical enemy" (White, 1966). Consider the situation in the Middle East. The Israelis have a very negative view of the Palestine Liberation Organization (PLO). As the former prime minister Yitzhak Shamir stated, "Even if we overlook the bloodthirsty modus operandi, [its] subservience to Soviet aims, and [its] key role in international terror, the PLO's very raison d'être is the denial of Israel's right to exist" (Shamir, 1982, p. 793). This type of perspective justified Israel's efforts to build strong armed forces and its swift and aggressive responses against Palestinians for acts of terrorism. Some Palestinians responded with further terrorism, which only strengthened the Jews' perceptions of the Arabs as dangerous and aggressive. The Israeli Jews characterized their actions as "defensive" while viewing the Arab's aggression as offensive. The self-fulfilling prophecy also was seen in the Palestinians. They viewed Israeli Jews as aggressive and dangerous: "Israel, in its capacity as the spearhead of this destructive movement (Zionism) and the pillar for colonialism is a permanent source of tension and turmoil in the Middle East" (National Covenant of the Palestine Liberation Organization, 1964, p. 378). With these expectations, the PLO justified its aggression as defensive, and it used the Israelis' responses as support for its view of the Jews as aggressive and dangerous. Therefore, a self-fulfilling prophecy being played out simultaneously on two stages keeps ethnic hatred and aggression alive and well in the Middle East. Two groups view themselves as defensive in their search for peace, each uses the other's aggression as "evidence" of violent intentions.

Expectations, then, focus our attention, affect our appraisal and interpretation of events, and invite us to respond in ways that lead to the confirmation of our expectations. Therefore, a question of critical importance for understanding ethnic group relations concerns how expectations about ethnic groups are formed. I will address this issue later in the chapter, when I explore the formation of stereotypes.

Lonely (But Simple) Planet:
No People, Only Groups

One morning, I opened the newspaper and glanced at the headlines. I intended to learn a bit about my world, but I actually learned more about how people (or at least people who write newspapers) organize my world. I read headlines proclaiming, "Hispanics Are Leery About Kemp," "Texas Democrats Give $6M to Clinton," "Blacks Concerned About Condition of Black Colleges," and "Australians Riot Over Tax Issues." Having identified with the Democratic party for years, I checked my bank account and found that there had been no draft of funds for Clinton. I next called several of my Hispanic friends to comfort them about the Republican nominee for vice president, but I found that Jack Kemp was the last issue on their mind. At lunch with a black colleague, I asked, "So, what are your worries about the condition of black colleges?" Her response was a delayed, "Huh? What black colleges are you referring to?" And finally, I e-mailed my Australian friends to inquire whether any of them had been injured in the riot. Response: "What riot?"

My newspaper had not embarked on a campaign to mislead. Rather, its headlines demonstrated a common tendency that we all have when dealing with our world. Our world is enormously complex. It is impossible to file each bit of information we receive in its own drawer; imagine the size of your dresser if you had a different drawer for each piece of clothing you owned. As a result, our minds use a system of filing together items (objects, events, or people) that share certain attributes. Just as you put all your underwear in a single drawer, your mind puts into a single category (*schema*) all people who have in common a characteristic such as ethnic origin. Hence, we form categories or groups based on the principle of "fit" (Campbell, 1958). Milgram (1970), for example, found that people in large cities tend to have two major categories for people they encounter: friends and strangers. In other words, we become cognitive misers: "We categorize people into groups as a means of reducing the amount of information we must contend with" (Hamilton & Trolier, 1986, p. 128).

John Turner (1991) argues that our categorization of people into groups is encouraged by our desire to develop our own self-identify (see Chapter 1) in addition to our need to simplify the world. We begin the categorization process by determining the groups or categories to which we belong. After taking stock of our characteristics, we put ourselves into the same categories as other people who share these characteristics. At the same time, we exclude people from our group who are not seen as sharing these characteristics. Collectively, these others become the "outgroup." But the process goes a step further, in many cases, as we place members of the collective out-group into their own specific groups and subcategories, based on perceived commonalities and differences.

According to Turner and his colleagues (Oakes et al., 1994), the categorization process is dynamic, sensitive to the context of the moment. The current situation determines which categories will be most accessible to us at a given time. If I'm engaged in a conversation about politics in the United States, I might form categories based on political parties: Democrats and Republicans. However, if the conversation turns to world politics, my categories will include democratic governments, communist governments, and dictatorships. There is also a tendency to make finer distinctions for areas we are familiar with. For example, when I consider the United States, I have many categories: Mainers, New Yorkers, Virginians, and so on. A German may have only one: Americans (everyone from the United States).

Categorization of people into groups sets the stage for stereotyping and prejudice. But it is not merely a cognitive process, involving only our minds. For, as we will discuss later, placing people into categories or groups guides our behavior. We often react to members of groups in a prescribed way, rather than reacting to individuals irrespective of their group identity. We not only put Miguel into our group labeled Hispanic, but we respond to Miguel in the same way we respond to other Hispanics. This occurs even though Miguel is a unique individual who possess many attributes not possessed by many other Hispanics.

"They" Are All the Same, But Each Member of My Group Is Unique

I have shown how we endow individuals with the characteristics of their groups. But the human mind is not a one-way street. We also assign to the group the characteristics of a few members. This is an interesting process, and it has far-reaching implications. Some years ago, I took my first trip to China. During my visit, I probably interacted with 20 to 30 Chinese for any length of time. Upon returning, I encountered a Chinese colleague, and during our conversation I proclaimed that I finally had a good picture of the Chinese people: "They are bright, hardworking, happy, and friendly." My colleague smiled and asked me to describe Americans. I was taken aback, but after considerable thought I politely informed him that Americans are so diverse that it is really impossible to describe them in a few words. He never stopped smiling as he reminded me that there are over a billion people in China, including 28 distinct minority groups, yet I had no trouble describing "Chinese people" after meeting only 20 to 30 of them.

There is considerable evidence that we often view out-groups as homogeneous, while we see considerable diversity within our own group. For example, Quattrone and Jones (1980) asked students at Princeton and Rutgers university to describe the student body at their own and the other university. In both cases, the students perceived considerably more variability within the student body at their own university. Linville, Fischer, and Salavoy (1989) found that residence of an elderly people's home and a student group rated the other age group as more homogeneous than their own group. There are some exceptions to this tendency. For example, people in minority groups often see their group as more homogeneous than the majority group (Simon & Brown, 1987), and members of new groups see their groups as more homogeneous than out-groups (Worchel, Coutant-Sassic, & Grossman, 1992). However, the inclination to see homogeneity in an out-group is very pervasive.

It has been argued that this effect occurs because we generally have more information from a greater variety of experiences with members of our own group than with members of out-groups. I've interacted with thousands of Americans in work, social, and religious settings, but my interactions with the Chinese were limited to professional situations in which we were strangers to each other. I failed to take this difference into account when forming my mental image of the Chinese. Another possibility is that because our in-group is more important to us and we have a higher motivation to perceive it correctly, we develop a more varied picture of it (Park, Judd, & Ryan, 1991).

But whatever the basis, consider the implications of this process. First, if I believe that members of other ethnic groups are similar, I will quickly form an impression of the whole group after meeting only a few of its members: "Know one, know them all." Second, I can justify limiting my interaction with an out-group because I'll know about the group and its members after only a few contacts. This reduced contact will ensure that my representation of the group is rarely challenged. I felt little need to return to China or meet other Chinese, because I now had a "good" picture of the group. I was ready to expand my growing knowledge of the world's people by taking a week's trip to Brazil.

Putting Groups in Their (Cognitive) Place: Stereotyping

One of the most wonderful aspects of youth is certainty. When I was young, I "knew" the characteristics of African-Americans, Hispanics, Jews, Russians, Turks, Arabs, and Germans. When that young black athlete entered my train compartment, I "knew" all about him because I could see that he was black. *Stereotypes* are our beliefs about the characteristics of people in a certain group. They allow us to draw inferences about an individual based on his or her group membership. In the final analysis, stereotypes form the foundation for our expectations about the behavior of members of ethnic groups. Once I categorize you as English, my stereotype of English people becomes the basis for my predictions about your behavior.

Stereotypes are a convenient cognitive shorthand for organizing our world (Table 3.1). But they play other roles as well. Stereotypes represent our causal model of the world (Yzerbyt & Schadron, 1994). If I view people's actions as being guided by their personalities or traits, developing a stereotype that is composed of traits enables me to explain their behaviors: "He failed the test because he is Italian, and Italians are not intelligent." So stereotypes can help justify our treatment of out-groups (Jost & Banaji, 1994). If we cheat a Jew in a business transaction, we can put salve on our guilt by concluding that he or she deserved it because Jews are greedy. I can recall an old landlord explaining his tardiness in fixing the plumbing in the apartment of a Greek family by stating, "Greeks are dirty, anyway. . . . They won't mind not having hot water for a while." Finally, stereotypes often describe the relationship that exists between our group and the other group (Ellemers & van Knippenberg, 1997). Poor educational opportunity for many African-Americans is reflected in the stereotype that this group is not motivated and is not easily educated. We generally hold more negative ideas about groups that we view as threats or enemies (Tables 3.2 and 3.3). Useful things these packages we call stereotypes! But what do stereotypes actually include?

TABLE 3.1   Ethnic Images of Groups Compared to Whites

Reported results of a survey asking people to rank certain ethnic groups on a scale of one to seven (one being most positive, seven being most negative). The results are presented relative to the perception given to whites.

Question/ranking (compared to whites)	Group	Mean difference
"How are certain groups rated concerning wealth (richer versus poorer)?"		
1st	Jews	+0.58
2nd	Whites	0.00
3rd	Southern Whites	−0.56
4th	Asian Americans	−0.77
5th	Blacks	−1.60
6th	Hispanics	−1.64
"How are certain groups rated concerning work ethic (hardworking versus lazy)?"		
1st	Jews	+0.38
2nd	Whites	0.00
3rd	Asian Americans	−0.19
4th	Southern Whites	−0.52
5th	Hispanics	−0.99
6th	Blacks	−1.24
"How are certain groups rated concerning violence (not violence-prone versus violence-prone)?"		
1st	Jews	+0.36
2nd	Whites	0.00
3rd	Asian Americans	−0.15
4th	Southern Whites	−0.23
5th	Hispanics	−0.75
6th	Blacks	−1.00
"How are certain groups rated concerning intelligence (intelligent versus unintelligent)?"		
1st	Jews	+0.15
2nd	Whites	0.00
3rd	Asian Americans	−0.36
4th	Southern Whites	−0.53
5th	Blacks	−0.93
6th	Hispanics	−0.96
"How are certain groups rated concerning dependency (self-supporting versus live off welfare)?"		
1st	Jews	+0.40
2nd	Whites	0.00
3rd	Southern Whites	−0.71
4th	Asian Americans	−0.75
5th	Hispanics	−1.72
6th	Blacks	−2.08

Source: Smith, T. W. (1991). *What Americans Say about Jews.* New York: American Jewish Committee.

TABLE 3.2 Perceived Power and Influence of Ethnic Groups

Reported results, in percent, of a survey asking people to give their opinion on how much political influence certain groups have.

Group	Response rate, %			
	Too much	About right	Too little	Don't know
Asian Americans	6.3%	41.0%	37.3%	15.4%
Whites	25.2%	64.2%	5.8%	4.8%
Southern Whites	10.4%	61.6%	14.7%	13.3%
Blacks	14.2%	31.4%	46.9%	7.5%
Hispanics	4.7%	36.9%	45.5%	12.9%
Jews	21.2%	54.5%	12.6%	11.7%

Source: Smith (1991), table 9, pp. 41–42; from *General Social Survey*, National Research Center, University of Chicago, 1990.

Stereotypes were initially viewed as being composed of traits (often physical) that characterized a group (Katz & Braly, 1933). In other words, my stereotype of the Chinese might include such adjectives as industrious, intelligent, happy, and friendly. This idea led to active research in human cognition, attempting to determine how we develop and store these characterizations. On the one hand, some theorists suggested that our stereotypes are stored as abstract representations of the typical or average features (the *prototype*) of a group (Cantor & Mischel, 1978). On the other hand, some investigators argued we store information in the form of concrete examples, or *exemplars* (Smith & Zarate, 1992). "The stereotype of African Americans as athletic, for example, is thought to be stored in the form of specific individuals (e.g. Michael Jordan, Carl Lewis)" (Hilton & von Hipple, 1996, p. 242).

Recently, investigators have returned their attention to the basic concept of the stereotype, arguing that a stereotype contains more than just traits (Worchel & Rothgerber, 1997). Stereotypes, they argue, also include a categorization of the group involved (Figure 3.2—see page 68). For example, my stereotype of the Chinese may involve all Chinese people, or it may involve only Chinese people in the People's Republic of China. Stereotypes also involve a belief about how homogeneous the target group is. Although I may characterize the Chinese as friendly, I might believe either that there is considerable variability among Chinese on this trait or that all or most Chinese are friendly. Finally, stereotypes involve an estimation of the centrality of each trait in describing the group. I might believe that friendliness is the most defining characteristic of the Chinese, or I might see it as a minor trait in the constellation that describes Chinese people.

I have argued that this multidimensional view of stereotypes is important because it reflects how stereotypes can change along any or all of these dimensions. I recall seeing the transformation of my friend John's belief about black people. When John arrived at college to play football, he proclaimed that blacks were lazy.

TABLE 3.3 Perceived Intergroup Relations

Reported results, in %, of a survey asking people to give their opinion on how they thought one ethnic group felt towards other ethnic groups

Reference group	Disliked by . . .			
	Asian Americans	Whites	Blacks	Hispanics
Asian Americans	1%	29%	17%	10%
Whites	13%	1%	56%	19%
Blacks	10%	53%	2%	18%
Hispanics	6%	36%	26%	2%
American Indians	4%	24%	8%	4%
Catholics	8%	3%	7%	2%
Jews	9%	14%	7%	8%

Reference group	Disliked by . . .		
	American Indians	Catholics	Jews
Asian Americans	4%	5%	8%
Whites	16%	2%	4%
Blacks	7%	6%	11%
Hispanics	4%	3%	7%
American Indians	1%	3%	4%
Catholics	3%	1%	24%
Jews	4%	16%	2%

Source: Smith (1991), table 23, pp. 62–63; from Princeton Survey Research Associates, May 1990.

However, we had a wonderfully skilled black West Indian player on the team who worked hard to develop his talent. After some time, John announced that it is only African-American blacks who were lazy. He broke down his category "black" into subtypes, which enabled him to maintain that his stereotype was still correct. Later John confided to me that there was really some diversity among blacks: *most* were lazy, but others were very hardworking. Throughout the year John maintained his view that blacks were lazy, but his stereotype underwent quite a bit of change.

A second expansion of the idea of stereotypes is that some investigators have viewed them as residing within a group as well as within individuals (Bar-Tal, 1994; Worchel & Rothgerber, 1997). Daniel Bar-Tal (1990b) coined the term *group belief* to describe beliefs that a group holds. For example, a group belief of citizens of the United States is that democracy is the best form of government. A stereotype might also be a group belief. The portrayal of Arabs as untrustworthy, dangerous, and lazy might be a group belief of Israeli Jews. Indeed, an Israeli Jew might feel that in order to be accepted by other Israeli Jews, he or she must hold this stereotype of Arabs.

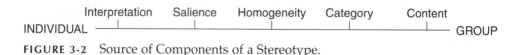

FIGURE 3-2   Source of Components of a Stereotype.

This view also helps explain why people hold stereotypes of groups they have no contact with. Murer (1996) pointed out a perplexing rise of anti-Semitism in Hungary in the last decade despite the fact that there are very few Jews in East Central Europe. Murer suggested that a negative view of Jews was an old attitude held by Hungarians as a group, and that its rise was a response to the trauma Hungary suffered after World War II. These events created a need to direct anger toward an out-group, and Jews were a convenient target because anti-Semitic views had been passed down through generations of Hungarians.

Developing Stereotypes: Who Is to Blame?

Given that stereotypes represent our view of other groups, how do we explain the content of stereotypes? This seems like a rather simple and straightforward question, but think for a moment before answering. Stereotypes have some unique characteristics that make finding their source an interesting journey. First, we often hold stereotypes of groups with which we have had no contact and little firsthand knowledge. I had a very clear view of Russians before I ever met one. Second, despite their tarnished reputation, stereotypes may be, in part, rather accurate representations (Judd & Park, 1993). As Ichheiser argued, "The stereotypes concerning characteristics of cultural and racial groups are a combination of truth and falsehood (1970, p. 76)." (We'll look at this issue in more depth later in this chapter.) Third, as I pointed out, stereotypes are often shared by whole groups of people. Fourth, as we will see, stereotypes are very resistant to change. We often hold on to the content of our stereotypes even in the face of mounting evidence that they may not be correct (Oakes, Haslam, & Turner, 1994). And finally, stereotypes form at a very young age. Jewish children as young as 4 years old were found to have stereotypes of Arabs (Bar-Tal, in press). Thus, finding the sources of stereotypes is a challenge.

INTERGROUP RELATIONS.   Bar-Tal (1996) has engaged in some detective work to identify how stereotypes are developed. His search has led him to implicate a number of sources that contribute to the development of our stereotypes and others that are responsible for transmitting this information to us. The relationship between our group and the target group tends to influence the development of our stereotypes.

As you might expect, a positive or cooperative relationship tends to develop positive content, while a negative, competitive relationship leads to a more evil picture. This point hit a responsive chord in me as I remember my past and present pictures of Russians. As a child of the Cold War, I remember viewing Russians as evil, untrustworthy, aggressive, cold, and unfriendly. My stereotypes were neatly confirmed by the Cuban missile crisis in 1961 and (much later) by the Russians' involvement in the Afghan war in 1992. But recent events, beginning with Gorbachev's overture of friendship to the United States and the cooperative atmosphere of the mid-1990s brought about slow and reluctant changes in my stereotype. In 1997 I even found myself waiting with growing anxiety for the new Russian team of "bright, capable, and concerned" cosmonauts to arrive at the Mir space station to begin repairs and save the visiting American astronaut there. I had come full circle. Now I view the Russians as being not such bad folks; they are bright and personally cautious but warm. I eagerly seek out my Russian colleagues. I'd like to think that the Russian people suddenly underwent a massive personality transformation in 1993. But, more than likely, they are the same as they were in 1992; only the relationship between my country and theirs has changed.

Although present intergroup relations are important for determining the content of stereotypes, past history is not irrelevant. "Can Poles forget at least five centuries of continuous active conflict with Germans, including two world wars? Can Bulgarians or Greeks forget at least three centuries of domination by the Turks? Can the Jews forget the Holocaust perpetrated on them a half century ago by Germans?" (Bar-Tal, 1996). Obviously, the Serbs did not forget their betrayal by the Croats during World War II. According to Bar-Tal, groups have a collective memory that includes the history of their relationships with other groups. This history is transmitted to new generations and helps define the individual's and the group's perception of these other groups. Although I may plead for my African-American friends to see that I have not discriminated against them, the shameful treatment of their ancestors by white Americans is forever etched in their collective mind.

Paul Berman (1994) illustrates how a combination of past history and the present situation can affect the nature of stereotypes. He reviews the writings of Jankelevitch, one of Freud's earliest translators, whose son was a hero in the French Resistance during World War II. Jankelevitch struggled to understand the sources of hatred between groups of people. He suggested that some of the most violent hatred resulted between groups that had much in common but at present had small differences—groups that were neither "other" nor "brother." Jankelevitch pointed to the negative stereotypes and conflicts that often occur between the Dutch and the Belgians; Berman applied this doctrine to the relationship between Jews and African-Americans. Similarities between groups (in history, characteristics, or other dimensions) leads them to compare themselves with one another. In order for each group to maintain its distinct identity, the group must amplify its differences from other similar groups—its uniqueness. Further, the desire for a favorable comparison with a similar out-group is threatened if the other out-group has positive attributes or is achieving success. Therefore, the success of a similar out-group excites more hatred and negative stereotypes because it indirectly reflects badly on one's own other group. (In Chapter 5, I'll expand on this ironic combination of history and present situation and illustrate how it leads to dislike between groups even under the microscope of the laboratory.)

But the nature of stereotypes is affected by more than just the groups involved in the relationship. In my own laboratory, we created three groups (Rothgerber & Worchel, 1997). Two of the groups (disadvantaged groups) had to confront a difficult environment; one group (advantaged group) had a very positive environment. All groups worked on a series of tasks and received reports on their own performance and that of the other two groups. At the end of the experiment, the participants were asked to give their impression of the other groups. Despite the fact that the performance of the advantaged group was *the same* in all conditions, that group was viewed more negatively by the members of one disadvantaged group when they believed that the other disadvantaged group was doing poorly than when they thought it was doing well. In other words, the performance of one out-group affected the impression people formed of another out-group. Reports from the participants

Violence against others becomes so much easier when individuals are perceived as members of a category and all members of that category are believed to be the same. Concentration camps were designed to exterminate groups, not individuals, and the line between the executioners and the executed was often very thin. (Gamma Liaison International)

indicated that those in the disadvantaged groups compared themselves with the other disadvantaged group. Only when they felt that their group was superior to the other disadvantaged group did they turn their attention to the advantaged group, hoping that a negative rating would elevate their own group further.

To look at it a different way, consider the old adage, "My friend's enemy is my enemy, and my enemy's enemy is my friend" (Heider, 1958). You have probably experienced the discomfort of trying to maintain a friendship with a person who is hated by another of your friends. Our life becomes more balanced when we like those whom our friends like and dislike those who are disliked by our friends. Similarly, when your country or ethnic group has a positive relationship with another group, there will be pressure on you to perceive the enemies of your new friend in a negative light. You may accept their stereotype of an out-group either as a show of friendship or because you now value their judgments more highly. Your perception of the third group may change even if its relationship with your group has not changed.

CONDITIONS OF THE TARGET GROUP.   It is clear that the distinct characteristics of the out-group have a profound effect on the content of our stereotypes. When the group's characteristics are different from those of our own group, our stereotype is likely to be negative. Kinloch (1974) suggested that some Anglo-Americans' negative stereotype of Mexican-Americans is partially the result of differences in language and religion and the fact that Chicano culture is typically collective and non-capitalistic. Anglo-Americans typically hold more positive views of Swedish, Dutch, and German immigrants because of the similarities in their religious and cultural practices and appearance.

Although possibly appearing to be blaming the victim, Ichheiser (1970; see Lee, 1996) does place some blame on the stereotyped group for the stereotypes formed by others. Addressing the stereotype of Jews as swindlers, Ichheiser argues as follows:

> The Jews, namely, for various reasons lend themselves extremely well to be used as an impressive symbol of the "swindler." In this context, it is of no importance to determine what, and how, the Jews "really are." We are only trying to explain why they lend themselves to be used as symbol and target of the fear of fraud. On the one hand, the Jews—by not being either workers, or peasants, or soldiers—symbolize the type of people who, although not working in a visible and tangible way, are nevertheless successful, and getting ahead, by performing more or less mysterious and superstitious manipulations behind the scenes. On the other hand, the peculiar history of Jews, the lack of their own country, their own state, their own army, the predilection, for whatever reasons it may be, toward living in cities in an industrialized and commercialized atmosphere, has engendered the Jewish attitudes of "worshipping the false intellectual values" of shrewdness and cleverness, and disparaging the "original biological values" of physical strength and physical courage. Thus in the hands of a diabolically clever propagandist, the Jews become an impressive and convincing symbol of the uprooted swindler. (1970, pp. 138–139)

This argument raises a very thorny issue—the accuracy of stereotypes. In our modern-day preoccupation with political correctness, stereotypes rank with racist jokes on the top-10 list of offensive behaviors. The prevailing thought is that stereotypes are bad, wrong, and that the world would be a much better place without them. But recently, several social psychologists have ventured into dangerous political waters by suggesting that there might be a "kernel of truth" in stereotypes, or, at the very least, that we should consider this possibility (Judd & Park, 1993; Lee, Jussim, & McCauley, 1995). If we ignore our concern of being on the popular side of this question, we might well entertain the possibility of examining how accurately stereotypes describe groups. But before we congratulate ourselves for our openness, let's consider some of the real obstacles we would face. Assume, for example, that we want to check the accuracy of the view that "French are passionate folks." Our first step is to decide who fits in our group of "French." Do we include all people living in France? This makes little sense, because France is a relatively diverse country, many of whose citizens have ethnic origins outside France (for example, Italy, Algeria, Morocco, Germany, Spain, Croatia, and so on). We might then decide to include only people of French ethnicity. But now we are faced with a host of mongrels who may have varying degrees of French ethnic strain, as well as other ethnic strains. Do we include only the relatively small group who are "pure French" (e.g. who can demonstrate that they have only French ancestors dating back to A.D. 1000) or do we set an arbitrary limit, say 50% French ancestors over the last 200 years?

Defining who is French is just the first issue. We must also decide how to define and measure "passionate." Each of us may have a slightly different view of what constitutes the dimension. Investigators have suggested that a wide range of measures, including the opinions of experts and results of standardized tests, must be used to assess the characteristics of a group (Judd & Park, 1993). But even if we could develop and apply such tests, we are left with the question of how high a group must rank on our critical dimension (passion, in this case) to merit receiving this distinction. To be described as passionate, do French people have to rank at the top of the "passion" scale, above 80% of the other groups, or only in the top half? We can see how determining the accuracy of stereotypes may be nearly as difficult as locating the beginning of a rainbow.

Finally, a hidden implication in stereotyping is that the traits assigned to a group are somehow rooted in its biological foundation. We conveniently overlook the possibility that the characteristics of a group may be garments that others forced it to wear. For example, even if the data supported the view that many Jews have gravitated toward certain professions such as banking, describing them as shrewd or money-oriented ignores the fact that in many parts of the world Jews were denied the opportunity to have their own army and to engage in many professions that represented "original biological values." The view of African-Americans as "dirty," even if supported by data, ignores the fact that they were historically forced to live in areas without basic services such as running water and electricity and were denied opportunities to better their condition. Suggesting that a group possesses a trait may have nothing to do with the unique characteristics of the group and everything to do with the conditions under which members of that group have been forced to operate till this point in time (Oakes & Reynolds, 1997). Therefore, because we are often cognitively lazy, we may latch onto the condition of a group to develop a stereotype without considering the circumstances that created the condition.

Of further importance is the recognition that a stereotype may not even be based on a large sample of the target group. The behavior of a single member or a few members of the group can invite stereotyping. Behind the turmoil and anguish of O. J. Simpson's trial was a fear that it would ignite a negative stereotype of African-American men as violent. Muhammad Nassardeen, founder of Recycling Black Dollars, worried that the portrayal of O. J. Simpson, a highly visible and admired African-American, as a wife-beater and jealous stalker would lead people to incorporate this view in their stereotype of African-Americans: "The perception is that African Americans are inferior, we're violent, we're people who need to be on a short leash because at any given time we can explode. That type of journalistic rhetoric perpetuates that image" (Foster, 1994, p. A5). The accusations against Simpson were highly publicized, and his ethnicity was emphasized in the press and in the courtroom. For example, there were several incidents in which the media were accused of portraying him as darker than he really was. Nassardeen commented, "The darker he is, the easier it is for them to say, 'Oh, just another black guy.'" When we combine these conditions with the tendency to view an out-group as homogeneous, we find the basis for the concern that the action of one can be used to characterize and defame the many.

CONDITIONS OF THE PERCEIVING GROUP.   Although the content of a stereotype is influenced by the characteristics of the target group, the situation of the *perceiving* group also contributes to the traits that are bundled into the description. Bar-Tal (1996) examined the sociopolitical structure of several national and ethnic groups with regard to their laws and norms concerning such factors as group structure, mobility within the group, and, especially, tolerance. For example, Nazi Germany was a highly structured society with little tolerance for deviance and little opportunity for mobility within the power structure. Such closed structures, Bar-Tal argued, are likely to create considerable frustration among group members. However, given the repressive character of the group, the resultant hostility could be expressed only by sanctioned means and toward sanctioned targets. Regardless of the actual source of frustration, the resulting aggression was displaced toward minority groups (Bettelheim & Janowitz, 1964). Closed, intolerant structures are often found in fundamentalist religious groups and dictatorships, and these conditions contribute to stereotyping and hatred of out-groups.

Other hardships within a group can also create fertile ground for negative stereotypes and displaced aggression. For example, economic crises and political chaos are likely to heighten the fear and frustration experienced by group members. They seek a target for their anger, and a minority group—ethnic, political, or religious—is often a safe choice. Hovland and Sears (1940) found that the number of incidents of whites' lynching blacks in the South between 1882 and 1930 increased as the value of cotton decreased. These investigators argued that the South's economy was closely tied to cotton prices, and low cotton prices created frustration. The aggression instigated by this frustration was displaced onto a visible and safe target, black people. This situation is similar to that proposed by Murer (1996) to explain anti-Semitism in Hungary. The trauma of seeing their empire torn limb from limb created a readiness to hate and encouraged the rebirth of old stereotypes.

PERSONAL EXPERIENCE AND CHARACTERISTICS.   We can't place the blame for the content of our stereotypes only on the backs of our group and other groups. Our own experience also plays an important role. The Dutch have always held a warm spot in my heart. My favorite story as a child was of the Dutch boy who prevented a flood by placing his finger in a hole in a dike. Although they hurt my feet, I cherished a pair of Dutch wooden shoes my father brought me. As I grew older, *The Diary of Anne Frank* took its place as one of my favorite books, and I marveled at the heroics of the Dutch during World War II. But against this background of admiration, I still remember an incident when I nearly got into a fight with a Dutch fellow over a chair in a restaurant in Amsterdam. It was a minor incident, but the experience opened the door for me to add "aggressive" to my stereotype of Dutch people. It also guided my eyes to focus on the graffiti on public buildings and aggressive drivers in Amsterdam rather than on Dutch art and energy.

Direct contact with members of a group often forms the basis of our impression of the group, even when the contact is very limited. We tend to perceive out-group members we meet as typical or representative of the group (Fiske & Neuberg, 1989). Since we perceive out-groups as homogeneous, "meet one, know them all" is a logical conclusion. In addition, our personal experiences are often the most salient and vivid pieces of information we have and may be accompanied by strong emotions. Indeed, research on changes in attitudes indicates that attitudes formed on the basis of personal experience are generally the most resistant to change (Fazio, 1986). Thus personal experiences have a central role in guiding our perceptions.

Although all of us hold stereotypes, there are considerable differences in both the content of our stereotypes and how readily we form and maintain them. In psychology, we call these *individual differences.* They can be explained by the fact that each of us has different experiences, as well as a unique personality and unique ways of dealing with information. After World War II, the American Jewish Committee sponsored a study of anti-Semitism in the United States (see Chapter 1). The investigators (Adorno et al., 1950) interviewed people who belonged to a wide range of groups—from college fraternities to prison inmates at San Quentin. The participants completed an "ethnocentrism scale" designed to measure the degree to which they rejected people who were culturally dissimilar to their in-group while blindly accepting people who were culturally similar. The investigators examined these responses in light of measures of the respondents' personalities and family patterns. They found that people who expressed anti-Semitic attitudes tended to have negative attitudes toward other religious, cultural, and ethnic groups. These people also tended to have a personality type, labeled "authoritarian," which included idolizing their parents and viewing the father as successful and influential and the mother as giving and helpful. "High authoritarian" people came from homes where discipline was severe and where parents had high aspirations for their children. They had high respect for people in authority and a need for order. The investigators went on to speculate about the relationship between the psychodynamics of this personality and prejudice. For our purpose, however, the important point is the finding that an authoritarian personality is related to the development of negative attitudes toward other groups.

Later work has focused on other individual differences. For example, cognitive psychologists distinguish between people who are high and low in cognitive complexity (Campbell, Chew, & Scratchley, 1991). People who are low in cognitive complexity tend not to discriminate between stimuli, and they organize information into a few simple categories. People high in cognitive complexity tolerate ambiguity and perceive fine differences between stimuli. They organize information into many subclasses and categories. Supposedly, learning accounts for differences in cognitive complexity. Of most interest is the finding that people with low cognitive complexity are more likely than people with high cognitive complexity to develop broad, rigid stereotypes of out-groups and to be negatively disposed toward them. In conclusion, our personalities may influence both the content and the structure of our stereotypes.

Now that we've examined the multitude of sources that guide and shape our stereotypes, let's look for a moment at how these sources transmit information to us.

Passing It On: The Transmission of Stereotypes

When I have a common cold, even though I know I have it, I'd also like to know who gave it to me. The same is true of stereotypes. The search for how stereotypes are transmitted implicates several sources. One source is obviously ourselves. We "catch" our stereotypes through our direct experience with members of other groups. But our own experience is not the only carrier of stereotypes.

FAMILY.   We can begin to share the blame by focusing on our families. Parents and other family members teach children stereotypic content in several ways. First, they may directly instruct children about an out-group: "You've got to watch those Jews because they are greedy and untrustworthy." Second, much learning takes place through imitation (Bandura, 1977). Imagine a child who overhears his or her father making disparaging remarks about blacks while watching the evening newscast: "Those blacks are just dangerous." The kid, wanting to be just like the father, adopts his position on blacks. Third, parents may reward their children, often unwittingly, for expressing certain views about groups. A friend confided, "I couldn't help smiling when Susie began imitating her Asian teacher. I was appalled by her actions, but she was so cute imitating the Asian accent and expressions. I told her she shouldn't make fun of people, but I did laugh." Susie may have heard her mother's admon-

Children are eager to learn from their parents. Just as a child might learn how to repair a chair, he or she may also be taught what others groups "are really like." (Myrleen Ferguson/Photo-Edit)

ishment, but she will also remember the smiles and laughter she elicited. These may be reward enough to stamp a stereotypic view of Asians on Susie's mind.

It is little wonder that parents are important transmitters of stereotypes. They are usually the first source of information that children come into contact with. Therefore, they face the comparatively easy job of implanting information onto a *tabula rasa* (blank slate), rather than the more difficult task of changing already held attitudes. Parents are admired by children. What child doesn't think his or her parents are the best, the brightest, the most successful, and the most powerful people in the world? (Having adolescent daughters, I can attest to the fact that this view disappears by age 12!). Parents control all the resources in the child's environment. They determine what the child eats, watches on television, or wears to school. Given these circumstances, it is hardly surprising that the degree of children's prejudice is highly correlated with that of their parents (Mosher & Scodel, 1960).

MEDIA.   Although it is politically correct in our times to blame all our ills on our parents, we must be kind and spread the blame outside the home. When I was a child, I remember rushing to turn on the radio to hear *Amos 'n' Andy.* I split my sides laughing at the characters in the program as they stumbled their way through life. But while I was laughing at their jokes, a message was sneaking into my mind. For Amos and Andy were portrayed as black, and their hilarious predicaments often resulted from their laziness, indolence, or stupidity. (Even more pointed is the fact that the actors were actually white, consciously acting in stereotypical ways.) Multiply this message by the fact that nearly every other program I was exposed to carried the same portrayal, and you can see that while I was laughing, I was learning that blacks were lazy and stupid. This message also appeared in newspaper and magazine advertisements. Dovidio and Gaertner (1986) found that almost all blacks appearing in magazine advertising in 1949–1950 were portrayed in low-skill jobs; in 62% of the cases they were shown in positions subordinate to whites. It was also customary until the mid-1960s for newspapers to report the ethnicity or race of people suspected of crimes *unless* the suspect was white.

Compare the history books of today with those of 30 years ago. In those early books, children rarely learned of the contributions of people of different ethnic groups (or women) to the development of the United States. It is little wonder that I grew up thinking that the great patriots, the great warriors, the great leaders, the great inventors, and the great states*men* of the United States had all been white men.

Even when the presentation of different groups began to change, there was still a subtle message of ethnic difference. Although more blacks and Hispanics began appearing in advertisements and television programs in the United States in the 1960s, they were still presented in very segregated formats. There were programs with all black actors, programs with all Hispanic actors, and programs with all white actors. It was as if each group lived in its own separate world. The message "them and us" survived. Today the situation has changed considerably. People of different ethnic groups frequently appear together, interacting from positions of equal status. But even today, it is rare to find ethnically or racially mixed families or couples. Although this may reflect common practices in today's world, it legitimizes these practices and implies that each group has its place.

POLITICS AND LAWS.   Who can forget President Ronald Reagan decrying the Soviet Union as an "evil empire"? Hearing one's leader characterize another nation as evil is likely to influence the impression one forms of its people. Going back some decades, we find pictures of Alabama's governor, George Wallace, standing in front of a school to block black students from entering and Georgia's governor George Maddox brandishing an ax handle to "protect" white schools. Recall, too, the venomous words of Khalid Abdul Muhammad, speaking to an audience at Kean College; he described Jews as greedy, untrustworthy rapists of black women (Berman, 1994). Bar-Tal (1988) studied the speeches of Israeli and Arab political leaders and found that each portrayed the other group in extremely negative ways. These are our leaders, the people we have chosen to take positions of power. Their words convey to us the image they think we should hold of target groups.

The laws and customs of our land also transmit to us a picture of certain groups. What impression was conveyed by laws that demanded that black people sit in the back of a bus, barred them from "white" schools and neighborhoods, and prohibited marriages between black and white people? What image was transmitted when Israel closed its borders to Palestinians following an act of terrorism? In each case, the laws implied that the excluded group was inferior and dangerous.

These images carry extra weight because they are officially sanctioned. It is for this reason that members of ethnic groups object so strongly when a leader makes a careless negative portrayal of their group. Even if the remark may be intended as a jest, its source confers a special degree of legitimacy. Laws define what is just and fair, and if the laws discriminate against a group, it must be just to view these groups in a negative light. Leaders and laws guide not only our behavior but our minds.

There are, then, a host of sources that influence the nature and content of our stereotypes. Some of these sources are among the most trusted in our societies. Who needs personal experience when we have our parents, the media, laws, and our leaders painting pictures for us? In their defense, these sources may only reflect prevailing views, but their actions are viewed as supporting these views. The power of these sources can be so strong that even members of targeted groups are enticed to adopt negative stereotypes of their own group (Clark & Clark, 1947).

More Than a Picture: The Influence of Stereotypes

After this discussion of stereotypes, you may still respond, "So what?" What harm can result if we hold generalized portrayals of groups, even if these portrayals are not completely correct? Why should I care if Chinese people see Americans as crass and shallow or if the Irish in the United States are pictured as dull-witted? In order to answer this question, we can explore the functions of stereotypes.

At a benign level, stereotypes help order our world and keep us from becoming overwhelmed by information. But this benefit comes at a cost. By putting people into categories, we tend to overlook differences between people in a category. And we tend to hold on to a stereotype as if it were our last friend on earth. Indeed, we humans have employed an elaborate array of mental activities to maintain our views.

First, we employ *selective attention*. Our stereotypes guide us to pay attention to certain details of a situation and ignore the rest (Schaller & Maass, 1989). For example, if my stereotype of your group includes the trait clumsiness, I will be quick to notice when you trip over a fold in the carpet. Without that component in the stereotype, I would most likely overlook this behavior. When I guide my attention to certain behaviors (and ignore others), my chance of finding support for my stereotype increases dramatically.

But we don't stop there. Next, our stereotypes induce *selective interpretation* of events, especially ambiguous events. In an early study, white participants watched either a black or a white person interacting with a white person (Duncan, 1976).

During an animated conversation, the first person gave the second an "ambiguous shove." When the observers were asked about the shove, they viewed it as playing around or emphasizing a point when it came from a white actor. However, when the actor was black, the shove was interpreted as hostile and aggressive. Other research has shown that we are most likely to interpret events in line with our stereotypes when we are busy and have little time to pay close attention to actions that are unfolding (Gilbert & Hixon, 1991). The point is that our stereotypes prime us to interpret events in ways that confirm our expectations. This tendency not only causes us to interpret actions at times but also helps our stereotypes resist pressure to change.

Stereotypes also affect our *memory* of events: we often recall details and situations that support our stereotypes. When I was a college student, a group of Brazilians lived next door. That year, I had attended Mardi Gras and came home with the impression that Brazilians were great party animals. Three years later I saw one of my former neighbors in medical school. I was quite surprised because all I remembered of him was the parties he and his roommates had during the year he lived next to me. I couldn't recall that he had ever studied or that there had been any moments of silence in his apartment. In an interesting demonstration of selective memory, Cohen (1981) showed people a video of a woman having a birthday dinner with her husband. When the viewers were told that the woman was a waitress, they recalled that she had a television set and drank beer. But when they were told that she was a librarian, they remembered that she wore glasses and listened to classical music during the dinner. All of the points recalled were correct, but the expectations of the perceivers influenced which points they remembered.

Not only do stereotypes affect how we store and interpret information; they also guide our attitudes and behaviors. Because many stereotypes involve out-groups and we are motivated to enhance the image of our own group, many, if not most, stereotypes are relatively negative. On the basis of negative information, we are apt to develop *prejudice* toward individuals from these out-groups. *Prejudice* is "a negative attitude toward, or evaluation of, a person based on his or her membership in a group other than one's own" (Worchel, Cooper, & Goethals, 1991, p. 360). In other words, we dislike an individual because he or she belongs to a different ethnic group, religion, sex, or nation. Our dislike is based not on the individual's behavior but on his or her group. From this base of prejudice, discrimination is likely to follow. *Discrimination* is action taken to harm a group, or a member of a group, on the basis of membership in the group. In its extreme form, the combination of prejudice and discrimination can lead to *delegitimization* of a target group (Bar-Tal, 1988), determining that it does not deserve fair treatment according to a code of norms calling for proper and decent behavior. This view opens the door for the exploitation of the target group and even justifies resorting to violence.

We've come a long way from a relatively innocent beginning. I began by showing some of the unwitting biases that silently creep into our perceptions. These included a tendency to emphasize disposition when explaining the actions of others and to see more variability in our own group than in out-groups. I also pointed out how we might influence the actions of others to support our expectations. These "mistakes" seem relatively harmless, but when they combine with our tendency to categorize our social world and develop stereotypes of groups, we begin to mix a rather dangerous cocktail. Using our stereotypes, we perform some intricate mental gymnastics to protect them and keep other people "in their place." The result is that we are primed to debase and mistreat members of a group solely because of their membership in it. Although our cognitive processes may prepare us to become soldiers of violence, it is the dynamics of groups that turn us into armies and send us into ethnic battles.

R E A D I N G   3 . 1

A Hispanic by Any Other Name Would Be Preferable*

EDUARDO MONTES

EL PASO—It hits me when I field yet another call from a salesman who wants to speak exclusively in Spanish.

It hits me every time I toss out another record club mailer offering great deals on Tejano music.

Too many people out there assume they know who I am simply because of my Spanish surname.

I can only speculate what they think when they assume that my primary language is Spanish. It's not.

Or when they assume that my taste in music tends toward the energetic songs of, say, Selena. I actually prefer more traditional rock 'n' roll.

Maybe they think I'm swarthy. I'm not. I have red hair and I'm fair-skinned.

Most likely, they consider me a "typical" Hispanic.

But what does that really mean?

The term used by the government and the press as a catchall for Americans who trace their roots to a Spanish-speaking country or culture has gained widespread acceptance over the years.

Yet it's inadequate in the eyes of many like myself who would prefer something else. Latino is my favorite alternative because it's something we picked for ourselves and not a label that was stuck on us.

The word Hispanic itself doesn't offend. Rather, it reflects an ignorance of the mul-

---

*Source: The Bryan-College Station Eagle, April 27, 1997, p. A15.

titude of Latino cultures that, despite some similarities, embrace many customs and philosophies.

The generalization also can lead to annoying stereotypes. Many people like me celebrate their heritage but don't necessarily fit the image used in some companies' misguided efforts to land Hispanic customers.

"Hispanic? That's painting with a pretty wide brush," says Avelardo Valdez, a sociologist and director of the Hispanic Research Center at the University of Texas at San Antonio.

"It's a term that is inappropriate to use for the entire Spanish-surnamed population of the United States because those populations are so distinct from each other from a whole variety of social and political factors."

Hispanic is alternately used to describe people with origins in Mexico, Cuba, Puerto Rico, Central and South America and the Caribbean.

It's almost as if these people are interchangeable. That's not the case.

So-called Hispanics run the gamut of physical appearances. Some are dark-skinned. Others are fair.

The Spanish language is essentially the same, though each group spices it up with dialects and slang.

Each group also has its own version of history, both in its country of origin and in the United States.

Many Mexican-American families, for example, were here centuries before they were swallowed up by an expanding nation. Many Cuban families, meanwhile, fled their nation's Communist dictatorship a relatively short time ago.

Using an umbrella term does nothing to encourage an understanding of any of this, says Alfredo Cruz, spokesman for the Southwest Voter Research Institute in Los Angeles.

"It closes down the perception of a diverse group of cultures," says Cruz, whose organization tracks Latino political trends. "To somebody who doesn't know anything about Latin culture, a Hispanic could be anything. `Hispanic' doesn't inform you of anything."

Not everyone sees it like Cruz. There are those who believe the term unifies Latino peoples, and some scholars think the similarities among Hispanic subgroups far out-weigh the differences.

Polling conducted in 1996 by Cruz's own research institute showed Latinos across the board do tend to agree on certain issues. For example, a majority favors affirmative action, and most think all children should be allowed to attend public school regard-less of their immigration status.

"If one isn't aware of the differences, one makes assumptions that can be quite in-accurate," says Blandina Cardenas, an educational leadership professor, also at UT-San Antonio. "But I don't sense enormous differences.

"I don't have a problem with a term that would seek to encompass all of the groups. At a very personal level, there is an affinity for other Hispanics that transcends our dif-ferences," she says.

Perhaps that's true.

Still, it would certainly be nice if people didn't make assumptions about me based on a surname and a generic term. It would be nice to be understood a little better than that.

Frenchman Fulfills Dream of Photographing Jewish Icons*

VERNA DOBNIK

NEW YORK—One night, French photographer Frederic Brenner dreamed he was in America with Lauren Bacall, Ruth Bader Ginsburg, Ralph Lauren, Arthur Miller, Mark Spitz, Dr. Ruth Westheimer . . .

Three years later, wide awake, Brenner peered at them through his camera lens as they stood bareheaded in the rain on Ellis Island, posing for him against the Manhattan skyline.

These prominent American Jews, all descended from immigrants who struggled in a new diaspora, are his "Jewish icons," as the photographer says in his book "Jews/America/A Representation."

Wednesday's rendezvous at the old gateway to the United States was part of Brenner's 17-year mission through 40 countries exploring the question: What does it mean to be a Jew at the end of the 20th century?

"There is no such thing as The Jew," concludes the 37-year-old photographer, who holds a Ph.D. in social anthropology. "My photographs raise questions, they don't give answers."

Many American Jews "became icons by breaking the icons," or stereotypes, Brenner said during an interview at the SoHo gallery where his photos are exhibited.

Barbra Streisand, for example. One of the 39 "icons" in the book, she "has obviously reinvented beauty. She is not beautiful, and she became beautiful."

To survive as a Jew is to be a chameleon, "always taking the shape and the color of the country where we are. It is to reinvent oneself, while anchored in tradition," says Brenner.

"And it's a very thin line, you walk like an 'equilibriste,'" he adds, using the French word for tightrope walker as he spread his arms precariously.

For the Ellis Island photo, his famous subjects stood in a labyrinth he built of white-painted wood, "the ultimate metaphor for diaspora, a place where the paths intersect, or merge sometimes, where the line is not straight, and there are many detours."

In one square of the maze was Westheimer, the sex therapist whose finger-wagging advice, delivered in German-tinged English, has made her a television celebrity.

---

*Source: The Bryan-College Station Eagle, September 22, 1996, p. A4.

She landed in America in 1956, "and I learned that you have to stand up and be counted," said the 4-foot-7-inch Westheimer, perched on a hidden box that raised her to camera level.

For Supreme Court Justice Ginsburg, the photo session was her first visit to the island where her Polish-born grandmother arrived in the early 1900s.

"Jewish people are sometimes called `the people of the book.' My grandparents' dream was for their children to become scholars," Ginsburg said.

The Supreme Court justice smiled when asked if she was an icon, saying she was just "a fortunate girl born in Brooklyn."

But there she was rubbing shoulders with the likes of business moguls Edgar Bronfman and his son, Edgar Jr.; violinists Itzhak Perlman and Isaac Stern; artist Roy Lichtenstein; composer Philip Glass; Olympic swimming champion Mark Spitz; feminist Betty Freidan; former CBS chairman Laurence Tisch; and former New York Mayor Ed Koch.

Holding her granddaughter's hand was another fortunate girl from Brooklyn, actress Lauren Bacall, born as Betty Joan Perske.

In two years of trekking through the country, Brenner also photographed Persian-born Jewish antique dealers in New Jersey, a Jewish family on Staten Island with a Christmas tree, students in a Hebrew day school in Las Vegas.

It's all part of his mammoth project, "Chronicle of Exile," which he says will be "the first visual anthology of the Jewish people in the 20th century." Publication is slated for 1999.

R E A D I N G   3 . 3

Black Activists: Frenzy Over O.J.'s Fall Feeds Racial Stereotypes*

DAVID FOSTER

As a sports star, O.J. Simpson rose above prejudice as gracefully as he dodged linebackers on the gridiron. To millions of fans, black and white, his skin color was irrelevant—he was The Juice.

But Simpson's new infamy as a man accused of murdering his former wife has proved less colorblind, some black activists say. They say that portrayals of Simpson as a wife batterer and jealous stalker, through police leaks and news stories, have reinforced stereotypes of black men as unpredictably violent.

"You have a person who was trusted by America suddenly being called an animal," said Muhammad Nassardeen, founder of Recycling Black Dollars, a Los Angeles self-help group. "It affects how people view African-Americans."

*Source: The Bryan-College Station Eagle, June 24, 1994, p. A5.

In the week and a half since the June 12 slayings of Nicole Brown Simpson and Ronald Goldman in the fashionable Brentwood section of Los Angeles, images of the still startlingly handsome Simpson and his vibrant, blond ex-wife have filled TV broadcasts and newspaper pages.

But the mainstream media have barely nibbled around the edges of race as a component of the story, exhibiting the conventional wisdom that this was a story about celebrity, passion and murder, not a black-on-white thing.

With two white victims and a black suspect, however, no matter who the individuals are, racial implications are perhaps inevitable. And an undercurrent of anger and resentment has been flowing among some blacks ever since the bodies were found outside Mrs. Simpson's condo and suspicion turned quickly to the ex-husband.

This week, they gave voice to that anger.

Half a dozen black organizations held a news conference Wednesday in Los Angeles, criticizing reporters, police and prosecutors as too quick to assign guilt to a black man and, more generally, to sensationalize crime involving blacks.

Their complaints were echoed by some prominent black leaders, including the Rev. Jesse Jackson, who objected to police briefly clapping handcuffs on Simpson and pinning his arms behind his back in full view of news cameras, days before he was arrested as a suspect.

"That seemed unnecessary," Jackson said Wednesday.

Nassardeen faulted reporters' reliance on anonymous police sources, who have supplied a steady stream of bloody—and often incorrect—details about a crime he said was being characterized with such loaded words as "brutal" and "savage."

"The perception is that African-Americans are inferior, we're violent, we're people who need to be on a short leash because at any given time we can explode," he said. "That type of journalistic rhetoric perpetuates that image."

Also under fire was this week's *Time* magazine cover, a "photo-illustration" that altered Simpson's police mug shot, darkening his skin tone and stubble by computer manipulation.

"The cover appeared to be a conscious effort to make Simpson look evil and macabre, to sway the opinion of the reader to becoming fixated on his guilt," said Dorothy Butler Gilliam, president of the National Association of Black Journalists, based in Reston, Va.

"They doctored it to look more menacing," Nassardeen said. "A lighter black man has more of an association with white Americans. The darker he is, the easier it is for them to say, `Oh, just another black guy.'"

In a message to readers who complained about the cover on the America Online computer network, Time Managing Editor James R. Gaines wrote, "To the extent that this caused offense to anyone, I obviously regret it."

But he rejected the notion there was a racial implication to the cover.

Los Angeles authorities also defended their handling of this most famous of murder suspects.

If anything, it was Simpson's celebrity that affected how officials acted, said Mike Botula, spokesman for the Los Angeles District Attorney's office.

"This whole case is different than most cases, because he's O.J. Simpson," Botula said.

Handcuffing Simpson was normal procedure, said Lorie Taylor, Los Angeles police spokeswoman.

"We don't treat anybody differently because of the color of their skin," she said.

But skin color was much on the minds of the excited crowd milling in the streets near Simpson's house last Friday night before he surrendered.

One black man in his 20s declared Simpson's arrest was yet another case of whites pulling down a black hero and role model to black youth.

A black woman in her 40s replied, "What kind of role model is he if he's beating our women?"

CHAPTER 4

LOOKING INWARD

The Dynamics of Groups and Interpersonal Relations

There is a certain quality to being Jewish that affects the mind and heart. Few Jews do not experience a quickened heartbeat on hearing the chanting of the Yom Kippur prayer Kol Nidre. News about Israel piques the interest, and even the least religious Jew cheers Israel's victories and is embarrassed by its shortcomings. But no issue or event penetrates the consciousness more than stories about Nazi Germany. Jewish children grow up hearing of the persecution of their people from the day the seven tribes entered the desert. Indeed, persecution is the bedrock of Judaism. But for modern Jews, it is the picture of bodies stacked like cordwood before the cold sinister smokestacks of Nazi concentration camps that haunts their minds. The picture dooms Jews to a pervading distrust of humanity and a deep sense of wonder and questioning. How could this have happened?

Such distrust and puzzlement are heavy burdens to bear, and many Jews have attempted to ease their minds by convincing themselves that those were the acts of a few misguided people at a difficult period in history. It could never happen again in this new world, this modern age. But that sense of security was shaken as the Berlin wall crumbled and Germany reunited. The ultimate nightmare moved from the dream world into the realm of reality when the unified Germany became the scene of scattered incidents of violence aimed at Jews, foreigners, and "non-Germans." Neo-Nazis and skinhead hooligans vandalized synagogues and defaced them with hate messages and swastikas. Jews were beaten and harassed. The terrorists found other helpless targets in foreign refugees from economically depressed or war-torn countries. The violence was justified by portraying these pitiful people as threats to German jobs and German society. Homes and camps were looted and burned. Gangs attacked, beat, and in some cases killed unlucky foreigners who happened to be in the wrong place at the wrong time. By New Year's Day 1993, there had been over 1,800 rightist attacks resulting in 16 deaths. In one of the more celebrated cases, a Turkish woman and two girls were killed in Moelln when their home was firebombed. Ironically enough, the first person arrested for the attack was a 19-year-old-youth named Christiansen. Five months later, there was a frighteningly similar incident which occurred like an echo on a silent night in Stolingen (see Reading 4-1). An arson attack killed five Turks, three of them children. Had the cycle started again? After a period in which Germany had inched open its doors to refugees and taken extraordinary steps to erase the blight of its Nazi past, was history to repeat itself? Were these acts of ethnic hatred only a few isolated incidents, or were they a spark that would ignite collective action in a new round of genocide? What forces are at play within a group, within a country, that lead to mass action? Are there patterns or cycles in group behavior that help us explain and predict it? How likely are we to fall victim to group-directed hatred? To answer these questions, we must understand the dynamics of groups.

Before I attempt to deal with these issues, let me make one point very clear. Although I chose to introduce group behavior by focusing on events in Germany, the situation is not confined to one country. A black colleague recently gave a stirring lecture to a group of spellbound students in my undergraduate class. She stated that as a child she had to sleep with the lights on in her room after seeing pictures in a history book of a lynch mob hanging and burning a black man. The lights went back on in her bedroom after she watched television coverage of policemen beating Rodney King, sparking riots in Los Angeles in 1992. She challenged the students to convince her that the racial violence that gripped the United States following the Civil War was not beginning anew. When she finished her lecture, a white student with tears streaming down his cheeks stunned the class with a halting story of how he and a group of white friends had placed a burning cross on the lawn of a black family some years ago. The young man trembled as he confessed that to this day he couldn't explain why he became involved or how the group decided on this cowardly course of action.

As sincere as this student was in his remorse for his actions, his experience may not be as isolated as we would like to believe. The summer of 1996 ushered in a series of burnings of African-American churches in the United States. By July of that year, 76 churches had been burned, and Congress was prompted to pass a bill raising the maximum penalty for church burning. An intense investigation began under the assumption that while one group was probably not responsible for the acts, many, if not most, were the cowardly work of individuals who belonged to right-wing groups. Like an intoxicating drug, group membership pumped these individuals full of ethnic hate and lit the fuse of action.

Chapters 1 to 3 focused on the individual psyche, the desire for self-esteem, the quest for identity, and the need for social comparison. Indeed, the seeds of ethnic conflict and hatred are sown deep within our psychology. But we don't build the fires of ethnic conflict alone. Ethnic hatred is played out in relationships between groups of people. Once we hitch our identity to a specific ethnic group, the social forces of the group join our inner forces to determine our ethnic relations: identification with our in-group and distaste for out-groups. Often, ethnicity is merely a category or label for defining ourselves and others. But at many other times, ethnicity is a magnet that draws people together to form a group ready to act for a common purpose. We rarely battle our ethnic enemies as a lone knight, carrying out a personal mission. Rather, we march into a fray either carrying the support and approval of our group or, more often, surrounded by fellow members rushing into the same battle. In fact, research suggests that simply viewing ourselves as acting as members of a group, rather than as isolated individuals, makes us more competitive and less willing to cooperate with an out-group (Insko & Schopler, 1987; Insko et al., 1990).

Ethnic conflict is intergroup as well as interpersonal, and even when it involves individual behaviors, the shadow of the group is clearly present. Both personal threats and threats to our ethnic collective motivate us to seek our ethnic relatives, to transform what has been only a label into a social reality of interacting individuals. Even in the relative safety of the laboratory, fear has proved to be a strong catalyst for motivating individuals to seek the comfort of others and form a group (Schachter, 1959; Morris et al., 1974). The formation of a group creates a new set of dynamics that shape behavior. For this reason, it is important to include a short lesson on group dynamics as we set out on our quest to understand ethnic conflict. Although the research on group dynamics has often concentrated on small groups in the laboratory, the principles that have been identified have implications for larger groups and collectives. The examination of group dynamics shows the power that groups have over us and how this power is wielded to influence our thoughts and actions. The influence of groups is often subtle, creeping upon us like mist blanketing a new dawn. The ultimate intent of this group influence is not necessarily sinister, but it can become a pervasive and important contributor to ethnic conflict.

The Foundation of Group Power

Whether it be the actions of Lars Christiansen in Moelln, Germany, or the young student in the cross-burning incident, where do we search for an explanation for such behavior? Are these evil individuals with hearts of stone? Our decidedly individualistic culture teaches us to locate the causes of behavior within the individual. Indeed there is a certain comfort in this viewpoint. If we desire to eliminate ethnic hatred, all we need to do is eliminate evil people, and then only good things will happen. But, alas, life and people are not that simple. There are few candidates for sainthood. Villains often have a streak of kindness, and even our most cherished heroes may lie, cheat, and steal. Can we believe that a nation such as Germany during the Nazi era was populated entirely by "bad" people? Clearly behavior is influenced by personal traits, characteristics, and even genes. But of equal, if not greater, importance is the power of the group. When it comes to human behavior, many hands chart the course. What is the foundation of the group's power over the individual?

The ability of groups to shape behavior springs from two sources. On one hand, we look to groups for *information* (Jones & Gerard, 1967). Our childhood experiences teach us that if most people hold a certain belief, it must be correct. The informative function of groups becomes especially important when we face new or changing situations. For example, the reunification of Germany created a new and confusing world for many Germans. How would the merging of East and West Germany affect their lives? At the same time these questions were surfacing, many refugees were entering Germany from Eastern Europe, Turkey, and the Arab countries. Many German citizens, especially young people who had known only a stable, prosperous country, naturally looked to others to help them make sense of the situation. While many groups could have supplied information, a climate of uncertainty and change is ideal for extremist groups. Whether a group is on the far left or the far right, the information it spews out can be music to the ears of confused, isolated individuals.

Why, we may ask, are wandering souls so often lured by the call of ethnocentrism and ethnic hatred espoused by extremists rather than by the messages of cooperation offered by mainstream groups?

If we analyze the message and the context, we can begin to see the appeal of extremism. Consider that the struggle to gain control of our ethnic souls often takes place in an environment of chaos, threat, and uncertainty. It is during such times that our ethnic identity becomes most critical to us, and we look to our ethnic groups for guidance. Within this context, the message of extremism recognizes and legitimizes our fear and confusion. In fact, the extremist often attempts to enhance and build upon an existing fear, raising our anxiety to higher levels. The message transforms personal fear into group fear. On several occasions Louis Farrakhan, Minister of the Nation of Islam, went to great lengths to outline threats to black people in the United States and then raised the ante by warning that the greatest threat was yet to come. The extremist message externalizes the source of the threat as an out-group. It is the Jews, the Arabs, or the immigrants who are responsible for our ills. Hitler's speeches masterfully painted the Jews as the cause of the economic problems of prewar Germany, vividly depicting them as a growing cancer that had already sapped the nation's strength. Finally, the extremist message prescribes a quick cure for the illness of the ethnic group: the elimination of the threatening out-group. The beauty of extremism is that its position is simple, straightforward, and action-oriented. It empowers the masses by recognizing their concerns, absolving them of blame, and identifying solutions. It asks for little thought or reason. In fact, by encouraging quick action, it entices the audience to suspend analytical reasoning. Individuals or groups who feel threatened and insecure want a quick, simple remedy—a bandage to bind their wounds. The extreme factions of ethnic groups offer just this type of "fix."

The message of moderation, on the other hand, has a very different character. It often minimizes a threat and minimizes the need for immediate action. It asks for reason, thought, and discussion. Its tone is more rational than emotional. And it is often evenhanded in identifying sources of personal and social problems, recognizing the contribution of both the in-group and the out-group. Compared with the fiery message of the extremist, the song of reason is pablum and milk-toast, hardly likely to inspire the confused, the threatened, or the hurt. Imagine getting excited by a message that exhorts you to "Rise up and be cautious!" Moderate messages may be welcomed during times of peace and prosperity, but they hardly offer comfort at times of stress and confusion. By failing to externalize blame, the moderate message is not likely to cause individuals to stress their ethnic identity or rush to the safety of their ethnic groups. We do look to our groups as sources of information, but our own condition determines the type of appeal that is most likely to influence us.

If information is the thunder of groups, then the threat of rejection is the lightning. We crave acceptance by others. Our groups form the foundation of our self-identity and esteem. But as children we learn an important, often painful, lesson about groups that remains with us throughout our lives: we will be welcomed by others only so long as we "behave ourselves," that is, conform to the group's rules and expectations. To deviate from these rules and expectations is to incur censure and rejection. And this rejection is painful to our psyche, even if it is not accompanied by physical harm. Rejection by important groups, such as our ethnic group, cuts deep, and we will go to great lengths to avoid it. Therefore, a second source of group power is *normative*, based on a real or imagined threat that the group will reject and punish those who do not follow its norms.

Indeed, groups do not take kindly to those who dare to chart their own course. For example, Roethlisberger and Dickson (1939) observed that work teams at the Western Electric Company in Hawthorne, Illinois, established clear but informal norms about how hard each person should work. If everyone followed these norms, management could not single out individuals as being better or worse than their coworkers. A worker who exceeded these standards ("rate buster") or failed to meet them ("chisler") was harassed by the others. The harassment began with good-natured kidding but then escalated to "binging"—a punch in the upper arm that was not intended to injure but did get the point across: conform or face rejection. In another situation, Stanley Schachter (1951) found that a group ceased interacting with, and voted out, a member who continuously disagreed with its position. Interestingly, one of the most popular members in the group was a convert who had started out disagreeing with the group but quickly changed his opinion to support the group's opinion. But remember that in the realm of ethnic identity, there can be no converts. We cannot change our ethnic group or entice new members to "join." Therefore, rejection by one's ethnic group often involves psychological or even physical death.

Groups have the power to guide our behavior because we fear rejection if we do not conform. The group need not make any explicit threat. Its power comes from our belief that rejection will result and our unwillingness to test this belief. Obviously, groups can enhance their power by clear, public punishment of deviates. The burning at the stake of heretics by the Catholic Inquisition, the public execution of individuals who disobey the laws of Islam, and the "shunning" of transgressors by some tribes and religions magnify the power of the group. The message that comes from dozens of empirical studies is a group has the greatest power when (1) the group is important to us, (2) there are few (or no) alternative groups we can join, (3) we expect long-term membership in the group, (4) we have low or uncertain status in the group, and (5) we feel threatened or insecure (Forsyth, 1990). These conditions apply beautifully to our ethnic groups, especially at times of threat or stress. It can also be suggested that ethnic groups will have the strongest hold over members who have fewer options—those whose ancestry includes few ethnic groups or whose society has determined that they must belong to a specific ethnic group.

The Group as a Dictator, the Group as a Shield

One of the troubling characteristics of ethnic violence is that often the most vicious acts are committed by people who acknowledge that they acted even though they knew they were doing wrong. Some of the most heart-wrenching stories coming out of the wars in the former Yugoslavia have involved neighbor slaying neighbor. A history of love and cooperation was forgotten once the individuals embraced their ethnic groups. The participants often stated that they "loved their neighbor" but turned to violence because "everybody else was doing it." Can the group really entice us to behave in ways we believe are wrong, or are these incidents simply cases of evil people grasping for any justification now that their wrongdoing has been uncovered?

Solomon Asch (1956) began his research with the latter assumption; he felt that people were unlikely to conform to a group position that they knew was incorrect. He constructed a most benign situation, one that involved a group of strangers meeting for only a short time to work on a task that seemingly had little personal relevance. He asked subjects in the experiment to compare the length of lines, and the correct answer was easily recognized. The "group" was actually composed of four confederates and one naive subject, who was to answer after several of the others had given their responses. On prearranged items, all the confederates gave an obviously incorrect answer. Asch expected that these incorrect answers would have little influence on the naive subject. To his surprise, however, the naive subject conformed to the group's incorrect opinion more than one-third of the time. The degree of conformity increased as the task became more difficult, as the group increased in size to a certain point (Mann, 1977), and as the subject's status in the group was lowered. On the other hand, conformity was nearly eliminated when one of the confederates deviated from the group's opinion (and was not punished) before the naive subject responded. Clearly, people do change their behavior to fit the group's behavior, because "everyone else is doing it."

Another common explanation for atrocities committed in the name of ethnic identity is "I was only following orders." The horror of the concentration camps led to worldwide outrage, based on the belief that "normal" people would not blindly follow orders to commit such terrible deeds. The war crime trials at Nuremberg rejected following orders as a legal defense. It was argued that individuals are ultimately responsible for their own behavior. Stanley Milgram (1963) set about testing the validity of this assumption that "normal" people would not follow orders to take part in actions they felt were wrong. He recruited citizens from New Haven, Connecticut, to take part in a "learning" study. The true subject was designated a "teacher" and was instructed to deliver purported shocks, of increasing intensity, to another subject—actually a confederate—each time he gave an incorrect response. During the study, the "teacher" heard the "learner" scream in pain after each shock and beg to be released from the experiment. If the "teacher" suggested that the study stop, the experimenter ordered him to continue delivering the shocks. How many people followed the orders and continued to deliver shocks to what they believed was the maximum (450-volt) level? Remember, the subjects were not soldiers on a battlefield or individuals caught up in a struggle for ethnic survival. Milgram reported that 65% of the participants followed the orders until the end! Does this surprise you? The figure surprised a panel of Yale students and psychiatrists, who predicted that only 1% would comply. (To relieve your mind, the "learner" in the Milgram study was an experimental confederate who, unknown to the "teacher," did not receive the shock, but acted in a scripted fashion.) The Milgram's study and other studies demonstrate that we often do follow the orders of authority figures even when these orders involve hurting others.

The group and its leader can play a dictatorial role in guiding our behavior. We do act because "others are doing it" and because "we are only following orders." We may wish to look like lions, but there is a lot of the sheep in each of us. This, however, is not the whole story. Although the portrayal of people as sheep may be unflattering, comparing them to weasels may be truer still. There is considerable evidence that we often hide behind (or in) a group. As members of a group, we relinquish our personal identity; we become "deindividuated" (Zimbardo, 1970). Our identity becomes only that of "another group member."

Deindividuation is achieved when any factor makes it difficult to distinguish individuals within a group and focuses our attention away from our own actions. For example, group members are more likely to feel deindividuated if they all dress alike, wear masks, or act under cover of darkness. On the one hand, such a loss of identity can be disturbing. It strips away our uniqueness. For this reason, we might conclude that people will avoid being deindividuated in group settings. But this is not always the case. Being deindividuated gives us an intoxicating sense of freedom—we realize that because we cannot be distinguished from other group members, we cannot be held personally accountable for our behavior. Being absolved of responsibility reduces our inhibitions about performing socially disapproved actions. In many cases the result is rather harmless, as when spectators at sporting events feel free to dress in outlandish garb and scream their support for their favorite team, believing that no one will recognize them. In other cases, however, this freedom from personal responsibility can have tragic consequences. It is no accident that the most cowardly and barbaric acts of the Ku Klux Klan were done at night, by people dressed in hoods and white sheets. The hood, the darkness, and the group concealed the individual's identity and released violent behavior. In a study of 200 cultures, Watson (1973) found that warriors who were deindividuated by masks and paint that concealed their faces were more likely to torture their captives than were warriors whose identities were not concealed. Similarly, a careful examination of "crimes of obedience" such as the My Lai massacre found that people hide behind their leaders. A strong leader frees us from feeling responsible for our behavior; we see the leader as responsible (Kelman & Hamilton, 1989). A similar outcome results when we reduce the humanity or individual identity of the targets of our acts. Reducing others to a group identity, especially an unflattering identity—such as gooks, spics, wops, kikes, or niggers—strips them of their humanity and individuality and encourages discrimination or aggression (Worchel & Andreoli, 1978).

One terrible result of deindividuation may be evident in ethnic violence. Individuals flock to their ethnic group—to like-minded people of similar appearance. They relinquish their personal identity and relinquish responsibility for their behavior to the group and its leaders. They are released from concern about basic

The power of leaders should not be overlooked. "I was only following orders" has been used to justify the most heinous acts of ethnic violence. (Popperfoto/Archive Pictures)

rules that govern human behavior such as justice, fairness, and compassion. Adding to the volatility of the situation is the tendency to dehumanize and deindividuate members of the other ethnic group. The "others" are portrayed as subhuman, both different from and dangerous to one's own group. Violence against the enemy is justified and not subject to punishment.

Throughout this discussion of group power and influence, I have mentioned the role of leaders. Leaders are used both to help define the situation and "correct" behavior and as figures who assume responsibility for our behavior. Although we cannot deny the power of the group to influence our actions and attitudes, we must not deny the role of leaders in this process.

Leadership and Power in Groups

For decades, the issue of leadership has been at the heart of research in psychology, political science, and management. Businesses spend millions of dollars every year training leaders, the military devotes considerable time and energy to identifying potential leaders, and in each election the voters search their hearts and souls, attempting to choose the "true" leader. Unfortunately, the success rate of all of these endeavors is far below what is desired. But our faith in the power of leaders remains unshaken. We are still guided by the wonderful misconception that if we can just find the right leaders, all the problems of life, of groups, and of organizations will be solved.

In the final analysis, leadership involves exerting influence over the activities of a group. Although most of us behave as leaders at some point, some of us rise to leadership more often than others. This point has not been lost on investigators, who have attempted to identify the factors that determine who will become the leader of a group. Early efforts focused on the individual's characteristics. According to the "great man" (or "great woman") theory, there are specific traits or sets of traits that "make" a person a leader. What a coup it would be to find a formula to identify those destined for leadership! Few stones have been left unturned in the eternal search for personal factors related to leadership. Studies have focused on personality, intelligence, and even height. But alas, no magic combination of traits has been discovered that can reliably determine who will become a leader (Forsyth, 1990). For example, Simonton (1986) reported that intellectual brilliance was one of the few traits linked to greatness among American presidents. But other studies have found that people who are much more intelligent than others in a group are rejected as leaders, presumably because they cannot relate to others (Loretto & Williams, 1974). Age, seniority, and being male have been linked to emerging as a leader in some situations, but even these traits are only weakly related to leadership.

One intriguing "trait" that continues to stimulate intense interest and arouse passionate disagreement is *charisma*. In our hearts we "know" that people such as Martin Luther King, Jr., John F. Kennedy, Adolf Hitler, and Franklin Roosevelt had a special quality that enabled them to enthrall the masses. I remember feeling electricity in the air when Martin Luther King spoke, and when John Kennedy spoke. It was not so much what they said as how they said it. They seemed almost able to cast a spell over large groups of people, exciting them to follow like sheep after the shepherd. Max Weber, the German sociologist, observed that some leaders have been able to turn the course of history through their power to influence. These leaders, he said, were endowed with "supernatural, superhuman, or at least . . . exceptional powers and qualities" (1947, p. 358). Weber adopted the term *charisma*, the Greek word for "gift from the gods," to describe these great leaders. The concept of charisma, however, has proved amazingly slippery, deftly resisting efforts to define it or isolate it operationally. Bernard Bass, an organizational psychologist, summed up the frustration with the concept: "In the popular media, charisma has come to mean anything from chutzpah to Pied Piperism, from celebrity to superman status. It has become an overworked cliché for strong, attractive and inspiring personality" (1985, p. 35).

If leadership is not determined by the individual's traits, perhaps it is determined by the situation—by being in the right place at the right time. Indeed, it has been argued that great leaders have been successful because they happened to have a receptive audience and circumstances conspired to ensure the achievement of their goals. But this situational approach does not explain why the same people often emerge as leaders in many different situations, and investigators have been unable to identify situational characteristics conducive to leadership. Most examinations of leadership (Hollander, 1985) argue that a combination of personal and situational characteristics determine who will emerge as a leader. The needs of the group influence which constellation of characteristics will be important. For example, a group experiencing a period of uncertainty, even chaos, will be most receptive to a strong, authoritarian leader who relies on emotional appeal and clear directives. However, a group enjoying stability and security will be most likely to seek a more democratic leader who adopts a reasoned approach and shows concern for individual welfare as well as group goals (Fiedler, 1978).

The Nature of Political Leadership

The fact that leaders use different styles to influence groups, and that the condition of the group often affects which style will be effective, is seen most clearly in the arena of political leadership. Blondel (1987) makes a number of interesting distinctions between political leaders that shed some light on this issue. According to his analysis, we can first divide leaders according to their *goals*. Some leaders—such as Winston Churchill, Dwight Eisenhower, and Charles De Gaulle—have been most concerned with maintaining or preserving an existing system that is in danger of collapse. These leaders—Blondel calls them "saviors"—were faced with a chaotic or deteriorating situation. Their efforts were aimed at restoring order and hope among their followers. On the other hand, some leaders are "transformers"—for example, Mao, Lenin, and Castro—whose aim is to modify and change the organization of society. Unlike saviors whose main concern is to build, transformers often begin by destroying the old order so that it can be replaced with a new system. Transformers are often the leaders of revolutions.

A second dimension along which to classify political leaders is the *scope* of their leadership. On the one hand leaders like Eisenhower, Reagan, and Thatcher had a relatively well-defined, narrow, focus. Their targets have included military and economic organization. A limited focus does not imply that the leader's efforts are not important or critical; what it does imply is that the leader's attention encompasses only one aspect of the group. Reagan, for example, was most concerned with the economic system of the United States, and even in other areas, such as foreign relations, he charted his course according to the expected impact on the economy. On the other hand, some leaders (such as Mao, Hitler, and Churchill) directed their efforts across a broad scope of issues, often including social, educational, political, and economic aims. These leaders viewed their mandate as encompassing all parts of the system. Mao, for example, attacked all aspects of Chinese culture, instituting reforms that "covered the waterfront," from personal thought to the structure of government.

Finally, Blondel suggests that we can differentiate leaders by determining whether their efforts are *focused internally* or more *globally*. Hitler, Alexander the Great, and Emperor Charles V wanted to change the world order; Mao and Lenin were largely focused on their own countries. Given this dichotomy, we might expect that global reformers would be involved in international wars while internal reformers would not. The first half of this assumption is correct—world reformers generally do force their will outside the borders of their countries. However, history is filled with examples of internal reformers (Reagan, Bush, Thatcher, Mao) who also led their countries into international conflicts. Still, the ultimate aim of the internal reformers in these cases was not world dominance but internal change and reform.

Trading group identity for individual identity may reduce concerns with personal codes of ethics and justice. The group, rather than the individual, assumes responsibility for behaviors when deindividuation occurs. (Gerrit Fokkema/Woodfin Camp & Associates)

An examination of political leadership is particularly interesting because it demonstrates very clearly the interplay between personal traits and situations. Churchill, with his strong will, had a rather dismal record of leadership before World War II. However, during the war, his style was effective in rallying the British people and bolstering their resolve. The fact that a rather inconsequential leader may suddenly be propelled into prominence can justify our concern about anyone who beats the drum of ethnic violence and hatred. Although such a leader's message may fall on deaf ears during periods of stability, it may be quickly embraced if the situation becomes more threatening. The crackpot of today may be the popular leader of tomorrow even though his or her message and methods remain the same. I recall as a graduate student listening to the host of a late-night talk show. His views were so extreme that they often caused my fellow students and me to roll with laughter. But the joke was on us when this fellow was elected to the United States Senate several years later. Times had changed, and now this extremist seemed to many people to be not so extreme.

Before we leave the subject of political leadership, there is another issue, relating to situational factors, that should be examined. Bureaucracies and constitutions are often developed with a double-edged purpose. On the one hand, their aim is to limit or circumscribe the power of the leader. On the other hand, the existence of order and structure helps ensure that the leader's decisions will be implemented and accepted. The law can be both a brake and an accelerator for a political leader. However, the skills needed to be an effective leader within a complex bureaucracy will be different from those needed within a less structured situation. So often a leader rises to power because he or she has shown brilliance in one type of situation but proves a dismal failure when faced with the other type. This note of caution was heard when Ross Perot, a successful businessman, made a run for the presidency of the United States. One can only wonder what would have happened had Perot been elected.

The Corrupting Influence of Power

A cynical friend once commented that "disillusionment is a sign of maturity." He lamented the fact that growing older is accompanied by a loss of heroes and heroines. Our first shock comes when we find that there is no tooth fairy, no Santa Claus, and no Easter bunny. Our next step toward despair is the fall from grace of our great leaders. Time and again our world is rocked when we find that our most cherished leaders have misused their power for their own aims. The position of "special prosecutor" has become almost permanent in the United States government, because so many of our leaders have been found to be involved in illegal activities. Scandals that bring down governments have visited nearly every democratic country. There is growing popular support for a law to limit the length of time a person can serve in political office in the United States. In some respects this is an admission that other means have failed to control power and curb corruption.

All of this lends credibility to Lord Acton's observation: "Power tends to corrupt; absolute power corrupts absolutely." Obviously, Acton was stretching the point; there are numerous examples of leaders with unblemished careers of selfless service. On the other hand, there are a disturbing number of cases where leaders have abused their power and positions. Rather than damn all leaders and severely limit their power for fear of abuse, it is instructive to examine the forces that can lead to abuse.

There is a seductive tendency for leaders to view themselves as responsible for the success of the group (Messe, Kerr, & Sattler, 1992). This perception justifies their taking whatever resources they desire from the group, even if they must break the law to do so. In their minds, they are taking only what they deserve. A second reason for abuse is that power separates and isolates the powerful from the powerless. This separation reduces the ability of the powerful to identify with or empathize with less powerful people. Having power makes one the center of attention and praise, and eventually a powerful person begins to believe all this adulation; leaders see themselves as being better than others. Finally, those with power begin to perceive that others want to take away their power. They distrust the powerless. Any gesture of goodwill or support by less powerful people is viewed as a manipulative attempt at ingratiation. The leader views the followers as a potential threat that must be controlled or eliminated. The leader, therefore, becomes increasingly isolated from those that he or she leads. As John Kennedy observed, "The position of the leader is the most lonely in the world."

Because power is so isolating and so easily corrupting, the relationship between group members and their leaders is often tense. In many cases, a group diverts its attention from the task at hand and becomes preoccupied with developing rules and regulations to control its leaders and curb their powers. The struggle becomes one of finding a balance that will give leaders the power necessary to lead but not enough power to invite corruption.

Ethnic Group Leadership: Charting an Untrodden Path

The existing studies of leadership shed light on how leaders rise to power and exert influence. But the overwhelming bulk of the research focuses on political or organizational leaders who act on a stage where they are constrained by rules (a constitution, bylaws, or job descriptions) and by an existing structure. Laws can be subverted or changed, but the leader must deal with them. Institutionalized group structures define who will be a follower and what the role of leader will be. In most cases, these rules and structures limit the power of the leader. You can imagine the uproar that would occur if the president of the United States tried to dictate how people would worship, or if the prime minister of Canada issued an edict declaring that all Canadians must wear shoulder-length hair. The citizens of the United States might be willing to give a president a third term, but the Constitution informs everyone that this is not possible.

In some cases, the situation of the leader of an ethnic group is similar to that of a national or business leader: The power of the leader of a tribe with a history of collective action, for example, is largely determined by custom or rule. But in other cases, the position of leader of an ethnic group is hardly defined at all. The ethnic group exists as a rather unstructured collective without rules that would delineate or govern leadership. For example, what is the "leadership position" for African-Americans, ethnic Germans, or ethnic Irish? In such cases, a pretender to the throne must create a collective spirit of ethnic identity, shape the structure of the resulting ethnic group, and define the position of leader. If we follow Blondel and categorize leaders on the basis of goals, the leader of an ethnic group must play the role of a "creator." He or she must create a sense of ethnic group, structure that group, and define the position of the leader.

This is a daunting task. The leaders must arouse the slumbering identity of many people, perhaps scattered in different nations and not even speaking a common language. Indeed, the scope of the task may be the major reason why there have been so few megaleaders of ethnic groups. But consider the position of the individuals who rise to the task and succeed. They are not bound with the shackles of laws that limit power. Their predecessors, if any, are likely to be immortalized in myth and endowed with superhuman qualities and limitless power. Thus, the group is primed to follow a new leader with unquestioning devotion. Ethnic group leaders can grasp for the brass ring of absolute power, extending their influence into every nook and cranny of life. Because there are few existing rules, they can write the rulebook. The mountain to be scaled is high, but once the ethnic leader has reached the pinnacle, the view and the power are breathtaking.

There are a few modern-day examples of ethnic group leaders that we can use as cases in point. Gandhi, Hitler, and Martin Luther King, Jr., though, could fit the description on a grand scale. The power of these men was extraordinary. Only death could limit their influence. Indeed, because of the nature of power and the lack of rules of succession, ethnic group leaders run a high risk of being assassinated, for how else can their power be contained?

Another unique quality of ethnic leaders is that their road to power is generally based on personality (charisma) and their skill in dissecting the world into a "we-they" dichotomy. Unlike political, religious, or business leaders, ethnic leaders rarely gain power because of a long history of contributions to the group or because of demonstrated skills of leadership. In fact, ethnic group leaders often come from out-side the recognized ranks; they rise from relative obscurity. The power of their personality and their uncanny insight into the fears, hopes, and aspirations of the ethnic group renders mute any group member who might ask, "So what are their qualifications?" Like no other type of leadership, ethnic group leadership has an urgent, fervent quality that stirs emotions and sets aside calculated reasoning. I still remember the electricity in the crowd when Martin Luther King, Jr., proclaimed, "I have a dream." This is not to say that leaders of other groups are not charismatic; they often are. But charismatic leadership is the rule in ethnic groups, rather than the exception. And this fever pitch of excitement may help explain why ethnic identity becomes so important to the followers.

This analysis of ethnic leadership paints a potentially troubling picture of the consequences of the world's fracturing into distinct ethnic groups. The power of leaders of ethnic groups can be tremendous. Their ability to set the agenda of ethnic relations may be limited only by their appetites and ambitions. Nations have developed prescribed rules for interacting with other nations, but no such rules exist to govern the relationship between different ethnic groups. Individuals often look to their leaders to define such rules. At this point, I only wish to plant these disturbing seeds in your thoughts, but I will return to this issue in Chapter 8.

The Making of an Extremist: Group Influence on Individual Attitudes

It's tempting to think that most of our social ills could be cured if we simply had good leadership. But this is not the case, because leaders are not the only source of influence in groups. There are strong currents within the group, quite apart from the leader, that toy with our minds and behaviors. Let's return for a moment to the fire-bombing in Moelln, Germany. When we hear of such incidents, our first reaction is that the perpetrators must be fanatics whose behavior should have been predicted. But in this case, like many others, we find the arsonist's neighbors and friends expressing surprise and shock. A former teacher of Lars Christiansen described him as a quiet kid who "at times wore combat-boots." The teacher did not think Christiansen was a neo-Nazi, and he expressed surprise that he was involved in the firebombings. As an individual, Christiansen did not appear radical or extreme. Indeed, haven't many parents sought to protect a child's image by explaining any wayward activities as resulting from the child's "getting mixed up with the wrong crowd." Maybe. But the crowd does not influence only our children. A friend recently confided that she was a bit disturbed by one of the books assigned to her fifth-grader. She intended to talk with the teacher about the book, but before she could do so, she attended a meeting at her church during which the education system was discussed. The issue of schoolbooks was raised, and a heated discussion took place. "I don't know what happened," my friend stated. "I went to that meeting a bit concerned about one book, and somewhere during the meeting I found myself demanding that several books be banned from the school curriculum and a citizens' group be set up to review all further decisions regarding books. I was horrified with myself!"

My friend's experience is not an isolated incident. Early thinking was that groups make us more conservative and thoughtful (Whyte, 1956). We don't want to make fools of ourselves by appearing too radical or extreme in a group. However, attempts to demonstrate this effect have found just the opposite. In fact, the initial results so often indicated that people become less cautious and more risky in groups that the effect was dubbed the *risky shift* (Wallach, Kogan, & Bem, 1962). More extensive examination revealed that people do not always shift their opinion toward risk, but rather that groups move individuals toward polarized positions representing the extreme of their initial beliefs. In the case of Lars Christiansen, we might speculate that he initially held some neo-Nazi ideas and that his interactions in groups pushed him to a more extreme neo-Nazi position, setting the stage for the firebombing. My friend went into her church group with some concerns about a single book adopted for the fifth grade. During the group discussion she was moved to a more extreme version of her initial attitude.

There have been many explanations for this effect. One is that we do not want to appear wishy-washy or unsure of ourselves in public (Myers, 1982). Therefore, when presenting our position in groups we attempt to strengthen our arguments by adopting a more extreme, clear-cut position. A second explanation is that the rhetoric available to express extreme positions is more forceful and persuasive than the rhetoric expressing mild, middle-of-the-road positions. Thus, people in groups who hold more extreme positions may be more persuasive speakers than moderates. Whatever the reason, groups do manage to move us toward extreme positions, both during group discussions and afterward. As a result, an individual who mildly dislikes or feels uncomfortable with members of other ethnic groups may be started on the road to racism after participating in discussions of ethnic relations with members of his or her own group. Gradually, without clear recognition or devious intent, a group discussion can polarize the ethnic attitudes of its members.

Two Heads Are Not Always Better Than One

Whether we focus on the cowardly act of Lars Christiansen or on Colonel George Custer's decision to attack Sitting Bull at Little Big Horn, we are tempted to classify such blunders as examples of poor thinking by isolated individuals. If only these

Ethnic leaders are governed by few conventions or rules. Their power to lead down the path of good or evil often has few bounds. (Gamma Liaison International)

people had talked over their plans with a group, their decisions would have been better and history books would be filled with happy endings! But would this be the result? Are groups able to utilize various perspectives and ranges of expertise to reach the best individual decisions?

Unfortunately, the case in favor of group decision making is weak at best. Irving Janis (1972; 1982) presents a fascinating analysis of some defective decisions by groups that affected the course of history. He examined such blunders as the invasion of the Bay of Pigs (in Cuba), the failure to defend Pearl Harbor before the Japanese attack, the escalation of the Vietnam War, and the Watergate burglary. Each case involved a decision by a group of highly intelligent people with a wealth of information and expertise at their disposal. Yet in each case the ultimate decision was flawed and resulted in disaster. All of us can add our own experiences of groups that made poor decisions. How does this happen? Why aren't groups better able to use their available talent and information?

According to Janis, even healthy groups are often infected by a "disease" that cripples their processes and renders them unproductive. This disease, called *groupthink*, is a mode of thinking that occurs when "members' striving for unanimity overrides their motivation to realistically appraise alternative courses of actions." There are many symptoms of groupthink. Individual members, fearing disunity, censor themselves; they avoid introducing critical, negative, or dissenting information. In some cases, a "mindguard" may emerge in the group. The mindguard takes it upon himself or herself to "protect" the group from disruptive information. The mind-guard may go so far as to take dissenting members aside and pressure them into silence. The group develops an illusion of unanimity, since the lack of open dissent leads members to believe that everyone is in agreement. A sense of assurance and confidence then overtakes the group, as members feel that the group can do no wrong. Rather than examine a wide range of alternatives, the group quickly narrows its focus to a few, often extreme alternatives. In the case of the Bay of Pigs, Janis reports that President Kennedy and his advisers saw only two courses of action—endorse the invasion plan or accept Cuba as a communist country forever. Finally, when the decision involves a response to another group, there is a tendency to underestimate the strength and ability of the out-group. Kennedy and his advisers considered Castro a weak leader and were unwilling to believe that he had the wide support of the Cuban people.

The frequency of groupthink differs from group to group. Janis identified several conditions that foster this virus. Interestingly enough, it is most likely to occur in cohesive, close-knit groups, whose members like and respect each other. Members in these groups want to perpetuate the good feelings, and they are therefore very reluctant to disagree with each other. A strong, highly respected leader who makes his or her opinions known helps set the stage for groupthink. No one wants to contradict or disagree with the leader for fear of appearing disloyal. Groupthink is most frequent in isolated or closed groups. In these cases, there is no opportunity to check decisions or introduce new information. Finally, groups that feel time pressure or perceive an approaching deadline are most likely to be afflicted with groupthink.

Fortunately, even in highly cohesive groups with strong leaders, groupthink is not inevitable. As an example, consider president-elect Clinton's health summit meeting on December 14–15, 1992, following his election in November of that year. Clinton took a number of unusual but effective steps to ensure careful consideration of a variety of issues and points of view. First, he built the group with individuals of diverse backgrounds (business, government, education), diverse political agendas (Republicans and Democrats), and diverse perspectives (blacks, whites, women, men). Second, Clinton refrained from expressing his own preferences and positions; he listened, probed, and questioned. He encouraged dissenting views and often asked group members, "What are the drawbacks of this position?" Third, he often stressed that the group's function was to examine information and positions and correct misperceptions, that there was no time pressure to make a decision. Finally, the discussions were broadcast to the public live, and viewers were given an opportunity to call in to express their opinions. The group, then, was not isolated but was a center of national and international scrutiny.

Do such procedures work? According to Janis and others (Flowers, 1977; t'Hart & Kroon, 1989) these steps are effective in avoiding groupthink. Janis examined another decision by Kennedy's cabinet, to illustrate this point. Just over a year after the disastrous decision about the Bay of Pigs, Kennedy learned that the Soviets were constructing bases for nuclear missiles in Cuba. This situation would represent a serious threat to the security of the United States. The Russian ships were steaming toward Cuba, and Kennedy had to stop them. However, this time Kennedy avoided making his position known. In fact, he absented himself from some of the meetings. People outside the group were called in to supply information and suggest alternative courses of action. Certain individuals, including Robert Kennedy, the president's brother, played the role of devil's advocate, questioning proposals and introducing dissenting positions. This time, the result was a "good" decision. A shipping blockade was imposed, and negotiations were begun with the Soviets that led to the removal of the missiles.

The lesson of the pitfalls of group decision making is that we cannot ensure ethnic harmony if we simply remove power from leaders and invite groups to chart the waters of ethnic relations. Groups, like individuals, may make poor decisions. We tend to want to believe that groups are better decision makers because of the wider range of experience and information they have at their disposal. However, as we have seen, it is not enough to have these resources available. Groups must take the steps to make use of them. Let's now look briefly at the factors that determine what information groups will use in their deliberations.

Who Influences Group Decisions?

Take a moment to watch a group—large or small—make a decision. If we expected the group to act in a rational way, we might expect all the members to present their positions and their reasons for holding those positions. As the group considered the problem, a slow process of elimination would occur: the members would discuss each position and narrow down the alternatives. Through this process a consensus would develop, which would be supported by the addition of new information.

But this seemingly reasonable route is not the process adopted by many groups. I became only too aware of this fact when attending a meeting of a school board of a small southern town. The board was attempting to decide whether or not to offer a course on multiculturalism in the high school. The meeting began with one person presenting a widely known incident of racial violence that had occurred in one of the district's schools. Many others added their views about this incident. At this point the discussion was usurped by the chairwoman of the board, the school superintendent, and the principal of the high school. They proposed offering a required course on African-American history. During this discussion I became aware of two other group members. One was a new member on the board, who tried to broaden the discussion by presenting information on the increasing numbers of Hispanic and Vietnamese students who were coming into the district. He suggested that the board members look beyond the black-white issue and broaden the scope of solutions to take into account many cultural groups. The other was a black vice-principal, who suggested that the new course should be only one step toward improving racial and cultural awareness and attempted to offer some of her personal experiences. Both of these people were largely ignored by the group as the discussion turned to how the course would fit into the schedule and who would teach it. The decision in favor of the course on black history was made almost by fiat. As you might expect, the course that was eventually offered was not well received by teachers or students. The students made every possible effort to avoid it, and tension remained at a high level—at one point, there was a fight in the dining hall between white and Vietnamese students.

The decision process exemplified by this group is not unusual. Research has long shown that group decisions are often influenced by the members with the highest status. In one early study, Navy bomber crews consisting of a pilot, a navigator, and a gunner were given the following problem to solve:

> A man bought a horse for $60 and sold it for $70. Then he bought the same horse back for $80 and sold it for $90. How much money did he make in the horse business?

The study found that even when one member of the group knew the correct answer ($20), the group did not always choose this answer. This depended on *who* knew the answer. Most of the groups chose the correct answer when it was introduced by the high-status member (the pilot), but only 65% of the groups settled on the correct answer when the lowest-status member of the crew (the gunner) suggested it.

A second interesting finding is that groups generally focus on *shared* information—information that is already known by most members. Little time is devoted to discussing unshared information—information that is known by only one or a few members. Even when unshared information is introduced, the members are unlikely to return to it as the discussion progresses (Stasser, 1992; Stasser & Stewart, 1992). This was clearly the case in the school board meeting, where much discussion was devoted to the widely known racial incident but little attention was given to the changing demographics of the student body, data known by only one member. When pertinent information is excluded in this way, group decisions often rest on a faulty or incomplete foundation.

Finally, it should come as little surprise that group decisions generally reflect the view of the majority; minority opinion is often rejected or ignored. Possibly the best place to see the power of the majority is in the deliberations of juries. Research (Kalven & Zeisel, 1966) has found that when 7 to 11 jurors in a 12-person panel initially felt that a defendant was guilty, a guilty verdict was returned to 90% of the cases (verdicts had to be unanimous in the cases that were studied). On the basis of our previous discussion about conformity and the power of the group, it is not difficult to understand why the majority is so influential.

However, the majority does not invariably determine the group's decision. The dissenting minority can be influential, even when that minority is not composed of high-status individuals. But the impact of the minority is more subtle than that of the majority. Consider the following experiment. Several five-person groups acted as a jury on a simulated personal injury case. One of the "jury" members was an experimental accomplice who had been instructed to favor a $3,000 award when the majority preferred a $15,000 award. On the final vote, the majority held steadfastly to $15,000. The minority dissenter apparently failed. But let's not jump to conclusions. When these same jurors were given a second case to consider, they chose a lower award than subjects who had not been exposed to the minority's low position during the first case (Nemeth & Wachtler, 1974). A minority's influence is often delayed and indirect, whereas the impact of the majority is more direct and immediate. Further research suggests that the presence of a minority opinion leads people to broaden the scope of their thinking and consider a wider range of alternatives. Rather than focus on the source of the message, people consider the merits and demerits of the message itself (Nemeth, 1992). When the influence of the majority prevails, people often confine their consideration to the single position being put forward by the majority; their thinking is convergent rather than divergent. Further, they focus as much on the source as on the message; they are as concerned with the question of how the majority will react to them as they are with the value of the majority's position. Finally, the minority is more likely to influence people's private beliefs than their public behavior. We may come to accept the minority position but remain very reluctant to publicly express it for fear of censure and rejection (Mucchi-Faina, 1994). This is not a hollow victory for the minority. It may not result in an immediate, dramatic change, but it creates an atmosphere for future change in public activity as well as private beliefs.

Obviously, the minority is not influential in all or even most cases. The style of the minority is critical. In order to be most effective, dissenters must take a clear position and remain consistent over time. They must convince the majority that they are confident their position is correct (Moscovici, 1980; 1985). Clear and consistent dissent has two immediate effects. First, the group members focus their attention on the minority (Moscovici & Mugny, 1983). Second, the minority becomes the target of intense efforts by the majority to force a change in opinion (Maass & Clark, 1984; Schachter, 1951). These efforts may range from increased communication to threats and actual physical harm. It is resistance to pressure to change that enhances the persuasiveness of the minority. Lest you plan to adopt this style on a whim, I must hasten to warn you that even when the minority is influential, it often remains unpopular and disliked. This is not a comfortable position for anyone, and minorities often choose to leave groups and find unions that are more supportive and hospitable.

There are many lessons to be learned from this work on group dynamics. However, one lesson is critical for understanding ethnic relations. A colleague of mine was a professor at the University of Zagreb. She was visiting the United States when troubles began to ignite in Yugoslavia. She made rather light of the situation, saying that much of the problem was caused by a few "hotheads" and that once large groups of people began to examine the situation, they would see the insanity of a civil war. Even if these groups were composed of people from the same ethnic background, reason should prevail. But to her amazement—and to the amazement of much of the world, the groups of rational citizens that did form often became fanatical, concluding that ethnicity was paramount, despite the cost. Whether the groups were in Croatia or Serbia, each felt their side would win, and each failed to heed the warning of the few who cautioned about the devastating impact of a war, even for the winner. The lesson from both research and the ethnic battlefield is that we cannot rely on groups to calm agitators or make the most rational and humane choices.

The Changing Nature of Groups:
To Everything There Is a Season

Although it is easy to become disturbed by the nuances of group behavior, there is an interesting pattern in the influence of groups, which may offer some solace. Consider the Basque people of northern Spain and southwestern France. The

Basques are distinct from their neighbors, having their own language (one of the most complicated in the world), history, homeland, and customs. Their history is one of constantly trying to distinguish themselves from their neighbors and gain recognition as an independent group (Ramirez & Sullivan, 1987). Since the sixth century, violence and nationalism have been followed by periods of peace and calm, in turn followed again by violence. Violence is preceded either by declining economic conditions or by perceived threats to Basque autonomy. These conditions lead to a rise in ethnic identity, accompanied by renewed attention to Basque history and increased emphasis on the Basque language. Calm returns when the Basque people feel they have achieved an acceptable degree of autonomy and self-rule. These periods of calm are associated with less emphasis on ethnic identity, greater concern for economic output, and increased willingness to cooperate with their Spanish and French neighbors. Interestingly, ethnic violence among the Basques has been more prominent in Spain than in France. Ramirez and Sullivan (1987) suggest that one reason for this is that "France has allowed external signs of 'Basqueness' to be expressed, such as folklore and customs" (p. 136).

Whether we examine a small group such as a family or a large group such as a country, one point is clear: groups are not static; they are in a constant state of change. At first glance, change may appear random, even frantic, like a crowd in Macy's bargain basement on the day before Christmas. Members move into and out of groups; group discussions sometimes focus on internal issues and sometimes focus on relationships with other groups; leadership is sometimes strong and central and sometimes weak and diffuse; at some times the group atmosphere is harmonious and at other times the group is torn by disagreement and disharmony. Although all this may appear to be based on whim, careful observations suggest that there is a reason for each change. Groups, like individuals, tend to develop through predictable stages or patterns. But unlike an individual, a group often repeats the cycle of development many times over its life. At each stage certain behaviors and events are more likely than others (Dunphy, 1968; Goodman, 1981; Tuckman, 1965).

Recognition of these cycles has prompted several investigators to develop models that describe group development and change. The aim was to determine if there are regular stages or patterns over time that shape groups and influence group behavior. If such patterns were uncovered, they would help us predict and explain the forces that propel groups toward violence or toward peace and cooperation. My students and I have attempted to construct such a model of group development (Worchel, Coutant-Sassic, & Grossman, 1992; Worchel, Coutant-Sassic, & Wong, 1993).

We began by sifting through thousands of pages of descriptions of the history of various groups, ranging from relatively small church and social groups to large groups such as political parties, social movements, and nations. We followed this search with observations of laboratory groups that met for extended periods of time. We were struck by the predictable cycle of behaviors that emerged in all the types of groups we examined, allowing us to construct a model of group development and change (Figure 4.1).

During the initial stages of formation, groups generally focus on the issue of *identification:* viz., the members attempt to give their group a distinct identity. During this

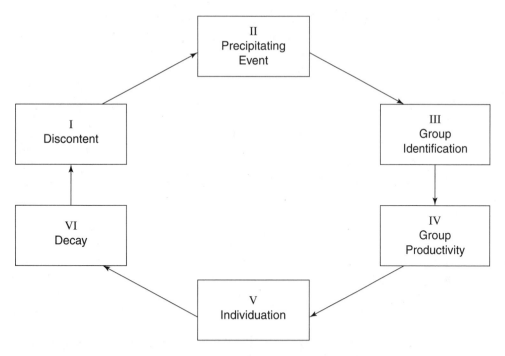

FIGURE 4.1   Preliminary Model of Group Formation and Development

period group norms and structure are identified, and leadership is centralized. There is a strong emphasis on harmony and conformity; minority opinions and dissenters are rejected. There is a high state of excitement and anticipation as members declare their loyalty to the group, adopt group symbols such as flags or dress, and sacrifice their own gains for the good of the group. Groupthink is likely during this period because of the emphasis on uniformity and harmony. Because of the high state of arousal and excitement, members are more easily influenced by extreme and emotionally charged appeals that advocate action. Although cooperation and interdependence rule internal behavior, the group often seeks conflict with out-groups. Such conflict serves to clarify the group's boundaries and to give the members a common enemy.

The identification stage occurs during the initial formation of the group, or when the group feels threatened by external forces, or both. The effect of external threats does not escape the attention of wily leaders. History is filled with examples of leaders, who, seeing their power and position slipping away, have taken steps to invite or manufacture conflicts with out-groups. Ronald Reagan sent American troops into Grenada at a time when questions were being raised about his leadership. George Bush committed troops to Panama and Iraq, countries which he portrayed as a direct threat to the United States. The result in both cases was a rapid rise in patriotism in the United States. In the case of Iraq, there was also a startling increase in Bush's public approval rating. As Bush's popularity began slipping before the 1992 election, there was a rash of rumors that he was considering renewing the battle with Iraq to regain momentum in his campaign. Hitler turned his wrath on Jews and Gypsies to excite the Germans, encourage them to identify with their in-group, and consolidate their support of the Nazi state.

Once a group is secure in its identity, its efforts turn toward *productivity*. Members set goals for the group. Concern moves away from distinguishing between the in-groups and out-groups and toward using the skills of group members to help the group achieve its goal. Leadership becomes more task-oriented and less socioemotional. The boundaries of the group become more permeable as it seeks to recruit new members or temporary members who can help it. Failure is attributed to external sources, and success is seen as resulting from internal efforts. There are cautious, often tentative, efforts to seek cooperation with out-groups, but failure results in a rush back to isolation.

During the initial two stages, the major concern of members is with the group. At each stage, individuals are willing to make personal sacrifices for the good of the group. But as the group begins to reach its productivity goals, attention shifts to the individual group members. As members attempt to *individuate* themselves, they begin to separate themselves from the group. Instead of pushing for equal distribution of rewards, members now want equity, giving rewards to those who have made the greatest contribution. Individuals demand to be recognized for their personal efforts. Members begin comparing themselves with other members. The push, now, is toward allowing greater personal freedom within the group. New members are invited into the group. Subgroups and cliques begin to form, and leadership is weakened. Most important, members begin to explore membership in other groups and use the threat of defection to enhance their position in the group. There is little concern with developing consensus, and minorities become very influential (Worchel, Grossman, & Coutant-Sassic, 1994).

The final stage of the process is *decay*. The group begins to disintegrate, and members leave it. Individuals demand compensation for past sacrifices, and competition arises between members. The honesty and ability of leaders is questioned; distrust fills the air. There is a growing demand to recruit new leaders from outside the group. Decay does not necessarily result in the complete destruction of the group. In fact, it can create fertile ground for change and for a rebirth of the group with a different structure, different leaders, and a different composition of members. As the group is reborn, it begins anew the identification process and the cycle of group development.

There are many points to be made about this development process. First, leaders generally have their greatest power during the identification stage. At this point, leaders are best able to guide and control the group—and the group is most vulnerable to the lure of a leader who stresses group identity and locates a threat in an out-group. Members are willing to follow a leader who promises action, who delivers the message of ethnic or national superiority. According to this model, it is no accident that Hitler rose to power at a time when German identity was battered and bruised. Likewise, there is little surprise in the fact that the various ethnic groups in the former Yugoslavia viciously demanded recognition and freedom after years of rule by Marshal Tito, who insisted that ethnic identity play a role secondary to that of the nation. Concerns with identity are a powder keg waiting for the smallest spark to ignite violence against an out-group. Once violence is ignited, it is very difficult to put out the fire, because groups concerned with establishing their identity have little interest in intergroup cooperation.

The model also suggests that voices of dissent are more likely to be heeded at some points than at others. Minorities are most able to influence the group during the latter stages, individuation and decay. They are most likely to be attacked and rejected when the group is establishing its identity or being threatened by an outside group. Finally, it is important to realize that individuals are more committed to groups at some points and will therefore be influenced by group-based messages at those times. At other points, their concern is more self-centered, so successful efforts to change behavior must have an egoistic appeal. Applying this approach to nations, we find interesting patterns in the nature of the laws passed at various points. During periods of concern about identification, laws are often aimed at protecting the nation, the group. Treason, for example, is most severely punished when the identity of a nation is being threatened, as during a war or an internal crisis. During periods of productivity and individuation, we find an increasing number of laws designed to protect the rights of the individual.

The general point of this approach is to suggest that groups, whether nations, ethnic groups, or smaller groups, develop in cycles in which the attention of the group is most focused on a specific issue. These cycles are predictable and are repeated several times over the life of the group. As the group moves through the stages of development, the behavior of the members changes, as does the nature of attempts by the group to control that behavior. Understanding these cycles opens our eyes and helps us explain a host of actions that seem, at first glance, to be random or unprovoked.

Beware of the Caged Tiger

Like a spider, a group weaves a beautiful web to ensnare members. But even though it may place its brand on the members' identity, a group is not always successful in enlisting members to fight for its goals. Members still remain torn between their personal needs and those of the group. Groups expend considerable effort to get members to see that these needs are the same, but a group cannot be successful without help. At the height of the "Black power" movement in the 1960s, I was surprised to find one of my black friends calmly studying in his office while the black community in Durham, North Carolina, was staging a massive demonstration. I asked him why he was not involved in the demonstrations. "Oh," he said, "I support the movement and recognize that it has legitimate goals, but, to tell you the truth, I've really not experienced much discrimination in my life. I've been accepted at the schools I applied for, and I've already received offers for several jobs when I complete my doctoral degree." I was shocked at his response, and as I rushed out carrying my banner in support of the demonstration, I said to myself, "He just doesn't understand." Several years later, I again muttered these words to myself as I watched Clarence Thomas, a conservative black jurist nominated for the Supreme Court, justify his color-blind position during his confirmation hearings.

But looking back on the incident, I find that quite possibly I was the one who didn't understand. The struggle between social identity and personal identity is a real one that consumes all of us. Research shows that while we may perceive and be disturbed by discrimination against our group, we are most likely to partake in collective action when we see the social system as closed to us personally. In other words, the belief that we can change groups or enhance our status cools the fires of activism. In an interesting study, Wright, Taylor, and Moghaddam (1990) led participants to believe that they had been rejected by a high-status group because of a quota system. Even when the quota was quite small, the rejected students preferred to take individual steps such as requesting reconsideration. Only when the quota system completely barred membership to members of their group (0% quota) were the subjects strongly interested in becoming involved in collective protest.

This finding has important implications for ethnic groups wishing to fight discrimination. From the perspective of recruiting members to do battle with the system, a group is in a better situation if discrimination is complete and affects all group members. However, programs such as affirmative action that offer hope (even only minimal hope) to some members of the group may reduce the resolve of members to become engaged in collective action to enhance the position of the group as a whole. Regardless of their intent, programs that offer mobility to some members of disadvantaged ethnic groups may, in fact, weaken the chance that the whole group can take action to raise its position. We might further expect that collective action is less likely from members who feel that they can leave a group or disassociate themselves from it. The light-skinned black or the Asian with multiethnic ancestry may be more reluctant to carry the group's flag into battle than the person who cannot "pass" as a member of another ethnic group. This possibility may also explain why many ethnic groups are less willing to accept individuals who are not clearly distinguishable as members.

Let me quickly point out that I am not suggesting that efforts to give members of disadvantaged groups hope and opportunity are misguided. But it is important to recognize that these programs can reduce the likelihood of collective effort to create a more widely equitable system, thereby reducing the immediate pressure on the group in power to continue moving toward ethnic equality. Any effort that moves us toward social justice is a positive step in the direction of developing long-term ethnic harmony. But we must realize that it is only one step in a long and continuing journey, and movement in this direction must continue even when the pressures of collective action are not on our doorstep.

Group Influence: Hands on the Puppet Strings

Although the seeds of ethnic conflict may be within the individual, ethnic groups themselves may become fertile soil for nurturing this conflict. Examination of group dynamics illustrates the forces within groups that conspire to push us toward extremes in attitudes and behaviors and invite us to suspend judgment regarding our actions. In their struggle for independence and recognition, groups help decide which issues and concerns will be important to us. The message is not that we should all become "group busters"—resolving ethnic conflict by guarding against the formation of groups. Rather, the research on groups demonstrates how groups can feed personal hatred and what conditions facilitate this process. It is easy to become sucked into the prevailing winds of groups and to become slaves to group power. However, just as groups can become forces for evil, they can also be catalysts for goodwill and harmony. It is, therefore, critical to understand how groups function if we are to appreciate why people act as they do when group membership is salient. Knowledge, in this case, is the best instrument for employing group dynamics as a balm to heal conflict rather than a breeze that fans its flames.

We've examined group dynamics under a fairly strong microscope. But we should not forget that just as our world is not populated by a single individual, it is not inhabited by a single group. Groups have a social landscape of their own; they coexist with other groups. Our focus on the group has given us an opportunity to move beyond the single individual and explore how individuals relate to each other. In Chapter 5, I will push the curtain back even further, venturing into the realm of intergroup relations. From many perspectives, the domain of intergroup relations is the real stage on which ethnic group relations unfold. However, as we examine the factors that influence relationships between groups, do not forget the backdrop, which includes the forces that are being played out within the individual and within the (ethnic) group. With this admonishment, let's head into the thorny territory of intergroup relations.

R E A D I N G   4 . 1

Murders Stun Solingen*

SOLINGEN, Germany—The Germans of Solingen said today they were bewildered by the arson attack which killed five Turks during the weekend, claiming that their city had always made foreigners welcome.

But civil rights groups said that in Solingen, as in many German cities, racism lurked below the surface.

Yesterday police arrested a youth in connection with the arson attack on the house occupied by the young Turkish family, the Federal Prosecutor's Office said.

The Prosecutor's Office in Karlsruhe said the arrested youth, whom it did not name, was being held on suspicion of several murders, attempted murder and arson.

While some residents say Solingen is a town at peace with migrants, others say it has a growing movement of hardcore neo-Nazis.

*Source: Waikato Times, Tuesday, June 1, 1993, p. 5.

A leaflet issued by human rights groups said skinheads and neo-Nazis had met regularly at the same places in the city for years.

The groups said Solingen had experienced racist violence, including a neo-Nazi attack on an asylum-seekers' home in May 1992 and an arson attack at the Turkish mosque in January this year.

Few residents can explain why anyone in Solingen should turn against the foreign workers who helped the city, destroyed in World War II, to rebuild its famous stainless steel and cutlery industry in the 1960s and 1970s.

"There is no right-wing scene in Solingen. Solingen is a very liberal, cosmopolitan city," said mayor Bernd Krebs.

German Chancellor Helmut Kohl said he and all decent Germans were appalled by the murders.

"Their crime displays an unfathomable degree of brutalisation and contempt for humanity. It is a disgrace that such murders can happen in the middle of Germany."

—Reuter

R E A D I N G 4 . 2

Jewish Influence a Mystery*

There has been one rare flash of unanimity in the heat of the Australian election campaign: applause from both sides for the decision to ban a visit by the controversial British historian, Mr. David Irving.

Mr. Irving was refused a visa for his determined defence of Adolf Hitler and his claims that the Holocaust never happened.

But behind the decision lay a continuing phenomenon of Australian politics—the influence of the Jewish community, which extends far beyond its size or power to decide even marginal seats.

The community's ability to sway the most powerful politicians in the land confounds political observers such as Dr. Clive Bean, of the Australian National University Research School of Social Sciences, and Mr. Malcolm Mackerras, one of Australia's most prominent electoral analysts.

"I must admit, I'm very puzzled by it," said Mr. Mackerras.

There is no doubt the influence is real, despite the fact that the Jewish community numbers less than 100,000, concentrated in Sydney and Melbourne, and with no deciding balance in any electorate.

---

*Source: NZ (New Zealand) Herald, February 25, 1993, p. 24 (section 1).

To put this into perspective, Australia has a migrant population of more than three million, but ethnic communities extend into generations of Australian-born descendants of original settlers.

For example, according to the Bureau of Statistics, there were about 260,000 Italian-born migrants living in Australia in 1986, but more than 500,000 people who considered themselves part of the Italian community.

And while politicians and lobbyists talk glibly of the ethnic vote, the creature remains largely mythical.

Said Dr. Bean: "The ethnic vote probably does exist, but beyond that we don't know a lot about it, or how it operates. Statistically, it's too small."

At best, analysts suggest that where ethnic groups appear to vote as something of a bloc, the vote is more likely to be determined by problems common to migrant groups—such as unemployment and access to social services—rather than membership of any community.

For these reasons Mr. Mackerras suspects that, such as it is, the ethnic vote will favour Labour.

Yet a relatively small group, with no direct electoral clout, can command attention about which other communities can only dream.

The Jewish lobby, spearheaded by the Zionist Federation of Australia, is constantly courted by Prime Ministers and Opposition leaders, is able to sway both domestic and foreign policy where it touches its interests, and last year even forced a senior minister to recant publicly.

Labour lost Jewish support in the 1970s when the former Prime Minister, Mr. Gough Whitlam, implied that Australia had not condemned the Arabs' Yom Kippur attack on Israel for fear of alienating Australian-Arab voters.

It returned with Mr. Hawke's rise to power, and his unwavering advocacy of Israel.

Zionist Federation conferences are routinely addressed by the leaders of both major parties, both of whom equally routinely pledge Australian loyalty to the Jewish and Israeli cause.

The Leader of the Opposition, Dr. Hewson, is "proud to be a friend of Israel" and promises "unshakeable support." The Prime Minister, Mr. Keating, lauds the Jews' "civilising influence" on Australia, Israel as a "great cause," and Jews as "great settlers, great Australians."

And when the Foreign Minister, Senator Evans, last year criticised Israel's Palestinian policies and human rights record, he was hauled over the coals.

Speaking to the students, Senator Evans at least gave an answer as to why the Jewish community enjoyed such extraordinary rapport with the Government. There was, he said, a "bonding experience" of shared democratic ideals, nurtured by schoolday friendships with the children of Holocaust survivors.

Dr. Bean is not so sure.

"My speculation would be that it has money," he said, "and money is influential. Also, the Jewish influence is a worldwide phenomenon and to some extent its international presence may make Australian parties feel that it is a group that cannot be ignored."

Chinese in Indonesia Fear Officials Won't Protect Them from Attacks*

PASURUAN, Indonesia—Rioters hurled stones at shuttered storefronts and shouted: "Chinese, you dogs. Come out, we'll kill you."

They looted this town, shattered windows and lit alcohol-soaked tires, then propped them up outside a Chinese-owned shop. Two hours later, police swinging truncheons broke up the mob and the violence subsided.

Yet many anxious Chinese, the scapegoats of scattered protests against price increases such as last week's in Pasuruan, 400 miles east of Jakarta, question whether authorities can shield them from growing unrest.

"They'll protect us, but not 100 percent," said Chandra Winata, 39, a Chinese businessman in Jember, one in a string of towns in eastern Java island hit by violent protests.

So far, no one has been killed and most of Indonesia remains peaceful. But as the economic crisis fueling increases in the price of staples such as rice and cooking oil grinds on, the government is stepping up security.

Police patrolled the streets of Bima, 875 miles east of Jakarta on Sumbawa Island, on Sunday, the day after rioters burned two Chinese-owned shops. They also were out in force in the Java town of Bojonegoro, 350 miles east of Jakarta, following rumors of a planned protest.

Bojonegoro officials have arranged special markets so villagers can buy staple foods at a cheaper price, police Lt. Budi Winarto told The Associated Press. Officers were also searching for vendors who were hoarding food, which is illegal, he said. The protest did not materialize.

Thousands of security personnel ran anti-riot drills in the Indonesian capital last week in a show of force designed to deter troublemakers. Jakarta's military commander has even tried to reassure jittery expatriates, whose money is a valuable source of foreign exchange.

"I assure all foreigners living in Jakarta not to worry about their safety," the official Antara news agency quoted Maj. Gen. Sjafrie Syamsuddin as saying Saturday.

In small Java towns, the affluent ethnic Chinese minority is relatively isolated and vulnerable to the resentment among the poor. Many police garrisons lack the mobility and numbers to respond forcefully to a riot.

Some officers may even sympathize with the rioters and prefer to allow them to let off some steam before intervening.

"In many cases, the local cops are far more hesitant to take violent action," said John Sidel, a lecturer in Southeast Asian politics at the School of Oriental and African Studies in London. Sidel has conducted research on riots in Indonesia.

---

*Source: Portland Press Herald, February 9, 1998, p. 12A.

"Lower the prices" and "Wreck the Chinese" read slogans spray-painted on a few boarded-up Chinese shops in East Java, a region with a strong conservative Muslim influence.

About 90 percent of Indonesians are Muslim, while many ethnic Chinese are Christian and Buddhist. Chinese, who make up 4 percent of Indonesia's 202 million people, run 70 percent of the economy.

The Feb. 2 riot in Pasuruan broke out after a rumor that a Chinese shopkeeper had raised the price of kerosene.

Rioters, all of them men, waited until a police patrol passed by, then began flinging stones at stores along a stretch of road. Police waded in eventually.

Some people suggest that the government, beset by economic turmoil, is trying to fan the perception that the Chinese are responsible for Indonesia's ills. "All the signs are encouraging people to blame the Chinese," said Sidel, the researcher.

CHAPTER 5

EXPANDING THE SCOPE

The Relationship between Groups

Several years ago, a peaceful afternoon of yard work was interrupted when my daughter, Leah, asked me to tell her about her "identity." I stammered a bit, then assured her that she was not adopted or illegitimate. She cut me short, saying that her class was studying family origins and she wanted to know the "roots" of the family and the family name. "This," she proudly proclaimed, "will tell me who I really am." I told her to go look in the mirror to find out who she was, but she pressed her point. As I thought about her question, I realized I had little knowledge of our family origin, and I suggested that she write to her grandparents. When the response came, I found myself as interested in our history as my daughter was. My pedigree was largely Polish and Lithuanian, and my true surname was not Worchel but Warsalevski. "Worchel" was a result of my grandparents' attempts to become more American when they arrived in this strange country. Leah was enthralled with the newfound identity, and she began signing her school papers "L. Warsalevski." Although her teachers were thrown into utter confusion, I didn't think much about this incident until I was invited to give a talk in Poland years later. As I disembarked from the airplane in Warsaw, a strange feeling came over me. I felt that somehow I belonged here. I walked the streets of Warsaw wondering whether my ancestors had walked the same streets a century before. And I cheered the freedom movement that was under way in Poland at the time of my visit. I left Poland with an odd sense of sadness, much like that of a child who leaves home for the first time to attend school.

Ten years later, I experienced similar feelings as I watched Lithuanians struggle for, and finally achieve, independence from the Soviet Union. Their fight suddenly became my fight, and their freedom was my freedom. I began to feel that I was merely a visitor in the United States. I searched out other people who had Polish or Lithuanian origins. In fact, my view of myself underwent a transformation.

The novelist Milan Kundera wrote, "People usually escape from their troubles into the future; they draw an imaginary line across the path of time, a line beyond which their current troubles will cease to exist" (1984, p. 164). I had been one of these people, always looking toward the future with eager anticipation; I'd even considered visiting a fortuneteller during times of strife. But now I began to realize that the future told me little about myself. It was my past, the groups from which I sprang, that answered the incessant question, "Who am I?" "I" am, in fact, the sum total of

116

the groups (ethnic, religious, family) from which I came and the groups to which I presently belong. My uniqueness is in the combination of these groups—with, of course, a dash of my personal characteristics. Comfort was to be found not in knowing my future but in understanding my past. The accomplishments of the groups to which I belonged were my accomplishments; their pain and struggles were mine. These groups gave me safe harbor as I navigated through life.

Had my story stopped here, it would have been rather benign. What can be more harmless than finding one's lost family roots? But this was not the end of my saga. Not only did I view myself and the people with whom I shared a common origin differently; I also viewed others, the outsiders, differently. During my travels through Europe, I found myself looking for flaws in the character and countries of these outsiders. I was especially hard on Germans and Russians, the neighbors and traditional antagonists of "my people." I remember passing up an opportunity to buy a beautiful painting at a bargain price after finding out that the painter was Russian. The intensity of my prejudice cooled as the years since my rebirth passed, but I still find myself reading the news about Europe with less than an open mind.

Conflict between Groups

Dislike, distrust, discrimination, and violence between people of different groups is as common as leaves on a tree. No country or region of the world is free from group hatred, and no period of human history is untainted by it. In some areas, group conflict has raged openly for centuries. In others, such as the former Yugoslavia, group violence erupts suddenly between people who have lived in relative harmony for decades. Tracing the causes of group conflict can be as difficult as finding the beginning of a circle. In many cases, even the participants are unaware of (and often do not care about) the origin of their conflict. Several years ago, I interviewed an inmate serving 20 years for burning the home of a black family. I asked him what had provoked him to this cowardly act. His answer was simply, "They were black." Did he know these people? "No." He then closed our conversation: "Hey, what are you getting at? These people were black, and they moved into a white neighborhood. What other reason do you need?"

I left the meeting condemning this lout as stupid and unthinking. Then I remembered my own thoughts about Russians. I hadn't burned down any of their homes, but I had an uneasy feeling about them. Why? The answer was simple. I had Polish origins, and "they" were Russian.

The process of loving and supporting our own group because it is our group and discriminating against the out-group is at the heart of *ethnocentrism*. Ethnocentrism is so commonplace that it may be viewed as a universal human characteristic. The sociologist William Graham Sumner described the process in his book *Folkways* in 1906:

> *Ethnocentrism* is the technical name for this view of things in which one's own group is the center of everything, and all others are scaled and rated with reference to it. Folkways correspond to it to cover both the inner and outer relation. Each group nourishes its own pride and vanity, boasts itself superior, exalts its own divinities,

Groups often go to great lengths to draw their boundaries. According to social identity theory, the seeds of discrimination are sown when the in-group and the out-group are defined. (Nathan Benn/Woodfin Camp & Associates)

and looks with contempt on outsiders. Each group thinks its own folkways the only right ones, and if it observes that other groups have other folkways, these excite its scorn. . . . For our present purpose the most important fact is that ethnocentrism leads a people to exaggerate and intensify everything in their own folkways which is peculiar and which differentiates them from others. It therefore strengthens the folkways. (pp. 12–13)

We cannot deny the existence of preference for our own group and conflict between groups, whether we term it racism, prejudice, ethnocentrism, or discrimination. But we must ask why it occurs. In searching for the roots of group conflict, we can begin with the individual. For the most part, our focus in earlier chapters has been on the individual, and I will take a moment to review some important points.

Identity: Beyond the Mirror

Birth is the beginning of two journeys. One involves the struggle for survival. The other is the search for identity. The French philosopher René Descartes (1596–1650) argued that the first issue that each of us faces in the search for identity is to determine that we exist. How do we know that we actually exist as an entity? His answer was: "I think, therefore I am" (*cogito, ergo sum*). Newborns have no idea who they are or how they look. One of the most interesting human drama occurs when an infant first sees his or her reflection. At first, the infant is delighted to have found a playmate and goes through an elaborate routine, inviting the "other baby" to play. But as the "other" steadfastly refuses to emerge from the mirror, the frustrated infant slowly learns that the reflection is an image of himself or herself, and the search for identity begins.

This search quickly progresses beyond the mirror, but the mirror remains important. William James (1890) pointed out that much of our personal identity is derived from our experiences with others. As we discussed in Chapter 1, Charles Cooley (1902) emphasized the importance of others in developing a self-image by using the term "looking-glass self." Cooley suggested that we wander the pathways of life imagining what others think of us. We then use the "imagined" image to help form our own impression of ourselves. We also undertake an elaborate process of social comparison, comparing ourselves with others on a variety of dimensions ranging from physical appearance to attitudes and skills (Festinger, 1954).

OUR SOCIAL IDENTITY.   Although we develop much of our identity through our own individual actions, some of it is more deeply rooted in another social dimension—our group membership. When you are asked to describe yourself, chances are you will give a response something like this: black, male, Baptist, American, father of four children, a carpenter, a Texan, and so on. You might sprinkle a few other details into this description, such as: bald, 6 feet tall, weighing 200 pounds. Much of your self-description will include groups or categories to which you belong (black, male, Baptist, and so on). Although this seems a relatively benign act of self-definition, the British psychologist Henri Tajfel and his colleagues (Tajfel, 1970; 1982; Tajfel & Turner, 1986; Turner, 1975; 1987) pointed out its sinister side. According to their "social identity" theory, we have simultaneous desires to develop a self-identity *and* to establish that identity as positive (see Chapter 1). This position is similar to that of humanistic psychologists such as Carl Rogers and Abraham Maslow, who argued that humans have a need for positive self-regard or esteem. Because much of our identity is based on the groups to which we belong, we strive to join "positive" groups and avoid "negative" groups.

In some cases, however, we cannot choose our group; we are born into some groups and endowed with lifetime membership (Baumeister, 1986). These groups include our gender, race, ethnic group, and family of origin. This could become an uncomfortable situation, but the human mind is inventive and flexible, and therefore, our identity need not suffer irreparable damage when two or more of our groups are in conflict. According to social identity theory, as members of a group or category we strive to enhance the position of that in-group and reduce the position of out-groups. In some cases, this feat is accomplished by assigning greater rewards to our own group than to out-groups (Tajfel, 1970).

We can enhance the position of our own group through our perceptions as easily as through rewards. Reality is as we see it, and research shows that we bias our perceptions in favor of our own group (Hinkle & Schopler, 1986). This bias is nowhere more evident than in the evaluation of group performance. Let us examine two experiments that illustrate this point. In one, boys at summer camp were divided into two groups, which were placed in a number of competitive situations (Sherif, Harvey, White, Hood, & Sherif, 1961). At one point, dried beans were scattered around a campground and the boys were told to find as many as possible in an allotted time. The beans collected by each group were placed in separate jars, and at the end of the period the boys were asked to estimate the number of beans in each. It should come as no surprise that there was a consistent tendency for the boys to overestimate the number their own group had collected and underestimate what the out-group had collected.

Let's now move from the campground to the football field. In 1954 students at Princeton and Dartmouth witnessed a particularly violent game between their two schools. The game was marred by numerous penalties and injuries. Both starting quarterbacks left the game with broken bones. During the game Dartmouth was flagged for more infractions than Princeton. Some time after the game, Al Hastorf and Hadley Cantril (1954) asked students from both schools to watch a film of the game and record the number and severity of infractions they saw. Although they saw the same film, the students' perceptions were very different (Figure 5.1). Dartmouth students saw the teams as having committed the same number of in-

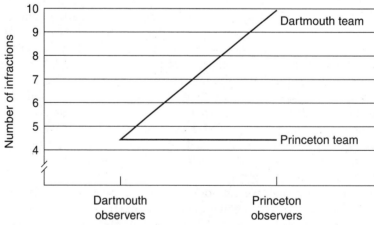

FIGURE 5.1   Number of Infractions Recorded by Dartmouth and Princeton Students while Watching the Film of a Dartmouth-Princeton Game.
Source: Hastorf & Cantril, 1954.

fractions, but Princeton students saw the Dartmouth players commit twice as many infractions. "Apparently, the Princeton observers' preference for their own team distorted their perceptions of the group interaction" (Forsyth, 1990, p. 30). Here is another case of advantaging our own group by the way in which we perceive or interpret events and performance.

What does social identity theory tell us about group conflict? Most importantly, the theory suggests that one root of group conflict can be found in the simple act of grouping. Putting people into groups by design or at random creates an in-group and an out-group, and this seemingly innocent distinction sets the stage for group conflict and discrimination. Second, the underlying dynamics of this process do not reside only within the group. Rather, the fountainhead of conflict and discrimination is the individual's desire to develop a positive self-image. This positive image is built, in part, by enhancing the position and reputation of the in-group relative to the out-group. This can be accomplished by actual acts of favoritism in the division of resources, rewards, opportunities, and power as well as through the perceptions and evaluations of groups and their products. But the process extends beyond the individual and his or her relationship to a group. It also involves the collective action of the group itself to establish its identity.

GROUP IDENTITY: THE GROUP AS A WILLING PARTNER.   Sean O'Grady was a young lion in the Irish Republican Army (IRA). He had a reputation as being one of its most daring and violent members, directly responsible for the death of three Protestants in Northern Ireland. A colleague of mine interviewed O'Grady and reported a rather surprising statement: O'Grady observed that he did not grow up hating Protestants but had adopted the hatreds of his chosen group. He said: "They [the Protestants] are the enemy of my people. The IRA targeted these people, and I was their instrument of death. I carry the hatred of my own group." This is a very revealing observation, critically important for understanding intergroup relations.

Psychology, because its mission is to study the individual, focuses on individual thought and behavior. Social identity theory, for example, explains how individuals in a group discriminate against out-groups in order to advance their own identity. The group, in this approach, becomes a stage for the actions of the individual. Psychologists are loath to endow groups with the ability to think or feel, apart from the capacities of individual members. Floyd Allport (1924) summarized this position: "Nervous systems are possessed by individuals; but there is no nervous system of the crowd" (p. 5).

But there is another stream of thought, deep within the roots of sociology, that considers a group an entity in its own right. Emile Durkheim, for example, spoke of the "will of the group," the group mind, which dominated and controlled members. Asch (1952) also accepted that a group may be something different from the sum of its members. He pointed out that while water (H_2O) is composed of hydrogen and oxygen, the characteristics of water cannot be understood by studying the properties of the separate elements. Such an analogy implies that although individuals affect a group, they are also affected by it.

This point has become evident to me in my own observations of a wide variety of groups—from small laboratory groups to large social movements and political parties (Worchel, 1996; Worchel, Coutant-Sassic, & Grossman, 1992; see also Chapter 4). Of interest here is the finding that groups develop through rather predictable phases or stages, each dominated by a particular concern or focus. One of the most pronounced phases is *group identity*, during which a group strives to establish its identity, its boundaries, and its independence from other groups. At this stage, a group demands conformity from its members, centralizes its leadership, and seeks competition and conflict with other groups. A group, like an individual, attempts to establish an identity that sets it apart from—and above—other groups.

A group in this phase becomes a dictator, demanding that members act in concert to advance its goals. It requires members to reduce or cease contact with out-groups, and to compete with members of out-groups. Echoing Sean O'Grady, groups demand that members dislike (or even hate) other groups. Therefore, individuals who embrace group membership to enhance their own identity may find themselves being forced to adopt measures that will help the group establish its identity. In this case, the goals of both the group and the individual may be nurtured by conflict with an out-group.

Fanning the Flame: Catalysts for Group Formation

Social identity theory may strike a responsive cord, but it isn't the whole tune. Although there may be only one in-group, there are always several out-groups, only some of which are targeted for hate and discrimination. The major conflict in Northern Ireland is between Protestants and Catholics, not between men and women, Irish and Turks, or carpenters and stenographers. The Serbs are battling Muslims and Croats, not Italians and Austrians. Obviously, there are factors that influence which groups an individual will target as enemies.

As we examine these points, a fascinating and revealing pattern takes shape. Each force that leads us to form a union with certain people also aids and abets intergroup conflict. Each factor that attracts individuals to a group helps drive a wedge between that group and other groups. And each variable helps determine which out-groups we will choose as our enemy. This fact is a key to understanding why ethnic conflict is so enduring and so hard to resolve. In order to reduce conflict between groups, we may need to mute the forces that attract us to and keep us within our own groups. But any move in this direction will meet stiff resistance from the group. The ability to attract and hold members is the lifeblood of a group. Therefore, groups will feel threatened by any effort to limit this ability.

As we examine these variables, keep in mind that groups are products of the mind. There is no set of rules devised by some supreme being that dictates which groups will be formed or who will be placed in them. We (using some input from others) decide when and where to draw the boundaries around a set of people and label it a group. As we will see, there are psychological "rules" that guide us in this endeavor, but each of us is the ultimate architect of our social categories. Human groups exist within our minds, although we react to them as if they are physical reality (Turner, 1987). This explains why assigning members to groups can differ between people: I may define an individual as Asian if he or she looks Asian, while another person may do so only if the person's parents are both Asian. The importance of these cognitive contributions is further seen in the fact that we often change the way we categorize our world. At one time, I may divide people by gender; at another time, along ethnic lines.

PROXIMITY. Proximity is a critical factor in the creation of groups, both from a cognitive perspective and from the standpoint of interacting people. We live in a universe of information. Like a planet in a solar system, we are constantly bombarded by asteroids in the form of information and events. Being mere mortals, we have limited capacity to comprehend, store, and react to this plethora of information. But being adaptive, we enhance our ability to survive by organizing the information and packaging it into chunks that we can handle. Cognitive psychologists, who consider "chunks" a rather ignoble concept, have dubbed these bundles of information *schemas*. As we saw in Chapter 3, schemas are formed by certain psychological rules that lead us to bundle certain events or information together. These schemas are like file drawers in the mind (Fiske & Taylor, 1984), helping us create an organized, uncluttered world.

According to this cognitive approach, one of the rules that lead us to file information together is proximity. Events or objects that frequently appear close together in time and space are bundled together. For example, several years ago, I succumbed to social pressure to take up jogging. I carefully chose my chamber of horrors (my jogging route) to take me through a wooded area before the home stretch, which led through a residential neighborhood. After a few weeks of jogging, I suddenly found that I had picked up a companion. While I was going through the serene woods, a ragged mongrel dog appeared from nowhere and trotted along for the remainder of my route, keeping his distance about 10 feet behind me. People along my route began asking me about "my dog." At first, I explained quickly that the persistent mutt was "not my dog." But after a week or so, I caved in. "Mutt" became my dog. I was soon feeding him, singing to him, and then building him a small mansion in my backyard. His constant presence next to me led my neighbors, and later me, to perceive that the dog and I belonged together; we were a group.

Proximity, then, is one of the rules that guide us to create specific categories and put people into categories; people who are close together (physically) are put into a common group. This suggests that when people of a common ethnic origin live close together, we (and they) are likely to classify them as a group. In addition to facilitating cognitive work, physical proximity enables us to interact with others, determine if they share similarities with us, and negotiate the formation of a group. The rule of proximity may help explain why ethnic identity is more salient in such countries as Switzerland, Canada, and Indonesia than in the United States. In the former countries, members of ethnic groups tend to reside together, even to the extent of having their own provinces or islands. In the United States, ethnicity has not been much of a factor in guiding people's choice of residence; there is no designated state for Germans, Poles, or Dutch. We can also see the effect of proximity in maintaining ethnic salience in the establishment of ghettos in countries gripped by fear, uncertainty, and crisis. In such cases, ghettos (or, in the United States, reservations) have been established where members of a targeted ethnic group are herded together and forced to remain. Proximity heightens one's identification with the ethnic group, and, as we will see, it fans the fires of ethnic conflict and stereotyping.

Proximity can also excite conflict between groups. At first glance, we might expect groups that are physically proximal to be categorized together and love to blossom. But once groupings are formed, proximity deals a more confusing hand. Several ethnographic studies have been conducted in cultures ranging from northern Canada to the South Pacific to West Africa. In these studies, respondents were often asked to evaluate their own group (culture, tribe) and several out-groups along a series of dimensions. Brewer (1986) examined these responses in terms of physical distance between the groups. Overall, there was a tendency for people to see physically close out-groups as being more similar to the in-group. However, proximal out-groups were also rated as potentially more hostile and untrustworthy than distant out-groups. There was greater reported conflict between groups in close proximity than between more physically separate groups.

Overall, we are likely to form groups with people who are physically close to us. But if our neighbors are not included in our group, their proximity may lead us to target them as our enemy. This occurs because the closeness of these nonmembers may be viewed as a threat to our group's independent identity, and proximity affords an opportunity for direct confrontation and conflict. Under the right (or wrong) conditions, ethnic neighbors may become ethnic enemies.

SPILLING OVER: THE IMPACT OF ETHNIC GROUP DISTRIBUTION ON NATIONALISM.
The proximity of ethnic groups plays an important role in directing ethnic conflict. But relationships between ethnic groups do not develop in a vacuum. Ethnic groups often find themselves guests in the domain of a larger group, the nation. And nations, like ethnic groups, compete for the loyalty and services of their people.

A great deal has been written about national loyalty and national identity. One definition of *nationalism* is the desire to enhance one nation's superiority and dominance over other nations (Gellner, 1983). Like ethnic conflict, national conflict is often played out on the battlefield as one country attempts to take the land and citizens of another. However, one curious aspect of nationalism is that it varies so widely between nations. Some nations, such as Japan and the United States, have a long history of nationalism. Their physical landscape is strewn with national symbols such as flags. Athletic contests open with the national anthem, and students begin each school day by pledging allegiance to their country. In fact, one group of investigators (Rajecki, Halter, Everts, & Feghall, 1991) related nationalism in the United States to the number of times the flag appeared on the covers of the World Series program. In some other nations, however, nationalism is rather muted. A Japanese colleague remarked that he was surprised to see so few national symbols in New Zealand and Australia. After having spent a month in each of these two countries, he observed that he had never heard the national anthem of either country.

Although proximity can foster attraction, the most violent acts often occur between groups that live close together. Ethnic hatred is grown within communities rather than imported from outside. (Anthony Potter Collection/Archive Photos)

How can we explain such differences? Many investigators locate the cause of nationalism within the individual. The nation, they argue, is a father figure or a maternal figure, and love and respect for the parent is transferred to the "fatherland" or "motherland" (Feldman, 1959; Feshbach, 1987). Nationalism, therefore, is a result of the basic Oedipus or Electra complex, played out at a group level. Regional differences in nationalism are the result of differences in child rearing in various countries.

However, we need not turn to psychodynamic theories of the individual to explain observed differences in nationalism. My colleague Dawna Coutant and I

(Worchel & Coutant, 1997), examined nationalism relative to the distribution of ethnic groups within and between countries. We reasoned that nations must compete with ethnic groups to occupy a central role in the people's identity. In some countries, there is little competition between these two entities, either because the boundaries of the ethnic group and nation are similar or because there is little recognition of ethnic identity. When these conditions exist, the nation plays a central role and is free to seek dominance over other nations.

Japan is an example of a country where ethnic group and national boundaries are similar. It is populated largely by people of Japanese ethnicity, and relatively few ethnic Japanese are found in large concentrations in other countries. What benefits the nation benefits the ethnic group, and vice versa. Japan, as a nation, has little internal competition for the identity of its individual citizens, and it is therefore free to focus on its relations with (and dominance of) other nations.

On the other hand, the United States is an example of a country in which ethnic identity is largely muted and, except for relationships between blacks and whites, plays a relatively minor role. Although many people suggest that the "grand experiment" of the United States has been the mixing of people from different ethnic groups, in reality the goal has been to eliminate ethnic identity from the social and political landscape. The Constitution of the United States guarantees people the freedom to practice any religion, but there is no mention of the freedom to identify with an ethnic group. The early history of the United States involved a tragic but largely successful effort to eliminate the indigenous ethnic group, Native Americans. As new immigrants came to the United States, they were generally scattered throughout the country rather than remaining in ethnic enclaves. The policies, practices, and laws of the United States were designed to ignore old ethnic distinctions and either build a new ethnic identity ("American") or depreciate the importance of ethnic identity altogether (see Chapter 7). As a result, nationalistic feelings were incubated, and the nation focused on becoming a global power rather than on internal characteristics. The point is that when a nation is composed of a single self-contained ethnic group or when ethnic groups have been so dispersed that they are hardly recognizable, national attention turns to global influence.

A very different pattern of ethnic concentration exists in such countries as North and South Korea, China and Taiwan, Ireland, and (the former) East and West Germany. In these examples, neighboring countries share a common ethnic group, which dominates each nation, so the goals of the ethnic group and the nation are in direct conflict. The nation is most concerned with developing its identity and encouraging citizens to identify themselves as its citizens. But at the same time the common ethnicity acts like a magnet, exerting a pull toward ethnic unification. Since unification can be achieved only if the two countries unite into one new nation, political leaders are tempted to provoke conflict between the two nations to counter this pull toward ethnic unity. No matter how high the walls between the nations or how well-guarded the boundaries, though, the forces of ethnic identity and unification keep pulling. This pattern of settlement often creates enmity between ethnic kinfolk and limits the nation's attention on global influence.

Yet another proximal arrangement occurs when an ethnic group occupies a minority status in two neighboring nations, each populated by a different majority ethnic group. An example is the Kurds, who exist as a distinct ethnic minority in Iran, Iraq, and Turkey—all of which are neighbors. This pattern is unfortunate for the Kurds. Each nation finds that it can promote nationalism and unite its majority ethnic group by directing hatred against the Kurds. The intensity of this hatred is most likely to increase when the nation faces external threats or domestic turmoil. The nation may attempt to force the minority group into a neighboring country. This strategy, however, is likely to create conflict between the two nations. A commonly adopted alternative that avoids conflict between nations is for each nation to obliterate the minority group through genocide.

Finally, another situation exists when a nation is populated by ethnic groups each occupying a circumscribed area. The proximity of the ethnic groups to each other sets up the conditions for ethnic friction within the nation. The nation is forced to turn its attention inward to preserve itself and deal with this conflict. The tugging of ethnic identity may eventually rip the nation apart, resulting in several new ethnically defined nations. This was the case in Yugoslavia and Czechoslovakia, both of which disintegrated into separate independent nations. In some cases, the larger nation may grasp for survival by creating ethnic states within its boundaries and adopting a policy of multiculturalism that recognizes each ethnic group. This is the situation in Switzerland and Indonesia, which have semiautonomous ethnic regions or states. In many cases, this solution is likely to be only temporary, because the various ethnic groups will continue to strive for dominance or greater independence. Such tension can be seen in Canada, which has struggled to deal with Quebec's threat to develop an independent state.

I could go further with this reasoning, but for now, it is necessary to make only one point. Just as proximity can influence conflict between ethnic groups, the physical location of ethnic groups within and between nations has a profound effect on both intergroup conflict and national and international relationships. And the ultimate foundations for this conflict are the desire of the individual to establish an identity and the desire of the ethnic group or nation to create its own identity.

SIMILARITY.   In Chapter 3, I pointed out that we are attracted to groups composed of people similar to us. We also use similarity to place people together into categories or psychological groups. Not only does this grouping soothe our overworked minds, but being with similar others validates our attitudes, our values, and even our physical characteristics. Imagine that you are a Muslim student studying at a university in South Carolina. Most of the other students are Protestant who find your beliefs strange; some even suggest that your beliefs are wrong but that you can be "saved" if you adopt Christianity. Within this framework of doubt, you meet other Muslim students. What a relief it is to find others who believe as you do and give you the comforting message that your beliefs are correct! Similarity draws us to form ethnic groups to please our schema that "likes belong together," and we rush into the warm bosom of these groups of like-minded and like-bodied others to validate our being.

But just as similarity helps us define our group, its unique identity is threatened by similar others who belong to different groups (Turner, 1987). We struggle to support the belief that our group is the best, the grandest, the most beautiful. We can depreciate other groups by believing that their attitudes and beliefs are wrong and their appearance is ugly. Differences help us define the boundaries of our group (who is one of us and who is one of them), and these differences offer us an opportunity to debase the out-groups.

Similarities between different groups threaten our own group by making it difficult to draw clear distinctions between groups. Consider the fact that the bitter hatred between Jews and Arabs involves two groups of people who trace their roots back to Abraham. There is a certain irony in the fact that Khalid Abdul Muhammad's anti-Semitic speech at Kean College, which characterized Jews in a most unkind light, reminded the black audience that they were the "true Jews" (see next section). A minister at an interfaith meeting suggested that one reason for segregated black and white Protestant churches is that white people do not want to be reminded that they share a common faith with the objects of their scorn. Likewise, the Jews in Nazi Germany shared many of the traits that the Nazis ascribed to gentile Germans (they were hardworking, loyal, and intelligent). A terrible dissonance arises within us when we find that people we hate share important beliefs or characteristics with us. Our similarities to out-groups threaten our sense of order and psychological comfort.

Therefore, it is not surprising that some of the most violent conflicts arise between similar groups. Small differences between the groups are amplified and used to justify hatred and violence. All this reminds us of the episode in *Gulliver's Travels* when Gulliver finds himself in the middle of a feud between the Big Enders and the Little Enders. The warring factions were nearly carbon copies of each other *except* that the Big Enders cracked their boiled eggs on the big side and the Little Enders entered their breakfast delight from the small end.

Thus, while similarity may be the glue that bonds friendship and forms groups, it may also be a match that ignites intergroup conflict and discrimination.

ETHNIC HATRED BETWEEN MINORITY GROUPS: A SURPRISING CASE OF SIMILARITY = HATRED.

In most countries, minority groups have a rather difficult hill to climb. They suffer constant uneasiness because they "stick out"—owing to their physical characteristics, their beliefs, or their practices—like a weed in a garden of flowers. It is often hard for them to feel that they are a true part of the social landscape. Imagine how Mexican-American kids feel when their class in Texas history reads about Mexican savagery during the battle of the Alamo. Or imagine how a Muslim child feels sitting through a class prayer that begins "Dear Jesus" and ends "in Christ's name, we pray." Members of minority ethnic groups often share the painful experience of being excluded, discriminated against, and characterized in the most negative terms within their own countries.

On the face of it, we would expect that sharing a fate might lead members of different minority groups to become allies and friends, or at the least develop a certain understanding and empathy for each other. But surprisingly, this is often not the case; the seeming similarity of experience often breeds contempt and hatred between such groups. This hatred and distrust often simmers just below the surface, but at times it rears its ugly head in public. For example, in the Los Angeles riots of 1992, some of the African-Americans who participated in the riots targeted Korean shopkeepers in their area. On November 29, 1993, Khalid Abdul Muhammad, an assistant minister in Louis Farrakhan's Nation of Islam, delivered a hate-filled speech at Kean College in Union, New York. According to Muhammad, the Jews had crucified Jesus, dispossessed the Palestinians, and exploited the Germans before World War II; they now controlled the Federal Reserve and the White House; they had participated in the civil rights movement in order to exploit blacks; they had supported apartheid in South Africa; they raped black women. Moreover, Muhammad informed his black audience, the Jews are in fact impostors: "For you are the true Jew. You are the true Hebrew" (Berman, 1994 p. 61).

It seems to be a cruel irony for an ethnic group that is itself an object of hatred and discrimination to engage in such behavior. How can we explain such seemingly irrationality? Recall, for a moment, our discussion (in Chapter 1) about how we compare ourselves with others to learn about ourselves. In order to determine if we are good students, we compare our grades with those of other students. But this social comparison (Festinger, 1954) does not involve random targets. Instead, we compare ourselves with similar others. As a student, you will probably compare your grades with those of others in the same academic major who have taken similar classes. To measure success in your career, you will compare your position with the position of others who have a similar education who began their professional life with similar resources. A close friend recently confessed that he was attending his 30th high school reunion so "I can see how far I've come in relation to those others who had Ms. Wiggins for algebra." In making such comparisons, our desire is to gain not only accurate evaluations about ourselves but also positive evaluations. This may be why high school reunions are generally attended only by those who are relatively successful.

Groups, like individuals, compare themselves with similar others to see how they measure up. Groups, like individuals, also want the result of the comparison to be positive. The significance of this process for minority ethnic groups is that these groups often use each other as standards for social judgment. If your group has been disadvantaged by society, you can determine how well it has coped by looking at groups that have suffered similar disadvantages. In other words, there is often a constant scrutiny between disadvantaged or minority ethnic groups. This comparison is itself a source of friction. But the friction can transform into dislike and resentment when one group determines that another is achieving greater success.

To demonstrate this process, Hank Rothgerber and I (Rothgerber & Worchel, 1997) designed a laboratory situation that involved two work groups (A and B) placed in a disadvantaged condition and one group (C) in a highly advantageous condition. The groups worked on similar tasks, and each was told how the other two groups were progressing. Members of one disadvantaged group (A) were then given the opportunity to hurt (economically damage) the out-groups. We found that when the other disadvantaged group (B) was doing as well as or better than the subjects' own group (A), they chose to injure the similar disadvantaged group. Anger and frustration resulted from finding out that another disadvantaged group was doing better than their own group. The group could not defend its relatively poor performance by blaming the situation, because another group in the same situation was

Surprisingly, ethnic violence often occurs between minority groups. These minority groups compare themselves with each other, and advances by one may be viewed as threats by the other. (Michael Newman/PhotoEdit)

doing well. Most interesting was the fact that members of a disadvantaged group chose to direct more injury toward the disadvantaged out-group (B) than toward the advantaged out-group (C) when both out-groups were performing at a superior level.

Therefore, suffering a common fate—such as discrimination—will not necessarily lead ethnic groups to like or empathize with each other. Rather, the shared fate may incite comparisons, and should these comparisons cast aspersions on one group, its hatred and jealously may be directed toward the other.

AMBIVALENCE.   There are many paradoxes in human behavior. One of the more interesting is that we often act most decisively when we are confused or unsure. I recall a large sign in the office of a safari company that warned patrons, "The Most Dangerous Animal Is One That Is Frightened." Research (Festinger, 1957) in psychology has demonstrated that people go to great lengths, in both their attitudes and their behavior, to erase "cognitive inconsistency"—attitudes or beliefs that are incompatible with one another. This dictum has been applied to individual and group identity (Worchel, Coutant-Sassic, & Wong, 1993). We found that people and groups of people who were unsure or uncertain of their identity reacted most strongly to threats to a secure identity. In one case, people learned that their group had both positive and negative characteristics. In another case, the position of their group as the best performer was threatened by another group. In both situations, group members responded by discriminating against and depreciating another group, even one that had not been involved in creating the initial threat.

The point is that ambivalence about ourselves or the identity of our group may impel us to attack another group. By destroying or damaging the other group, we create a more certain or more positive image of our own group. We may feel unsure about ourselves when we experience misfortune (losing a job, undergoing the destruction of an important relationship) or when we receive disquieting information. A group can experience a threat to its positive self-image when it faces economic decline, general anomie, or other conditions that tarnish its identity. These conditions of ambivalence, threat, or uncertainty can consequently light the fires of hatred toward out-groups. We might post a sign over everyone's ethnic bed that reads, "The Most Dangerous Ethnic Group Is One Whose Identity Is Confused or Threatened."

Ambivalence about ourselves and our own group is not the only type of uncertainty that prepares us to hate other groups. Ambivalence about out-groups can also lead us to hate. If we examine accounts of large-scale group conflict and violence, an interesting picture emerges. The protagonists often do not begin as bitter enemies; in fact, there may be a certain degree of admiration of the out-group (Toland, 1993; Turner, 1987). The Nazis focused their hatred on the Jews, a group who evidenced traits—such as industriousness and thrift—espoused by the Nazis themselves. Bitterness between Catholics and Protestants in Northern Ireland is sprinkled with reluctant words of praise or admiration for the out-group. An interesting quirk in the background of some of the most infamous anti-black racists in the United States is having been raised by a beloved black caregiver. It seems as if we hate most those whom we are afraid to love.

This is not a new observation. Sigmund Freud (1933) used the term *ambivalence* to describe loving and hating the same person. He argued that we cannot live with this internal conflict, and in order to resolve it, we draw energy from one impulse and add it to the opposite impulse: thus we exaggerate the opposite response. Irwin Katz and his associates (Katz, Wackenhut, & Hass, 1986; Katz, 1981) report a series of studies designed to test this ambivalence and amplification in a situation involving stigmatized groups ranging from the physically handicapped to racial minorities. In one study, the researchers developed an ambivalence scale that measured the subjects' favorable and unfavorable attitudes toward blacks; the highest ambivalence resulted when a subject had an equal number of favorable and unfavorable ideas. A group of white college students completed this scale. Then some of them read a vignette about a black student who faced an emergency. In some vignettes the black student acted bravely and altruistically; in other vignettes the student was timid and indecisive. Subjects then rated the black student on a series of dimensions.

How do you think the results turned out? If our behavior is solely dictated by extreme attitudes, we would expect subjects who had a wholly negative attitude towards blacks to rate the black student lowest. However, this was not the case. The

ratings were related more to the degree of ambivalence. When the black student behaved positively, the ratings were more positive as the subjects' degree of ambivalence increased. Likewise, when the black student was inept, subjects were more
negative as their degree of ambivalence increased. The ratings by ambivalent subjects were more extreme in both cases, but they were sometimes more positive and
sometimes more negative.

The investigators suggested that "holding both positive and negative attitudes
about a target group is potentially threatening to positive self-regard" (Katz et al.,
1986, p. 114). They argued that we are uncomfortable when we can't form a consistent impression of a group and that we compensate for this discomfort by increasing the extremity of our behavior toward members of that group. It may also be argued that the more positive the traits we attribute to an out-group, the more the
image of our in-group is threatened. Therefore, in an effort to differentiate the in-
group from the out-group, we increase the intensity and extremity of our behavior
toward the out-group. Regardless of the reason, ambivalence may increase the degree of discrimination toward the out-group.

SALIENCE.   I have always had a romantic image of Gypsies. Their free spirit and
endless wandering tug at my heartstrings, and many's the time I have longed to put
down the burdens of my modern world and join a Gypsy band. I was utterly amazed
to find that my view of Gypsies is not universal, especially among people who have
contact with them (Zolova, 1992). I visited Czechoslovakia when it was undergoing
the agony of cutting itself into two separate countries. Although much attention was
focused on this difficult surgery, I found both Czechs and Slovaks willing to put
aside their differences and speak in unison about their distaste for Gypsies. Their
prevailing view was that Gypsies were *the* criminal element, responsible for most of
their social ills. Although groups of Gypsies lived in both Czech and Slovak regions,
they were physically and culturally distinct and remained completely outside both
societies. It was these physical and cultural differences that kept Gypsies out of the
mainstream by making them a *salient* out-group, an easy target for hatred.

This experience reminded me of an early laboratory study I ran on reducing intergroup discrimination. The aim of the study was to examine the effect of cooperation on intergroup relations (Worchel, Axsom, Ferris, Samaha, & Schwiezer, 1978).
During the first period of the study, subjects were randomly divided into two groups
that competed. Later, they were combined into one group to cooperate on a task. In
some cases the combined group succeeded; in others, it failed. In order to get subjects into the spirit of the study, the plan was to have them all wear white laboratory
coats. One day, one of the experimenters found that someone had taken some of the
coats, and she searched around for new ones. The only coats she could find were red,
and so she had some groups wear white coats while others wore the new red coats.
To our surprise, this physical distinction not only increased the hostility between the
groups when they competed, but sabotaged our best efforts to reduce hostility when
the groups were later combined. The physical distinction kept the original groupings salient and defined targets for scapegoating and hostility. When things turned

TABLE 5.1   Changes in Attraction for the Out-group as a Function of Group Distinctiveness and Outcome of Interaction

	Uniforms of Two Groups	
Outcome of combined effort	Similar	Dissimilar
Success	3.79	1.29
Failure	−1.03	−2.26

Note: Positive scores indicate increase in attraction as a result of combined effort; negative scores indicate decreased attraction. Scores indicate that success led to increased attraction and failure reduced attraction. The greatest decrease in attraction resulted when the combined effort failed and the groups wore dissimilar uniforms.

Source: Adapted from: Worchel, Axsom, Ferris, Samaha, & Schwiezer (1978, p. 435).

sour in the combined group, the "whites" blamed the "reds" for their problems and the "reds" blamed the "whites." As can be seen from Table 5.1, this misdirected blame was most strongest when the groups wore different colored coats.

The results from all these studies demonstrate the pervasiveness of social identity. Because we are constantly in search of our identity, we keep our finger on a hair trigger as regards discrimination. Any event that questions or threatens our identity leads us to build solid walls around our own group, distinguish between it and out-groups, and enhance its relative advantage over those other groups. Features (such as physical or cultural distinctiveness) that distinguish out-groups help define the targets of our discrimination. And the features (such as proximity, similarity, and positive regard for an out-group) that make this distinction difficult conspire to intensify our behavior toward that out-group. These same factors also encourage our identification with our in-group and increase its cohesiveness.

The concept of salience may explain why there is chronic conflict in the United States between African-Americans and Anglos rather than between, say, ethnic Germans and ethnic Swedes. There are clear, salient differences—skin color and other physical characterisics—between African-Americans and Anglos. There are few salient physical distinctions between Germans and Swedes. In New Zealand, there are very evident physical distinctions between the Pakeha and Maori but few between people of British and Dutch descent. Conflict in New Zealand is mainly between Maoris and Pakehas. Thus salient characteristics help us decide which groups we will join and which groups we will hate.

STRANGENESS: FEAR OF THE UNKNOWN.   I love to travel, see new sights, meet new people, and experience different situations. This love of travel, however, is often accompanied by a certain uneasiness, a feeling of dread and discomfort. Before and during each trip, my insides are a battleground of competing emotions. I long for the comfort of what I know and fear the unknown, yet I'm attracted like a moth to a flame by the excitement of the journey.

I have witnessed a similar battle in my young twins. Hannah and Elise romp through the park close to our home, from time to time glancing over their shoulders to be sure I'm still there. The intrusion of a strange adult or child into the environment sends them scurrying to cling to me like barnacles on the hull of a ship. *Stranger anxiety*, or fear of strangers, begins to appear in infants around the age of six months (Sroufe, 1985). As a child ages, stranger anxiety is reduced. In fact, anyone who has raised a child through adolescence will swear that this fear becomes supplanted by a loathing of the familiar; I cannot now bribe, cajole, or threaten my adolescent daughter to spend time with me at home.

But does this fear of the strange ever really disappear? Robert Zajonc (1968) argued that the more familiar we are with almost any object, the more we come to like it. In one study, college students were shown a series of photographs of people. They saw some of the photographs more frequently than others. Later the subjects were asked to rate how much they liked the people in the photographs. The students indicated that they liked the people whose photographs they had seen often more than the people whose pictures they had seldom seen. This bias appeared even though all the people in the photographs were strangers at the beginning of the study.

Let's apply these results to intergroup relations. Think about your own life and daily routine. Chances are that you are exposed to people of your own race, culture, socioeconomic group, and occupation more often than people outside these categories. It is possible, therefore, that our attraction to the in-group results from mere exposure. The more we are exposed to a certain group of people, the more we like and value them. By contrast, those who are different from us and with whom we have little contact arouse our anxiety and suspicion. This process is accelerated as groups isolate themselves or are segregated into enclaves, where most of their interactions are with members of their own group and contact with out-groups is limited to role-determined interactions.

Because of this lack of contact, the out-group is viewed as strange and unusual. Its members may appear different—wearing strange clothing, speaking an unfamiliar language, worshiping a puzzling god, and practicing odd customs. In short, our lack of familiarity with a group causes us to classify it as "strange." Strangeness is threatening precisely because it is strange, and the sense of a threat leads to fear and hostility.

The Behavior of the Out-Group: Realistic Conflict

My focus so far has been on the situational variables that characterize groups. The accident of our birth, which marks us with certain physical characteristics, places us within a certain culture, and locates us in a specific geographic region, excites our tendency to like some groups of people and discriminate against others. None of the cases I have mentioned requires that members of an in-group or an out-group behave in any way to receive our love or scorn. The mere existence of groups is a sufficient condition for discrimination and conflict. You may wish to keep this thought in mind as you decide how to respond to an invitation to join one "exclusive" group or another. Although the intent of that group may be completely benign and its goals of the highest nobility, an undesired consequence of exclusivity may be to set into motion intergroup discrimination and conflict.

But let's not stop here in our effort to paint a bleak picture of groups. Not all group conflict is caused by factors outside the group's behavior and intentions. Not all group conflict arises within the boundaries of the individual psyche. Clearly, groups themselves can develop goals and engage in behaviors that fan the fires of conflict, discrimination, and prejudice.

REALISTIC GROUP CONFLICT.   Our world is not a cornucopia of endless resources. Territory, wealth, and other natural resources are limited. And societies and the psyche are structured to limit other, less tangible resources such as power, status, and prestige. As a group develops needs and appetites for scarce resources, it finds itself in competition with other groups. Many social scientists have argued that group conflict and hostility are a result of opposing claims to limited resources (Sears, 1993; Campbell, 1965; Sherif et al., 1961). The foundation of this realistic conflict theory is that competition makes enemies.

The history of nearly every colonized land demonstrates this principle. Looking at the United States, we find that the early explorers and settlers developed close cooperative relationships with the indigenous Indians. The land was bountiful, and there were plenty of resources for everyone. Pictures of the first Thanksgiving often show a harmonious gathering of Indians and settlers around a long table piled high with food. But as more settlers arrived, they too desired the rich land. Unfortunately, this was land occupied by the Indians.

The conflict thus became tinged with a moral hue—the settlers viewed themselves as "civilized" people guided to this land by a divine power. The Indians were merely savages who had no God-given right to the territory. Indeed, the Indians were viewed as subhumans, merely an unusual species of animal (deindividuated and dehumanized; see Chapter 4). A need, along with a view of the out-group as dehumanized, justified appropriating the valuable resources possessed by the Indians. Obviously, the Indians had another view, and conflict turned to competition, hatred, violence, and destruction.

Whether we examine the history of the United States, Mexico, the Middle East, Europe, India, China, or New Zealand, the story is the same. As humans, we have added an interesting twist to this tale of intergroup violence. We are uncomfortable seeing our violence and domination as unbridled greed, so we institute laws and norms that legitimize and regulate to our destructive ways. Our religions often aid this process by anointing our group as the "chosen people." Hence, intergroup violence and discrimination become institutionalized, and this rule of law allows hostility to continue long after there is anything left to compete for (see Chapter 7).

Examples of institutionalized efforts to keep certain groups from competing fairly can be found in almost every nation. In the United States, for instance, laws (some in existence well into the 20th century) prevented African-Americans from voting, holding political office, being employed in certain positions, and being educated in certain institutions. Not only were these laws designed to prevent "pollution" of the dominant white groups; they also ensured that African-American groups would not be able to compete for valued resources and positions in the United States. Religion can also be used to justify discrimination. I still remember a minister from my childhood who justified discrimination against African-Americans by pointing out that the Bible states that God put a *black* mark on Cain's forehead to signify his "evil character." For him, it was a small step to argue the supreme being had colored African-Americans black to show us they were evil and should be segregated. South Africa, to take another example, had an even more comprehensive set of laws and customs that kept black and colored groups "in their place," away from direct competition with the more powerful white group. Such laws legitimize discrimination and create an uneven playing field for interethnic relations. The unjust becomes just because it is written in law. And these laws give the dominant group the advantage in competition for resources, position, and recognition.

The tragic history of the treatment of Native Americans in the United States is testimony to this process. As the white population, and its greed, increased, the government adopted a moral and legal structure allowing, even encouraging, the appropriation of Indian lands and the destruction of Indian nations. This position was clearly outlined by the Big Horn Association in the *Cheyenne (Wyoming) Daily Leaders* (on March 3, 1870):

> The rich and beautiful valleys of Wyoming are destined for the occupancy and sustenance of the Anglo-Saxon race. The wealth that for untold ages has lain hidden beneath the snow-capped summit of our mountains has been placed there by Providence to reward the brave spirits whose lot it is to compose the advance-guard of civilization. The Indians must stand aside or be overwhelmed by the ever advancing and ever increasing tide of emigration. The destiny of the aborigines is written in characters not to be mistaken. The same inscrutable Arbiter that decreed the downfall of Rome has pronounced the doom of extinction upon the red men of America.

It may be easy to understand how groups develop animosity toward other groups desiring the same resources. However, the story does not end here. If we focus on limited physical resources such as money or territory, we deal with a situation referred to as *zero-sum*: one group's gain is necessarily the other group's loss (Thibaut & Kelley, 1959). Common examples of zero-sum conflict are cases where one group occupies territory that another group wants or members of one group take jobs desired by members of another group. However, many of life's conflicts are not of this nature. Rather, they involved *mixed-motive* situations, where solutions exist that will benefit both parties. A classic mixed-motive situation is the *prisoner's dilemma*. The prototype of this dilemma involves two people who are suspected of having committed a serious crime (murder). The district attorney does not have sufficient evidence for a conviction and therefore must obtain a confession from at least one person. The district attorney separates the two defendants and approaches each with a proposition. If defendant A confesses and turns state's evidence and defendant B does not confess, then A will be released and B will be given the maximum sentence—and vice versa. If neither defendant confesses, the district attorney will convict both of them of a lesser crime, and they will both serve a short prison term. If both defendants confess, they will both be convicted of the serious crime but will serve only a moderate prison sentence (See Table 5.2). If you examine the situation, it is evident that the best result for both A and B occurs if neither confesses. However, if you are in the situation, you will refrain from confessing only if you *trust* the other party to refrain. And even when there is such trust, you may be tempted to confess in order to achieve the highest personal advantage for yourself. However, if there is any degree of distrust, you must protect yourself and take the course of action that will be somewhat destructive for both parties (e.g., confess). Competition breeds distrust (Argyle, 1992), and this atmosphere of distrust motivates each party to take the safest, albeit most destructive, route. This course of action is even more likely when a situation involves groups rather than individuals, because groups are more likely than individuals to be competitive (Insko & Schopler, 1987; see also Chapter 3).

Another distinction that is often made is between conflict over goals versus conflict over means. In some cases, groups may have competing goals such as the desire to possess the same territory or to convert the other group to the "one true religion." Situations involving conflict over goals can be settled only if one group beats the other or if both groups yield for the common good and agree to compromise. It is easy to understand why such conflicts lead to hostility, discrimination, and the desire to overcome the out-group. However, in many cases the groups may agree on the goals but disagree on the means of achieving them. For example, during elections feelings often run high. Political parties emphasize their differences and portray their opponents as evil. Given this environment, it is little wonder that political

TABLE 5.2 Matrix Representation of the Prisoner's Dilemma

		Person B Not confess	Person B Confess
Person A	Not confess	4 years / 4 years	Freedom / 99 years
	Confess	99 years / Freedom	20 years / 20 years

Note: Cooperative responses (not confess) from both parties would lead to relatively light sentences for each, but each party must trust the other before he will make a cooperative response.

campaigns often deteriorate into "dirty tricks" and slander. What may be overlooked is that the goals of the various political parties are similar: economic stability and growth, national security, and a good education for the nation's children. Conflicts over means may be resolved by developing joint programs that incorporate the desires and programs of the various groups. Unfortunately, groups in conflict tend to view the conflict as being over goals even when the disagreement is really over means (Filley, 1975).

Perceiving Evil in Others:
The Diabolical Enemy Image

The human mind is wonderfully inventive, and nowhere is the scope of its inventiveness more evident than in actions taken during group conflict. No matter how widely I read, I have yet to find a situation where one side to an armed conflict proclaims that its actions were unprovoked naked aggression to further its own aims. When President George Bush sent 24,000 troops to invade Panama and crush the Noriega regime, he described his actions as "defensive." Noriega was portrayed as a power-crazed drug dealer who was planning to attack American citizens in Panama. Attacks on defenseless foreigners in Germany have been depicted as "defensive"—these immigrants are supposedly intending to destroy the German social structure and economy. Wars, it seems, are always fought between two defensive opponents.

Sigmund Freud (1933) coined the term *projection* to describe the process by which we perceive our own negative tendencies in others. In the same way, conflict and disagreement often lead us to project evil, aggressive intentions onto the opponent (Sande, Goethals, Ferrari, & Worth, 1989). Since the enemy is viewed as diabolical, we see ourselves as merely defending against this evil force. But our inventiveness does not stop here. Earlier, I suggested that nature's decision to focus our eyes outward and our familiarity with our own history lead us to view our actions as responses to environmental demands and others' behaviors as caused by their own traits and characteristics. As a result, we are very likely to decide that our enemies are diabolical because they are evil and mean-spirited. This perception reduces our openness to examining why other groups act as they do or to accepting our own group's contribution to the conflict.

Reap What You Sow:
The Case of Reciprocity

The ancient prescription of an "eye for an eye" should be altered slightly to describe ethnic relations. Here the formula is often "two eyes and maybe an ear for an eye." Moshe Dayan, the Israeli general, argued that the best way to protect Jews in Israel was to respond to Arab aggression with two and a half times the level of violence directed against the Jews. Aggression and conflict often beget more aggression and violence. Deutsch (1973) referred to this effect as a *conflict spiral*. Once conflict begins, it continually escalates, as each party resorts to increased levels of aggression in response to the other's transgressions.

The tendency toward reciprocity has profound implications for the progress of ethnic group relations. At the most basic level, it suggests that when one group resorts to aggression and violence, the other group will, when able, answer with aggression and violence (Patchen, 1993). Aggression is a long hard road to peace and understanding, for even if one side dominates, the other side may bide its time and seek revenge. The Serbs in Yugoslavia remembered the treacherous acts of the Croats during World War II, and a generation later, this aggression was used as a justification for revenge. In reviewing relations between the United States and the Soviet Union, Patchen (1991) concluded, "Cooperative behavior seemed to be more affected by the actions of the rival than as by the nation's own prior behavior" (p. 121). Hence, the behavior of one group guides the behavior of another.

This process can be especially troublesome in the ethnic arena when a small minority within an ethnic group adopts an aggressive mode of behavior. The target of the aggression may fail to distinguish between the small faction and the group as a whole. Many Israeli Jews perceive a terrorist act by the Arab militant organization Hamas as an attack by the greater Arab population. Reprisals, such as armed counterattack or closing the borders of the West Bank, are aimed at the larger Arab group, and it is the larger Arab group that now views the Jews as aggressive and vows to retaliate. The conflict, instigated by a minority group within one ethnic group, quickly escalates and draws in an increasing number of participants. Hence the conflict spiral involves not only increasingly aggressive behavior but an ever-widening group of people.

Indeed, this is often the goal of terrorists (Merari & Friedland, 1988). Their aggression is designed to invite reprisals from the target group. Reprisals help draw more distinct group boundaries and increase the importance of ethnic identity for people in the region. The spark quickly becomes a forest fire, as rival groups become more internally cohesive and intergroup conflict and hatred expand.

Patchen (1993) makes another intriguing observation about reciprocity between groups. Often it is not the absolute intensity of a behavior that provokes a response. Rather, groups may be more sensitive to *change* in each other's behavior. Therefore, an ethnic group that has been rather passive in the past may evoke a violent response if it begins to take a more militant approach to ethnic relations. On the other hand, an aggressive act on the part of an old antagonist who has a history of threatening action may invite a relatively minor response. This effect may explain the high level of threat perceived by many white people in the United States when the civil rights movement took a more militant, though still relatively nonviolent, turn in the 1960s.

Bringing It All Together

The main point of our discussion is that although the formation of distinct groups may set the table for ethnic violence and conflict, several other factors serve to ring the dinner bell. Some of these factors reside within each individual and group, including the security of self-identity or group identity, the salience and strangeness of the out-group, and the proximity of the groups. Indeed, the very factors that facilitate the formation of groups can also serve as the foundation for intergroup violence. In addition to these factors, the behavior of the groups and the situation in which the groups find themselves are also factors determining the likelihood of conflict. Competition over scarce resources can spark confrontation. The tendency to portray the competitor as evil or dangerous adds fuel to the fire. This tendency can be encouraged (or muted) by group leaders and opinion leaders. Finally, aggression on the part of one party is often met by aggression by the other party. Ethnic violence, then, is the result of a combination of individual, group, and intergroup forces.

One point that quickly becomes clear is that the actions involved in ethnic conflict are often the result of perceptions and characterizations as much as, if not more than, actual reality. We often endow groups with such characteristics as being evil and aggressive even when an uninvolved observer would not conclude that the group merited such a description. Indeed, uninvolved observers often have difficulty understanding what all the ruckus is about. For example, American newspapers' accounts of the conflicts in Yugoslavia and Northern Ireland often register disbelief. Many ask innocently, "Why are they fighting?" or "Why don't they sit down and talk the matter out?" At the same time, people in other countries have difficulty understanding the bitterness that exists between white and black Americans. Parties to a conflict are often quick to interpret the most ambiguous acts of an opponent as having evil intentions. An overture of friendship is viewed as an attempt to "sucker us in" or "lull us to sleep." We then respond to what we perceive as aggressive *intent*. The uninvolved observer fails to see the evil that these actions might represent.

Finally, it is important to recognize that responses to conflict may institutionalize that conflict, ensuring that it will be difficult to resolve in the future. I remember my neighbor spending thousands of dollars—money he could have used for vacations or a new car—to build a bomb shelter in his backyard. This would protect him from the evil Russians. I often wonder what this poor soul is doing with his bomb shelter now that the Russians are our friends! The movie industry of the 1950s spewed out films portraying blacks, Russians, and Native Americans as evil, stupid, or dangerous. The change in attitudes toward these ethnic groups required a revision of the industry. The economic system of the southern United States was built on the view that blacks and Hispanics were suited only for menial jobs. Many factors help create intergroup hatred; and once this hatred becomes institutionalized, social, political, and economic systems perpetuate it. Systems are ponderous beasts that change only slowly and with much pain.

I have attempted to identify the forces that flow together to spark ethnic tension and conflict. Together, these forces constitute a formidable power that seem to make ethnic confrontation inevitable. But as the basic laws of physics teach us, to every force there is a counterforce. Indeed, this is the case with ethnic relations. Just as factors at the individual, group, and intergroup level push us toward conflict, there are currents at each level that pull us back from the precipice. There are steps that can and have been taken to create ethnic harmony and peace. It is to these issues that I will turn in the closing chapters.

Can the Balkans Heal? A Tale From Croatia Shows What It'll Take*

ROGER THUROW

VUKOVAR, Serb-Occupied Croatia—An odd whiff of nostalgia rises from the ruins.

"Doughnuts," says Snezana Ciric, closing her eyes to savor the memory of a long-lost taste. "Our neighbors made the best doughnuts in the world."

Three autumns ago, house-to-house fighting between Croats and Serbs raged through this once-lovely Danube River city of 45,000 until none of the houses—or shops, churches or anything else—was left unscathed. The house of Mrs. Ciric, a Serb, was gutted by Croats; the house of her doughnut-making Croat neighbors was pummeled by the Serbian forces.

"I wonder," muses Mrs. Ciric, sitting beneath a new roof in an armchair pillaged from the rubble of another house, "does Danica still cook?"

In a refugee camp 200 miles away in Zagreb, the Croatian capital, Danica Sandor does indeed, on a tiny stove with second-hand pots and charity flour.

"Cakes and doughnuts," she says. "We would never eat a cake without sharing it with our next-door neighbors. We were as close as neighbors could be." She, too, wonders. "How are the Cirics?" she asks. "Are they all right?"

Such flickers of affection among friends-turned-enemies kindle hope that the people of what was once Yugoslavia can one day live together again in a civilized manner. But before you know it, the hurricane of ethnic hatred and mistrust that utterly leveled this town comes roaring back, snuffing out such illusions. Misty-eyed memories of warm pastries are trumped by the cold acknowledgment that former chums can never again close their eyes and sleep soundly knowing that the others are next door.

Thus, a day that these two neighbors shared in joy—the birth of Mrs. Ciric's daughter in May 1991—is now marked by bitter and divisive memories. "It was the day the Croats started the war, when Croatian policemen started shooting at Serbs," says Mrs. Ciric. Says Mrs. Sandor, whom the little girl would have grown up calling *baka*, or granny: "It was the day Serbs killed 12 Croatian policemen."

A Monster Unchained

These crosscurrents of emotions—old affinities that long for reconciliation and new enmities that prevent it—are what make peace so elusive. For even if diplomats can draft cease-fires and draw new maps, how will they put neighborhoods and families back together? They are discovering that once nationalism has been released from its box, it is nearly impossible to stuff back in again.

---

*Source: The Wall Street Journal, September 23, 1994, p. 1.

In Croatia, for instance, the Serbs and Croats signed a truce 2½ years ago, just as the war spilled into Bosnia-Herzegovina. But nothing has been done to soothe the forces that destroyed cities like Vukovar. Instead, both sides have waged a venomous *sitzkrieg*: The Serbs pledge to keep Vukovar; the Croats vow to take it back. Rather than time healing all, the turning of the calendar's pages has made things worse.

So it is that Snezana Ciric's husband, Goran, and neighbor Zeljko Sandor, born three months apart 28 years ago and buddies to the day they took up guns against each other in 1991, are ready to take aim again. Mr. Sandor, wounded in the chest and head after the fighting flared, remains with the Croatian army, bivouacked just several miles from Vukovar. Mr. Ciric, who was shot in the left leg, has returned to construction work but does a monthly stint in the front-line trenches.

"We grew up together. I remember good things about him and I hope he has good memories of us. But I don't think he can ever come back to Vukovar," Mr. Ciric says of his old friend. "If we see each other again, it will be in a battle."

He looks out the window at the yard in which they so often played as boys. "If this was a movie that could be reversed, everyone would reverse it," says Mr. Ciric. "But this isn't a movie. It's real."

Like mortar fragments and spent bullets, the ironies from this clash between nostalgia and nationalism are strewn all over Vukovar.

At the jagged shell of a building that used to be a museum, for example, Serbian curators are painstakingly trying to re-create the displays of the old multiethnic nature of Vukovar. (Before the war, Vukovar was 47% Croat and 32% Serb, with the rest coming from a dozen other European nationalities.) After all that has happened, these Serbs strain to shift concrete rubble and fallen beams to preserve works by Croatian artists and the relics from the Croats' Catholic monastery.

"Look at the exquisite detail. It's very good work. Beautiful," says Dejan Sokolovic, a member of the Serbian Orthodox faith, as he caresses a wooden crucifix that once adorned one of the monastery's altars. He found it months after the fighting had subsided, in a vineyard, with the wooden Christ missing a left foot and right arm but otherwise in fine shape.

The curators also have saved the paintings of a local Croatian extremist who was said to be among those who provoked Serbs into rebelling against Croatian rule. "They aren't just part of Croatian culture," says museum director Olivera Rokvic. "They are part of Vukovar culture."

But such beliefs end with the art: The curators argue that the Croats themselves should never again be part of Vukovar. "I can never forget that the Croats brought their army here and used the museum as a barracks," the director says.

Last Stand

Jovan Koledin, another curator, snarls at the prospect of Croats coming back to Vukovar. "Remember the words of Sitting Bull: 'It's a nice day for dying,' " he says. "If the Croats think this is their land, well, let them try to come and get it."

In the city's former commercial center, Darko Kovacevic sips a Coke among the ruins at his sidewalk cafe. "This wasn't a fight between Croats and Serbs, but between extremists," he says. "Evil can't last forever. Everything has its time."

But evil knows how to work the clock. Mr. Kovacevic, a Serb, has a Croatian wife who has remained in Vukovar with him and their children. The rest of her family has fled. They write regularly, always asking them when they can return.

Mr. Kovacevic scoffs. "Now isn't a good time for them to return," he says darkly. "Not yet."

It wasn't always so. Over on Stara Banijska, a narrow lane pockmarked by mortar blasts, the Ciric and Sandor families lived almost as one for 30 years. The Sandors were in house No. 4, the Cirics in No. 6, with a common driveway in between. The mothers worked together at the nearby shoe factory, Mrs. Sandor in the tennis-shoe section and Jovanka Ciric, Goran's mother, in the leather-shoe division. The children and grandchildren played and went to school together. The vegetable gardens overlapped, and the chickens, rabbits and goats knew no fences.

Idly sweeping the dirt driveway of her refugee camp, Mrs. Sandor, a 60-year-old widow, begins sobbing over the memories. "We had such a nice neighborhood," she says. "How could you ever imagine that we would fight amongst ourselves?"

Dabbing her eyes with a handkerchief, she continues: "There were six Croat houses and 29 Serb houses on the street. Even at the time of war, I was asking Goran what we should do. He said, 'Don't worry, Auntie Danica, no one will touch a hair on your head.' I said, 'I believe *you* won't harm me, but every night 50 people are in your house. I have no faith in them.'"

Then, she continues, "One night as I walked past a neighbor's house I noticed people sitting on the floor and I heard someone say they were going to kill my son. My son tells me, 'No, it won't happen. You're imagining things,'" she says. "Then he ran into a friend of his, a Serb, who said, 'Zeljko, don't go home tonight. They want to kill you.' He went to stay at another friend's house. That saved his life. A few days later, Yugoslav army tanks arrived in Vukovar. The war had started."

As shooting crackled in the distance on that not-so-distant day, the grandchildren, playing together in the Sandors' sandbox, were swept up by their mothers and taken inside their respective houses. Suspicions grew across the driveway: Were the Serbs next door to be trusted? Were the Croats? Goran and Zeljko, the only able-bodied men in the two families, left to fight on opposite sides. In late June and early July, as the skirmishing neared their block, the women left, too, going their separate ways. By September, the Yugoslav army and Serb paramilitaries besieged the city. The Cirics and Sandors haven't met since.

"Do they hate us?" asks Mrs. Sandor.

"Do they curse us?" asks Mrs. Ciric.

The mistrust, totally absent three years ago, has grown into a mighty wall. "I think Danica could come back tomorrow," says Jovanka Ciric, whose tired and weathered face belies her 55 years. "She's not guilty of anything. But her son, Zeljko, no, we couldn't trust him."

Jasna, her daughter, agrees. "How could we look at them?" she asks.

The only thing the two families now share is their misery. In Zagreb, the Sandors live in a flimsy wooden barracks that once housed construction workers. The rooms are smaller than those of a typical college dormitory; Mrs. Sandor occupies one with a daughter, two grandchildren and a huge Pink Panther doll. There are communal toilets and showers, and the bland food is donated by international relief organizations.

Spoils of War

In Vukovar, the Cirics—who moved back into the house several days after the fighting eased—sit on furniture, sleep on beds and eat on tables plundered from destroyed Croatian houses. "Why not?" Mr. Ciric asks. "Croat soldiers destroyed all our things." A recent swine disease forced them to kill their two pigs, which they were counting on for food for the winter. They spent all their money to buy a calf so they will have milk for their children. The bullet holes in the walls still need to be filled. Rats, which have taken up residence in the Sandors' damaged house, scurry in the yard.

When cold weather comes, the Cirics and their two children will move into the smaller brick house that the Sandors were building behind their main house. The rooms are smaller, and need less heat. The Cirics finished the construction, laying the roof and putting up curtains.

"Take some pictures for Danica," suggests Jovanka Ciric, who shoos away her goats from eating the crumbling plaster of the Sandors' battered house. "She can see that we're looking after her place, that we didn't take anything."

The Cirics pose, smiling.

A few weeks later, looking at the photographs, Danica can't take her eyes off the images. "That's my tree," she says, pointing to an evergreen. "Planted it myself. Look, they put a tin roof over the door."

"Of our house!" reminds her daughter Jazminka.

Mrs. Sandor puts the photo of the house in a frame and hangs it on a wall of her refugee room. She drapes two strands of rosary beads over it. "My house, my walls," she says. "As long as I have my walls, I will go back."

Jazminka tells her to stop dreaming; the only way they will ever return to Vukovar is if the Serbs leave, including the Cirics. "And that would take another war," she says.

The mother scolds the daughter. "Hating each other is an affliction we have now," she says. "We have to get over it."

But a terrible fever still burns even in this gentle woman. "When we see the Cirics again, we will roast a goat together," she says. "But it will have to be one of theirs. I'm sure they have already eaten all of mine."

R E A D I N G   5 . 2

Black-Jewish Relations Still Tense*

CLARENCE PAGE

Washington—It was a heart-warming scene that Rep. Jesse L. Jackson, Jr., D-Ill., son of the famous civil rights leader, presented in speaking to a gathering of 60 officials from leading Jewish organizations in New York City last week.

---

*Source: The Bryan-College Station Eagle, June 1, 1996, p. A11.

Many Jews remain skeptical of his father, who once famously referred to New York City as "Hymietown" and later apologized. But that was precisely why a Jewish-led group called the Foundation for Ethnic Understanding had invited the young Jackson to help rebuild bridges.

Speaking in the Seagram Building on Park Avenue, sharing the stage with Seagram's chairman Edgar M. Bronfman, who is also president of the World Jewish Congress, "Junior" Jackson even sounded like his famous father at times.

But, for all his eloquent appeal to brotherhood and coalition between these two historically oppressed and embattled minorities, when question time came the issue that came up quickest and most forcefully was the Farrakhan Question: Why are black leaders so reluctant to denounce the anti-Semitism of Nation of Islam Minister Louis Farrakhan?

How frustrated the younger Jackson must have felt. As much as Americans of all colors need to work together on common problems these days, it is the insensitive few who cause the most hurt, not only to individual feelings but also to our ability to work together as groups.

I sympathize with "Junior" Jackson and I sympathize with those who ask the Farrakhan Question, too. Both feel a hurt. The Jewish hurt may have been best expressed by a young Jewish student at UCLA who columnist Nat Hentoff heard say aloud, to no one in particular, "Why do the blacks hate us so?"

Why? It's not "hate" as much as it is resentment. As the headline on a famous essay James Baldwin wrote in the late 1960s put it, "Blacks Are Anti-Semitic Because They're Anti-White." Many Jews, recalling the days when blacks and Jews organized, marched and sometimes died together for civil rights, see themselves as fellow victims.

But, as Baldwin explained, blacks have watched Jews assimilate quite rapidly into mainstream white America, compared to black folks, and many of us feel hurt, left behind, resentful and not as sensitive as we otherwise might be to how much our words (or our reluctance to denounce the hurtful words) can wound.

Ironically, the more Farrakhan is attacked, the more it enhances his image as "unbought and unbroken." This puts other, more egalitarian black leaders into a trick bag. If they attack Farrakhan, they risk being misunderstood by blacks. If they try to ignore him, they risk being misunderstood by whites.

So they walk a delicate line, as the young Jackson tried to: Condemn the objectionable parts of Farrakhan's message, while expressing solidarity with his positive values: particularly self-help, self-reliance, strong families, rigorously moral behavior and strong spiritual values.

Trying to explain, the young Jackson arched a lot of eyebrows in his New York audience when he described "the enormous influence that this organization (the Nation of Islam) exerts on a whole new generation of young African-Americans—to the tune of 100,000 tapes a week in the prison system of speeches given by Minister Farrakhan, and the distribution of newspapers all over."

Prisons are full of young black people seeking bold, audacious in-yo'-face voices that speak directly to them and their experience. So, ironically, are colleges. Racism, contrary to many expectations, is felt more acutely by middle-class blacks than it is felt by poor blacks. So, it turns out, is the feeling of resentment many blacks feel toward a seemingly increasingly indifferent white society of which many Jews have become a part.

But, despite the bad news, most African-Americans and American Jews still tend to agree far more than we disagree. In Congress, for example, black members still vote consistently in favor of Israel and Jewish members still vote consistently in favor of affirmative action. Hillels and black student unions are meeting together on various campuses.

And we also have voices like those of the two Jesse Jacksons, walking the tightrope of strained ethnic relations, but still finding ample reason to keep hope alive.

Clarence Page's e-mail address is cptime@aol.com.

Nigerian Ethnic Divisions Widen*

MICHELLE FAUL

LAGOS, Nigeria—Like many Nigerians, Rufus Emeribe thought life had gotten as bad as possible. Then it got worse.

First he lost his job of 19 years making car-seat covers at the Volkswagen factory, which cut back because of Nigeria's foundering economy. Now his landlady wants to evict him because he is an Ibo and she is a Yoruba.

The 54-year-old tailor traces his decline back to June 1993 when generals annulled a presidential election that was to restore civilian rule. It picked up speed when a new dictator seized power a year ago.

Since ousting the previous military regime, Gen. Sani Abacha has jailed dozens of opposition leaders. Among them are Moshood Abiola, the businessman whose expected victory in the election had raised hopes of an end to the tribal and regional strife that divides Africa's most populous nation.

Abacha has since solidified ethnic divisions among the country's 90 million people, fueling animosities that grow while the oil-dependent economy shrinks. It is rich against poor, tribe against tribe, north against south, all against a backdrop of dashed hopes as people worry more about getting their next meal than getting rid of their current dictator.

"It's like scratching a wall. At some point you lose your nails and climb down," said financier Roberta Folahan, expressing a weariness typical of many people in Lagos, Nigeria's biggest city and business center.

A year ago, Nigerians were rioting and striking to demand democracy. Today, they shrug at the thought of Abacha and are more concerned about the price of rice, which nearly doubled this month.

"The standard order is for soldiers to go out there and shoot them," said Clement Nwankwo, head of the pro-democracy Constitutional Rights Project. "So it would take someone looking for a form of suicide to want to go there and demonstrate."

---

*Source: The Bryan-College Station Eagle, November 21, 1994, p. B6.

CHAPTER 6

REDUCING ETHNIC VIOLENCE

Heal Thyself

Often, rather small events lodge themselves in our minds, stubbornly refusing to be forgotten, as if they were resolved to teach us a lesson. For me one such event involves a therapy client I had during my graduate school training. During an early session, I listened as he described his family, one of the most dysfunctional I had encountered. As I followed the tortured history of this family, I was gripped by two impressions. The more comforting impression was that my training allowed me to understand how events of the past 20 years had conspired to create this family system of twisted roles and hatred; I understood how and why the members felt as they did. However, this impression was undermined by my second thought: I had no idea what could be done to repair the situation!

In many ways, my situation was similar to the state of affairs that exists with ethnic conflict; theories help us understand its roots better than they guide us toward preventing or resolving it. We often find ourselves conducting an autopsy of a tragic ethnic situation such as the fracturing of Yugoslavia, struggles in Central Africa, or ethnic violence in South Africa. We can trace the steps that led to confrontation and understand how the cancer of hatred took its destructive course. Theories of evolutionary psychology, social psychology, political science, and sociology give us insight into the cause of the conflict. But we are strangely naked when it comes to developing a plan to improve the situation. Each direction we follow is filled with roadblocks. As gruesome pictures of death and starvation in Zaire (Democratic Republic of Congo) filled our news reports, I was dumbstruck by the inability of relief agencies and nations to act. While thousands of people starved to death, the world debated various options for responding. Political, economic, logistical, and ethical flaws were found in each proposed plan. This situation illustrates the terrible complexity of ethnic conflict and the difficulty of finding ways to reduce or control it. The first, and possibly the most difficult question, concerns where to begin interventions to reduce ethnic hatred and strife.

"A Journey of a Thousand Miles Begins with a Single Step"

In searching for a starting point, perhaps we should remember the *Samyutta Nikaya*, which tells the story of Pasenadi, king of Kosala, and his queen, Millika. In an effort to entice the queen to express her love for and devotion to him, Pasenadi asked her, "Is there anyone who is more dear to you than yourself?" To the king's dismay, Millika replied, "There is indeed no one more dear to me than myself." His plan having backfired, Pasenadi pondered the question. After considerable thought, Pasenadi admitted that he, too, knew of "no one who is more dear to myself than me." Troubled by this exchange and more than a little worried about the depth of the queen's love for him, Pasenadi sought the counsel of the Buddha and recounted the conversation with his wife.

The Buddha listened patiently and then replied, "If you thoroughly search in ten directions of your mind, nowhere will you find anything more dear to you than yourself. In the same way, the self is extremely dear to others. Therefore, one who loves himself should cause no harm to another" (p. 75).

The message expresses a foundation of Buddhist philosophy: love for others begins with love for oneself. When we realize how important we are to ourselves, we will also see how dearly others value themselves. With this understanding, we will be reluctant to injure something that is so important to another: his or her self. To this doctrine, Buddhism adds a second: events are interrelated. For example, Kraft (1992) points to the paper on which the words of a book are written. The piece of paper is the product of a host of factors, including a tree, rain that nurtured it, the logger who cut it down, the truck that transported the log to the mill, and so on. If we break the chain at any point, we will not have a piece of paper. According to engaged (activist) Buddhism, if we desire to influence an event, we should break the chain of interrelated factors at the point over which we have the greatest control.

What does this have to do with the reduction of ethnic conflict? If we recall our earlier discussion, we find that ethnic conflict is a result of interrelated factors involving the individual, the group, and the relationship between groups. According to the Buddhist doctrine of interrelatedness, we can reduce or avoid ethnic conflict if we break into this chain of interrelated events. The link over which we have greatest control is the one involving the self; we have the greatest ability to influence ourselves. Hence, Gomez (1992) counsels: "Refraining from lying, for example, would take precedence over public verbal activities such as issuing proclamations in support of world harmony" (p. 46).

The Buddhist perspective is valuable because it gives us guidance about where to begin our search for ways to reduce ethnic conflict: begin with the individual. Change at the personal level may then foster change at the group and intergroup levels. Therefore, we will begin our discussion of the reduction of ethnic conflict by examining ways to effect individual change.

Securing the Individual's Identity

Abraham Ashkenasi (1996), a political scientist, argues that ethnic violence will continue to afflict society so long as individuals fear for their personal safety or feel insecure in or uncertain of their personal identity. Fear arises when we view our situation as unpredictable and uncontrollable. In many parts of the world, people do not know how long they will have their jobs or whether tomorrow they will be excluded from schools or neighborhoods because of their ethnicity, religion, or political views; or whether their night's sleep will be interrupted by gunmen bursting into their homes to kill them or kidnap them. They feel powerless and afraid, and these ingredients motivate them to find something or someone they can control (Boulding, 1989).

Having power enhances our esteem and gives us a sense of personal security. Although there are many ways for us to build and demonstrate our power, destruction is one of the most seductive. In an intriguing analysis of vandalism, Allen and Greenberger (1978; 1980) argue that the ultimate demonstration of power is destruction. Who can question our power over objects or people when we can end their existence? Vandalism appears to be senseless—the vandal destroys property but seems to gain nothing from this act. Allen and Greenberger suggest, however, that what the vandal gains is a feeling of power. They found that people whose self-esteem and sense of power were threatened were the most likely to engage in vandalism. We could, therefore, argue that discrimination is a desperate act to demonstrate one's power over others and that a feeling of security and enhanced self-esteem results from discriminating against or destroying members of an out-group.

If people must hate and destroy to feel powerful, we should be able to reduce the need to hate by enhancing their esteem and power in less destructive ways. This thought is echoed by humanistic psychologists. For instance, Carl Rogers (1980) argues that confusion about one's self-concept creates discomfort, anger, and alienation. He suggests that a distressing situation arises when we are unable to accept ourselves or feel worthless. Society plays a central role by condemning a person as a whole for isolated shortcomings. Thus each time we act, we feel that our whole identity is on the line. A single failure or misstep may relegate us to the category of "worthlessness."

In addition to blanket condemnation, Rogers was concerned about another tendency: our social environment often conspires to prevent us from developing a clear vision of ourselves. Society tells us "who we should be," i.e., it gives us an image of the self we "ought to" be or "should" be (Higgins, 1987). We cannot acknowledge who we are or accept ourselves because we feel driven to meet the expectations of others and fear rejection when we do not. By contrast, we have a sense of security and comfort when we form a clear picture of ourselves and are able to accept ourselves. Once we have achieved these goals, we will feel less anger and be less motivated to depreciate others. Recall Buddha's words: "One who loves himself should cause no harm to another."

Rogers argues that to facilitate adjustment our social environment should include unconditional positive regard, giving individuals the message that they are accepted and valued regardless of their behavior. Unconditional positive regard does not require that all behavior be accepted or defined positively. Rather, it entails separating specific behaviors from the total image of the individual. An offending individual may be told that society is upset about a specific action, but society should not say that the individual is "bad." Rogers suggested that within such an environment of positive regard, people will strive to learn about themselves, will be willing to recognize and accept their shortcomings, and will be less likely to view others or differences between themselves and others as threatening.

This may sound like pie in the sky, but there is a glimmer of hope that societies could move toward this goal. The first step concerns child rearing. Investigators at the University of California at Berkeley examined how a child's family environment affected his or her creativity and willingness to experiment with new ideas later in life (Harrington, Block, & Block, 1987). They determined the nature of preschool children's family environment through interviews with the parents and observations of the parents working with their children on a series of tasks (see Table 6.1). The investigators followed the children through their school years; their sixth- and ninth-grade teachers were then asked to describe their performance and classroom behaviors. They found that children who experienced unconditional positive regard during their early years showed more signs of creativity and personal openness than children who did not. The value of a supportive family environment was underscored by studies of the development of interpersonal trust. This research found that infants raised in a setting where the caretaker is responsive to their needs and offers them an accepting, supportive environment not only become secure in their attachment to

TABLE 6.1 Behaviors That Build (or Inhibit) a Creativity-Fostering Environment

Items consensually judged most typical of Rogers's creativity-fostering environment	Items consensually judged least typical of Rogers's creativity-fostering environment
Parent encouraged the child.	Parent tended to overstructure the tasks.
Parent was warm and supportive.	Parent tended to control the tasks.
Parent reacted to the child in an ego-enhancing manner.	Parent tended to provide specific solutions in the tasks.
Child appeared to enjoy the situation.	Parent was hostile in the situation.
Adult derived pleasure from being with the child.	Parent was critical of child; rejected child's ideas and suggestions.
Parent was supportive and encouraging of the child.	Parent appeared ashamed of child, lacked pride in child.
Parent praised the child.	Parent got into power struggle with child; parent and child competed.
Parent was able to establish a good working relationship with the child.	Parent gave up and retreated from difficulties; failed to cope.
Parent encouraged child to proceed independently.	Parent pressured child to work at the tasks.
	Parent was impatient with the child.

Source: Harrington, Block, and Block (1987).

loved ones but also show readiness to trust and accept strangers (Farnsworth, 1966; Ainsworth, 1979). Individuals raised in a more controlling environment develop anxious relationships with those close to them and are rejecting and distrusting of strangers. The freedom to explore without fear of incurring punishment and disapproval helps individuals develop a sense of self-worth and a trust of other people.

Another piece of evidence indicating the importance of self-concept in interpersonal relations comes from Bandura's (1982) research on *self-efficacy*, the belief that we can perform behaviors that are necessary to bring about desired outcomes. People who develop a strong sense of self-efficacy are more willing to engage in difficult or unusual behaviors and more open to relationships with a variety of others. Children who are rewarded and praised for *attempting* difficult or unusual behaviors develop a sense of personal power and efficacy. They are less threatened by the strange and the unusual than individuals who have a low sense of self-efficacy. It is important to recognize that we learn this belief about ourselves just as we learn other beliefs. Therefore, how we are rewarded and punished and what models we have during early childhood are important for developing our esteem and thereby our sense of security.

Although childhood is a crucial time for establishing and recognizing our identity, experiences later in life also play a role. One of my fondest childhood memories was the annual summer trek my family would make to Bethel, Maine, where my father served as a trainer of T-groups. The history of the "T-group" movement is interesting, but our present concern is the aim of these groups. The T-group was the brainchild of Kurt Lewin (1947). To examine the development of groups, Lewin devised a technique that involved groups of 8 to 15 members (often strangers) and 1 or 2 trainers. Since a group had no preestablished structure or task, its members had to "build and guide" it. As the members struggled to establish their group and the rules that would govern it, they learned about group behavior and their own impact on the group. The experience was designed to help the participants develop a greater sense of efficacy in groups.

The technique was later adapted to focus more on personal growth by encouraging group members to experiment with new behaviors and seek feedback about others' on their effectiveness. This new type, called a *sensitivity group* or an *encounter group*, attempted to create an environment of unconditional positive regard: Members could criticize the behavior of others but had to refrain from blanket condemnation. The basic aim was to recognize adults' needs to learn about and become more secure with themselves and to develop their willingness to accept others. The popularity of these groups has diminished over the last few decades, but the concept of creating opportunities for a large number of people to engage in self-learning is still viable.

Poverty: A Culture of Hate

Regardless of the steps we take to develop people's sense of personal identity, Ashkenasi (1996) argues, we will be doomed to failure unless we can meet their basic needs for physical security, health, and education. Without progress in these areas, individuals will remain threatened and frustrated, and they will seek a scapegoat. They will be easily swayed by extremists advocating hatred and violence against an ethnic minority group that is identified as the root of their problems. Addressing these issues requires concerted efforts by governments and public organizations to guarantee that individuals will not go hungry, unclothed, uneducated, or in need of medical treatment. Although these actions must occur at the societal and political levels, their impact will be to enhance personal security, individual worth, and self-esteem.

Michael Argyle (1994) has argued that poverty produces its own culture, setting into motion a host of destructive tendencies. The fear that we cannot meet our basic needs diminishes our self-image. Desperate individuals facing the bleakest prospects seek safety and order by identifying with a group, often their ethnic group. The search for structure and meaning often leads to rigid forms of child rearing and a worldview that demands strict compliance with rules and demands of authority figures (Kohn, 1976). Violence is accepted, both as a way of disciplining children and as a means of dealing with people who belong to different groups. The culture of poverty, in sum, is characterized by personal insecurity, rigid attachment to one's own group, loathing of others who are different, and acceptance of violence as a re-

The foot soldiers of ethnic violence are often the poor and downtrodden. Poverty may lead to rigid patterns of thinking and sow the seeds for hatred. Raising the standard of living within a community should reduce the likelihood of ethnic violence. (Wally McNamee/Woodfin Camp & Associates)

sponse to frustration. On the basis of this argument, it is not surprising to find that ethnic violence and hatred often flourish in an environment of poverty. Whether we turn to Nazi Germany, Northern Ireland, Central Africa, Yugoslavia, or the southern United States of the early 1900s, the foot soldiers of ethnic violence are often the poor and the insecure. For people experiencing a marginal existence, violence serves two purposes: it diverts attention from the immediate problem—poverty—and it holds a promise that one's own deplorable condition can be improved by depriving someone else.

Interestingly, poverty can be especially injurious to self-esteem in democratic societies. These societies proclaim that everyone is created equal and that one's position in life is a result of one's own efforts. To understand the dangers that lurk in such a view, place yourself in the shoes of someone living in poverty. Despite your greatest efforts, you and your family remain on the lowest rung of American society. Your situation, on its own, is cause for frustration and despair. But now let's add some background music—the constant reminders that "America is a land of opportunity and freedom," and "You are what you want to be." If you accept these myths, you create a dilemma for yourself. On the one hand, you can adopt the self-image of a failure: you are too stupid, too lazy, too unskilled to take advantage of the opportunities that are offered to everyone. This self-image will encourage you to accept your impoverished condition and willingly take any type of welfare the system has to offer. The result is a state of *learned helplessness*, in which people stop trying to influence outcomes, often bringing on a state of severe depression (Abramson, Seligman, & Teasdale, 1978). This is obviously not an appealing alternative, but it does help explain why some members of disadvantaged groups give up trying to improve their position in society.

This is not the only option available to people who find themselves in an unfortunate condition, but a second option is equally unattractive. You can protect your self-image by adopting the belief that those who control the system (the powerful ethnic group, in many cases) are denying you opportunities because of the ethnic group to which you belong. Your desperate condition, therefore, is a result of your group membership, not of lack of effort or skills on your own part. This position is likely to evoke hatred toward the group in power. A plethora of research on the self suggests that we manage our environment and attributions to develop or maintain a positive self-image (Goffman, 1959; Greenwald, 1980; Tedeschi, 1981). Blaming external events (including other people) for our dismal condition allows a positive self-image, but it guides our actions toward attacking the external barriers.

Now let's turn the situation around and say you are an affluent person in the same society. You too have a desire to hold a positive self-image, and you too are aware of your society's views about opportunity and the rewards of hard work. How do you account for your affluence? You could decide that it has resulted from your membership in a favored group, but this perception does little to build your self-image as a capable individual. On the other hand, you could adopt the myth that your condition is solely the result of your hard work in a land of equal opportunity and that your group membership had little to do with it. If your hard work created your riches, the corollary is that lack of effort is responsible for the condition of the impoverished. This is a seductive option because it allows you to envision a *just world* view: good things happen to people who are good and hardworking, and bad things befall people who are bad (Lerner, 1980). This is certainly a comforting position . . . if good things fill your stocking in life!

This discussion suggests that our status will affect how we explain our success or failure. Indeed, Lorenzi-Cioldi (1996) found that members of a dominant group believed that their position was a result of personal effort and that they saw considerable variability within their own group. However, individuals in a low-status group blamed group membership for their difficult condition, and they saw their group as very homogeneous. These perceptions enable both high-status and low-status people to develop a positive self-image. Further evidence of the divergent perceptions of the fortunate and unfortunate can be found in a Gallup poll of 1985, which asked black and white Americans to indicate what was to blame for poverty: lack of individual effort or social, political, and environmental circumstances. More than twice as many whites (35%) as blacks (15%) cited individual effort, whereas more than twice as many blacks (67%) as whites (30%) cited circumstances. In light of these views, it is not surprising that in 1990, 32% of blacks, but less than 9% of whites, lived below the poverty line.

What is interesting about these different perceptions is not only that they allow people to maintain a positive self-identity but also that they lead people to detest outgroups. Members of the impoverished group grasp for an acceptable self-image by blaming the dominant group for their poverty: I work hard, but "they" keep me down (the system keeps me down). They also tend to see everyone in their group as suffering from the same conditions, and this enhances cohesion among the downtrodden. Members of the dominant group, on the other hand, protect their image by attributing their success to hard work and the failure of others to a lack of personal effort.

If poverty helps sow the seeds of ethnic hatred by encouraging both dominant and subordinate groups to paint a negative picture of each other, the formula for reducing ethnic conflict seems fairly straightforward. Eliminating poverty, or at least reducing it, should enhance the self-image of the poor and reduce ethnic tension. Taking this step seems so simple that we can ask why greater national and global effort is not immediately focused on it.

There are several answers to this question, not least the concept of fairness and justice prevalent in many societies. The quickest way to reduce poverty is to distribute more resources to the impoverished. This approach, however, uses economic condition rather than personal effort as the justification for distributing resources. This is the fly in the ointment for societies whose social physics is based on the principle of equity. *Equity* is achieved when one party's ratio of input to outcome is equal to the ratio achieved by the other party (Austin, 1986). Input can be measured in terms of effort, money, status, time, or other variables; outcomes can be measured in terms of money, material gains, position or status, and freedom. Equity dictates that "good" (efforts or other positive inputs) be rewarded. Inequity is viewed as unjust. If we view poverty as resulting from individuals' lack of effort, then rewarding these individuals with resources is inherently inequitable. The principle of equity is further violated if supplying resources to the poor requires that those in a more fortunate condition are denied resources.

You may soon notice that violating the principle of equity smacks of the welfare state. Indeed, one foundation of communism is: "From each according to his abilities; to each according to his needs." Political ideology, therefore, is a major obstacle to any solution that begins to "mess" with distribution of rewards. We must recognize this perspective. However, at the same time, it is important to take a broad approach. No matter how much money we have, our own quality of life will be severely tarnished if we must live in constant fear of others who are impoverished. Therefore, improving the condition of others can be viewed as egocentric if these improvements ultimately increase the quality of life of even the most advantaged people.

In large systems, radical changes are notoriously difficult to achieve, even if the resources needed to effect the change are available. One reason is that the process involved is likely to insult the norms and customs on which the system is built. A second reason is that the system generally defines people's roles and purposes (see Chapter 5), so changes to the system often require people to adjust their behavior and self-image.

At a societal level, the *elite* theory of intergroup conflict (Taylor & Moghaddam, 1987) argues that many societies are organized on the assumption of an elite and a nonelite, each with a clearly defined role. Leadership comes from the elite group, which also has responsibility for the "care" of the nonelite. The existence of the nonelite defines and gives purpose to the elite. Conflict between the two groups remains low as long as the nonelite believes that the boundaries of the elite are permeable, that deserving members of the nonelite can move up to the elite. For our present purpose it is important to see that an intervention that radically alters the structure of social system can have consequences well beyond its intended effects. Eliminating or greatly reducing the size of an impoverished class would require changes throughout the society. When I raised the possibility of eliminating poverty in the United States in a speech to a group of government officials, one of them quipped that it would result in massive unemployment in the civil service. He observed, only half joking, "At least half the government jobs are aimed at dealing with issues related to poverty!"

These issues aside, it seems clear that poverty and the damage it does to the self-image contribute to ethnic violence. Therefore, reducing people's fears and uncertainty about meeting their basic needs is one step that can be taken to reduce ethnic conflict. But this is only one step in a long journey. As we saw in Chapter 3, even when we feel threatened, our hatred is not directed equally against all out-groups. We learn whom to hate. As a result, our instructors must join our quest to reduce ethnic conflict.

Learning: Developing Responsible Teachers

PARENTS.   One burden of parenthood is that a child's transgressions are laid at the parent's doorstep. In fact, many communities in the United States fine or even incarcerate parents for the misdeeds of their offspring. While parents must certainly share some of the blame for passing on ethnic hatred and prejudice, they must also be given some of the credit when their children are accepting and open in interethnic relations. In one of my undergraduate classes on ethnic conflict, David, a student, burst out, "I can't believe the number of people I dislike and distrust even though I haven't met them. I don't like blacks, Hispanics, Russians, Cubans, Mexicans, Chinese, or Indians. Gee, that's probably more than half the world!" When another student challenged David to explain his feelings, he began digging into his past.

His first suspects were his parents. David admitted that they were prejudiced, but he defended them: "They never directly instructed me to hate people in these ethnic groups." On further consideration, though, he was able to identify several indirect methods his parents had used to influence him. His examination of his childhood experiences sounded like a review of basic psychological theories of learning. One of the earliest principles of learning is that we repeat behaviors that bring us rewards and avoid behaviors that are punished (Thorndike, 1913). David recalled situations when he had made disparaging remarks about a group, bringing a mild re-

Cooperation and positive social interaction may not make newspaper headlines, but they are a vital step toward reducing rigid group identity and intergroup conflict. (AP/Wide World Photos)

buke from his parents—but, "They were smiling when they told me 'Don't.' I think I got the message that they thought I was cute or funny when I expressed those views." In retrospect, David realized that he had been rewarded for expressing negative attitudes toward certain groups. But this was not the end of his schooling. According to social learning theory (Bandura & Walters, 1963), we learn by observing others; like our primal ancestors, we are excellent imitators. We ape the behavior (and attitudes) of others, especially powerful and important others. David recalled overhearing his parents describe blacks as lazy and Jews as stingy. He remembered his father proclaiming to a friend, "We should bomb the hell out of those damned Russians."

David's experience illustrates how our parents can teach us prejudice and hatred. But this lesson is not inevitable. After David's self-examination ended, another student (Jessica) discussed her childhood. She had grown up two blocks away from David, but she had a very different family experience. "I don't know if I'm prejudiced or not, though I guess everyone is prejudiced to some degree. But I don't dislike people from those groups that David named. When I see a Chinese person, my reaction is more one of curiosity. I wonder what Chinese people think, how they live. Differences intrigue me." Her family situation involved the same learning principles, but the lesson was very different. She, too, recalled making negative remarks about ethnic groups, but she did not elicit smiles *or anger* from her parents. Instead, they stated that they did not feel that way and asked her to explain why she held those opinions. "I didn't like those long discussions, but they made me think why I felt certain ways." She recalled that her house had literature and pictures of many countries and many groups. Her parents had friends from many ethnic groups: "I remember attending the bar mitzvah of the son of my father's friend. I didn't understand a word of the service, but the food was great and he raked in the presents." She remembered family discussions about Nazi Germany. Her parents characterized Hitler as an evil man, but rather than condemning the German people, they wondered how so many people could be induced to become involved in such terrible deeds.

These two students demonstrate how important learning is in the development of ethnic hatred or tolerance. Reinforcement and modeling occurred in each home, but with very different results. Jessica's situation is interesting because it shows how parents can guide children from fear and dislike to curiosity and thoughtfulness. Interestingly, Jessica's parents did not punish her statements; while punishment may lead children to refrain from expressing certain views, it also creates the sense of "a forbidden fruit." Brehm (1972) argues that actions, attitudes, or objects that are withheld from us often acquire greater importance. The withholding creates a psychological state of reactance, which motivates us to show that we can possess the forbidden object, hold the forbidden attitude, or engage in the forbidden behavior. My own research on censorship found that withholding information led people to place greater importance on it, desire it to a greater degree, and change their attitude toward the censored position (Worchel & Arnold, 1973; Worchel, Arnold, & Baker, 1975). Using my own home as a laboratory, I find my young children devising ingenious and persistent schemes to entice me to tell them "taboo" words when I refrain from answering their inquiries directly. Punishment may push forbidden attitudes into the mind's closet, but they will still lurk there, ready to spring into action when the time is ripe.

Jessica's parents avoided either approval or punishment. They set themselves up as a model by stating that they did not hold certain negative attitudes, and they encouraged her to explore why she had adopted these ideas. Their response acknowledged that Jessica had a right to her opinion but challenged her to think about its basis. By adopting this approach, her parents gave themselves many options for reacting to her response. If she reported that she had experienced a negative interaction with a member of a group, her parents could question the wisdom of leaping to characterize a whole group on the basis of limited experience with a few members. If she responded that others held negative views of the group, her parents could question the basis for their position or point out that others often hold different opinions on a variety of issues. The opinions of others may be wrong or misleading. In fact, her parents could have illustrated this point by showing that people had different views of Jessica; she would probably feel uncomfortable if someone adopted an opinion of her just because others held that view.

A second characteristic of Jessica's home situation was the variety of friends and literature in her environment. By inviting diversity into the household, her parents demonstrated that they were open to and comfortable with different ideas, customs, and people. The silent message was that there was nothing to fear in diversity and difference. Jessica had contact with different people, different beliefs, different practices, and different literature and art. She may have perceived others and their customs as unusual, but she did not perceive threats or danger. Robert Zajonc (1968) has repeatedly found that our attraction toward other people (and toward words and tunes) increases the more frequently we are exposed to them. The home can be a place where children learn fear and hatred of other groups, or it can be a classroom that teaches openness, reflection, and acceptance.

Parents can also model constructive ways for dealing with failure. Children observe how parents respond to losing a job, missing out on a promotion, or dealing with a difficult neighbor. Their response can teach children to blame others for problems or to analyze the situation and develop alternative plans. Harry Truman recalled an incident in which his father beat up another man in a fight over a debt. His mother quietly pointed out to him that his father had now "made an enemy for life." Instead, she suggested, he could have tried to discuss the situation. In this case, he might have left with both some money in his pocket and a friend (Miller, 1973).

The list could go on, but the point is that parents and other caregivers play a critical role in charting children's course on many journeys, including their regard for and relationship with people of other ethnic groups. Their children watch their actions, hear even whispered words, and embrace these lessons. Given the vital role of parents in child rearing, the scanty and informal training we receive in parenting is disturbing. Our school days are spent learning about the history and government of our nation so we can be good citizens. We learn to use a computer, solve math problems, and write business letters so we can be good employees. We even take courses and take a test to be licensed to drive an automobile. But nowhere in the required curriculum are there courses that prepare us to rear children. These lessons are left to be learned from our own parents or friends, whose knowledge was obtained through trial and error or by observing others who also had no training. Quite interesting!

SCHOOLS.   When we think of sources of learning, we obviously think of schools. In fact, it is in schools that I have found the widest variance in teaching about culture. My daughters attended school in New Zealand for one semester. At both the kindergarten and fourth-grade levels, my kids received a healthy dose of lessons about the Maori culture. Whether the subject was history, literature, or music, my children were taught to appreciate Maori as well as other cultures in New Zealand. When the youngest children began printing, they carefully wrote words in both English and Maori. When my fourth-grader had to write a composition, her assignment was a Maori theme. The various cultures of New Zealand seemed to fit comfortably into the classroom at all grade levels. This experience was in stark contrast to the debate that raged at my own university (Texas A&M) some years later about the role of culture in the curriculum. This university, which had recently anointed itself a "world class" institution, was faced with a proposal by the faculty senate that some courses on cultures be required for a bachelor's degree. The proposal met strong opposition from some faculty members and students. The proposal was eventually killed by the administration.

Schools can play an important role not only in teaching students about others but also in making the point that learning about other ethnic groups is valuable. Obviously, integrating information about cultures into the school curriculum raises many questions, not the least of which is what cultures or ethnic groups should be included. In fact, one of my colleagues commented, "If we include courses on African-American culture, we'll also have to have courses on Hispanic, Asian, German, Czech, and other ethnic groups." Although this position may have some merit, the more critical point is that lessons on any culture not only legitimize cultures as a topic of study but also demonstrate to students how they can learn about other cultures. Students learn that different groups are just that—different—not wrong or something to be feared. Further, students who happen to be members of minority ethnic groups are given the message that their uniqueness is an asset that can be studied rather than a liability that should remain hidden or unspoken. Schools, then, can play the dual role of imparting knowledge about other ethnic groups and establishing the value of learning about these groups.

MEDIA.   I don't consider myself old—just middle-aged—but I get a kick out of examining the newspapers I've saved for various reasons over the years. Sometimes I look to see how ethnic groups were portrayed at different time periods. In Chapter 3, I discussed how the media teach us who is our enemy and what are the characteristics of various ethnic groups. For many groups the media are the only source of knowledge we have. How many of us have ever met a Kurd, talked with a South African, or interacted with a Native American? Our impression of these groups is based on what we read in newspapers, hear on the radio, or see on television. As anyone can determine, the media of 40 years ago often took an unabashed role in conveying stereotypes of various groups. African-Americans were portrayed as lazy, unintelligent, and dangerous. Russians were pictured as cold, distant, unfriendly, and untrustworthy. Other messages were more subtle. For example, television programs of 30 years ago rarely depicted African-Americans and whites living in the same neighborhood or working in the same office. Jones (1972) calls attention to the subtle technique of attaching traits to colors. He analyzed the popular movie *The Three Faces of Eve*, an account of a case of split personality. To disguise the patient's identity, her therapists used the names Eve White and Eve Black for two of her personalities. This is an interesting choice, because any two names could have been used: Eve Yellow and Eve Green, Eve One and Eve Two, Eve Sharp and Eve Dull, and so on. The choice of "black" and "white" does not seem to have been random. As you can see in Table 6.2, the characteristics of the two Eves reflected common stereotypes of blacks and whites.

Times have changed, and so has the media's portrayal of groups. Our television programs portray ethnically mixed groups in all walks of life. Blatant stereotypes are no longer easy to find in newspapers or television programs. But there are still subtle messages about ethnic relations. After returning from a trip to Israel, I paid special attention to television news programs about the area for a week. Every program I saw focused on conflict and tensions between Jews and Palestinians. On my trip, I had witnessed several tense interactions between Jews and Palestinians, but I had many other experiences as well. I observed a team of Jewish and Palestinian surgeons perform a new technique to save the life of a Catholic priest. I visited a school established by Jewish and Palestinian mothers. I played a spirited game of soccer on an ethnically mixed team in an old creek bed in Jerusalem. And I shopped in a large antique store run by an old Jewish man and a young Palestinian.

When we examine news reports from almost any part of the world, we find a similar situation. Conflict and violence attract attention as a rotting carcass attracts flies. When conflict in an area subsides, the place disappears from the news like the morning fog. Examples of ethnic cooperation and peace receive little, if any, attention, unless they are presented as unusual or unexpected. If you want a demonstration of this preoccupation with violence and conflict, simply look at your local newspaper and compare the number of stories on ethnic conflict with the number that discuss cooperation between ethnic groups. Certainly ethnic conflict and fighting exist in many parts of our world. But just as certainly, our social landscape is filled with incidents of ethnic harmony and examples of groups adopting measures to rise above their differences. Better coverage of these incidents would not only reflect existing situations but convey the message that ethnic harmony is as natural and common as ethnic conflict.

Suggestions aimed at guiding media, literature, and art usually provoke concern that freedom of expression is being threatened (Jowett & O'Donnell, 1992). Indeed, freedom of expression is vital for maintaining a free world and, consequently, for protecting ethnic groups. On the other hand, our media, art, and literature are important teachers. Those who would fill the shoes of societies' teachers must accept the cloak of responsibility. Many countries have codes and standards to guide the portrayal of violence and sex in entertainment programs and news reports.

TABLE 6.2 Characteristics of Eve White and Eve Black	
Eve White	Eve Black
Demure, retiring, in some respects almost saintly.	Obviously a party girl. Shrewd, childishly vain, and egocentric.
Face suggests a quiet sweetness; the expression in repose is predominantly one of contained sadness.	Face is pixie-like; eyes dance with mischief as if Puck peered through the pupils.
Voice always softly modulated, always influenced by a specifically feminine restraint.	Voice a little coarsened, "discultured," with echoes or implications of mirth and teasing. Speech richly vernacular and liberally seasoned with spontaneous gusts of rowdy wit.
An industrious and able worker; also a competent housekeeper and a skillful cook. Not colorful or glamorous. Limited in spontaneity.	All attitudes and passions whim-like and momentary. Quick and vivid flares of many light feelings, all ephemeral.
Though not stiffly prudish and never self-righteous, she is seldom lively or playful or inclined to tease or tell a joke. Seldom animated.	Immediately likable and attractive. A touch of sexiness seasons every word and gesture. Ready for any little irresponsible adventure.
Her presence resonates unexpressed devotion to her child. Every act, every gesture, the demonstrated sacrifice of personal aims to work hard for her little girl, is consistent with this love.	Dress is becoming and a little provocative. Posture and gait suggest lightheartedness, play, a challenge to some sort of frolic.
Cornered by bitter circumstances, threatened with tragedy, her endeavors to sustain herself, to defend her child, are impressive.	Is immediately amusing and likable. Meets the little details of experience with a relish that is catching. Strangely "secure from the contagion of the world's slow stain," and from inner aspect of grief and tragedy.

Source: Adapted from Thigpen and Cleckley (1954) by Jones (1972).

Watchdog groups monitor programs to ensure that specific ethnic groups are not portrayed unfairly. Freedom of the press is already interpreted within the domain of responsibility. That responsibility could be extended to include a balanced and fair depiction of ethnic relations: show the good with the bad in news stories and fictional programs.

Professors are often depicted as having their heads in the clouds, failing to acknowledge the "reality" of market forces. For example, I recently participated on a panel at a mass media conference where two of the panelists were news directors.

Both readily accepted the position that the media have a responsibility to the public. But one panelist observed, "I've got to consider the audience. I must give them what they want. If I don't, I won't have an audience." I could empathize with his problem, but I could not help responding: "You know, I feel the same way sometimes. I'd probably be the most popular professor in the university if I taught my students only what they wanted to know. I can't ignore their concerns and interests, but I also can't ignore my responsibility as a teacher."

Our media, our art, and our literature can play several critical roles in soothing ethnic conflict and fears. First, they can teach us about the customs, practices, and beliefs of other groups. The strange can become the familiar. Faceless groups can be transformed into individuals. Learning about the hopes, lives, and fears of individuals who happen to be Russian, Chinese, Native American, or Maori breathes life into what may have been perceived as a group without a heart or soul. Achieving this aim does not require that people in these groups be presented as "just like us." It is their unique characteristics and unique approaches to problems that humanize them and illustrate their special contributions to our world. Second, our media and literature can carry the message that ethnic harmony is as natural and noteworthy as ethnic conflict. By reporting instances of cooperation, they can teach us effective methods of promoting ethnic harmony. As an illustration, examine the story in Reading 6.1 about one community's efforts to fight ethnic hatred. The story indicates that cooperation is as newsworthy as conflict and outlines the methods that one community undertook to protect itself from ethnic strife.

Personal Experience: Teaching Ourselves

I have taught university students for 30 years, in which time nearly 15,000 students have attended my classes. I usually begin each course by trying to learn something about my students. I ask how many of them have traveled abroad, lived next to people of a different ethnic group, or been the object of prejudice and discrimination. My students typically come from middle- or upper-middle-class white families. They are generally in their late teens or early twenties and were ranked in the top quarter of their high school classes. They will be our country's future leaders. Though they are thus the "cream of the crop," with considerable financial resources, I never cease to be amazed at their limited personal experience with members of other ethnic groups. Less than 15 percent have visited a foreign country and less than 5 percent speak a second language—although some have tried to convince me I should consider "computer" a second language. I'd estimate that less than 15 percent of these students have been inside the home of someone from a very different ethnic group. And after much soul-searching, only a few students, mostly members of minority groups, recall being the object of discrimination, although I have noticed an increasing trend for students to argue that they have been victims of reverse discrimination.

Assuming that my figures are not unusual for the United States, they have profound implications for understanding ethnic relations within our country. Limited personal experience with members of other ethnic groups makes us dependent on sources such as friends, teachers, and the media for information about those groups. The information on which we base our impression of those other groups is filtered through such sources. And it is our impressions, based on secondhand information, that will guide our behavior toward members of those ethnic groups.

I lived in Greece during the height of conflict between the United States and Iran in 1979–1980. I remember being outraged at the Iranians' violation of the United States embassy. I saw pictures of hordes attacking the embassy and massive demonstrations in Iran calling for "death to the Americans." On the basis of these stories, I readily supported plans to bomb Iran and a total trade embargo to starve the country into submission. I hated Iran and Iranians. While the conflict in Iran was raging, a student at the University of Athens invited me to give a series of lectures on psychology to his study group. The group met at different members' homes on different evenings. When I arrived for my first lecture, I was horror-struck to find that many of the students were Iranian. I was among the enemy with no place to hide! Because my invitation had come from a Greek student, most of the Iranian students were equally surprised to find out that I was American. There was a pregnant pause lasting a few moments (though I could have sworn that it lasted for hours)—silence, dripping with tension and punctuated with wary glances. Just as I was about to dash out the door to save my life, the twin four-year-old sons of the host (an Iranian student) shyly approached and offered me a cup of tea. As they vied with each other to be the one who handed me the refreshment, the hot tea spilled on my lap. No one moved, but as I sought to determine if this attack was an evil Iranian plot, I suddenly burst into uncontrollable laughter. This reaction opened the floodgates, and everyone joined in a chorus of laughter. The host gave me a pair of his pants to wear, and we spent the evening (with me wearing the pants of my sworn enemy) talking not about group dynamics but about stereotypes and the development of group impressions. Family photos were exchanged, fears were discussed, and I learned a great deal about everyday life and attitudes in Iran. I left our meeting in the early morning hours with a decidedly different picture of Iranians than I had gotten from the newspapers and television. I was still angry about the attack on the embassy, but now my anger was directed solely at the outlaws who had participated in the act. And though I was angry with the participants, I had a better understanding of why they had been involved in the incident. I also examined subsequent news accounts of the Iranian situation with a much more critical eye.

Another function of personal experience with people of different ethnic groups is that it enhances our confidence in our ability to deal with different and unusual people. The realization that we can handle, even enjoy, interactions with other people builds our sense of self-efficacy. We can approach others with a sense of challenge and curiosity rather than fear. Fear prepares us to hate and to become aggressive. Fear often leads to "autistic" hostility (Newcomb, 1947), which motivates us to withdraw and cease interaction. Challenge and curiosity, on the other hand, invite us to approach, study, and seek understanding. Personal contact and experience with members of other ethnic groups can enhance our understanding of and comfort with

Developing friendships across ethnic group lines has been shown to reduce prejudice. (Jeff Greenberg/PhotoEdit)

those groups. As we will see, though, some types of contact are more effective than others in building ethnic harmony.

NOT ALL CONTACT IS CREATED EQUAL.   The effect of contact between individuals from different groups has been widely studied by psychologists (Allport, 1954; Brewer & Miller, 1984; Worchel, 1986). While contact is vital for reducing prejudice and discrimination, it is often the *nature* of the contact rather than contact itself that is important in reaching this goal.

The gentle hills of Oklahoma were the scene of an instructive drama during the late 1950s. Muzafer Sherif and a group of social scientists (Sherif et al., 1961) invaded a peaceful summer camp for boys to study the relations between groups. They began by having boys who lived in one bunkhouse engage in a series of competitive interactions with boys from the other bunkhouse. The kids played softball against each other, competed to see who could keep the neatest bunks, and so on. Soon the camp was a hotbed of hostility and aggression between boys from the two bunkhouses. Friends who happened to live in different bunkhouses came to hate and avoid each other. The social scientists had anticipated this outcome and were ready with a series of steps to reduce this hostility.

The prevailing wisdom of the time was that hostility between groups could be eliminated by bringing the members of the groups into frequent contact with one another. Indeed, the plan for desegregating schools in the United States was based on the premise that if white and black children could only have more direct contact with each other, relations between the groups would improve, trust would develop, and blacks and whites would come to respect and value the other culture. Sherif and his colleagues put this belief to the test by bringing the warring factions together. The kids ate together in a common dining hall and attended joint functions. The result of this planned contact was the same at the camp as it was in the schools: it did not improve relations and trust between the groups. In fact, contact often gave the kids an opportunity to act out their hatred. The dining hall became a battleground, for food fights and joint functions were disrupted as members of the two groups heckled and fought each other.

The lesson was that contact *alone* will not reduce hostility between groups. Indeed, some of the most violent fighting in Yugoslavia erupted between people who had lived side by side for nearly a generation. Daily contact was not enough. Later research found that contact would reduce hostility and open the door for understanding if that contact was between groups (or individuals) of equal power or status. A significant factor in school desegregation in the United States was that it increased contact between advantaged whites and disadvantaged blacks, and later also disadvantaged Hispanics. The black and Hispanic kids performed more poorly in classes, reinforcing the whites' prejudiced view that blacks and Hispanics were inferior.

Research that followed the study by Sherif and his colleagues found that hostility could be reduced and mutual understanding increased if care was taken to ensure that both groups had equal status or power in the situation in which contact occurred (Amir, 1969). For example, when Israelis were finally allowed to visit Egypt, an experimental program was instituted in which Israeli travelers were given information about the richness of Egyptian culture and the advances that had taken place in Egypt. The information highlighted the power and standing of Egypt. Travelers who had both the information *and* contact with Egyptians developed much more positive relationships with Egyptians and more attraction for Egypt than travelers who had only contact or only the information. The overall lesson from the research on contact is that relations between ethnic groups can be improved by contact if that contact brings people together on a basis of equal status, encourages them to interact personally with one another, and is preceded by positive information about the other group.

A COMMON PREDICAMENT.   After finding that contact alone was not successful in promoting intergroup understanding at the boys' camp, Sherif and his colleagues tried several other approaches. One that looked quite hopeful in the beginning involved setting up a common enemy for the warring factions to face. A team from another camp was invited to engage in athletic competition. This strategy worked for awhile, as the two previously feuding groups combined to meet the invading foe. But once the common enemy left, the old hatred and hostility reemerged. It is not difficult to find examples of the failure of the "common enemy" approach in our world today. Following bitter and bloody battles, the Serbs and Croats turned their attention toward devouring Bosnia. For a short time, these former foes coordinated their efforts; but as Bosnia began to crumble, the Serbs and Croats quickly resumed their fighting as if their cooperative efforts had never occurred. On a smaller scope, black and white fishermen in a small coastal town in Texas briefly combined forces to frighten away a contingent of Vietnamese fishermen who had attempted to set up an operation in the town. After months of violence, and a failure to scare off the Vietnamese, the blacks and whites returned to their former feuding and hatred. A common enemy may serve as a temporary bandage, but it will not promote the development of trust and understanding between ethnic groups.

However, in the case of the boys' camp all was not lost. Sherif and his colleagues eventually found a formula for reducing the animosity between the two groups of campers. They set up a number of predicaments that required the combined efforts of the two parties to solve. In one case a truck carrying water to a campsite became stuck and could be moved only if all the campers helped. In another case, a water line broke, and all the campers had to search together to find and repair the break. These situations had two points in common. First, they required members of the two groups to work together to deal with a common problem. Second, the two parties shared equally in the outcome. Even with these elements, though, Sherif found that old hostility was slow to ebb; many combined efforts were required to begin building trust, communication, and understanding. And later research added another caveat to this approach; hostility is reduced when the combined efforts result in success (Worchel, 1986).

There are several examples of a common predicament leading to greater intercultural understanding. Elliot Aronson and his colleagues (Aronson, Bridgeman, & Geffner, 1978) formed mixed groups of black and white children in an elementary school classroom. Each group was given problems to solve, but the solutions could be found only if each child learned his or her part of the puzzle. The success of the group required the successful cooperation of all parties. As the semester progressed and the groups succeeded in solving the problems, tension between black and white students dropped and interaction outside the problem situation increased. Recent efforts to form economic alliances between nations that were once competitors are another example of this approach. A side benefit of the European Union has been greater understanding and acceptance between member nations. History classes in each country have been expanded to include the other member nations. There has been an upsurge in people's willingness to learn the language and culture of other member nations.

Contact may work its magic through a number of channels (Stephan, 1987). It may destroy our stereotypes of a group or show how dysfunctional they are. We may learn that we are more similar to members of the other ethnic group than we suspected. We may learn positive ways to respond to members of other ethnic groups. Having such a positive encounter may create considerable cognitive discomfort for us: "How can we have a positive interaction with people we fear and hate?" An obvious answer to this question is that those people are not as bad as we first thought. The encounter may cool the flames of negative affect we felt toward the group.

This is quite a distinguished list, but before we embrace contact as a cure for ethnic strife, we must exercise some caution. Unfortunately we can find instances in which contact has either had no effect or has actually inflamed ethnic conflict (see Chapter 4). Prejudice, like the common cold, stubbornly refuses to go away, despite the array of "medicines" we use to dislodge it. We may try to preserve a prejudice even in the face of personal experiences that argue against it. Contact, even equal-status contact involving cooperation, will have little impact on our views of other ethnic groups if we decide that our experience is unique or that we are dealing with an "exceptional" case (Wilder, 1986). The owner of a clothing store in my hometown took every available opportunity to express his prejudice against African-Americans. I recall him ranting, "They are lazy and will steal you blind." His attitude was quite shocking given that the manager of his store for 20 years was an African-American whom I'll call James. James was one of the most honest, hardest-working people I have ever encountered. When the discrepancy between the owner's attitude and his experience was pointed out, the owner replied, "There is no inconsistency at all. James is an exception. He comes from a good family and has avoided picking up 'those' ways." When contact is made at the personal level, then, it is important to make a connection with the group so that the experience is not dismissed as an exception. This is often a delicate maneuver because of the danger of reinforcing the tendency to view all out-group members as the same. In other words, it is important to avoid creating the impression that we can judge a group simply by having contact with one member of that group. One way to achieve this aim is to ensure that individuals have contact with a variety of people from other ethnic groups in a variety of situations. Although it is relatively easy to discount interaction with one person in one situation, it is more difficult to deceive ourselves when we have experience with many people in many situations. How many "exceptions" break a rule?

FRIENDSHIP: A SPECIAL CASE OF CONTACT?   As our world becomes increasingly diverse, most of us will have a variety of contacts with people from many ethnic groups. As a child, I lived in an ethnic bubble. I could go for several days without encountering someone from a different ethnic group. But today, I have students and professional colleagues from many groups, I go to an Asian physician, I buy my gas from a Hispanic store owner, and I've learned to work my new computer from the patient lessons of an Indian technician. But despite the frequency of these contacts, my stereotypes may remain untouched. Thomas Pettigrew (1997) suggested that a special type of contact is necessary to pierce the fortress of our prejudice: We need to form friendships with members of other ethnic groups. Friendship, he argues, allows us to empathize and identify with members of the other group. Spending time with friends from other groups enables us to better understand their customs, norms, and lifestyles. It also gives us an opportunity to step outside our in-group identity and view the other group from a different perspective.

On the basis of a large European survey, Pettigrew concluded that personal friendship did generalize to feelings about other groups. Friendship, of all types of contact, was most effective in reducing prejudice. These findings support research indicating that non-Jews who reported close friendship with Jews as children were more likely than others to risk their lives to save Jews during World War II (Oliner & Oliner, 1988). These and other findings (Cook, 1984), are encouraging, though they don't tell the whole story. Some of the most disheartening incidents that occurred during the disintegration of Yugoslavia involved friend turning on friend because of their different ethnicity. Another problem is how we might go about enticing people with extreme prejudice to strike up friendships with members of groups they hate. Therefore, with regard to overcoming ethnic hatred, we can include friendship as one (but not the only) arrow in our quiver.

Talking the Talk

A result of personal experience with people of different ethnic groups is to increase understanding and reduce the perceived threat posed by "strange" people. Contact helps achieve both these aims, but it is not the only route toward building a greater understanding and appreciation of other ethnic groups. One defining characteristic of many ethnic groups is language (Edwards, 1985). Language is not just a means of communication; it defines how people perceive and understand their world. One of the earliest demonstrations of this point was the observation that Eskimos have many different words for "snow" while people in warmer climates have only one (Whorf, 1956). The Eskimo differentiates between wet and dry snow, large crystals and small crystals, and several other characteristics. These distinctions are important for people who must use types of snow to predict environmental conditions, but the distinctions also imply that the Eskimos perceive their environment differently from people in another climate. Some languages have a formal and polite form of address, indicating that people in these cultures are sensitive to status and relationship when they interact with others. Some languages have an extensive dictionary of terms to describe kinship, while others, like English, have relatively few terms. These differences suggest that family and the relationship between family members may be more important in some cultures than in others. Some languages like German and Spanish distinguish between masculine, feminine, and neuter nouns; others, like Thai, have different forms for addressing a man or a woman. English speakers often find these distinctions difficult to grasp because our language fails to make them.

Knowledge of a group's language gives us deeper insight about how people in that group perceive their environment, relate events, and process information. Understanding a language helps us understand those who speak it. Interestingly, this same statement can be applied to the newest member of our family, the computer. I've marveled at the wonderful things my computer can do. I give it a few simple commands, and, like magic, it gives me the answers I am looking for. But at times I find myself sitting back and wondering, "How does it do that?" or, more frequently, "Why isn't it responding?" In order to comprehend how the computer works, I must understand its language. Knowledge of basic computer language demystifies the computer. I can appreciate how and why it functions. Therefore, fluency in computer language serves to facilitate communication *and* understanding.

A similar observation can be made about knowledge of the language of other ethnic groups.

Given the value of language for enhancing ethnic understanding, it seems ironic that many schools are willing to drop or reduce the study of foreign language from the curriculum. As school budgets become increasingly constrained, foreign languages are among the first courses to be eliminated. One justification frequently offered is that English is understood by most of the world's people. Therefore, it is less necessary for native English-speakers to learn other languages if they desire to communicate with others. Although this position has some merit, it overlooks the point that language facilitates communication and understanding. Therefore, as the world becomes "smaller" and we interact with a greater variety of people, knowing foreign languages will become more, not less, important.

Up to this point, I have presented a rather benign view of language, focusing on its function in communication and understanding. But language plays another very important role in ethnic relations. Language is a defining characteristic of many ethnic groups, the focus of ethnic identity and pride (Citrin, Green, Reingold, & Walters, 1990). In an interesting book entitled *Power in Language*, Ng and Bradac (1993) argue that the expectation that all people should speak the same language carries a hidden message of power and legitimization. Because language is a defining characteristic of an ethnic group, requiring people in that group to speak a different language serves to delegitimize that group. It eliminates a basic symbol of the group's identity. It shouts out, "My group is the most powerful, and my language is the one that will define us all." Sears and his colleagues (Sears, 1993; Sears & Huddy, 1993) present an insightful analysis of the importance of language in symbolic politics. They point out that language is at the heart of ethnic conflict in Canada, Sri Lanka, Malaysia, the former Soviet Union, and other countries. According to Sears, racism and ethnocentrism have moved from the arena of blatant discrimination into the more confusing dimension of symbolism. Symbolic politics involves stripping away the symbols that characterize minority ethnic groups and emphasizing the dominance of the majority group. Because the process is often veiled with other principles, it is characterized by misunderstanding. For example, the "English-only" movement that took hold in the United States during the 1980s was defended by proponents as a way of maintaining American identity and a practical means of facilitating communication and education in the United States. Opponents and members of non–English-speaking groups viewed it as a racist policy aimed at delegitimizing them. Once again, this issue involves the various functions of language: as a vehicle of communication, as a means of understanding a group, and as a symbol of an ethnic group.

Knowledge of other languages can facilitate the understanding and appreciation of other ethnic groups. The study of language represents one step that can be taken at the individual level to promote ethnic harmony. From the perspective of people in other cultures, an individual's efforts to learn their language signals a willingness to recognize that culture as valuable and important. The most immediate test of this can be seen in the smiles that engulf the faces of people from another culture when they are greeted in their own language by someone from another group.

Individuals Make a Difference

The importance of individual action in reducing ethnic conflict cannot be overemphasized. Each person has an opportunity to add to ethnic conflict or push the balance toward ethnic harmony. Individual action has been stressed by a variety of world leaders. President George Bush struck a responsive chord with his "thousand points of light," in a speech that stressed individual responsibility and action to combat the world's problems. Shortly before receiving the Nobel Peace Prize in 1989, the Dalai Lama stated:

> The question for real, lasting world peace concerns human beings, so basic human feelings are also at its roots. Through inner peace, genuine world peace can be achieved. In this the importance of individual responsibility is quite clear; an atmosphere of peace must first be created within ourselves. (1989, p. 4)

In recognizing the importance of individual action, we should not overlook the fact that individuals often behave within the context of a group. As we found in Chapter 4, group forces can guide and shape individual behavior and attitudes. For this reason, the drive toward greater ethnic harmony must also include efforts aimed at the group. These programs should complement, not replace, individual-based efforts. Next, we turn our attention to changes that can be effected at the group level in the quest for ethnic harmony.

READING 6 . 1

A City Cries, "Not in Our Town!"*

TOM LACEKY

BILLINGS, Mont.—Police Chief Wayne Inman has seen what happens when racism and anti-Semitism are allowed to fester. As a cop in Oregon, he watched skinhead hatred turn murderous.

When the swastikas appeared in Billings, Montana's largest city, Inman was determined to halt the hatred early. He and others stirred the community to a roar of outrage that appears to have cowed the racist groups, at least for now.

"Hate crimes are not a police problem, they're a community problem," he said in an interview. "Hate crimes and hate activity will flourish only in communities that allow it to flourish."

The first signs came last year, when fliers started showing up in Billings mailboxes, on doorsteps, under windshield wipers. The fliers and anonymous phone calls vilified Hispanics, Indians, blacks, gays, lesbians and welfare recipients but reserved special venom for the city's Jewish community of 48 families.

---

*Source: The Bryan-College Station Eagle, February 20, 1994, p. B7.

Then, a series of seemingly random, isolated incidents:

- In January, a few skinheads slipped into a Martin Luther King Day observance; afterwards, participants found their cars papered with Ku Klux Klan material.
- In the spring, skinheads began showing up in twos and threes at Wayman Chapel African Methodist Episcopal Church, glowering in the back pews. As the Rev. Bob Freeman recalls it, "They were trying to intimidate us with 'the stare,' you know."
- In August, a black swastika painted on white posterboard was nailed to the door of Beth Aaron Synagogue, and tombstones were toppled in its cemetery.
- In October, swastikas and racial slurs were spray-painted on the home of a mixed race couple, white and Indian.

From his previous job, Inman recognized an emerging pattern—hate literature to intimidation to vandalism to personal attacks—which in Portland had culminated in the November 1988 beating death of Mulugeta Seraw, a young Ethiopian. Seraw's three skinhead attackers were fresh from a meeting of East Side White Pride at which two agents of White Aryan Resistance, a supremacist group, gave a spirited "recruitment" speech.

The skinheads pleaded guilty, and, in a trial two years later, WAR founder Tom Metzger and his son, John, were convicted of inciting Seraw's murder by recruitment.

"I saw the emergence of the hate groups and a community's denial, and I saw a wakeup call that was the death of a black man . . . by baseball bat because he was black," Inman said. "That's what it took to wake up Portland. We didn't have to go through that here to get the wakeup call."

What was different in Billings, a metropolitan area of about 100,000 people, was the united public reaction to the early ugliness.

"There was not silence," Inman said. "There was community outrage, saying, 'If you harass and intimidate one member of this community you are attacking all of us.'"

Inman kept repeating a message to civic groups and community leaders: Hate groups must be resisted, not ignored.

And the resistance was more than bluster. Within five days of the spray-painted vandalism, 27 volunteers from Painters Local 1922 swarmed over the defaced house and obliterated the slurs in 45 minutes.

Bigotry resurfaced the next month. On Nov. 27, a beer bottle was hurled through a glass door at the home of Uri Barnea, conductor of the Billings Symphony. Five nights later, a cinder block thrown through a window sent shards of glass spraying over the bed of 5-year-old Isaac Schnitzer.

Both houses were decorated with Hanukkah menorahs. Both houses had children at home with baby-sitters.

The threats to children aroused a fierceness in the city. Christian churches distributed photocopies of menorahs. The *Billings Gazette* published a black-and-white picture of a menorah with an editorial, then a full-page version in color. Several businesses began providing paper menorahs.

Within days, the nine-candled symbol of Jewish perseverance and resistance from second century B.C. was displayed in thousands of windows across the city.

The menorah idea started with the Rev. Keith Torney of the First Congregational Church and Margie MacDonald of the Montana Association of Churches.

"This was just getting to be too much," Torney said. "At first the homosexual community was being harassed. First the gays, then the black community, but it seemed to me they kind of hit their stride in the Jewish community. It's like they're searching around to get attention."

Civic leaders, churches and businesses declared their revulsion. Universal Athletics replaced its billboard display on a busy thoroughfare with this message:

"NOT IN OUR TOWN! NO HATE. NO VIOLENCE."

But the hatemongers returned. Over two weeks in December, they broke windows at two Jewish homes and two churches that displayed menorahs, shot bullets through windows at Billings Central Catholic High School, and stomped and battered six vehicles at homes displaying menorahs, telling two owners in phone calls, "Go look at your car, Jew-lover."

The spasm of hate only created more resistance.

"The result was that many more people put menorahs in their windows," Inman said, allowing himself a rare grin at the memory. "It became physically impossible for the hate groups to harass and intimidate thousands and thousands of Billings citizens."

On Dec. 10, about 100 people attended a Hanukkah service at Beth Aaron Synagogue. Outside, other neighbors discreetly stood vigil in the dark.

The city is not proclaiming victory, but Inman thinks the hate groups have backed off. No vandalism has occurred since the incidents in December, and the literature and anonymous calls have diminished.

"I would hate to predict we have stopped the influence and impact of hate crimes, but something appears to be working," Inman said.

A grimmer outlook comes from Clinton Sipes, a former skinhead who did time for assault, armed robbery and burglary, and now runs a program to help youngsters leave racist groups. He thinks the gains are temporary, the solutions not nearly so simple.

"A year from now," Sipes predicts, "we're going to have racial assaults, vandalism, all kinds of violence."

Yellowstone County Sheriff Charles Maxwell remains optimistic.

"It may happen again," the sheriff acknowledged. "But the reaction will be the same."

READING 6.2

Two Workers Fired for Speaking Spanish*

AMARILLO, Texas—Rosa Gonzales and Ester Hernandez were hired by Allied Insurance for their Spanish-speaking ability. They were fired for the same reason.

The two were "being very rude for speaking in a language we don't understand,"

---

*Source: The Bryan-College Station Eagle, August 15, 1997, p. A14.

said Allied co-owner Linda Polk, who says she and other employees were frustrated by the women's intraoffice Spanish conversations.

Gonzales and Hernandez said they regularly spoke to the agency's large Hispanic customer base in Spanish. But when they used the language to speak to each other, they said, they were discussing work and not conducting personal chats or secretly talking about their co-workers.

"Being able to speak Spanish is an advantage to us. We don't want our heritage taken away from us," Gonzales told the *Amarillo Globe-News.*

Allied co-owner Pat Polk issued a memo stating that "this be an English-speaking office except when we have customers who can't speak our language . . . If you can't live with the rules here—Draw your pay and make the rules at your next job."

Three women in the office were handed the memo. One signed it, while Hernandez and Gonzales refused and were fired.

"When we read it, we were very upset," Gonzales said. "They never warned us."

Gonzales was hired in November and Hernandez in March "to speak Spanish to non-American-speaking people" and not to each other, Polk said.

"It would be just like getting over in a corner and whispering," she said.

The incident is the second major language-related conflict here in the last three years. In 1995, a judge ordered a woman to speak English as well as Spanish to her 5-year-old daughter.

In a hearing, he said a Spanish-only environment at home was tantamount to abuse. He told the woman, "You're abusing that child and you're relegating her to the position of a housemaid," words for which he later apologized.

R E A D I N G   6 . 3

Interracial Marriage Rises, Acceptance Lags*

ISABEL WILKERSON

In another era, Tom and Yvette Weatherly might never have known each other. They grew up in opposite worlds in Atlanta, his white and affluent, hers black and working-class. But as the children of integration, they met when she was bused to his virtually all-white high school and sat behind him in English class. They helped each other with class work and goaded each other to raise their hands.

Eight years ago they were married. They have survived their families' shock and disapproval and the stares and unwelcome comments of strangers. They know not to stop in small towns or rural areas when they travel.

They are part of a small but rapidly growing corps of interracial couples who, wittingly or not, have put themselves on the front lines of American race relations, staring

---

Source: The New York Times, December 2, 1991, pp. A1, A10, A11.

into the face of age-old stereotypes and painfully aware that their public embraces can unsettle all but the most tolerant Americans.

Nightmare, and Role Model

The number of black-white marriages has more than tripled since 1970, according to the Census Bureau. And while interracial marriage is far more common between whites and members of other minorities, no pairing hits as raw a nerve as unions between blacks and whites. "We are a segregationist's worst nightmare," said Mr. Weatherly, a 30-year-old systems analyst. "But to other people, we're the perfect example."

As the nation confronts persistent racial bigotry, fanned by a stagnant economy and politicians like David Duke, these couples are quietly trying to bridge two increasingly alienated worlds.

Many manage a veneer of civility with once hostile in-laws. Others find acceptance from more tolerant families, particularly with the arrival of the firstborn.

But a few have not even told their parents that they are married and have children. Some say that even after decades of marriage, they are made to feel as if their relationships are illicit or unseemly. Many suffer indignities like being spat upon or refused services. And most say they want the one thing society seems not quite ready to give them: acceptance as ordinary couples.

"It has not passed the 'no blink' test," said Dr. Tom W. Smith, a researcher on social issues at the National Opinion Research Center at the University of Chicago. "It's clear that the majority of whites are not prepared to accept this as just another couple. The minimum you get is a look and a stare."

According to the General Social Survey, an annual polling of 1,500 American adults of all races directed by Dr. Smith, a significant proportion of whites—1 in 5—still believe interracial marriage should be illegal, as against 2 in 5 whites asked the question in 1972. "They feel so strongly about it that they don't even want to leave it up to the individual," said Dr. Smith, who has conducted the survey for 19 years.

Further, 66 percent of whites said they would oppose a close relative's marrying a black person. Only 4 percent said they would favor it; the remainder said race was not a factor one way or the other. (The margin of sampling error in the poll was plus or minus three and a half to four percentage points, and six to seven percentage points for blacks.)

Intensity and Indifference

No other ethnic or racial group engenders as intense a response from whites. About 45 percent of whites said they would oppose a close relative's marriage to an Asian or Hispanic person and 15 percent said they would oppose a marriage between a close relative and a Jew, according to the survey.

Blacks, on the other hand, exhibited indifference to intermarriage, with nearly two-thirds saying they would neither favor nor oppose a relative's marrying someone from another race.

To be sure, some white opposition has melted. The beaming faces of interracial couples appear with little protest on the wedding pages of Southern newspapers like

The Augusta Chronicle in Georgia, a state where such unions were illegal until the 1970's. Television shows like "The Days and Nights of Molly Dodd" and movies like "Jungle Fever" have brought interracial relationships to living rooms and theaters across the country, usually in a more realistic fashion than in the 1967 film "Guess Who's Coming to Dinner?"

And in the contentious confirmation hearings of Clarence Thomas to be Supreme Court Justice, his marriage to Virginia Lamp, a white woman from Nebraska, drew little comment. The two were seen every morning of the hearings holding hands and giving each other good-luck kisses on national television.

But these new signs of openness do not necessarily translate into approval for most of these couples.

Teresa Johnson, a white social worker, has been married to Ralph Johnson, a black actor, for 17 years. They have two teen-age children and a house in the Hyde Park section of Chicago. Her relatives are miles away in Cleveland, and all but the very closest of them know her by her maiden name; they think she is single and childless.

To protect this secret, she has not been to a family wedding or funeral since she married, for fear that the topic might come up. For years, only her parents knew. But they were horrified at the news and dared not let it slip. She didn't even bother to tell them she was pregnant the last time.

"They were so upset about the first one," said Mrs. Johnson, 40 years old, "because that meant I wasn't turning back."

For years her parents would not let her children enter their house, preferring instead to meet them at the airport or at a pizza parlor in some other neighborhood. Now her parents let the children visit—but only at night so the neighbors won't see.

"To this day," said Mr. Johnson, "I can't go to their house because of the neighbors."

Mrs. Johnson said she felt caught in a cruel paradox because people cannot get beyond the color of her husband's skin. "Here we are, a typical middle-class family," she said. "Ralph's a Little League coach. He's on the local school council. I have cousins who have kids out of wedlock, who are juvenile delinquents and in the Hell's Angels. But I'm the one on the outs. If my husband was white and beat me, that would be O.K."

Marriages between blacks and whites make up a tiny fraction of all married couples in the country—about 4 of every 1,000. But the numbers are rising, as well as the ratio, which was 1.5 out of 1,000 in 1970. There were 65,000 black-white marriages in 1970 and 211,000 in 1990, according to Census figures. While these figures are not broken down by state or region, researchers say such marriages are more common on the East and West Coasts than elsewhere, and far more common in cities than in suburbs or rural areas.

Threshold for Integration

The rise in intermarriage and whites' almost primal feelings against it are an important measure of the threshold for integration, social scientists say.

"Intermarriage is like the tip of the iceberg," said Dr. Richard D. Alba, chairman of the sociology department at the State University of New York at Albany, who is a specialist in ethnic intermarriage and race relations. "It is the visible expression of a host of attitudes and informal contacts that are otherwise hard to measure. Whites have difficulty accepting blacks as neighbors and co-workers, and all the more as members of the family."

Still, things are far different than in 1958, when Richard Loving and Mildred Jeter were married in Washington and promptly arrested back home in Virginia. The groom, who was white, and the bride, who was black, were accused of violating the state's anti-miscegenation law, a felony, and faced up to five years in prison. In exchange for a suspended sentence, they were forbidden to set foot in Virginia for 25 years.

Their case, *Loving* v. *Virginia*, went to the Supreme Court, which in 1967 overturned miscegenation laws in Virginia and 15 other states, most of them Southern. Some states kept the laws on the books well into the 1970's, however, and only in recent years have some interracial couples there felt safe.

Indeed, a black woman in Georgia gave her son a gun when he married a white woman in the early 1970's. The son, Nathaniel Brown, now a physician's assistant, never had to use the gun, but he was stopped by state troopers on a quiet stretch of rural Georgia road.

"They thought my husband had abducted me," Mrs. Brown said.

Mr. Brown thinks life is easier for the couple now, but not by much. "People now say, 'Maybe I can't shoot this person like I could before,'" Mr. Brown said. "Now that you see pictures of interracial couples in the newspaper and on television, you can feel free to walk in the malls and out in the street, doing what other people do and enjoying each other."

Couples as Pioneers

Last August, a Methodist minister in Pennsylvania refused to marry a white beautician to a black army private after meeting the groom-to-be. It was four days before the wedding.

Douglas and Marcia Drumright of San Pablo, Calif., were terrorized for four years by a neighbor who was infuriated by the sight of them, a black man and white woman, together. The Drumrights are now suing the neighbor.

In court papers, they say the neighbor, a professed member of the white supremacy group Aryan Brotherhood, cursed at their children, threatened to kill the husband, poured motor oil in their swimming pool and spat on the family car as Mrs. Drumright drove her daughter to school. "I'm going to get you," they say the neighbor told them. "I'm going to get your whole family."

It would seem to take extraordinary strength of will to bear that kind of stress, and sociologists say that people who enter into these kinds of marriages tend to have an open, pioneering way about them.

Women as Symbols

Some say the most common black-white pairing—a black man married to a white woman—may be more frequent because of shared feelings of powerlessness. "They both occupy an incongruent status in society," said Prof. Charles Willie, a black sociologist at Harvard University, who is himself married to a white woman. "They both should be dominant, he because he is male, she because she is white. But because of racism and sexism, they are not respected as dominant."

Others say that some black men gain a sense of membership in a white-dominated culture through such marriages. "The white woman becomes the supreme symbol of acceptability," said Dr. Naim Akbar, a psychologist at Florida State University, who has counseled black men in interracial relationships.

For the white spouses, the marriages often become a crash course in what it is like to be black in America. They begin to measure their movements and be alert to discrimination in much the same way blacks do.

Margriet Daniels, a white bookstore owner in Evanston, Ill., who is married to a retired black chemist, worries about their two grown sons simply because of the disproportionate danger faced by young black men. "I hear police sirens, and I immediately think, Where are the boys?" she said. "This is something you don't learn growing up white."

CHAPTER 7

ALL FOR ONE OR ONE FOR ALL?

Managing Group Identity to Reduce Ethnic Conflict

Ethnic cleansing is one of the most horrible human behaviors no matter where it takes place. But it seems particularly shameful when it occurs in one's own country. During the middle 1800s, the United States was the scene of a coordinated effort to eliminate the Native American population and relocate those who escaped destruction. Tribes such as the Wampanoag, the Chesapeak, the Chickahominy, the Potomac, and the Montauk disappeared, their bones buried beneath a thousand burned villages. Other tribes such as the Modoc, the Nez Perce, and the Northern Cheyenne were reduced to tiny remnants. A once proud people were classified within the new legal system as "nonpeople."

But even during this terrible period of American history, there were incidents that showed another side of human behavior. During some of the darkest times, a light seemed to show through, even if for just a moment, hinting that people of different ethnic groups could live together in harmony and peace.

In 1878, Chief Standing Bear of the Ponca people and 66 members of his clan left their miserable reservation on the west bank of the Arkansas River to honor the last request of Standing Bear's son—to be buried in his Nebraska homeland. Through the long cold winter, the ragged group made their way over trails chosen to avoid soldiers and white settlers. The group finally reached the Omaha reservation, only to be arrested by General Crook on orders from the Bureau of Indian Affairs. The Ponca were supposed to be sent back to their reservation immediately. Crook, however, was so moved when he saw the stoic courage of the Ponca, that he held up their transfer. Crook enlisted the aid of a local newspaper, which published stories about the plight of Standing Bear.

The Indian Affairs office was unmoved and reiterated its order that the Ponca be forcibly returned. By this time, however, two attorneys had volunteered their services and obtained a writ of habeas corpus requiring Crook to bring Standing Bear into court to show by what authority he held the Ponca (Brown, 1971). The U.S. district attorney argued that the Ponca had no right of a writ because Indians were "not persons within the meaning of the law." During the trial that followed, the

Ponca's attorneys argued that the Indians were persons with rights under the Constitution and that they and any other Indians had the right to separate themselves from their tribe.

At the end of the trial Judge Dundy ruled that the Indian was a "person" and in the eyes of the law had the same natural, inherent, and inalienable rights as the white race. When the judge announced that Standing Bear and his Ponca band were to be released and allowed to stay in Nebraska, the courtroom erupted in cheers. The band took possession of a few hundred acres and worked along with the white settlers to build a community. Justice was served in this case, and one result was that the clear ruling from Judge Dundy helped set a foundation for whites and a small band of Native Americans to work together as equals on the land and in the eyes of the law.

Both the Ponca and the white settlers recognized the right of the other to exist. Each recognized the differences between the groups, but each group pledged to protect the other. For a time, the peaceful coexistence of the two groups was nurtured by a sharing of ideas and resources and a mutual commitment to a pledge to be good neighbors.

This incident is important—even though the number of people involved was small—because it illustrates the positive role groups can play in creating ethnic harmony. Chapter 6 discussed how individuals can improve ethnic relations. Now our attention turns to the importance of collective efforts in achieving that goal. Although General Crook and Judge Dundy played major roles in the drama on the Nebraska plains, the ultimate resolution of the problem was the result of actions by the Ponca and the white settlers. Although the two groups were different on nearly every dimension, both were determined to find a peaceful solution that would allow the Ponca to remain on their Omaha homestead. In the final analysis, ethnic relations involve groups of people. Our concern now is to explore how interventions that involve the condition of groups affect the relationship between groups.

Although many issues are raised in this endeavor, one of the most basic is the degree to which the identity and uniqueness of each group should be emphasized. A farmer in one of Robert Frost's poems suggests that "good fences make good neighbors." If we were to follow this line of reasoning, we would work toward positive intergroup relations by creating clear boundaries between groups. But according to social identity theory (Tajfel & Turner, 1986), a demarcation of an in-group and an out-group sets the stage for intergroup discrimination. This theory recommends tearing down the fences that encourage people to perceive themselves as belonging to different groups. Rather, we should work to develop a common identity that will bind people together into a common group or category.

As we will see, attempts by nations to deal with ethnic diversity and work toward ethnic harmony can be divided into these two approaches. It is, therefore, important to dissect each position, examining its theoretical foundation and its implications for social behavior. This review will help explain why both approaches have met with some success, as well as some failures. Let's begin by analyzing attempts to promote ethnic harmony by protecting independent group identities.

Building Better Fences: Maintaining Separate Group Identities

In Chapter 1, I argued that we all struggle to establish ourselves as independent, unique, and important. The struggle for identity is as basic to human existence as the struggle for survival. The desire to establish a positive identity leads us to join attractive groups and to depreciate those outside our group. Threats to either our independence or our positive self-image are met with anger and hostility. Insecurity prepares us to hate.

A similar description applies to groups. A group, too, strives to establish its identity and its independence from other groups. In my own observations of laboratory work groups, I found that a group's first order of business was to secure its identity (Worchel, 1998). A new group often adopted a name, rearranged furniture to demonstrate its control over a territory, and developed a structure and boundaries. Determining what it was and establishing its position became a critical first step before the group began working on tasks. Whenever the identity of a group was threatened by internal strife or another group, its members became preoccupied with reestablishing its identity and reconstructing its boundaries.

This same process repeats itself in the world beyond the laboratory. New nations strive to gain recognition from the international community. They are often willing to make considerable concessions, such as relinquishing control over territory, altering their political structure, or adopting specified economic policies just to have others recognize them as legitimate nations. The posturing for recognition seems like a child's game, with one party "pretending the other does not exist" unless it meets certain demands. Israel spent nearly half a century after it declared independence attempting to gain recognition from its Arab neighbors. As strange as this process might seem, it gives us insight into forces that drive group behavior.

Denying a nation's right to exist has not only political and economic implications but also important psychological consequences. The bold statement that one group will "not recognize" another delegitimizes the unrecognized group and strikes at its basic identity (Bar-Tal, 1990). Tucked within the folds of a group's identity are its history, its heroes and heroines, its home, and its right to embrace its members. Denying recognition to a group denies the legitimacy of these dimensions. All this suggests that the existence and identity of a nation result from a combination of the efforts of its citizens and the willingness of other nations to acknowledge its existence. Only when a nation feels that its identity is secure and recognized by other nations can it begin to turn its attention toward other issues, such as productivity and international cooperation.

If group identity and legitimization are so important for a sovereign nation, which occupies a defined territory and has a definite political structure, concern with identity must be even greater for an ethnic group. Unlike nations, many ethnic groups do not reside in specified regions with clear boundaries, and many lack political organization. But since gaining recognition of one's ethnic group is often critical for establishing one's personal identity, it is easy to understand why individuals may feel threatened by those who would injure or deny their group's identity.

Because ethnic groups often exist as vague constructs in the minds of members, a threat to the group can act as a magnet that draws its members together and impels them to give solid form to their group. Anger and hostility arise within the group, and a readiness to reject or attack other groups develops. A revival of customs and native dress, the erection of shrines, and the emergence of centralized leadership endow the ethnic group with a physical reality designed to induce others to recognize it. Several psychologists have suggested that the hostility felt by many African-Americans is based as much on the unwillingness of others to recognize them as a unique ethnic group as it is on the disadvantaged position they occupy (Sidanius, 1993; Jones & Morris, 1993). In this sense, they are cut with both edges of the ethnic sword: they are treated shabbily because of their membership in a group that fails to win recognition as "legitimate."

If we accept the view that groups can function effectively only after they have established a secure identity, we find a rather clear formula for enhancing harmony between ethnic groups. Building a positive relationship between groups should begin by ensuring that all ethnic groups have a positive and unassailable identity. Each group needs to feel that its right to exist is guaranteed by law or custom. Each group must be free from the fear that cooperation with others will jeopardize its identity. In some cases, a secure identity will require the freedom to practice its own customs, religion, and language; in others, it will be linked to territory. Once groups are freed from threats to their existence, they will be more willing to accept and cooperate with other groups. Assuming that group identity has been secured in this way, we can now proceed to examine the ideal conditions for developing positive interactions between groups.

But before turning to that issue, we must address a factor that has the potential to undermine the formation of a group identity in a community of several groups. A group can feel safe only if it *trusts* other groups to respect its identity and security. Lack of trust of its neighbors forces a group to remain preoccupied with its own safety and existence. Interactions with other groups, if they take place at all, will be tentative and egocentric. Therefore, developing a secure group identity depends on an environment of trust.

Trust: The Guiding Light

If we systematically strip away the layers of a conflict, we eventually uncover a common element at the rotten core of conflict: distrust. William Webb and Philip Worchel (1986) observe, "The perception of the other group as untrustworthy is a major source of tensions leading to conflict" (p. 213). Similarly, Alexander Gralnick (1988) suggests, "Trust is the critical link of any policy designed or meant to prevent nuclear holocaust" (p. 182). More poignant is the observation by Chief Red Cloud of the Oglala Sioux: "The white man made us many promises, more than I can remember, but they never kept but one: they promised to take our land, and they took it" (Brown, 1971, p. 347).

Trust is an expectation that someone else's word, promise, or statement—written or oral—can be relied on. Another way of describing trust is as an expectation that someone else will act helpfully rather than hurtfully. Trust is excruciatingly slow to develop between people or groups. In most cases trust grows when one party is willing to let down his or her guard to see if the other party will abuse that vulnerability. The greater the vulnerability, the greater the resulting trust *if* the other party does not take advantage of the situation for personal gain.

Even in an atmosphere of relative safety and positive feelings, making ourselves vulnerable is frightening. The fear of becoming vulnerable can paralyze us when vulnerability may lead to instant destruction or when the antagonist is already viewed as sinister or strange, as in the case of relations between ethnic groups. This point is brought home in the simple but informative, battle cry of Israeli soldiers: "Never again!" The message is that Jews had once trusted (the Germans) and allowed themselves to be vulnerable only to find that their trust brought them to the verge of extinction. The point can also be seen in the remarks of Yehuda, an elderly shopkeeper in Tel Aviv: "I'd like to learn from the Arabs and have them learn from me, but I can't afford to. One sign of weakness and the Arabs will swoop onto me and destroy me like crows in a field of corn. It is my Jewishness, my culture, that makes me strong. Any compromise in this will weaken me, and that will be the beginning of the end. I am afraid that these recent compromises [plans for Palestinian self-rule] are the beginning of the end for Israel."

One other point is worth noting: although trust is slow to develop, distrust strikes with lightning speed. It takes only one transgression to arouse distrust. One of the most infamous feuds in American history illustrates this point. The Hatfields and McCoys had lived for nearly a century in relative peace, secreted in a valley of the Appalachian mountains. Intermarriage between the families was commonplace, as was the sharing of grazing and hunting land. All this came to an abrupt end in 1873, when Floyd Hatfield rounded up an unbranded pig that belonged to his brother-in-law Randolph McCoy. Randolph was stunned that Floyd would "sink so low" as to take advantage of their cooperative grazing arrangement (Jones, 1948). Randolph called Floyd and all other Hatfields untrustworthy scoundrels; cooperation between the two families ceased immediately; and the hills rang with intermittent gunfire. The feud lasted over 50 years, left over 100 dead, and almost brought Kentucky and West Virginia to civil war.

Whether we focus on an intimate relationship between two people or on interaction between nations or ethnic groups, trust is a vital ingredient. Without trust, the relationship will be a powder keg, waiting for the tiniest spark to ignite conflict and hatred. The seeds of trust must not only be carefully planted, but constantly nurtured and tended. But how can we create an environment in which trust and understanding can develop?

Deflating the Balloon of Conflict: A Mutual Reduction of Threat

Lessons on conflict can be found in strange places. Dr. Seuss (1984) describes a fictional conflict between the Yooks and the Zooks that begins with a disagreement over which side of the bread should be buttered. The conflict progresses through successive stages until each side develops the "ultimate weapon" to destroy the other. While Seuss's rhymes are witty and enjoyable, the events he describes have been played out in every corner of the world, with tragic consequences. Most clearly, the United States and the former Soviet Union entered into an arms race that lasted nearly 50 years, consumed vast resources and energy, and brought the world to the brink of destruction. The recent history of Northern Ireland is marred by repeated episodes of terrorist violence as Protestant and Catholic militants battle for control. Jews and Arabs have been engaged in a series of wars and confrontations since the formation of the state of Israel in 1948.

The typical course of conflict begins with each side seeking an advantage by raising its level of threats and weaponry. We are easily sucked into thinking that the object in a conflict is to win: there must be a winner and a loser. And the quickest way to win is to beat the opponent into total submission. Beating the opponent—whether an individual or another ethnic group—gives us an immediate "high," reinforcing the belief that "might makes right." The vision of conflict as a win-lose situation entices us to augment our strength and our ability to threaten. In our best-case scenario, the opponent may simply cut and run in fear at the very sight of our vast arsenal. But if saber rattling doesn't do the trick at least we've constructed a wall to protect us from attack. What we don't realize is that this wall of power and threat may intensify the conflict and increase our chance of being destroyed. The increased threat results in growing distrust and distance between the two parties. Even if one side whips the other and brings it to its knees, the resolution is usually only temporary, as the vanquished side awaits its chance to become the conqueror. Witness the violence against whites in South Africa that occurred immediately after blacks achieved some power after a century of domination and degradation. Centuries of dominance and control by the Pakeha of New Zealand have failed to erase the Maori cry for recognition and respect. Ethnic conflicts cannot be "won" through power or threat.

Charles Osgood (1962) recognized that the increasing threat so often associated with escalating conflict is a recipe for disaster. To break the spiral of conflict, he proposed a plan he called *graduated reciprocation in tension reduction* (GRIT). GRIT asks one side to take a calculated risk by publicly announcing and then carrying out its intention to reduce its "threat potential" by destroying weapons, pulling back from strategic territory, and offering greater freedom to a dominated group. The action is unilateral. The other party is invited to reciprocate, but even in the absence of reciprocation, the first party must follow through with its stated action. The initial reduction of threat must lead to increased vulnerability, though not so much that the initiating party loses the ability to protect itself. Also, after a period of time, the initiator must take other steps to reduce its threat potential, even if its initial actions have not been reciprocated.

Osgood suggested that this plan would have at least two consequences. First, it would put public pressure on the adversary to reciprocate, since failure to reciprocate would label the adversary as an aggressor. Second, and possibly more important, the increased vulnerability of one side would set the stage for developing trust between the two parties. One party sees the other as willing to take risks, and the other learns that the adversary will not take advantage of the increased vulnerability.

Will GRIT work? There are numerous examples to suggest that it could. General

Crook's interaction with Standing Bear was a case in point. Crook ordered his soldiers to take only sidearms when visiting the Ponca camp, making them vulnerable to the Ponca braves. Standing Bear saw that Crook was willing to jeopardize his career by refusing orders to relocate the Ponca. On the other side, Crook's troops found that the Ponca not only did not take advantage of their increased vulnerability but went further, offering the soldiers food and shelter. Local settlers no longer feared raids from the Ponca, and the two groups were soon working side by side on their farms.

Lindskold (1986) reviewed many studies, both simulations and laboratory experiments, designed to examine how one party responds to threat-reducing behavior by an adversary. Although most of the research studied relations between individuals, the results have important implications for intergroup relations. The studies often placed experimental subjects in situations where they faced an opponent over a series of interactions. The opponent began by responding competitively, generally eliciting competition in return. The opponent then began making cooperative responses, taking a less threatening stance. In many but not all cases, the more cooperative stance elicited cooperation from the subjects. As cooperative encounters con-

Communication between members of groups in conflict is an important step toward reducing intergroup conflict. However, the tendency to distrust the words of an antagonist requires training to develop effective communication. (Reuters / Win McNamee / Archive Photos)

tinued, subjects began to trust the opponent. Although these results support the wisdom of GRIT, several studies reported incidents where subjects responded competitively to the opponent's cooperative behavior. These subjects were suspicious of the opponent's seeming cooperation. Interestingly, the competitive responses were based on two premises. Some subjects felt that the opponent was attempting to manipulate them; their competitive response was a signal that they would not "fall into a trap." In other cases, subjects interpreted the switch to cooperation as a sign of weakness, which they viewed as an opportunity to take advantage of the opponent and enhance their own position. This latter response is often seen in international situations. For example, in October 1979, the Soviet president Leonid Brezhnev stated that the Soviet Union would reduce the number of medium-range nuclear carriers threatening western Europe and the number of Soviet troops in East Germany. The United States distrusted this overture and responded by deploying more missiles in Europe. Brezhnev scrapped his plans to reduce the Soviet threat, and the arms race escalated. We cannot know the intention behind Brezhnev's proposal, but the incident demonstrates how difficult it is to reduce our own threat potential when our opponents react by increasing their threat.

It is puzzling that overtures consisting of cooperation and a reduced threat are met by cooperation in some cases and by competition and distrust in others. This is a particularly troubling inconsistency in the arena of ethnic relations, where a miscalculation about the intentions of the other group can result in total destruction of your group. Fortunately, we can identify some of the factors that can help ensure that overtures of cooperation are met with cooperation rather than suspicion and aggression. One important issue concerns the contribution of communication between the groups.

Let's Talk about It: The Role of Communication

On fall weekends I often take my children to a park not far from my home. As is common throughout the United States, there is usually a football game under way. The games are hotly contested, and each kid throws his heart into the contest. But quite often the game comes to an abrupt halt when the sides start bickering over a relatively minor infraction. The arguing begins with a minor rumble, "You interfered with my efforts to make that catch." "No, I didn't. I just guarded you closely." The crescendo builds: "You're crazy. You've been pushing and shoving me all morning. I'm sick of it!" Just when it seems that World War III will break out, one of the kids states, "If they can't play fairly, let's quit. I'm taking my football and going home." The game breaks up and the sides cease talking to one another. (I never learn whether there really was interference.) Newcomb (1947) observed that conflict and anger often lead to *autistic hostility:* each side withdraws from and ceases communicating with the other.

In one respect, we might view this as a positive development, since the withdrawal seems to dampen the conflict for the moment. But if we examine the situation more closely, we find that this is not a desirable solution, because the lack of communication ensures the conflict will never be resolved. Each side retreats into its own domain, disliking and distrusting the other group. If the groups happen to encounter each other, anger and hostility are quick to flare. In the case of the friendly football game, the absence of communication ensures that the participants will not be able to develop rules for future games. Therefore, the same unfortunate scenario is likely to unfold next weekend.

Communication is important for resolving conflict, developing understanding, and creating an atmosphere of trust (Rubin, 1980; Rubin, Pruitt, & Kim, 1993). If ethnic groups retreat behind their borders (physical or psychological), there is little hope that they will learn about or be willing to work with other groups. Suspicion grows in a culture of silence. Communication allows each side to explain its actions and intentions, so the sides can learn about each other. Given these points, the solution to conflict seems simple: provide ethnic groups with forums to communicate with each other.

Unfortunately, this solution is not so simple. In an important study, Deutsch and Krauss (1962) placed two opponents in a conflict. In some cases, the opponents had no opportunity to communicate with each other; in others, they could communicate and explain their intentions and plans for future behavior. The results showed that having an opportunity to communicate did little to reduce competition. In fact, many of the opponents did not communicate, even though they had the option to do so. "Autistic" hostility was alive and well. But the investigators did not stop there. They included a condition under which opponents were required to communicate with one another (Krauss & Deutsch, 1966). Forced communication led to some increase in cooperation, but not as much as we might expect.

If we give careful thought to the situation, we can not only explain these results but frame an intervention that would reduce conflict. Last year I undertook the American ritual of buying a new automobile. I had my heart set on a red BMW; I even dreamed about cruising the highways in it. But when I arrived at the dealership, I moved from my dreamworld to reality: I would have to drive a hard bargain before driving "my" car. The obstacle between me and my car was the surly salesperson who approached me. For a moment I considered reacting like a patient in clinical therapy, disclosing the content of my dreams (and my finances). But I quickly decided that he would use this information against me, and I was determined that he would never peer into my soul or my bankbook! So I spent the first 10 minutes informing him that I had little desire and little money to purchase a BMW. As he began waking away from me, desperation overtook me and I blurted out an offer well below the sticker price. He obviously caught the scent of fresh meat and quickly responded that he couldn't sell the car for my price. After telling me how much demand there was for *my* red BMW, he made me a counteroffer, indicating that this was "as low as he could go." I felt like a firehouse during a three-alarm fire—bells began going off in my head. I didn't believe a word he said. I was certain that no one else had an interest in the car of my dreams and that he could meet my price. Our interaction ended abruptly, and I left the lot. Two days later a red BMW passed me as I chugged down the highway in my old wreck!

The point in this example is not to gain sympathy but to illustrate why communication does not always resolve conflicts. In my unfortunate experience, I viewed information as a weapon. If my adversary had information about me, he would use it against me. Therefore, I was motivated to withhold my true desires and intentions. Likewise, I was not disposed to trust the information I received from my adversary. I figured that he felt I would use accurate information about his situation against him, and that therefore he would not be truthful. Hence, conflict can lead us to withhold information or supply inaccurate information. Being a party to conflict also invites us to distrust information we receive from our adversary. Therefore, even when parties to a conflict are required to communicate, they are apt to offer misleading information and to be distrustful of information they receive.

Despite these pitfalls, accurate communication is necessary to resolve misunderstandings and build relationships, research has concentrated on how to develop effective communication in conflicts. Several points have been made. First, parties to a conflict must often be strongly encouraged or forced to communicate. Second, communication must be ongoing, so that each party has the opportunity to test the truth of the other's message (Grzelak, 1988). Third, the most effective communication includes information about the group's desires and planned behaviors, the behaviors it would like to see the other group take, and how it will respond to transgressions (Caldwell, 1969).

Clearly effective communication must be developed by considering the impact on the recipient. In adopting this perspective, we enter the realm of *face saving* (Goffman, 1967). An individual's face or a group's face is a public image. For most individuals and groups, independence and strength are components of that image. As we have seen, a group's image is critical to its pride and even its survival. Therefore, a group will react swiftly and negatively in any situation that may make it lose face. Demands that a group behave in a certain way are quick to arouse resistance, even if the group would like to comply. Following the command of another implies weakness (Wilson, 1992). Even suggesting a meeting with an opponent may be viewed as a sign of weakness and result in a loss of face (Pruitt, 1971). Therefore, communication in a conflict must save face for both parties if it is to lead to a successful resolution.

The interactions of the United States government with the various Indian nations clearly illustrate lack of sensitivity to face. For example, after the Battle of the Washita in November 1868, General Sheridan ordered the Kiowa, Commanche, and Cheyenne to surrender or face extinction. Chief Satanta of the Kiowa agreed to meet with General Custer to discuss a peaceful settlement. However, when the two met, Custer refused to hear Satanta's suggestions, ordering him instead to take his people to Fort Cobb. The command was accompanied by a threat to hang Satanta if he did not comply. Although Satanta kept his temper, he replied, "It don't alter my opinion a particle if you take me by the hand now, or take and hang me. My opinion will be just the same. What you have told me today has opened my eyes" (Brown, 1971, p. 198). Although the Kiowa came to Fort Cobb, their resentment burned under the surface, and the peace was short-lived. The Kiowa felt humiliated by Custer's treatment and were determined to resist, even though they knew that resistance was likely to lead to their ultimate destruction. In their advice to mediators, Pruitt and Johnson (1970) suggest that face-saving communication involves acknowledging the power and importance of each party and giving each party an opportunity to make concessions in a way that suggests they were the result of free will and desire rather than force or threats.

Students of communication also point out the differences between threats and promises in communication (Putnam & Holmer, 1992). A *threat* draws clear distinctions between groups, implies differences, and suggests that compliance is a sign of weakness. For example, Custer's threat that he would hang Satanta unless he surrendered his people created a situation in which compliance by the chief could be interpreted only as an indication of personal fear. A *promise* is less disruptive and less likely to create concern over saving face. A different atmosphere in the negotiations might have prevailed if Custer had told Satanta that the government would feed and clothe his people if they surrendered. In this case, Satanta's agreement would have demonstrated concern for his people rather than weakness and fear.

The critical point is that the structure of messages can determine the long-term success of efforts to resolve conflict. Although threats and commands may result in compliance, the atmosphere will be poisoned with hatred and resentment, creating the powder keg described earlier. Communication that allows both parties to save face can help lay a foundation for future cooperation.

It may seem that these suggestions about how to structure a communication are vague and general. I plead guilty to this charge, but my guilt is intentional. As tempting as it is to write a "how to" recipe for communication, we must remember that in the case of ethnic conflict we are dealing with different cultures. Cultures often have very different styles of communicating (Wiseman & Koester, 1993). For example, Anglo-Americans prefer a direct, open style. Almost from birth, we (especially men) are instructed to take a stand on issues and express disagreements openly. However, in many collective cultures, such as Japan, the preferred manner of communication is indirect. Disagreement is conveyed by avoidance. Harmony is of utmost importance, and therefore one says what the other wants to hear (Hofstede, 1991). It would be impolite for me to tell you that your behavior bothers me. Instead, when you act offensively, I will avoid you and simply expect you to "get the message." Similarly, if I do not like your proposal, I will avoid discussing it rather than tell you directly that I disagree (Nakanishi & Johnson, 1993). Therefore, there is no single formula for effective communication—the clear transmission of information requires sensitivity to a culture's style of communication.

In most cultures, however, parties to a conflict tend to reduce or cease communicating. In these cases, the participants need to be encouraged to engage in discourse *and* taught how to communicate effectively. Training should involve teaching how to frame messages to invite (rather than demand) cooperation, to let both parties maintain a positive self-image rather than risk losing face, and to help develop an understanding of why others may not readily trust one's message even when its intent is noble. Finally, these programs must develop an understanding of the communication styles of people in different cultures, so we can frame our own messages for better understanding and receive the intended messages from others. Toward these ends, several investigators have developed cultural training programs and other exercises to develop effective communication between ethnic groups (Landis & Brislin, 1983; Landis & Bhagat, 1996).

Revisiting Contact: The Importance of Interaction

In Chapter 6, I discussed the importance of contact for personal acceptance of other ethnic groups. That prescription also applies to groups: equal-status contacts promote communication between groups and often reduce conflict and fear. Let's dig a bit deeper into this issue at the group level.

HELPING OR COOPERATION.   One of my favorite countries in all the world was the Yugoslavia that existed before 1990. It had a beautiful coastline, Norwegian-like fjords, medieval towns, and fabulous mountains. My first experience with the people of this beautiful land had an unexpected twist, though. As a college student in the 1960s, I spent a summer backpacking across Europe to "find myself." Yugoslavia held a special allure for me. A certain excitement was aroused by venturing into a then-communist country. Also, a short time before my visit, the country had been devastated by an earthquake and the United States had helped rebuild many areas; as a result, I expected that the Yugoslavs would greet me with open arms. But when I entered a small village in southern Yugoslavia, the greeting was anything but warm. The children scurried into their homes, and the adults gave me cold, sullen stares that seemed to say, "Get out." I was not going to stay where I wasn't wanted, so I quickened my pace and headed out of the village. But as luck would have it, in the middle of the town I stepped into a hole and twisted my ankle.

As a small crowd gathered around me, I half expected them to hack me to pieces. But I was gently carried into a home, my ankle was wrapped, and I was told I should stay there until it healed. I was thoroughly confused, because this kindness was so different from the unfriendly welcome I had received shortly before. During my convalescence, I had several long conversations with my host, Igor. I asked him why people had reacted in such a distant way when I arrived. Igor told me that his village had been severely damaged by the earthquake and that the Americans had come quickly to its aid. In the beginning, the villagers were grateful, but their joy quickly faded when the rebuilding began. "The Americans came in and cleared the streets with their bulldozers, rebuilt the houses, and repaired our utility system. They did everything on their own. When we offered to work with them, they told us to stay back; they could handle this on their own. They ignored our suggestions and even refused our gifts of food. We were strangers in our own home, and we felt rather worthless. I guess this gave us a bad feeling about ourselves and about Americans." I have reflected on this incident several times over the years. My countrymen had tried to help, but despite their best intentions they had created ill will. Being the recipient of help had left the villagers feeling powerless and incompetent.

This experience led me to conduct a study that began with two groups in competition with each other (Worchel, 1984). After the competitive interaction, one of the groups was given an opportunity to work for an extra incentive. The task was clearly difficult, and success was unlikely if the group worked alone. In some cases, the group that had been the opponent offered to help by working on part of the task. Their stated message was, "We'll work on the first half of the problem so you can get your reward." In a second condition, the previous opponent offered to combine efforts with the chosen group if both could share the reward: "We'll work with you on the task so we can share the reward." The chosen group was more likely to reject the offer of aid in the first instance, and to resent the other group for making the offer. This seemed quite odd, because the offer was well intended and the group need not share the reward. But the members reported that the offer of aid suggested that they could not do the job on their own, and even if they succeeded they would feel an obligation to "return the favor." The second type of offer was viewed as indicating that neither party could complete the task on its own. This offer of mutual cooperation also openly stated that the group would receive something for its efforts, eliminating the uncertainty about the obligation of the recipient.

If we analyze helping situations, we can see why charity does not necessarily lead to intergroup harmony. Helpful interactions establish clear group boundaries between the recipient and the donor, and differences in power and competence are implied. The donor is powerful and competent; the recipient is powerless and incompetent. The recipient's self-esteem and self-confidence are damaged (Fisher & Nadler, 1974). In addition, the recipient feels obligated to "return the favor." As we know from personal experience, feeling obligated to another is often an uncomfortable position to be in. Tension remains until we balance the scales and restore equity. These negative reactions are especially likely to occur when helping goes beyond what is absolutely required, when aid is unsolicited, and when there is no immediate opportunity for reciprocation (Schwartz, 1977). I am not suggesting that help should always be withheld or that a recipient will always resent a donor. However, we must understand that help may not reduce tension. By its very nature, help involves contact between parties with unequal power.

A more successful alternative to helping may be cooperation toward a superordinate goal, the second condition in my study (Worchel 1984). Cooperation requires a combination of efforts to achieve a goal desired by each party; input from each group is critical. Cooperation does not burden either party with an obligation to reciprocate. Instead, the success that results often motivates the two parties to continue cooperating.

It is not difficult to find areas where groups can cooperate without sacrificing their independence or incurring an obligation to reciprocate. For example, there have recently been international efforts to draft global laws that crack down on child prostitution, abduction, and slavery. The initiative came from Thailand and other Asian nations alarmed by the increasing child prostitution in their countries. The problem was international because many of the clients who supported the industry came from western nations and Japan; in some countries travel agents organized sex tours focused on child prostitutes. Not only did child prostitution go against the moral grain of most nations, but it threatened to spread AIDS and other sexually transmitted diseases throughout the world. Therefore, all nations stood to benefit from the elimination of child prostitution. In 1993, nations around the world organized to draft laws and policies to deal with the problem. This cooperative effort not only brought the problem to world attention and served to stem its growth, but also led to further international action—to control the spread of AIDS and to develop laws

Just as leaders can excite ethnic hatred, so too can they take their follow-ers down the road of peace. Dr. Martin Luther King, Jr., is an example of a leader whose message of vision and hope changed the course of ethnic relations. (AP/Wide World Photos)

regulating child labor. A similar example can be seen in international efforts to re-duce global pollution. Both cases allowed people from different ethnic and national groups to come together to find solutions to a common problem. The individuals in-volved were not only government officials and political leaders. Rather, people from a variety of professions and ethnic groups participated in the meetings. Although the large conventions were the most publicized, dozens of ongoing committees were set up. There was no threat to the identity or sovereignty of any group, and as all worked together, each group learned about the others.

There are, then, nearly limitless possibilities for developing cooperative interactions between members of different ethnic groups either within nations or internationally. Common problems in areas such as education, health, and the environment can be the focal point of cooperative efforts. Interactions designed to deal with these issues can take place at all levels, from small community meetings to large national and international conventions. As these interactions open up new perspectives on the problem at hand, they will offer greater understanding of the ethnic groups involved and create new channels for communication between groups. The independence and value of each group can be retained within a climate that recognizes the interdependence of goals and outcomes. The model for intergroup cooperation already exists; we must simply expand and build on it.

CONTACT BETWEEN WHOM?   I have suggested that contact at the individual level can reduce an individual's prejudice and lead to greater acceptance of an outgroup. In the case of individuals such contact is easy to conceive and arrange. But what does it mean to suggest equal-status contact between groups? If we are dealing with small groups—as in the study of the boys' camp by Sherif and his colleagues, contact between all group members is feasible. But if we are dealing with large ethnic groups, it is difficult to create a forum that results in contact between many members. Laws can be changed to integrate neighborhoods, schools, and job sites, but such sweeping changes are generally laboriously slow and require that a large segment of the society desire greater understanding and contact.

Therefore, we cannot rely only on these large-scale events to develop greater interethnic harmony. It is important to create smaller approaches, in more limited domains and involving a more limited number of people, to set the stage for the broader efforts. Given these restraints, we can ask what type of approach will be most useful. Fortunately, several social scientists (Burton, 1969; Doob & Foltz, 1973; Kelman & Cohen, 1986) have developed a method designed to meet these objectives. The *problem-solving workshop* has proved effective for dealing with interethnic conflicts in a variety of conflicts: Greeks and Turks in Cyprus, Protestants and Catholics in Northern Ireland, Jews and Palestinians in Israel. There are slight differences between the various workshops, but the principles are basically the same.

The workshops involve having members of the groups in conflict meet in an isolated setting under the guidance of a social scientist. The participants are chosen on the basis of their positions in their respective groups. Formally recognized leaders, such as people holding high political office, are rarely included. These people have often taken public positions on the issues and are concerned with being reelected or reappointed. Therefore, their attitudes may be entrenched and open dialogue may be difficult to achieve. Instead, people who have access to these leaders are asked to be participants. These include business and religious leaders, newspaper correspondents and television newscasters, and educators. These people are influential, but compared with politicians they are less carefully scrutinized and are not expected to represent official positions or the views of specific groups.

The participants generally begin by meeting with their own group members and organizers in a preworkshop meeting. At this meeting the purpose and structure of the workshop are explained to the participants, who have a chance to become acquainted with their fellow group members outside the presence of their traditional adversaries. The participants are able to present their views of the conflict without having to worry about igniting a debate with the other group. Participants are told that the purpose of the workshop is to have members of different groups work on developing solutions to problems that are of interest and concern to both sides. Such problems may involve developing an economic plan for the region, devising a school curriculum that can teach children about both ethnic groups, or dealing with an environmental hazard (such as pollution of a river) that affects both groups.

After these preworkshops, the two groups are brought together to select a specific problem and come up with solutions. The participants are instructed to take an analytical perspective rather than advocate a particular position. There are few formal rules, and the combined group can determine how it wants to proceed. The third party (the social scientist) serves as a group facilitator, helping focus the discussion and suggesting new interpretations or implications of the proposals. The facilitator may also interject comments about the patterns of communication. For example, he or she may point out that certain people in the group are being overlooked or have failed to express an opinion.

The workshop generally lasts several days. As the participants struggle to develop creative solutions, they also deal with their views of the other group. Kelman (1993) points out that in one workshop, the Israeli participants convinced themselves that the Palestinian participants were "non-PLO" and the Palestinians tried to convince themselves that the Israelis were "non-Zionists." However, as the workshop progressed the Palestinians made it clear they identified closely with the PLO, and the Israelis revealed they were dedicated Zionists. "Thus, the Israelis had to confront the fact that the Palestinians whom they had come to trust, at least to the extent of accepting the sincerity of their commitment to peace, were PLO loyalists; and the Palestinians had to confront the fact that the Israelis whom they had come to trust were loyal Zionists" (p. 252).

The stated aim of the workshop is to have the participants develop solutions to common problems. But because of their position within their respective groups, there is a strong likelihood that the participants will be able to influence policy makers to consider these plans. In addition, the workshops allow members of each group to learn about the other group, break down stereotypes, and develop trust. These lessons may not be directly reflected in the policies advocated by the groups, but they may find indirect outlets when the members return to their respective groups. The participants may discuss their new views with others and serve as role models of more openness toward the other group. A newscaster may tone down the intensity of a story attacking the other group; an educator may not adopt a textbook that vilifies the other group; a businessperson may expand trade with members of the other ethnic group. Kelman suggests that these indirect effects do occur and that they may be the most important achievement of the workshops.

Although the workshop approach has been used as an intervention when ethnic groups are in conflict, it is interesting to contemplate using the technique as a pro-phylactic for groups not currently experiencing conflict. Participants in workshops under these conditions would have less resistance and suspicion to overcome. They might be more willing to cooperate with members of the other ethnic group and might carry messages back to their own group that could prevent ethnic conflict. Unfortunately, the prevention of conflict and violence is more difficult to measure and less dramatic; our concern with intergroup relations seems to be piqued by crises. The important point of this discussion is that intergroup contact may reduce (or pre-vent) conflict between ethnic groups while still preserving the identity of the groups.

Multiculturalism: Intergroup Harmony between Independent Groups

The basis for increasing ethnic harmony by ensuring the secure identity of various groups is found in theory and laboratory research, often involving relationships be-tween individuals. But we do not have to rely on laboratory studies alone to confirm the wisdom of this approach. Countries that have pursued a *multicultural* political and social system have adopted this premise as well. New Zealand, Canada, Switzerland, and Indonesia have implemented multicultural policies to deal with their ethnically diverse populations. Recognizing that there is value in diversity, they have sought to preserve it. Ethnic groups maintain their distinct identities, practice their own customs, speak their own languages, and in some cases control their own territory. Schoolchildren are taught about all the ethnic groups of their land. They are encouraged to learn all the languages, and the entire country often celebrates the holidays of each ethnic group.

New Zealand is an especially interesting example of this approach because its government has embarked on a renewed effort to establish multiculturalism. The settlement of New Zealand by white settlers during the early 1800s was accompa-nied by violent confrontations with the indigenous Maori people. The fighting abated only after the signing of the Treaty of Waitangi in 1840, which granted the Maori sovereignty over certain territory and matters relating to tribal issues. The in-tent was to recognize the Maori as a sovereign people in New Zealand. But the en-suing years were characterized by increasing dominance by whites (the Pakeha), who eroded the Maori's sovereignty, appropriated their lands, and nearly destroyed their culture. In the last 30 years, however, the climate has begun to change, as the Maori have mounted an effective campaign to demand their rights granted by the Treaty. The protest had a violent beginning—each side searched for advantage and threatened the legitimacy of the other. The Pakeha feared that "giving in" to any of the Maori's demands would spell doom for their own position in New Zealand. But slowly—very slowly at times—each side diminished its threats. A Department of Maori Affairs was set up to administer claims. Land guaranteed to the Maori by treaty but subsequently taken over by the Pakeha was returned to its rightful own-ers. The Maori were given a greater voice in government, including reserved seats in Parliament. As each step was undertaken, each party held its collective breath, waiting for the other to exploit the new advantage.

But the expected exploitation never came. Both Maori and Pakeha began to realize that they had a common interest in seeing New Zealand economically and socially sound. As the threatening rhetoric dimmed, appreciation for each other's culture began to take hold. Public schools offered courses in Maori culture and language. Public holidays celebrated events important to both Pakeha and Maori. The rebirth of the Maori culture gave new vitality to the country, and an attitude of multiculturalism which respected the coexistence of multiple cultures dominated all aspects of daily life. The last 30 years have not been entirely smooth or without setbacks and conflict, and the final chapter has not been written. But the tone of ethnic relations has been transformed from distrust, hatred, and threat to acceptance, interest, and curiosity.

Change in attitudes and policy has not brought full equality to all of New Zealand's people. The Maori are overrepresented in the lower socioeconomic classes. The average Maori worker earns only 78 percent of what a non-Maori worker earns. Although they constitute 12 percent of the population, the Maori make up 45 percent of the male and 67 percent of the female prison population. Their average life expectancy is 10 years less than that of non-Maori (Nairn & McCreanor, 1990). Some Maori children struggle with determining their identity: are they New Zealanders or Maori? When the interests of the country conflict with the interests of the ethnic group, which should predominate? The problems are especially acute for individuals of mixed ethnicity. And we must realize that New Zealand is a rather isolated nation with two major ethnic groups. Could a policy of multiculturalism work in a country with four or five large ethnic groups, or a country located next to other nations with large concentrations of some of the same ethnic groups?

On the whole, maintaining separate ethnic group identities while promoting cooperation between groups must be given mixed marks as a strategy for achieving ethnic harmony and understanding. Rigid group identities always have the potential to provoke conflict and discrimination. Ethnic pride may give way to interethnic conflict, especially during periods of turmoil, uncertainty, and scarcity.

One Big Family: Creating a Common Group Identity

Critics of the multicultural approach scoff at its basic foundation and suggest it is doomed to failure. Understanding and harmony between people cannot be achieved in an environment of high walls and secure identities of separate groups. The boundaries between groups become a lightning rod for intergroup conflict. Social identity theory (Tajfel, 1970) has made a strong case that the human tendency is to identify with distinct groups *and* to enhance this personal identity by discriminating against out-groups. According to this theory, the more we accentuate the differences between groups, the more fuel we add to the fire of ethnic conflict and discrimination.

Good fences may make good neighbors in poetry, but in the actual social landscape, fences between groups define the sides in a conflict and separate them.

If achieving ethnic understanding and compassion does not rest on building fences, can it be found in reducing or eliminating distinctions between groups? Several social psychologists have argued that conflict between groups can be reduced by diminishing the salience of group boundaries. The ultimate aim is to recategorize our social environment, viewing people as members of one common group rather than several separate groups (Turner, 1987; Gaertner, Mann, Murrell, and Dovidio, 1989; Worchel, 1986). With ethnic groups, this approach involves inducing people to ignore or greatly minimize their ethnic distinctions, embracing a common group identity instead.

As I pointed out earlier (Chapter 3), groups exist largely in our minds. We organize our world by putting people into groups, and these categories guide our subsequent behavior and perceptions. Once we place people in separate groups, we treat them differently, depending on that placement. Although people can fit into many groups or categories at one time, each situation determines which category is salient. We strive for simplicity, and therefore we react to others on the basis of which category is salient at the moment. We hate ambiguity.

An interesting example of the lengths to which we go to achieve clear definition of categories is found in an interview between Marvin Kalb and Jesse Jackson on *Meet the Press* in 1984, when Jackson was running for the presidency.

> KALB: The question is . . . are you a black man who happens to be an American running for the presidency, or are you an American who happens to be a black man running for the presidency?
>
> JACKSON: Well, I'm both an American and a black at one and the same time. I'm both of these.
>
> KALB: What I'm trying to get at is something that addresses a question no one seems able to grasp and that is: Are your priorities deep inside yourself, to the degree that anyone can look inside himself, those of a black man who happens to be an American, or the reverse?
>
> JACKSON: Well I was born black in America. I was not born American in black! You're asking a funny kind of *Catch-22* question. My interests are *national* interests. (Jones & Morris, 1993)

The point is that when we interact with people, only a few categories are salient—often, only one category is salient. We generally view people as belonging *either* to an ethnic group or to a larger group. (Marvin Kalb, for instance, was attempting to determine whether to classify Jesse Jackson as a black or as an American.) According to social identity theory, if we perceive people as members of our own category, we will respond positively to them. However, if we perceive them as members of another category, we will avoid, dislike, and discriminate against them. For example, I will respond positively to my neighbors to the extent that I perceive them as Americans. I will be less kind to them when their ethnic identity as, say, Chinese is salient.

On this approach, ethnic conflict can be reduced to the extent that individuals categorize themselves and others as belonging to the same group. To promote intergroup harmony, ethnic identity must be overlooked or made less salient. Interestingly, the methods used to reduce the salience of ethnic identity and create common categories are similar to those used in the multicultural approach. However, the aims and the emphasis are very different.

CONTACT REVISITED.   Equal-status contact in the service of reaching a common goal is a linchpin of both the multicultural approach and the recategorization approach. The multicultural approach prescribes contact only when the separate identities of the groups involved can be maintained, and the contact serves as a forum for learning about the other groups and finding value in their unique perspectives. However, the recategorization approach argues that contact will be effective only if it breaks down identification with the old groups and creates identification with the new common group. Efforts in this case should be aimed at reducing the salience of the previous groups.

Although physical differences are the most visible way to distinguish between groups, they are not the only dimension that should concern us. Differences in language, customs, economic condition, or status may work against creating a common category. When such differences exist, intervention may be necessary to reduce them or make them less salient. In one study I undertook with a colleague (Norvell & Worchel, 1981), two groups began by competing against each other on a series of tasks. In half the conditions, one group was designated the winner and the other the loser. In the remaining conditions, no determination of winning or losing was made. The groups were then brought together to work on a common task. By itself, the distinction between winner and loser had categorized the groups and worked against recategorizing them as a single group. Cooperation led to greater attraction between the two groups when no previous winner-loser distinction had been made. To determine whether we could counter the effect of the previous categories, we then included an additional intervention. In some cases, one of the groups was given an advantage (additional information) that could help the combined group achieve its goal. Possessing this additional information raised the status of the group. As Figure 7.1 shows, when no distinction had been made between winner and loser, giving one group additional information led to greater dislike of this group in the cooperative setting. This additional information distinguished between the two groups, which had previously been equal. However, when a winner and loser had been identified, giving the losing group additional information (higher status) before cooperation increased the attraction for that group. In this case, the status associated with possessing the information "erased" the previous status and facilitated recategorization. Interestingly, subjects viewed giving one group additional information as being unfair in both cases. Nevertheless, the additional information and the resulting balanced status led to increased attraction in the case when a previous loser had been distinguished.

In this light, contact between group members is important to the extent that it reduces the salience of original distinctions between in-group and out-group and be-

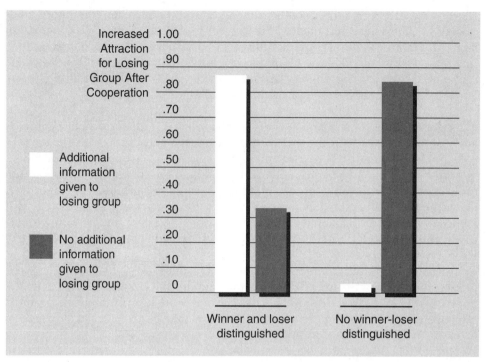

FIGURE 7.1   Attraction for Out-group as a Result of Distinguishing Winner and Loser and Giving the Losing Group an Informational Advantage

gins to build a new in-group that encompasses previously separate groups (Gaertner et al., 1993). Extensive research has identified many of the conditions under which contact is most likely to lead to recategorization and, consequently, to reduce intergroup hostility (Hewstone & Brown, 1986). First, reduction of hostility generally requires a number of contacts over an extended period of time. It takes some time to eliminate old distinctions and form a common group identity. Second, contact that results in success rather than failure is more likely to enhance intergroup attraction. Failure often leads to scapegoating—members of one group blame the other group for the failure. Third, contact that highlights group differences and supports stereotypes will not reduce intergroup hostility. For example, a student recently told me that he was uncomfortable around Asian students. He felt that he had little in common with them, "But I've tried to have discussions with them." As it turned out, he had tried to engage a group of Asian students in a conversation about his favorite topics: American football and breeding horses. Since the Asian students had little to say, the interaction was uncomfortable for all parties. The student left the contact convinced that his first impression was correct: he was uncomfortable with Asians and had little in common with them. Had the student chosen to discuss any of a host of other subjects, he might have found that he had a great deal in common with these Asian students. Contact, then, can emphasize group differences, or it can create an impression that two groups are actually members of the same larger group. Only the latter type of contact can reduce hostility.

THE MELTING POT: EMPHASIZING A COMMON GROUP IDENTITY.

The recategorization approach has been adopted by some nations. The United States, for instance, has struggled for over two centuries to institute recategorization as a means of creating ethnic harmony. The United States is an interesting example because most of its ethnic groups are rather recent interlopers with shallow roots in its soil. The early history of the United States involved a program of deliberate and accidental genocide aimed at ridding the land of its indigenous people. The Native Americans were starved and slaughtered, and the remnants were carefully swept up and deposited on isolated reservations. As the land was being cleansed of its native inhabitants, immigrants from over the world rushed in. The immigrants came in waves from England, Scotland, Germany, Ireland, Southern and Eastern Europe, Mexico, China, India, and more recently Vietnam and Cambodia. Many came of their own free will, eager to settle in a new country. Others were dragged here in chains, many from Africa and the West Indies.

The United States became a country of ethnic visitors with no enduring claim to territory and no long lineage giving them a right to claim themselves "Americans." The framers of the U.S. Constitution set about to create a country in which people were free (in theory) to practice the religion of their choice. But no such freedom was granted for people to engage in the cultural practices of their choice. In fact, a new ethnic group, "American," was gradually created. The stirring words of the Declaration of Independence, "All men are created equal," implied that America would be a society blind to an individual's ethnicity. In fact, it was expected that those who wished to reside in the house would leave their ethnic identity at the doorway and become American. "American" was viewed as both a nationality and an emerging ethnic group. Harmony between people would be achieved by ignoring their differences and having everyone become a member of the same group. Because people would speak the same language, obey the same laws, follow the same customs, and identify with the same group, there would be no need to take steps to reduce ethnic conflict. The United States would be the melting pot that blended previous ethnic identities and loyalties.

In theory, this approach appears to be the ideal method for solving the problem of ethnic hostility and discrimination. But as we know, things have not worked out as planned. Ethnic prejudice and hostility have always been alive and well within the melting pot. The Irish, the Poles, the Italians, the Jews, the Asians, the Africans, the West Indians, the Mexicans, the Puerto Ricans, and the Arabs have all felt the cruel lash of prejudice and ethnic hatred. Indeed, the cynics among us may describe the American brand of equality this way: "In America, equal opportunity means that every group has a chance to be the target of discrimination." What went wrong with this grand experiment?

One problem was that some people did not want to relinquish their ethnic identity and others were not allowed to shed it. As we discussed in Chapter 1, ethnic identity was at the core of their self-image. Asking people to deny or subjugate their ethnic identity was like asking them to deny their existence. Some people clung to their ethnic identities and their customs, and this was viewed by others as a sign of disloyalty to their new homeland, sparking anger and even hatred. In other cases people were not allowed to shed their ethnic identity. Skin color, the shape of the head, or the slant of the eyes branded them as being of another ethnic group. They were non-American, and their assurances that they were loyal to their new country and their new ethnic group were viewed as lies. Being "non-American" was bad enough, but lying about it was even more treacherous! Hatred toward members of these other ethnic groups rose to its highest level at times of stress, including economic and political hardship and war. Ethnic identity cannot always be "taken off" like an old coat and discarded. While justice might be blind, people are not. They could see the differences between ethnic groups, and these differences led to hatred.

But this was not the only issue that roiled the melting pot. In theory, the contents of the melting pot—the new combined group—reflect the ingredients of the stew. As new ingredients are added, the flavor changes. But this was not what happened in the United States, nor does it happen in many other groups that add new members. Instead of having all groups contribute to the structure of the society, minority ethnic groups were told that they must *assimilate* into the dominant culture (Sidanius, 1993). They were forced to relinquish their identity, language, and custom and adopt those of the majority. Thus not all members of the national group were equal. Some established rules and group boundaries, while others were required to accept and assimilate.

Therefore, despite the claim that all people were equal members of the same group, this goal has proved elusive. Distinctions are made within the group. Individuals cling to characteristics that give them a distinct identity. Group members view differences within their group with alarm and concern. Being part of the same group means appearing, talking, acting, and believing the same way. And human desires rebel against homogeneity. Certainly there are times when differences can be and are overlooked. But at other times, differences become salient, and prejudice and hostility result.

Finally, lurking in the background is the nagging question about the value of differences. The ocean is beautiful, but when you're surrounded by miles of calm water, it can become boring and monotonous. So it is with our social landscape. If we all thought the same, behaved the same, and were physically homogeneous, we would surely all die of boredom. As Deutsch (1973) points out, differences and conflict light the fires of creativity and problem solving (see Chapter 9). It is the differences between members of the human species that allow us to adapt to a changing environment. A social policy that strives to ignore differences between people will doom them to extinction. To ignore or mute these differences not only denies some people their unique identity but prevents us from learning potentially lifesaving lessons. We may, therefore, question the wisdom of a policy that seeks to overlook differences between ethnic groups, especially with regard to customs, in an effort to create a common group with a rigid system of universal norms.

Which Path to Take? Fitting the Solution to the Situation

All this seems to paint a rather discouraging picture for promoting ethnic harmony at the group level. So far I've discussed approaches, both with impressive theoretical foundations and backed up by research. However, both have imperfections, and neither has proved completely satisfactory in practice. On second glance, however, we have the classic question: Is our glass half full or half empty? If we look on the bright side, we find we have two viable approaches to slowing the hemorrhaging of ethnic conflict. Each can boast some degree of success.

On one hand, the experiences of New Zealand, Switzerland, and Canada demonstrate that multiculturalism can work. Each of these countries faced a potentially explosive situation involving several ethnic groups with different customs, languages, and aspirations. Recognition of these groups and efforts to promote widespread learning about them resulted in considerable cooperation. In fact, the mosaic of these groups has shaped the personality of these nations and enriched them all. There have been violent ethnic conflicts, and in each country certain ethnic groups struggle with low status and difficult economic conditions, but each nation can point to progress and extended periods of peace and harmony.

A similar case can be made for recategorization—the melting pot illustrated by the United States. The United States is composed of a multitude of ethnic groups. People from these various ethnic groups live side by side, interacting with considerable frequency. Although prejudice and discrimination exist, we can still marvel at the fact that our melting pot only simmers with conflict rather than constantly boiling over with violence.

There is always a temptation to ask which approach is best. The evidence alone does not give us a basis for choosing a winner, but an observation may shed light on the issue. The cases where multiculturalism has been most effective share some commonalities. Canada, Indonesia, Switzerland, and New Zealand, for example, all have a relatively small number of ethnic groups. New Zealand consists largely of the Maori people, the Pakeha (mostly British and Dutch), and Pacific Islanders. Switzerland is largely composed of German, Italian, and French people. A second common feature is that the ethnic groups generally occupy rather separate areas. The French in Canada reside largely in Quebec and New Brunswick; the Native Americans (First Nations) are mostly found in British Columbia and the western provinces. In Indonesia, whole islands are largely the domain of a single ethnic group. These conditions may well promote an approach that gives the various groups separate recognition and seeks a cooperative federation. Indeed, under these conditions, ethnic groups may be able to develop enough cohesiveness to mount an effective campaign to preserve their unique identities.

On the other hand, the United States has a large number of ethnic groups, generally spread throughout the nation. Although the various groups may live in enclaves in some cities and may be more numerous in some regions than in others, there are few regions that consist predominantly of a single ethnic group. This physical arrangement works against creating a cohesive ethnic group that would be able to demand an independent identity. The dispersal of individuals across the landscape also facilitates the development of a blanket common identity that cuts across subgroups. Therefore, the recategorization approach may be best suited to situations involving several ethnic groups that are interwoven throughout an area.

Before leaving this issue, let's consider a "middle ground"—a hybrid of these two approaches. John Berry (1991) suggests that there are actually four options for constructing a group. In addition to multiculturalism and the melting pot, groups may adopt integration (identifying with both subgroup and superordinate group) or marginalization (weak identification with both subgroup and superordinate group). The marginalization model suggests a rather bleak picture of isolated souls plodding through life guided only by selfish interests. This alternative is unappealing even in individualistic cultures, so we will reject it. However, the integration approach has a certain appeal. Research has shown that individuals who are able to identify with both a subgroup and a larger superordinate group become less concerned with their personal outcomes and value justice systems that are perceived as fair and respectful of the larger superordinate group (Huo, Smith, Tyler, & Lind, 1996). These investigators argue that a condition of dual loyalty allows authorities to "worry less about providing desired outcomes to group members and to concentrate on achieving the greater good and maintaining social stability" (p. 44).

At first glance the integration model seems to be the perfect way to resolve ethnic conflicts. In fact, in a speech in August 1997, President Clinton stated that his goal was to develop an America that encouraged multiculturalism while preserving the overarching identity of "every citizen as an American." Although we may set this model up as a goal, we should not ignore the lessons of decades of research on human identity—that we are rather myopic in our identification with groups, focusing on specific categories as situations bring them to prominence. Multiple identifications may reside comfortably in your psyche until something or someone disturbs their roost and the different personas come into conflict, demanding that you choose one or risk being rejected by both. We need only look back a few years to a time when Serb, Croat, and Muslim lived in peace in Bosnia, each individual accepting a subgroup (ethnic) and superordinate group (country) identity.

Although true integration may be difficult to achieve, we need not send the model to the scrap heap. Rather, we should work to create superordinate groups, recognizing that identification with a subgroup may be particularly strong at times and teaching people ways to identify with a subgroup that do not require destructive discrimination against members of other subgroups. This is obviously a tall order for any society, but we can ask our leaders to promote movement in this direction.

The Importance of Leaders

Nature is fickle. By stamping each of us with the identity of different ethnic groups, nature confronts us with an eternal choice: to work for the superiority of our ethnic group or to work for intergroup cooperation and understanding. As a result, we stand suspended between two competing motivations, waiting for the slightest breeze to push us in one direction or the other. Forces outside the group's control—economic conditions, natural disasters, or changing situations in neighboring regions—can tilt the balance toward ethnic harmony or away from it. But there is also a force within our own groups that can move us toward ethnic cooperation and acceptance or toward ethnic competition, hostility, and destruction. That force is the leaders of our groups.

I have cited Switzerland as an example of multiculturalism that promotes harmony and understanding. German, Italian, and French Swiss have their own territories, their own representation in parliament, and the right to speak their own language and engage in their own cultural practices. Each group is encouraged to learn about the others, and cooperation between the groups is generally high.

Before 1990, I might have used Yugoslavia as another example of cooperation under multicultural policies. Its constitution of 1946 recognized five ethnic groups: Serbs, Croats, Slovenes, Macedonians, and Montenegrins. The Muslims in the Bosnia region were considered a separate group, but without national identity. An ethnic Croat, Tito, ruled the country with an iron hand, but giving the various ethnic groups some degree of representation. Late in his rule, Tito relaxed his hold, giving more freedom and autonomy to ethnic groups. By the time of his death, a collective presidency was ruling the country. A representative from each region was elected every fifth year to serve as president of the assembly. The vice presidency of the country rotated each year; as a result, each region had its representative serve as vice president every fifth year. When Tito died in 1980, the system of rotating members was elevated to include the presidency. Despite old animosities dating back to World War II and earlier, Yugoslavia enjoyed relative ethnic harmony for over 45 years.

After 1980, the Yugoslavian government became more decentralized, with each ethnic group gaining increasing autonomy. But trouble waited in the wings. Economic problems began to mount, and in 1983 Premier Markovic instituted measures that taxed the wealthy Croats and Serbs more heavily than people in the poor regions. Economic conditions worsened, and ethnic groups began to take matters into their own hands. Two routes were open to them: cooperation to combat a common problem or ethnocentrism and ethnic conflict. In Serbia, the populist Slobodon Milosevic rose to power. He saw an opportunity in the chaos and began rallying Serbs with strong ethnocentric rhetoric. He preached the right of Serbs to control their destiny and urged them to celebrate their ethnicity. He first targeted the

Albanian minority in southern Serbia, branding them traitors and initiating efforts to remove them from the region. Milosevic's favorite slogan was "Strong Serbia, strong Yugoslavia," and he based his rise to power on ethnic hatred. Milosevic became a folk hero, and other ethnic groups in Yugoslavia began to fear him. By 1990 the assembly ruling Yugoslavia was beginning to crumble. The final blow came in 1991, when Serbia voted against allowing a Croat, Stipe Mesic, to take his rightful turn as president of the assembly. Yugoslavia broke up into ethnic states, as Slovenia, Croatia, Bosnia, and Macedonia broke off. War erupted between what was left of Yugoslavia and Croatia when a predominantly Serbian area of Croatia tried to reunite with Milosevic's Yugoslav remnant. The war spread into Bosnia and other regions as the various ethnic groups carved their own ethnic states, free from the "contamination" of other ethnic groups.

Compare Milosevic's demagoguery with the words of a stocky 34-year-old minister who rose to address a crowd of 250,000 in Washington, D.C., on August 23, 1963. Tension was high in the United States as the country grappled with establishing equality between its white and black citizens. Several in the black community had called for a direct confrontation and the formation of a black state. But Martin Luther King, Jr., did not believe in ethnic confrontation and separatism. Instead, King proclaimed, "I have a dream that one day on the red hills of Georgia the sons of former slaves and the sons of former slaveowners will be able to sit down together at the table of brotherhood" (King, 1969).

Regardless of the structure of intergroup relations, there is a delicate balance between competing motivations and emotions, and leaders can tilt the balance in one direction or the other. Ethnic groups waver between the path of withdrawal, separatism, and discrimination against other ethnic groups and the path of cooperation, contact, and understanding. Each path holds both danger and promise for the group. Leaders need only move the group slightly in one direction to create a snowball effect: fear and hatred accumulate on top of more fear and hatred; but cooperation and openness often bring further cooperation.

As I pointed out in Chapter 4, leaders of ethnic groups are rarely subjected to the system of checks and balances faced by many national leaders. Without a formal system to control their power, ethnic leaders often exert tremendous influence. From the group's perspective, the best measures of control include an informed populace committed to ethnic harmony and cooperation. Various organizations within the ethnic community could work to steer leaders onto a constructive course. This role is often played by religious leaders who have encouraged both ethnic and national leaders toward the path of cooperation. However, leaders devoted to creating ethnic conflict often have the support of the majority of their group, or at least the powerful members. In these cases, pressure on the leaders to follow a constructive course of action must be applied by forces outside the control of the group. When we move beyond the level of the group, we find important vehicles that can influence group leaders and help protect powerless ethnic groups from abuse and discrimination. The forces available at this level are an important resource in the struggle to create understanding and harmony between groups. Let's next turn our attention to these forces.

World Unites in Fight Against AIDS*

SUE LEEMAN

In Rome, taxi drivers distributed AIDS leaflets. Across Thailand, gas stations offered free condoms. In South Africa, Nobel laureate Desmond Tutu went on TV to urge people to practice safe sex.

World AIDS Day was marked with renewed vigor around the world Sunday after a U.N. agency reported an accelerating death toll, with nearly a quarter of the 6.4 million AIDS deaths to date occurring in the past year.

In 1996, 3.1 million people were infected with HIV, the virus that causes AIDS, bringing the total number of people with HIV or AIDS to 22.6 million, UNAIDS said.

In Asia, the site of an AIDS explosion, the war on the disease got graphic.

Activists posted photos of an emaciated AIDS victim in Beijing's central Zhongshan Park near the ancient imperial palace, along with posters that read, "The risks of careless sex and lifestyle hygiene."

Health officials have warned that more than 1 million Chinese—10 times the estimated present number—could be infected with HIV by 2000 if preventive measures are not taken.

In Thailand, which has an active sex industry, 420 gas stations distributed 3 million condoms to customers with the warning, "Be careful of AIDS when feeling naughty."

The health ministry and state-owned Petroleum Authority of Thailand sponsored the program. An estimated 800,000 of Thailand's 60 million people have the HIV virus, and 50,000 more have died of AIDS.

In the Philippine capital of Manila, about 250 government officials, activists and at least four HIV patients joined in the 1 1/4-mile "First National AIDS Walk."

In Taipei, an AIDS awareness group displayed memorial quilt patches to honor victims of the disease.

Photo exhibitions carried the message in India, which volunteer organizations say has Asia's worst AIDS epidemic, with an estimated 1 million or more HIV cases.

Charity organizations sponsored marches in Bombay.

More than 400 people gathered in Tokyo for the lighting of a 20-foot tree bearing 12,000 red ribbons, symbol of the fight against AIDS.

Europe warned against complacency.

In central Paris, several hundred AIDS activists marched with signs reading, "AIDS: The Epidemic Isn't Over" and "Zero Equals the Number of AIDS Survivors."

In Rome, two taxi companies distributed AIDS information leaflets to passengers

---

Source: The Bryan-College Station Eagle (December 2, 1994), pp. A1, A3.

and included similar messages on their telephone answering service. Some players in Italy's top soccer league wore red bows on their uniforms.

Dozens of candles were lit at Madrid's Puerta de Alcala monument in memory of the estimated 5,000 AIDS victims to have died in the Spanish capital since 1981.

In South Africa, retired Archbishop Tutu, who won the Nobel Peace Prize in 1984 for his fight against apartheid, appeared in a TV advertisement to warn, "Our wonderful country faces a major crisis with HIV and AIDS spreading so fast. Please use a condom!"

Algeria had another solution. Reminding audiences that AIDS has no cure, state-run media recommended sexual abstinence as the only sure method of avoiding the disease.

R E A D I N G   7 . 2

The Quota Culture's Slow Demise: Return to Self-Reliance*

JASON L. RILEY

Washington—On an unseasonably mild evening here last week, a smartly suited middle-aged gentleman stood before a crowd of 3,000 or so and said in a forceful but measured tone: "The endgame in a capitalist democracy like ours is economic power."

For most Americans, this utterance falls somewhere short of divine insight into the rudiments of success under capitalism. The fact that success in free-market societies presupposes a firm economic foundation is nearly intuitive. In this instance, however, two observations made the statement noteworthy: First, the speaker, Hugh Price, heads one of the nation's premier black organizations, the National Urban League. And second, Mr. Price was addressing a mostly black audience, at the league's annual convention, encouragingly themed "Economic Power: The Next Civil Rights Frontier."

A sad truth of late–20th-century black history is the lack of emphasis black leaders have placed on economic independence, opting instead to funnel resources toward integrating predominantly white institutions, be they political, corporate or educational. Such was not always the thinking; indeed, blacks left bondage with a very different mind-set.

"When you think back to the situation right after the Emancipation Proclamation, African-Americans did a couple things coming right out of slavery," Mr. Price said recently in an interview. "They started up colleges and they started up businesses, like independent farms and burial societies that led to the creation of insurance companies. And as black folks moved into the cities, they started everything that came with living there—barber shops, grocery stores, hotels."

---

*Source: The Wall Street Journal, August 13, 1997, p. A14.

Part of the reason blacks were able to do these things despite the racial barriers of Reconstruction and, later, Jim Crow, was the guidance and support of individuals such as Booker T. Washington. The pre-eminent black leader of the late 1800s and early 1900s, Washington was a shrewd self-help advocate and educator, and a relentless promoter of black economic independence. In 1901, the black novelist Pauline Hopkins called him "probably the most talked of Afro-American in the civilized world today."

A famous William Johnson painting of Washington shows the former slave addressing a class full of attentive black children. The blackboard behind him depicts a plow, a shovel, books and writing instruments—symbolizing the "tools" Washington realized were essential to the postslavery progress of his race. Demonstrating a keen understanding of the central role money and wealth accumulation play in advancing a people, Washington said: "No race that has anything to contribute to the markets of the world is long in any degree ostracized."

Mr. Price believes blacks are poised to pick up where his turn-of-the-century brethren left off. "The traditional civil rights movement was about knocking down barriers and pushing into employment and politics. What we haven't done with the same focus, but what we must do in the final analysis, is get positioned in the American economy as full-time players."

In his remarks, Mr. Price emphasized the critical role education will play in positioning blacks to compete, going so far as to issue a warning to the urban education establishment. After declaring both the charter school movement—which already includes some Urban League affiliates—and voucher programs viable alternatives to public schools, Mr. Price said: "If urban schools continue to fail in the face of all we know about how to improve them, customers will be obliged to shop elsewhere for quality education." (National Education Association President Robert Chase was seated just a few feet from the lectern, and he smiled nervously at this remark.)

Most significantly, parents are not absolved of their responsibilities. Mr. Price urged parents to focus single-mindedly on education and to denounce as often as necessary "the antiachievement peer culture" affecting too many black youngsters.

The decision of an organization with the size and influence of the Urban League—114 affiliates in 34 states, serving more than two million people annually—to reassert its efforts in education and economic development is significant. The difficulties, however, will be formidable, not least because history shows that most formerly downtrodden minority groups have gone about changing their fortunes in exactly the reverse order that blacks have gone about changing theirs. While political clout seems to be a natural byproduct of economic clout, the reverse is seldom the case. Jews, Japanese, Germans, Italians and others acquired political strength only after advancing economically. As economist Thomas Sowell has documented, "Those groups which have acquired political power and attempted to use it to advance themselves economically have not come close to duplicating the success of non-political minorities.

Another and perhaps greater obstacle is the civil rights mentality even someone as thoughtful as Hugh Price brings to the task. Mr. Price firmly but mistakenly links most black advancement to college entrance quotas and government contract set-asides. This era of rollbacks distresses him. "What will replace set-asides?" he asks, apparently not realizing this is akin to a Southern segregationist in the 1940s wondering what would replace Jim Crow, both being forms of government-sanctioned racial discrimination.

Blacks have won the battle for political equality, thanks in no small part to groups like the NAACP and the Urban League. But these groups have neglected what today is clearly black Americans' greatest need: to enter the economic mainstream through entrepreneurship and educational achievement. Mr. Price calls this the new frontier for black America. "We're getting reacquainted with the rudiments of self-reliance," he says. "We have a history of understanding the importance of it."

R E A D I N G   7 . 3

The Quota Culture's Slow Demise: We're All "Disadvantaged" Now*

VINCENT CARROLL

Two years after the U.S. Supreme Court gave Randy Pech hope that racial preferences for government contracts would be abolished, the U.S. District Court for Colorado has dealt him an ironic but bitter surprise. Judge John Kane has declared Mr. Pech, a white man who was a central figure in the Supreme Court's landmark case *Adarand Constructors Inc. v. Peña,* eligible for the preference program he had sought to dismantle.

All Mr. Pech has to do, Judge Kane told him late last month, is apply to the state of Colorado for certification as a disadvantaged business enterprise. At that point he'll presumably receive the preferences previously restricted to racial minorities. Meanwhile, Judge Kane left Colorado's racial spoils system for highway contracts intact.

Mr. Pech says he will apply for disadvantaged status, but this was not the ending he hoped for when he began his quixotic battle with the U.S. Department of Transportation back in 1989. If nothing else, his ordeal is a cautionary tale of the power of bureaucratic mendacity. It is also a lesson in the risk of relying on the judiciary to roll back racial preferences in the absence of executive and legislative support. Yet even with this unexpected turn of events, the latest twist in the *Adarand* case gives opponents of preferences an unprecedented opening, if they but understand how events arrived at their present pass.

Mr. Pech, Adarand's owner, originally challenged a federal Department of Transportation program that awarded bonuses to prime contractors who hired minority subcontractors. Adarand had submitted the low bid for the guardrail portion of a highway project in Colorado, but because of the bonus program, a Hispanic-owned firm won the contract instead. In the litigation that followed, the Supreme Court said such race-based preferences, even when adopted by Congress, must meet the strictest

---

*Source: The Wall Street Journal, August 13, 1997, p. A.14.

constitutional test: They can only be used to remedy proven past discrimination, and must be narrowly tailored to that goal.

The court refused, however, to rule specifically on the merits of the federal program that had cost Mr. Pech the guardrail job. He would have to wait two more years to hear Judge Kane confirm what had been obvious from the Supreme Court's decision: that the various statutes and regulations that support race-conscious policies in highway contracts are unconstitutional violations of the Constitution's Equal Protection Clause. Judge Kane struck down those statutes this past June. But, just as in 1995, the ruling was a limited victory for opponents of preferences.

The reason is that most federal highway money flows through the states, which then award the contracts that impose the federal Department of Transportation's preference policies. Those race-conscious policies may be federally conceived and federally enforced, and federal highway revenue may be the bludgeon Washington wields to keep states in line, but a contractor is certified as a disadvantaged business enterprise by the state in which the work takes place, unless that work occurs on federal lands. And Colorado Gov. Roy Romer simply refused to suspend his state's preference program even though a judge had just said that its statutory basis was illegal. Apparently Mr. Romer—who's also chairman of the Democratic National Committee—does not consider a federal court ruling binding in his state unless he's presented with a direct judicial order to obey it. Mr. Romer left Adarand with no choice but to sue Colorado, which it did in mid-June.

What happened next illustrates the extremes to which those who defend racial quotas will go to protect their programs. First, the federal government sought to intervene on behalf of Colorado in the new lawsuit, with the transparent goal of retrying the very issues it had just lost after years of litigation. An obviously irritated Judge Kane called the federal play "fatuous" and its reasoning "fallacious," and ordered the Department of Transportation to pay Adarand's legal fees. Next, Colorado Attorney General Gale Norton, a Republican, told the governor that she could not, which is to say would not, defend the state against Adarand. Mr. Romer then hired private lawyers for the task.

These were but warm-ups for the most brazen spectacle of all. Representatives of the same state that for years awarded contracts meeting the Department of Transportation's strict but unconstitutional conditions now told Judge Kane that Colorado was an independent agent and that it had, moreover, reformed the program so that it now met Supreme Court guidelines. In the future, they said, no minority would be certified as owning a disadvantaged business enterprise before the state asked him whether he has been socially and economically disadvantaged. One can imagine the responses this lame query will elicit. Narrowly tailored, indeed.

Yet however implausible the state's assurances that its revised program meets constitutional muster, they were apparently enough to convince Judge Kane that he could not simply rule summarily in Adarand's favor. He would have instead to slog through another lengthy inspection of the facts. That is when he seized upon the neat scheme of offering Adarand the opportunity to benefit from the very preferences its lawsuit had sought to abolish.

Judge Kane did hold on to the case, so he can intervene should Colorado deny Mr.

Pech preferential status. And Mr. Pech is hardly the only nonminority contractor Colorado has discriminated against for years. How will the state react if the others also seek designation as disadvantaged business enterprises? If everyone is certified as disadvantaged, the program self-destructs.

Beyond that, there is an even more interesting question. William Perry Pendley of Mountain States Legal Foundation, which has represented Adarand from the outset, points out that the Department of Transportation has defeated every previous attempt by a state to alter the terms of its highway preference program. Now the department is in a bind. It cannot order Colorado to revert to the old requirements without, in effect, flouting a federal court ruling. But it can hardly concede Colorado's independence without also conceding the independence of the other 12 states controlled by its Central Federal Lands Highway Division.

What, Mr. Pendley asks, is to prevent a governor of one of those 13 states—say, Mike Leavitt of Utah, George W. Bush of Texas, or Peter Wilson of California—from discarding the Department of Transportation's entire racial preference program? If Roy Romer is free to adjust the program as he likes, then so are they. And if just one of them does, the real fallout from *Adarand* will have only begun.

CHAPTER 8

WHOSE WOODS ARE THESE?

Expanding the Responsibility for Reducing Conflict

The war did not spring up here in our land; this war was brought upon us by the children of the Great Father who came to take our land from us without a price, and who, in our land, do a great many evil things. The Great Father and his children are to blame for this trouble. . . . It has been our wish to live in our country peaceably, and do such things as may be for the welfare and good of our people, but the Great Father has filled it with soldiers who think only of our death. Some of our people who have gone from here in order that they may have a change, and others who have gone north to hunt, have been attacked by the soldiers from this direction, and when they have got north have been attacked by soldiers from the other side, and now when they are willing to come back the soldiers stand between them to keep them from coming home. It seems to me there is a better way than this.—Sinte-Galeshka (Spotted Tail) of the Brulé Sioux. (Brown, 1971, p. 97)

"It can't happen here!" I can rely on eliciting this response from my class whenever I discuss ethnic violence in Nazi Germany, Iraq, Central Africa, or Bosnia. "Nicht hier!" was the response I heard from students in a class in Konstanz, Germany, when I spoke of the tortured history of black-white relationships in the United States and the present tensions between these groups. Although I found it hard to contain my disbelief, I asked students in both countries to explain why they believed "*it*" could "*not happen*" in their country. The responses were very similar. Some students cited their country's strong moral fiber. Others cited their country's legal system as a safeguard: "Today we have laws and moral codes that protect people and groups. Our laws, our court system, and our religious establishments would stop blatant ethnic discrimination and violence before it could reach massive proportions."

It seems cruel to dampen such wonderful optimism. So I generally refrain from taking a slash-and-burn approach, choosing rather to explore the assumptions on which the students base their comforting conclusions. Some argue that ethnic violence today is confined to regions that have no laws against discrimination. They suggest that Northern Ireland, South Africa, Yugoslavia, the Soviet Union, and Rwanda failed to develop a legal code to deal with violations of human rights. Although this assumption offers them some comfort, it is totally incorrect. Each of these regions had extensive laws prohibiting the atrocities that occurred there. In some cases, a system broke down, allowing violence to go unhindered. But in other cases, ethnic discrimination and violence have taken place under the nose of the authorities, an intact legal system. The seeds of ethnic hatred can germinate and thrive in the most civilized and orderly societies as well as in those characterized by chaos.

My students' outlook is not unusual. Most of us would argue that justice is the hallmark of our country's legal system. We might admit that abuses do occur, but we will be quick to add that society would function perfectly well if people abided by the law. Law and order sit on the throne next to godliness. Our symbol of justice is a beautiful woman protected from bias and discrimination by a blindfold. We all sleep better believing that the laws of our land are just and fair, although sometimes those who apply the law may be flawed. But is this really the case? Is the law—even the law of countries founded on a creed of equality—designed to prevent discrimination and abuse?

The Emperor's New Clothes: The Legal System as Protection against Discrimination

Arguably the greatest blot on the history of the United States was the shameful treatment of Native Americans. Schoolchildren are told of the first Thanksgiving, when the English settlers sat down with the Indians to give thanks for a bountiful harvest. But it was not long before the table guests became bitter enemies. As more settlers arrived and pushed westward, the Native Americans were first pushed off their lands into more remote areas. But soon even this was considered insufficient. General Philip Sheridan's categorical proclamation, "The only good Indians I ever saw were dead," set the tone for a deadly campaign against the Indians that began in earnest after the Civil War. The slaughter was not the work of jackbooted ruffians and outlaws. Rather, it was supported—in fact, encouraged—by the law of the land.

It is ironic that at the height of efforts designed to exterminate the Indian, Congress overrode President Andrew Johnson's veto and passed a Civil Rights Act on April 1, 1866. The act gave equal rights to all persons born in the United States *except Indians.* And on June 14 of that year, the Fourteenth Amendment to the Constitution was ratified, extending the rights of citizenship to many groups, including Negroes. The series of laws designed to promote equality enacted during this time systematically stripped Indians of their human rights and supported efforts to take care of the Indian problem, once and for all.

Rather than serving as stepping-stones for lofty principles, laws may be instituted to justify the status quo. Throughout human history, the ethnic groups in power have sought to solidify their position by passing laws, establishing a "friendly" political system, and developing customs to protect their power. These efforts keep minority groups at a disadvantage and reduce their threat to the group in power. In many cases, these attempts are transparent, even blatant. For example, the political history of the United States is littered with laws that withheld voting rights from less powerful groups including blacks, Indians, and women. When these laws were shown to be dissonant with the principle of equal rights for all, more subtle means of discrimination were adopted, such as enacting a poll tax, requiring voters to pass literacy tests, or giving the vote only to people who owned property. These rules denied the vote to groups who were less educated or poor. Not surprisingly, these groups were usually minority ethnic groups that had little power and few opportunities for education. Disenfranchising certain ethnic groups is not unique to the United States. Countries such as Canada, South Africa, Germany, England, and Mexico find this legal skullduggery in their legal history. More subtle "legal" steps have included gerrymandering voting districts so that the members of minority ethnic groups are dispersed among many districts or concentrated in just a few. As a result, they are able to elect few or no representatives to legislative bodies.

In addition to being denied the vote, members of minority ethnic groups are often denied educational opportunities by law or custom. They are forced to live in dilapidated areas that fail to provide the basic necessities of life, let alone comfort or security. Denied access to attractive jobs, they are funneled into menial, low-paying positions. In most cases, each of these steps is undertaken in the most proper legal way. As a result, the advantaged group can innocently claim, "We too must abide by these same laws. How can there be discrimination if the laws apply to everyone?"

These skillfully orchestrated programs to keep minority ethnic groups "in their place" have a number of consequences. One is a self-fulfilling prophecy (Rosenthal & Jacobson, 1968), which reinforces stereotypes and maintains the status quo. In essence, the law creates the very behavior it aims to eliminate. To understand how this might work, let's reexamine the basic process underlying the self-fulfilling prophecy.

As a high school student, I had a high aspiration: to make my mark on the tennis world. I delighted in hearing the gasps from the audience when I hit a booming serve. But one summer, in a tennis clinic, I met my match. Henry was a tall, lanky fellow who moved like a cat across the court. When he served, I expected to hear a sonic boom or see flames erupt behind the ball. After one match with Henry, I couldn't stretch my powers of self-delusion any longer: Henry was headed to tennis stardom, and I was on my way to the junkyard of tennis also-rans. But Henry had one strike against him. He was an African-American. Our coach made no bones of his belief that "Negroes can't play tennis." As an afterthought he explained, "I'm not prejudiced at all, but after twenty years of coaching, I have to give you the facts as I see them. Name me one Negro tennis star." (This was before the days of Arthur Ashe.) At first I thought he was joking, but even if he was serious, how could he really hurt someone with Henry's obvious talent? I soon found out. During the summer, the coach spent time helping me and the other white boys improve our game. He didn't ignore Henry; each time Henry made a mistake, he would yell, "Come on, Henry. Can't you do anything right?" When we were paired for matches, the coach always put Henry against the worst player on the team. Since Henry could beat the worst player easily, he could learn little from the experience. By midsummer, Henry came to the lessons only sporadically; his enthusiasm for the game was gone. His serve no longer boomed, and his catlike movement across the court was gone. By the end of the summer, there were two ex-tennis players—Henry and I. And the coach's parting words were, "See, I told you Negroes can't play tennis. Henry, maybe you should think about going out for basketball."

The self-fulfilling prophecy—in this case and in many others—begins with a viewpoint or stereotype: "*They* are lazy." "*They* can't play tennis." As we discussed in Chapter 3, the expectation conveyed by the stereotype guides behaviors toward the target. If "they" (the targeted group) are lazy, dumb, and unmotivated, they should not be given skilled or important jobs. Why waste education on lazy, unmotivated, unintelligent people? So opportunities are denied, and "they" are constantly reminded that they are lazy and unintelligent. With few job opportunities and little education, the targeted group recognizes that there is little reason to work hard or try to advance. Their efforts will get them nothing. As a result, hard work and education are not emphasized, and they become unmotivated. The powerful group pounces on this behavior, "See, we were right. They are lazy, unmotivated." They can't play tennis!

The powerful group fails to recognize that its own attitudes, behaviors, and rules have created the situation that confirmed their expectations. The result of the self-fulfilling prophecy is that negative stereotypes are supported; inequality between groups widens; and there is little motivation for members of the two groups to interact or cooperate. As I pointed out in Chapter 7, a critical requirement for reducing hostility and increasing understanding between groups is equal-status contact. But when a powerless group is caught in the web of the self-fulfilling prophecy, there can be no equal-status contact.

It's important to understand that all this takes place quite legally, without explicit malice or intention. We're a law-abiding people who pride ourselves on following the law. We remain blind to the fact that just laws can perpetuate unjust conditions. Although our laws include procedures for changing statutes, those in power are the ones favored by the designated process. By excluding certain groups from the political process or from protection of the law, it becomes lawful to take their lands and exclude them from the best schools and employment opportunities. And through disenfranchisement or gerrymandering, these groups are denied a legal forum for expressing protests. In the United States, for example, blacks, Indians, and Asians have all at one time or another been moved outside the umbrella of the law and the political system.

Today many countries face an intriguing legal conundrum. The laws in question are not specifically aimed at minority ethnic groups, but their effect is felt most strongly by these groups. The laws involve people who have entered the country illegally—illegal immigrants. The legally established punishment for illegally entering a country is deportation. But for illegal immigrants who are not caught, the "punishment" is often greater. They are denied the protection of the country's legal system and the rights of the country's citizens. Not only do they live in constant fear of being deported, but they also must endure the whims and mistreatment of those who wish to take advantage of their situation. In effect, for these people there is no minimum wage, no standard of housing, and no right to education. We can argue that this situation is fair, given that these people have chosen to disobey the immigration laws. Few would argue that a nation does not have the right, even the responsibility, to regulate immigration. On the other hand, the result is to create a group of people who will remain impoverished. Their situation also entices others to take advantage of them, sometimes engaging in the most inhumane activities, which ultimately bring disgrace to the country. Once again, we see a situation where just and well-intentioned laws help create unjust conditions.

Once a situation of inequality between groups becomes institutionalized, it is very difficult to reverse within the prevailing conditions. A low-status group has little power to effect change; in some cases, such groups may even accept their unfortunate position as legitimate. And a high-status group has little motivation to change the existing arrangement, so it too accepts the situation as legitimate. As a result, the traditional system of justice is often ineffective for improving ethnic relations.

This argument is at the heart of an emerging theory of race relations known as *critical race theory* (Bell, 1992; Monaghan, 1993). These theorists hold that racism is endemic in American life and that existing laws could not eliminate it even if they were to be applied fairly. For example, the constitutional guarantee of free speech protects "hate speech," aimed at minority groups. The law itself is not unfair, but within the existing framework it can be used to perpetuate ethnic hatred. The powerful group has little to fear from "hate speech" directed at it, but the minority group is not in such a comfortable position. Some proponents of critical race theory have called for a radical overhaul of legal doctrines, even suggesting that those affected by discrimination should be the ones to craft a new legal system. In any case we must look to forces outside the groups involved in ethnic conflict to pave the path toward better ethnic relations. It is to these "other forces" that I will now turn.

My Brother's Keeper

Recently, I was involved in a discussion with several Israeli colleagues about the security of Israel. They began arguing among themselves over the best way to preserve the Jewish state. Some held that the only way to prevent another holocaust was for the Israelis to build up their military power and be stronger than the Arab states in the area. Others took another view. They argued that the tremendous expense of building an ever-stronger military would destroy Israel from within. Money needed for schools, medical facilities, and infrastructure would not be available, and the country would become rotten at the core. Besides, they concluded, "Countries such as the United States would not allow another holocaust. If things really got bad, they would step in. Our ability to call on our friends gives us an opportunity to build bridges between the Arabs and the Jews." Their opponents quickly responded, "Where were our friends in Germany, in the Soviet Union, and during the Six-Day War?"

Although that question remained unanswered, the discussion illustrates one way to create harmony between ethnic groups, or at least to protect one group from the ravages of another. That way involves relying on a third party who is willing to guarantee the safety of an ethnic group explicitly or implicitly. There are many reasons why a third party might agree to intercede. In some cases, the targeted ethnic group may have significant representation within the third party. For example, there is a powerful Jewish presence within the United States that has actively advocated the protection of Jews in Israel and in countries where they are persecuted. The island nation of Fiji has a population that is nearly 50% Indian. When tension is high and the Indian population is threatened, the possibility arises that India will intervene to protect it. When the Muslims of Bosnia were fighting for survival, their troops were aided by volunteers and supplies from Muslim Iran. And African-Americans kept up constant pressure on the United States to take vigorous action to end discrimination against blacks in South Africa. But although many ethnic groups have a strong presence in countries that can act as protectors, many others do not. As a result, the Native Americans of the United States had no champion to save them from mistreatment; the Kurds in Iraq, Iran, and Turkey and the Tajik and Panjshiri in Afghanistan are left to fend for themselves. These unfortunates have little presence outside the regions where they are the subject of discrimination.

Still, even without friends in high places, an ethnic group may find itself the recipient of help from outside. In some cases, intervention is based on humanitarian grounds. The slaughter of Tutsis and Hutus in Central Africa, the ethnic battles in Somalia, and the human carnage in Bosnia reached such terrible proportions that several nations were impelled to intercede. Whose heart could fail to be touched by the terrible pictures of the victims of those conflicts? On the other hand, as one of my Hungarian friends observed, "The cemeteries of the world are filled with the

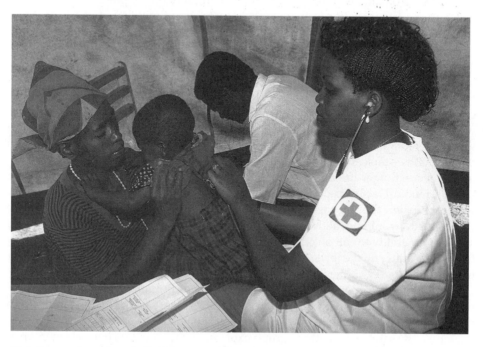

Outside agencies such as the Red Cross can work effectively to reduce the suffering of ethnic conflict without taking sides. Staying neutral in a highly charged situation is often a very delicate task. (Betty Press/Woodfin Camp & Associates)

bodies of those who counted on the altruism of their neighbors." Relying on others to act out of altruism and a sense of justice (or guilt) is a risky strategy for any group. A wrong bet can mean doom and destruction.

Fortunately (or perhaps unfortunately, for those of us who believe that humans are inherently caring) there is another motive that may lead to action: *egoism,* or self-interest (Cialdini et al., 1987). In many cases, mistreatment of an ethnic group within one country can be viewed by another country as an opportunity to gain territory or influence in the region. In fact, the superpowers historically divided the world into domains of influence to ensure that no one power would gain a foothold in another's territory under the guise of altruism. The Monroe Doctrine staked the claim of the United States to bar intervention by European powers in Central and South America. If help was to be given there, it would come from the United States. The Soviet Union was the self-designated champion in Eastern Europe, many Arab states, and of communist nations in Asia. France assumed the role of a benevolent third party in North and Central Africa. Interestingly, the ethnic violence between the Hutus and Tutsis tested this implicit "sphere of influence." As the violence engulfed the region, a United Nations peacekeeping force was sent to the area. However, Rwanda had traditionally been protected by the French, and in June 1994 France sent an armed force into Rwanda to "protect refugees." The U.N. commander promptly warned the French to stay out of certain areas, interpreting France's "altruism" as an egoistic action to assert its own influence.

Rescue by a third party, regardless of its motive, has saved many ethnic groups from persecution and destruction. A threatened group, like a drowning person, is in no position to refuse a lifeline. Yet history shows that a third party is rarely a source of lasting ethnic harmony. There are several reasons for this. First, the outside party often imposes a settlement based on force and fear. As a result, some of the internal parties are likely to view the resolution as unfair. An unjust resolution to one conflict often leaves embers that can ignite future conflicts (Deutsch, 1973). In 1990, for example, France intervened in Rwanda to quell ethnic violence. Although the French stopped the violence, their forcible attempt to settle the conflict probably set the stage for the tribal massacres that erupted in 1994 and continued until 1997. Forced resolutions often last only as long as the third party maintains a presence in the area (Rubin et al., 1993).

Second, in many cases the parties involved in an ethnic conflict can call in their own "bulldogs," champions who have pledged to protect them. In such cases, outside parties enter on both sides, widening the scope of the conflict. The world has been brought to the brink of world war in just such cases. For example, the conflict in the Middle East brought the United States and other Western powers, on the side of Israel, face to face with the Soviet Union, which supported the Arabs. The struggle between the Croats and the Serbs sucked in the world's major powers, which aligned themselves on different sides. In these cases, the focus often shifts away from finding a resolution to the ethnic conflict and toward posturing by the major powers.

A third danger is that the champion may become a permanent resident of the area, reducing or destroying the independence of the indigenous ethnic groups. The third party's intervention may be so complete that the protector becomes the enemy, or at the least demands a high price for protection. The United States intervened in the Philippines, Guam, and Cuba only to decide that its continued presence was strategically necessary after the conflict ended. Residents of Guam and Guantanamo Bay, Cuba, now find that it is impossible to dislodge their "guest." I'm reminded of a friend whose mother moved into her home to help her with her newborn; the mother is still there 20 years later, even though the child she helped raise has gone off to college! The message is: Beware of inviting people into your home, lest they adopt it as their own.

Aside from this concern, there is also the uneasy relationship that generally characterizes coalitions formed to deal with a specific conflict (Thompson, Manniz, & Bazerman, 1988; Komorita & Kravitz, 1983). Coalitions are notoriously unstable—largely because of disputes over how to divide the spoils. Weaker members propose an even split, because, they argue, nothing would have been gained without their involvement. Stronger parties typically demand a division on the basis of equity; since they contributed the lion's share (strength, resources, manpower) to the partnership, they should be rewarded in proportion to their contribution. The intervention of a strong outside party to protect a weaker ethnic group can result in a similar conflict.

Finally, third parties are often fair-weather friends. A nation that promises protection at one time may be unwilling or unable to give it at another time. For example, the United States gave both explicit and implicit support to the white ruling minority in South Africa prior to 1985. But as political currents in the United States changed, its support for the white ruling minority ebbed. The British helped the Jews establish a toehold in Palestine in the 1940s, but at a critical juncture in the struggle to form an independent nation, British support evaporated. Britain had found itself faced with an increasingly complicated political situation, and the cost of rebuilding Great Britain after the World War II had mounted. The British abruptly pulled out of the area, leaving the Arabs and Jews to achieve their own bloody solution to their conflict. Taiwan, a country built with the support of the United States, now floats like a sitting duck off the shore of China, wondering when an invasion will come and, when it comes, who will come to its aid. The United States's support for Chiang Kai-shek (Jiang Jieshi) was based on his fight against communism and on Americans' fear of Red China. But as relations developed between the United States and China, strong support for Taiwan was sacrificed.

Intervention is also a risky strategy when considered from the position of the third party. Intervention may be based on a desire to protect, and the third party may wish to serve only as a neutral mediator. Such mediators are being called on with increasing frequency to settle civil disputes that once clogged our court system (Duffy, 1991). A mediator is an adviser who helps the parties identify issues and agree on a solution to the conflict (Carnevale, 1985). The mediator is generally viewed as neutral, supporting neither side but creating an environment where the opponents can come together to exchange information and develop better mutual understanding. The mediator helps the disputants develop their own settlement to the conflict without resorting to force or invoking legally binding rules (Kleiboer, 1994). In theory, the mediator moves out of the picture once the parties have resolved their conflict. This process works well in civil matters such as landlord-tenant disputes or the division of property in divorce cases. But theory and practice are often at odds when a dispute involves ethnic or national groups and the mediator is another country. In many of these cases, the mediator is forced to commit to a long-term presence in the area, even after the conflict is "resolved." This presence is often costly in terms of money, material, and lives, and it is politically risky both at home and on the international front. We can see clear examples in the aftermath of the United States' involvement in Haiti, Somalia, Bosnia, and Nicaragua. The British government has also found how costly the position of mediator can be, as it has attempted to take on the role of a neutral in the Protestant-Catholic conflict in Northern Ireland. Another problem for would-be mediators is that mediation is based on the premise that the parties in a conflict can be clearly identified and have accepted leaders who represent them. This is not always the case in ethnic conflicts. It is often unclear who speaks for an ethnic group. Even when an identifiable leadership structure exists at the beginning of the conflict, it may dissolve during the process, so that conflict exists both within the ethnic groups and between them. The structure of ethnic conflict is often not neatly defined, looking more like a rat's nest than a carefully constructed spider web.

In sum, the intervention of third parties to protect less powerful ethnic groups is a double-edged sword. We can point to cases where groups have been rescued from the brink of destruction by third parties. In other cases, the entry of third parties has widened and prolonged a conflict, hastening the demise of one or more groups initially involved. Even when the motives of the third party are pure as the driven snow, intervention has often exacted a large toll. This is certainly an unsavory dilemma for those interested in ethnic harmony and peace. For these reasons, relying on the intervention of powerful third parties to promote ethnic cooperation must be considered a relatively undesirable option, to be chosen only when other options have failed.

Depersonalizing Conflict

In our examination of third-party intervention, I presented the third party as a gunslinger who comes to town to whip the bickering ethnic groups into shape. The success of the third party in these cases depends on a quick draw and deadly aim—on power. Might becomes right, and acquiescence is a sign of weakness. This is obviously a rather shaky foundation on which to build a relationship. But there is another alternative, one that may involve a third party but is not based on threat and power.

Elementary school teachers in multiethnic classes have the challenging task of teaching students course material while developing a sense of acceptance and group cohesion among the students. The trials and tribulations of teachers in undertaking the latter endeavor are legend, but an interesting success story was presented at a national conference by a fourth-grade teacher from Los Angeles. A group of Hispanic students were assigned to give a presentation on the history and customs of Hispanics in California. When the group members were ready to speak, several other students did everything possible to disrupt the presentation and show that they had no interest in it. The Hispanic students and the teacher were obviously frustrated with the situation, which began to deteriorate further when one of the Hispanic kids warned the rowdy students that they would be "sorry" if they didn't listen. The immediate response was an increase in the rowdiness and a counterthreat: "We'll see who'll be sorry." The explosive situation was not defused when the teacher intervened to chide the audience that if they didn't listen when others were talking, no one would listen to them when it was their turn. Both of these approaches were very personal—they involved trying to force the students to listen and learn because otherwise they would suffer.

The teacher's aide had a different strategy. She deflected attention away from the particular situation by getting the students to talk about general feelings and general rules of human behavior. She guided the class toward a discussion of fairness, equality, and openness. She had students talk about their beliefs on these and other issues. Surprisingly, the fourth-graders were able to relate to these issues. The aide then suggested that since the students had agreed that fairness and openness were generally pretty good rules to follow, the class should adopt these principles. No student disagreed, and the presentation by the Hispanic students proceeded smoothly, with the audience attentive and interested.

If we examine this situation, a number of points become apparent. The initial attempts to get the students to participate, even passively, involved personal threats and veiled references to power. "*You* do this, or else." Conflicts and disagreements that focus on individuals tend to cause them to draw clear lines, and focus in turn on their own power in the relationship. Thus any compromise or acquiescence comes to be viewed as a loss of face. The aide was able to change the confrontation from one between individuals to one involving principles or norms. At this level, any modification in behavior was not an admission of personal defeat or caving into the demands of an adversary, but a matter of following more noble principles.

John Thibaut (1968) presents a cogent case for resolving conflict and promoting understanding by depersonalizing the situation and appealing to general norms of behavior. It is difficult to mount a successful attack against the position that people should be open to new ideas, or that equality and fairness should prevail in human interactions. Ethnic conflict often occurs between people who hold similar values. But these values get lost as the individuals focus on a particular issue or on the implications for their own well-being. Thibaut argues that people can be encouraged to interact by stressing general, impersonal norms and reinforcing the idea that any actions are based on such norms instead of on factors related to the particular interaction—such as fear, power, or threats.

The wisdom of this approach has been apparent in many ethnic conflicts. Martin Luther King, Jr., was a master of this technique. He took great pains to avoid suggesting that racial problems in the United States were the result of conflict between blacks and whites. King stressed that the core of the civil rights movement was to uphold the principles of democracy on which the United States was founded: "I still have a dream. It is a dream that is deeply rooted in the American dream. I have a dream that one day this nation will rise up, live out the true meaning of its creed: We hold these truths to be self-evident, that all men are created equal." Who could argue that the United States should not honor its creed, its Declaration of Independence, its Constitution? Granting equality to blacks was not a matter of whites' giving up something. It was a matter of living up to the nation's values—values that even the most conservative white person held. In a similar manner, the development of New Zealand into a multicultural nation was presented as upholding the Treaty of Waitangi on which New Zealand had been founded—not as yielding to the demands of a vocal Maori minority.

A World Court, a World Policeman

So far I have discussed two approaches to resolving ethnic conflict, the intervention of a third party and an appeal to normative rules of fairness to depersonalize the conflict. If we combine these two approaches, we find a third strategy, one that currently enjoys some popularity. This procedure involves developing a regional or global body—existing outside the control of any nation or ethnic group—that examines and attempts to resolve conflicts.

After World War I, the president of the United States, Woodrow Wilson, was concerned about preserving world peace. He felt that future world wars could be avoided if there was a body to guarantee the security of nations. This body had to be outside the control of any one nation, and potentially stronger than any single nation. Wilson proposed the League of Nations to serve this purpose. The League, founded in 1920, was joined by most of the world's nations, which committed themselves to protect nations from external aggression.

The League of Nations was the prototype for today's United Nations. Although both the League and the United Nations were originally designed to protect nations from outside aggression, it was recognized that some of the most terrible conflicts arise within nations, often between ethnic groups. These conflicts not only were devastating to the nation involved but could serve as a match to ignite international conflict. For example, the struggle between Israeli Jews and Palestinians induced the world powers to take sides and threatened to bring them into armed conflict.

Since that time several bodies within the United Nations have been set up to handle issues of human rights, often associated with ethnic group conflicts: the Commission on Human Rights, the Sub-Commission on Prevention of Discrimination and Protection of Minorities, and the Sub-Commission on Indigenous Populations. The United Nations also reestablished the International Court of Justice at the Hague. Although the Court has largely dealt with economic and territorial issues, it has also been involved in disputes between ethnic groups. In addition to the United Nations, there are multilateral treaties, such as the International Covenant on Economic, Social, and Cultural Rights, aimed at protecting groups from discrimination. These treaties are designed to bind member nations to follow an agreed-upon code of behavior.

For the most part, all of these agencies and treaties have one point in common: they involve established nations. Recognized nations sit in the United Nations General Assembly, and recognized nations enter into treaties and covenants. This arrangement makes several implicit points. First, nations are the legitimate participants in these world forums for resolution of conflict. Ethnic groups, gender groups, or religions do not have clear representation, even though these groups may be larger than any single country and their domain may cross several national boundaries. There is no seat in the United Nations reserved for a representative of Native Americans, Maori people, Jews, Catholics, or women. This does not mean that the United Nations ignores the needs and condition of these groups. It does, however, imply that for the most part the concerns of these groups must be raised by and will be considered by representatives of nations. This can be a ticklish situation because, as we saw in Chapters 1 and 5, the concerns of ethnic groups may conflict with the interests of a nation or nations. We must also realize that many ethnic conflicts are domestic, occurring totally within the boundaries of a single nation. In these cases, the United Nations's hands are tied because its charter precludes it from intervening in domestic affairs: "Nothing contained in the present Charter shall authorize the United Nations to intervene in matters which are essentially within the domestic jurisdiction of any state" (Article 2(7) U.N. Charter).

Fortunately, country-based bodies are not the only umbrella for protecting group rights. Organizations such as the International Red Cross, the International Rescue Committee, and Amnesty International spread their influence across national boundaries and are not controlled by nations. By their charters, nongovernmental organizations address the needs of people both within nations and across national boundaries. They define a code of acceptable behavior based on views of fundamental human rights, and they report violations of this code. But they have no means of enforcing remedies. For example, Amnesty International monitored the rise to power of the Taliban in Afghanistan in 1996. In the first few weeks after the group gained control of Kabul, Amnesty International reported that 1,000 people had been arrested and the new rulers were violating the human rights of women and the Tajik and Panjshir ethnic groups. It publicly labeled the new regime a "reign of terror." Although Amnesty International was able to bring the situation to the world's attention, it could not punish the perpetrators of the atrocities or protect victims from abuse. It must rely on world opinion to bring pressure on parties to reduce violence and abuse. This approach is often effective, but it is far from certain.

At first glance, such multinational organizations or neutral global groups seem to be the perfect solution for controlling ethnic violence and mistreatment based on ethnic identity. But let's take a closer look at these groups and their record in addressing the three daunting questions they must always address.

What to Protect?   Let's tiptoe through the world of human misery. Our journey uncovers some incredible examples of man's inhumanity to man. In the United States we find that in 1990, less than 9 percent of whites but nearly 32 percent of blacks lived below the poverty line. In Israel, we find that an incident of terrorism leads authorities to close national boundaries, depriving thousands of Palestinian Arabs from earning a living. In Central Africa, Tutsi and Hutu slaughter each other by the tens of thousands, simply because of their ethnicity. In Germany, a Turkish family are burned in their home. And in Tibet, the Chinese government has undertaken a systematic program since the mid-1950s to destroy the area's natural environment. Tibetans are becoming a minority in their own homeland as a result of the resettling of thousands of Han Chinese in the area (Van Praag 1986).

Each of these examples represents an injustice, but do all involve denial of basic human rights? Are there global rights that each of us inherits as a human being? What rights accrue to us because we are human, and what rights are endowed to us because of the nation to which we belong? For example, is deciding the type of government one will have a basic human right? Is deciding what language one will speak or the type of job one will have a basic right, or is it the right of a nation or some other group to determine this? If there are "human rights," what are they and how do they apply to ethnic identity and conflict? The history of the United Nations is a story of the struggle to deal with these questions, as Asher and his colleagues (1957) note: "The evolution of the United Nations's activities in the field of human rights is the story of early agreement on objectives and general principles, followed by prolonged, serious, and unresolved disagreement on translating those principles into precise commitments" (p. 1060).

After a two-year effort to deal with these and other issues, the United Nations adopted the Universal Declaration of Human Rights on December 10, 1948 (see Box 8.1). This declaration was a major step because most of the world's nations agreed to declare that there were rights that all people share, and it identified these rights. The Declaration was a statement of goals and principles; it did not have the weight of a law or treaty that could be enforced. Vague and general in many places, it left large areas open to interpretation.

Holsti (1996), for example, points out that distinctions can be made between the levels at which human rights exist. One level is personal and involves acts of bodily injury and personal degradation. The second level concerns economic and political rights. The third level concerns global issues such as ecosystem rights. Holsti asks how we are to prioritize the list of human rights. Are those involving bodily injury more important (and deserving of greater punishment when violated) than those involving the economic or political freedom of a group? Such questions illustrate the difficulty of developing a consensus on what rights should be considered "basic."

From the standpoint of relations between ethnic groups, the hope was that the Declaration's clear definition of human rights would promote peace and harmony between ethnic groups. Protecting people from ethnic discrimination should set the stage for promoting greater willingness to accept and learn about ethnic groups. However, progress toward this lofty goal has been painfully slow in the 50 years since the Declaration was issued. It is true that many new agencies, both within the United Nations (such as Special Committee on Apartheid, Committee on Human Rights) and within regional alliances (the Organization for Security and Cooperation in Europe, and the European Commission on Human Rights, for example), were created to define human rights more clearly within a regional context. However, the authority and scope of these different agencies are often unclear and conflicting. For example, a committee of the Organization of American States (OAS) attempted to return democratic rule to Haiti in 1991. After making little headway, it passed the problem on to the U.N. Security Council, which authorized military intervention by a force provided predominantly by the United States—a member of both the Security

UNIVERSAL DECLARATION OF HUMAN RIGHTS

United Nations
Department of Public Information

These are the human rights of

_____

**as set forth by the United Nations
in the Universal Declaration
of Human Rights**

On 10 December 1948, the General Assembly of the United Nations adopted and proclaimed the Universal Declaration of Human Rights, the full text of which appears in the following pages. Following this historic act, the Assembly called upon all Member countries to publicize the text of the Declaration and "to cause it to be disseminated, displayed, read and expounded principally in schools and other educational institutions, without distinction based on the political status of countries or territories".

Javier Pérez de Cuéllar
SECRETARY-GENERAL

All human beings are born with equal and inalienable rights and fundamental freedoms.

The United Nations is committed to upholding, promoting and protecting the human rights of every individual. This commitment stems from the United Nations Charter, which reaffirms the faith of the peoples of the world in fundamental human rights and in the dignity and worth of the human person.

In the Universal Declaration of Human Rights, the United Nations has stated in clear and simple terms the rights which belong equally to every person.

These rights belong to you.

They are your rights.

Familiarize yourself with them. Help to promote and defend them for yourself as well as for your fellow human beings.

Universal Declaration of Human Rights

Preamble

Whereas recognition of the inherent dignity and of the equal and inalienable rights of all members of the human family is the foundation of freedom, justice and peace in the world,

Whereas disregard and contempt for human rights have resulted in barbarous acts which have outraged the conscience of mankind, and the advent of a world in which human beings shall enjoy freedom of speech and belief and freedom from fear and want has been proclaimed as the highest aspiration of the common people,

Whereas it is essential, if man is not to be compelled to have recourse, as a last resort, to rebellion against tyranny and oppression, that human rights should be protected by the rule of law,

Whereas it is essential to promote the development of friendly relations between nations,

Whereas the peoples of the United Nations have in the Charter reaffirmed their faith in fundamental human rights, in the dignity and worth of the human person and in the equal rights of men and women and have determined to promote social progress and better standards of life in larger freedom,

Whereas Member States have pledged themselves to achieve, in co-operation with the United Nations, the promotion of universal respect for and observance of human rights and fundamental freedoms,

Whereas a common understanding of these rights and freedoms is of the greatest importance for the full realization of this pledge,

Now, Therefore,

The General Assembly

proclaims

The Universal Declaration of Human Rights

as a common standard of achievement for all peoples and all nations, to the end that every individual and every organ of society, keeping this Declaration constantly in mind, shall strive by teaching and education to promote respect for these rights and freedoms and by progressive measures, national and international, to secure their universal and effective recognition and observance, both among the peoples of Member States themselves and among the peoples of territories under their jurisdiction.

Article 1

All human beings are born free and equal in dignity and rights. They are endowed with reason and conscience and should act towards one another in a spirit of brotherhood.

Article 2

Everyone is entitled to all the rights and freedoms set forth in this Declaration, without distinction of any kind, such as race, colour, sex, language, religion, political or other opinion, national or social origin, property, birth or other status.

Furthermore, no distinction shall be made on the basis of the political, jurisdictional or international status of the country or territory to which a person belongs, whether it be independent, trust, non-self-governing or under any other limitation of sovereignty.

Article 3

Everyone has the right to life, liberty and security of person.

Article 4

No one shall be held in slavery or servitude; slavery and the slave trade shall be prohibited in all their forms.

Article 5

No one shall be subjected to torture or to cruel, inhuman or degrading treatment or punishment.

Article 6

Everyone has the right to recognition everywhere as a person before the law.

Article 7

All are equal before the law and are entitled without any discrimination to equal protection of the law. All are entitled to equal protection against any discrimination in violation of this Declaration and against any incitement to such discrimination.

Article 8

Everyone has the right to an effective remedy by the competent national tribunals for acts violating the fundamental rights granted him by the constitution or by law.

Article 9

No one shall be subjected to arbitrary arrest, detention or exile.

Article 10

Everyone is entitled in full equality to a fair and public hearing by an independent and impartial tribunal, in the determination of his rights and obligations and of any criminal charge against him.

Article 11

(1) Everyone charged with a penal offence has the right to be presumed innocent until proven guilty according to law in a public trial at which he has had all the guarantees necessary for his defence.

(2) No one shall be held guilty of any penal offence on account of any act or omission which did not constitute a penal offence, under national or international law, at the time when it was committed. Nor shall a heavier penalty be imposed than the one that was applicable at the time the penal offence was committed.

Article 12

No one shall be subjected to arbitrary interference with his privacy, family, home or correspondence, nor to attacks upon his honour and reputation. Everyone has the right to the protection of the law against such interference or attacks.

Article 13

(1) Everyone has the right to freedom of movement and residence within the borders of each State.

(2) Everyone has the right to leave any country, including his own, and to return to his country.

Article 14

(1) Everyone has the right to seek and to enjoy in other countries asylum from persecution.

(2) This right may not be invoked in the case of prosecutions genuinely arising from non-political crimes or from acts contrary to the purposes and principles of the United Nations.

Article 15

(1) Everyone has the right to a nationality.

(2) No one shall be arbitrarily deprived of his nationality nor denied the right to change his nationality.

Article 16

(1) Men and women of full age, without any limitation due to race, nationality or religion, have the right to marry and to found a family. They are entitled to equal rights as to marriage, during marriage and at its dissolution.

(2) Marriage shall be entered into only with the free and full consent of the intending spouses.

(3) The family is the natural and fundamental group unity of society and is entitled to protection by society and the State.

Article 17

(1) Everyone has the right to own property alone as well as in association with others.

(2) No one shall be arbitrarily deprived of his property.

Article 18

Everyone has the right to freedom of thought, conscience and religion; this right includes freedom to change his religion or belief, and freedom, either alone or in community with others and in public or private, to manifest his religion or belief in teaching, practice, worship and observance.

Article 19

Everyone has the right to freedom of opinion and expression; this right includes freedom to hold opinions without interference and to seek, receive and impart information and ideas through any media and regardless of frontiers.

Article 20

(1) Everyone has the right to freedom of peaceful assembly and association.

(2) No one may be compelled to belong to an association.

Article 21

(1) Everyone has the right to take part in the government of his country, directly or through freely chosen representatives.

(2) Everyone has the right of equal access to public service in his country.

(3) The will of the people shall be the basis of the authority of government; this will shall be expressed in periodic and genuine elections which shall be by universal and equal suffrage and shall be held by secret vote or by equivalent free voting procedures.

Article 22

Everyone, as a member of society, has the right to social security and is entitled to realization, through national effort and international co-operation and in accordance with the organization and resources of each State, of the economic, social and cultural rights indispensable for his dignity and the free development of his personality.

Article 23

(1) Everyone has the right to work, to free choice of employment, to just and favourable conditions of work and to protection against unemployment.

(2) Everyone, without any discrimination, has the right to equal pay for equal work.

(3) Everyone who works has the right to just and favourable remuneration ensuring for himself and his family an existence worthy of human dignity, and supplemented, if necessary, by other means of social protection.

(4) Everyone has the right to form and to join trade unions for the protection of his interests.

Article 24

Everyone has the right to rest and leisure, including reasonable limitation of working hours and periodic holidays with pay.

Article 25

(1) Everyone has the right to a standard of living adequate for the health and well-being of himself and of his family, including food, clothing, housing and medical care and necessary social services, and the right to security in the event of unemployment, sickness, disability, widowhood, old age or other lack of livelihood in circumstances beyond his control.

(2) Motherhood and childhood are entitled to special care and assistance. All children, whether born in or out of wedlock, shall enjoy the same social protection.

Article 26

(1) Everyone has the right to education. Education shall be free, at least in the elementary and fundamental stages. Elementary education shall be compulsory. Technical and professional education shall be made generally available and higher education shall be equally accessible to all on the basis of merit.

(2) Education shall be directed to the full development of the human personality and to the strengthening of respect for human rights and fundamental freedoms. It shall promote understanding, tolerance and friendship among all nations, racial or religious groups, and shall further the activities of the United Nations for the maintenance of peace.

(3) Parents have a prior right to choose the kind of education that shall be given to their children.

Article 27

(1) Everyone has the right freely to participate in the cultural life of the community, to enjoy the arts and to share in scientific advancement and its benefits.

(2) Everyone has the right to the protection of the moral and material interests resulting from any scientific, literary or artistic production of which he is the author.

Article 28

Everyone is entitled to a social and international order in which the rights and freedoms set forth in this Declaration can be fully realized.

Article 29

(1) Everyone has duties to the community in which alone the free and full development of his personality is possible.

(2) In the exercise of his rights and freedoms, everyone shall be subject only to such limitations as are determined by law solely for the purpose of securing due recognition and respect for the rights and freedoms of others and of meeting the just requirements of morality, public order and the general welfare in a democratic society.

(3) These rights and freedoms may in no case be exercised contrary to the purposes and principles of the United Nations.

Article 30

Nothing in this Declaration may be interpreted as implying for any State, group or person any right to engage in any activity or to perform any act aimed at the destruction of any of the rights and freedoms set forth herein.

Council and the OAS. The confused mosaic of international organizations dealing with human rights reminds one of the old Keystone Cops colliding with each other in their rush to a crime scene. B. G. Ramcharan (1979), the Special Assistant to the Director of the U.N. Division of Human Rights, observed, "This proliferation of instruments and institutions . . . gives even the most optimistic an impression of confusion and weakness, and to others a feeling of failure" (p. 207). Even more depressing is the fact that the definition and protection of human rights abroad are generally given low priority by both American leaders and the general public (Tonelson, 1994; Holsti, 1996). Indeed, evidence suggests that concern about human rights is declining in the United States. Respondents to a national survey reported being most concerned with issues that applied directly to themselves or their country and were pressing at the moment. If these feelings are reflected in other countries, it is little wonder there have been so many difficulties developing a strong international program to protect human rights and deal with ethnic conflict.

WHOM TO PROTECT?   Even if we could develop a clear statement of basic human rights and the rights of ethnic groups, we would still be faced with the issue of how violations would be identified and at what level solutions would be applied. Most world bodies (such as the United Nations) and regional alliances (such as the Organization of American States) are composed of recognized nations. As a result, the avenue for raising issues is through one of the member nations. This is also the case for the World Court, as the International Court of Justice is usually called. Nations may submit their disputes to these bodies. But what happens when a problem occurs within the boundaries of a nation, as is commonly the case with ethnic problems? What are you to do if you feel that you are being denied a livelihood because you are a Kurd, especially if you live in a country that has no national laws protecting Kurds from discrimination? We certainly cannot expect an offending nation to request intervention. One avenue for raising intranational issues is for the victim to convince another nation to bring the problem to the international body. The United States, for example, might have asked the U.N. to examine the treatment of Jews in the Soviet Union. But nations are obviously reluctant to interfere in the domestic affairs of another nation. The accepted modus operandi is that conflict occurring within a nation will be handled by domestic agencies.

But Kleiboer (1996) points out another problem with this hands-off approach. How can it deal with conflicts like the Vietnam War that occur within one nation's borders but involve several nations? "Does domestic conflict such as in the former Yugoslavia turn into international conflict simply become some of the competing regions declare themselves independent and are recognized by some parts of the international community?" (p. 10). Treating domestic conflicts differently from international conflicts shuts many ethnic groups out of international protection.

At first glance, the solution to this problem seems simple: allow international bodies to intervene in all conflicts, whether domestic or international. But this "solution" would threaten the sovereignty of nations. Granting a nation international recognition implies that the global community will recognize its sovereignty, including its right to settle internal disputes. Creating global organizations that could ignore national sovereignty would imply that human rights are more important than national identity. A second alternative may be to create national ombudsmen offices, independent of political organizations, to deal with domestic ethnic conflicts. These agencies could receive support from an international body like the United Nations and function with an international agenda and an international definition of human rights. But this alternative would still threaten national sovereignty and could function only as long as a nation agreed to abide by an ombudsman's rulings.

Hence, for ethnic conflicts involving domestic groups, we must make do with unofficial organizations like Amnesty International, which are not constrained by national borders or by concerns with national sovereignty. But because these organizations are not officially sanctioned by nations, they have no official methods for dealing with conflicts or punishing groups that violate human rights.

HOW TO PROTECT?   If I haven't painted a bleak enough picture, let me add one more nail to the coffin. Let's take a group of Mexican-American farm workers and assume that their plight has been brought to the attention of the United Nations by a member nation. It is deemed that this group has been discriminated against and its basic rights have been violated. Further, it is determined that the U.S. government has not taken sufficient steps to redress the situation. Now what? Who should be punished, and how? The agency, the United Nations in this case, can demand fair treatment. But this demand will most likely fall on deaf ears if the offending nation tolerates the discrimination. The agency may next condemn the government of the offending nation, but there is obvious reluctance to interfere with governments and the sovereignty of nations.

Another step may be to have member nations agree to stop trading (either on selected items or completely) with the offending nation until the discrimination is eliminated. A trade embargo will injure the offending nation and may persuade it to take remedial action. This sounds like a fine solution until we consider it further. First, if the offending nation is strong or has products (such as oil) that other nations need, the avenging nations may suffer as much as the target. In this case, nations are unlikely to agree to a self-destructive action. Hence, trade embargoes are most likely to be selectively directed against poor nations or ones that have few essential goods. Second, trade embargoes affect everyone within the target nation, including, and sometimes especially, the group that was the object of discrimination. This is an uncomfortable prospect for all parties and makes embargoes an unattractive option in many cases.

Finally, an agency may use armed intervention to protect the injured group, as in Bosnia, but there are obvious drawbacks to such an action. It threatens the principle of the sovereignty of nations and places the peacekeeping force in harm's way. Casualties suffered by the force may lead people within the concerned nations to question the wisdom of involvement. Maintaining a peacekeeping force is costly. We must also consider whether a violation of human rights such as denying an ethnic group economic opportunities is sufficient to merit intervention.

There are then many issues involved with the implementation of procedures to protect human and group rights. These include defining what those rights are, how violations will be determined, and what actions will be taken when violations are identified. These issues are complicated because we must deal with these problems at many levels, including the individual, the group (ethnic, religious, political), and the nation. Finally, Banton (1997) raises an intriguing issue with regard to the United Nations' efforts to combat racism. He points out that the approach one adopts to deal with a social issue is ultimately based on how one views the causes of that problem. In the 1960s, when the U.N. was struggling to develop a response to racism, two different perspectives became evident. Some nations viewed racism as a crime that merited punishment. Others perceived it as a social sickness that afflicted some societies but not others. The treatment of a sickness is very different from the response to a crime. But even those who saw racism as a social illness had different perspectives. The Soviets argued that racism was a result of capitalism, while the newly independent nations of Africa traced the cause to colonialism. European states saw racism as resulting from doctrines of racial inequality adopted by some nations. Each of these views suggested a different approach to eliminating racial (ethnic) discrimination.

AN OUNCE OF PREVENTION . . .   All the options I have discussed are designed to deal with conflicts that have already broken out. But there is a better option: prevention. Conflicts and confrontations are notoriously difficult to resolve; even when they are dealt with, there is often a residue of negative feeling between the groups, which can serve as a foundation for future conflicts. In the area of ethnic relations, we need measures designed to promote understanding and harmony, measures that will *prevent* destructive confrontation before it starts.

I recently found a letter from my county sheriff taped to my door. The letter included a note from a citizen who had seen several children riding their bicycles carelessly on a busy street. The sheriff pointed no finger of accusation. Instead, he stated that this event was a formula for tragedy and requested the neighborhood's help to prevent it. His letter made people aware of the situation, pointed out what would be likely to happen if steps were not taken, and requested help. No law was evoked and no threat of punishment was raised, but I have not seen a single unaccompanied child riding down that road since the letter was sent.

Prevention can take many forms. As in any program designed to avoid a problem, steps can be taken to identify conditions that may be ripe for ethnic conflict. Careful study of past ethnic conflicts might find, for example, that ethnic conflict is most likely to flare up when an ethnic group is a minority in two contiguous countries, or when one ethnic group occupies the lowest rung of the socioeconomic ladder within a country. A second step is to identify the types of interventions that are most successful in reducing ethnic tension. Such interventions might include increasing contact between schoolchildren of different ethnic groups, education about the history and customs of ethnic groups in a country, or basic lessons in conflict resolution. Such programs could be made available to countries along with incentives (economic or other) to implement them. A similar approach is used to motivate countries to adopt vaccination programs. In these cases, it is recognized that the outbreak of an epidemic in one country has global implications. Such is also the case when an outbreak involves ethnic conflict; strife within one country is likely to infect other countries.

An obvious question is what body would be responsible for developing and implementing such programs. The U.N. Security Council has a major role in ensuring world peace. Its role has been reactive, responding to the outbreak of conflicts. It is not too far-fetched to suggest that the Security Council could take a lead in prevention, since preemptive programs may prove equally effective in securing world peace.

There are many issues surrounding the prevention of ethnic conflict. The point to keep in mind is that the topic is as urgent, and deserves as much serious consideration, as efforts to "treat" ethnic conflict once it erupts. Indeed, an ounce of prevention may save pounds of suffering. Ceasefires, imposed peace, and peacekeeping troops are not necessarily the only or the best way to build bridges between ethnic groups.

A Global Culture: The Concept of a World Village

Whether we look to strong third-party nations to rescue ethnic groups or to international bodies to intervene, we always seem to run up against the same obstacle: national sovereignty. We must step lightly around the boundaries of nations, lest they feel threatened or become agitated. We have neatly carved up our world into 150 or so nations. National boundaries often make little geographical or cultural sense, but we humans go to great lengths to protect these sacred units. We fly flags, sing songs, and pledge allegiance. We entrust our nations with protecting us and our groups, defining what is correct and incorrect behavior, and creating economic and political systems that rule our lives. At times we seem to forget that nations are the creation of humans. We allow nations to grant us an identity (citizenship) rather than realizing that it is we, the people, who hold the power of life or death over our nation's existence. But unlike our ethnic identity, which is ingrained in our physical fiber, national identity is invented by humans and is worn like a suit that can be changed at will. If obsessive concern with national sovereignty gums up the machinery of global bodies, why not simply do away with the concept of the nation?

Wallerstein (1990) suggests that people can be defined along three dimensions. Our idiosyncratic character makes us different from any other person: this is the individual perspective. Then there are the characteristics that define the person as a member of a series of groups such as nations, religions, and ethnic groups. Finally, there are the universal characteristics of the species that bind all humans together. For the most part, our discussion—and indeed the history of the world—has focused on people as individuals or members of groups, including nations.

Nations are critical because they create social order and protect their citizens. Elias (1987) argues that the emphasis on nation-states made good sense when groups could protect themselves by banding together, when economic realities restricted the size and scope of business, and when communication between people was limited. But today's world is different. Human ingenuity has developed weapons so terrible that the entire human race can be vaporized into oblivion. No group can protect its members from the power of "the bomb." Economics knows no national boundaries. Multinational companies spread into every corner of the world without respect for national boundaries. And communicating with someone across the world is nearly as easy and quick as talking to your next-door neighbor.

The opportunities and demands of our world have changed dramatically. Why then do we cling to a division of people into nation-states—a division that was de-

Business knows no boundaries. Can politics follow the same route? (Reuters/Claro Cortes/ Archive Photos)

signed to adapt to the world situation of 350 years ago? This question becomes especially critical if we determine that our division into nations inhibits us from developing greater harmony between each other and between ethnic groups. The boundaries of nations often slice through the heart of ethnic groups, separating members by high walls and barbed-wire fences. Even when ethnic groups are contained within national boundaries, national governments sit idly by as these groups scramble for power and dominance; and these same groups scream about violations of national sovereignty if another power seeks to intervene.

The possibility of eliminating nations or reducing their importance has been suggested by proponents of a *global culture,* a culture designed to unite all people on the basis of characteristics they share as human beings (Featherstone, 1990; Smith, 1988). There are a wide variety of suggestions about the shape a global culture would assume. Some see a world without boundaries, where everyone speaks a common language, obeys a common set of laws, and shares a common identity and destiny (Smith, 1990). "We, the people" would apply to the world's people. With no boundaries or nation-states, there would be no barriers to travel, no concern with citizenship, and no national sovereignty. Other people would retain nations but make them subservient to the global will. Nations would help organize people and provide some means for order, but people's allegiance would be to the global community of humanity. National boundaries would be loose social constructs or simply geographic reference points. Social and economic problems would be addressed by a global body unrestrained by considerations of national sovereignty.

The idea of a global culture builds nicely on psychological theories of recategorization, which suggest that the reduction of interpersonal and intergroup conflict can best be achieved by changing group boundaries so that all parties view themselves as belonging to the same group (Gaertner, Mann, Dovidio, & Murrell, 1990; Worchel, 1986). We have conflict and discrimination, it is argued, because we have groups. If we eliminate the group boundaries that separate people and encourage people to see themselves as belonging to a single supergroup, a major source of conflict would be eliminated. In this view nations are a major cause of conflict and an impediment to reducing it.

On a recent trip to the Rio Grande Valley in Texas, I was struck by the intrusive presence of immigration agents, who patrolled the highways like an army of angry ants. They seemed so serious and so intent on keeping illegal immigrants out. But the absurdity of the situation was made clear when one agent confided that they were fighting a hopeless battle in which deterring even a small number of illegals would be considered a victory. Indeed, both the hopelessness of the situation and its warlike quality were underscored by the fact that during my trip a grand jury was considering a case of a mistaken, fatal shooting by border guards of a Mexican-American teenager herding his goats. My companion contributed additional irony when she remarked that the economic system of the southern United States would collapse if the battle against illegals were really won: "Several economists point out that there would be no one to take up the menial, but critical, jobs performed by the illegal aliens." But the band plays on because national boundaries are lines in the sand (or rivers in a valley) that separate people and dictate who is legal and who is not.

The idea of a global culture evokes images of the old Coca Cola commercial in which people from around the world held hands and sang, "I'd Like to Teach the World to Sing." There is a simple elegance to a plan that seeks to bring people into harmony by stressing their universal characteristics and inducing them to see themselves as belonging to a single group. Although most such plans go no further than eliminating nation-states, we could dream about a world purged of all distinctions that divide us. We might eliminate our religious differences and our linguistic differences. And with a few generations of selective breeding, we could confuse ethnic lineages to such a point that ethnic differences would become meaningless too. Once we reached this point of homogeneity, conflicts would center on individuals rather than groups, and social scientists tell us that people are less competitive when they act as individuals rather than as members of a group (Insko et al., 1990).

Tempting, isn't it? But could it work? The world has seen experiments of this nature, albeit on a limited scale. The aim of the Soviet Union was to create a superstate in which people were loyal to and identified with the new community (Fedoseyev et al., 1977). The Soviet Union was to incorporate several nation-states into one union that would disregard the old boundaries. Religion, which tended to divide people, would be eliminated and replaced by atheism and communist ideology. And ethnic communities, after a period of growing cooperation, would "fuse together to produce a truly 'Soviet culture'" (Smith, 1990, p. 173). It was a grand goal, and progress was made toward it, although many Western observers argued that the loss of personal freedom did not justify the accomplishments. But in the 1990s, the grand union foundered in a bloody sea of ethnic and national conflict. Ethnic hatred and regional identification remained, even during the height of the Soviet Union's power. The experience of the Soviet Union, then, gives us little reason to believe in the success of bringing multitudes of people into a common tent.

For another example of an attempt to create a grand union that would reduce or avoid ethnic, regional, and religious animosities, let us raise the stars and stripes. We must concede that the United States began with an advantage over the Soviet Union because it was not faced with unifying many indigenous groups with long-standing attachments to specific regions. The land was cleared of any human flotsam that might stand in the way of the waves of immigrants. The initial formula was rather simple: All were welcome as long as they shed or submerged their ethnic identity, embraced the identity of their new country, and agreed to let others worship freely. By many measures, the experiment has been a success. With the exception of the bloody Civil War fought over the issue of slavery and states' rights, there have been no major wars between ethnic, religious, or racial groups. But American society is obviously not free of these conflicts. Poverty is not color-blind, and certain ethnic groups (African-Americans, Hispanics, Native Americans) are disproportionately represented in the lower economic echelons. Ethnic hatred simmers just below the surface, ready to boil over with the slightest provocation such as an isolated incident of police brutality toward a member of an ethnic group. O. J. Simpson's trial for the murder of his ex-wife and her friend became consumed with the issue of white and black racism. The beating of an African-American motorist by several white policemen in Los Angeles set off a firestorm of ethnic violence involving Asians and Hispanics as well as Anglos and African-Americans. The country holds its collective breath when violence breaks out between people of different ethnicity, because these incidents are so readily viewed as intergroup rather than interpersonal conflicts. Members of minority ethnic and religious groups still find discrimination in the workplace, schools, and neighborhoods.

In an interesting study of national and ethnic identification, Sidanius, Feshbach, Levin, and Pratto (1996) found a considerable degree of ethnic identity in the United States. Most interesting was the finding that attachment to an ethnic group was positively related to nationalism *for the dominant white group.* That is, the more strongly white respondents identified with their ethnic group, the stronger was their attachment to the United States. The pattern was reversed for minority groups (Asians, African-Americans, Hispanics). Strong attachment to these ethnic groups was associated with less identification with supergroup, the United States.

Therefore, we must withhold judgment on the success of the United States in creating a superculture, a single identity for all its people. It is unclear whether the United States is a country of people or peoples. Certainly there is reason to feel encouraged. But there is a cloud on the horizon. It may be argued that what has united the United States has been its opposition to other nations, first the British and later the communist nations—the Soviet Union, China, even Cuba, North Vietnam, and North Korea. As outside threats recede, will the nation turn upon itself, exaggerating ethnic distinctions among Americans?

What about Europe, which is moving—in fits and starts—toward a superidentity? The European Union is a hot issue, and there are many different visions of what will be involved in a European Community. Is it merely an economic alliance among nations, or will it involve the development of a superculture and a common language that would eventually eliminate the need for separate identifiable nations. The process of creating such a union is filled with minefields, reflecting the prejudices of the groups involved.

CURRENTS AND CROSS-CURRENTS.   As yet there is no example we can cite of elimination of conflict and animosity between ethnic groups. Some countries have taken steps in this direction, none has come close to the goal. If we examine the aims of these grand unions, we can identify some of the reasons for failure. As we pointed out in Chapter 1, we humans dance to two fiddlers. One plays the tune of inclusion and belonging, while the other offers the melody of uniqueness. The theme of uniqueness leads us to demonstrate how we are different from (and hopefully better than) others. Our identity is partly defined by the groups to which we belong *and partly by the groups to which we do not belong.* Emphasizing that we all belong to the same large group eliminates an important dimension of our identity—the out-group. In a truly global village, there would be no out-groups. This can be uncomfortable and dissatisfying, given our need to be unique.

So even if a band plays beautiful music, we tend to separate the drummers from the trombone players. This categorization not only helps us describe the band but gives the various players unique identities. While we might accept and enjoy our membership in a world community, we constantly want to make finer distinctions, to place ourselves and others in some recognizable category within that community. The category may be based on place (physical or social), function, appearance, language, or some other identifiable feature. Once this categorization occurs, we sow the seed for conflict based on groupings.

The global culture, therefore, runs counter to our basic need for uniqueness. To this countercurrent we can also throw in all those other human failings, such as the striving for power, control, and recognition, that also pave the streets of human conflict. The result is that any global culture, like the supreme Soviet Union, will soon begin to fissure and crack along group and category lines.

A Concluding Comment

Although I have painted a rather pessimistic picture of the use of outsiders or supergroups to resolve ethnic conflict and develop ethnic harmony, we should not become completely discouraged. The bottom line is that we cannot rest assured (as my students did) that ethnic conflict and genocide "can't happen here." The formation of powerful police groups or a global culture is not *the* solution to ethnic violence and conflict. But it may be *a* solution. In other words, these measures can help and have helped to reduce strife between ethnic groups. Each "super" solution has weaknesses that prohibit it from being a cure-all. But each measure also has strengths that enable it, under certain circumstances, to contribute. As we will see in Chapter 9, the problem of ethnic relations is complex and requires complex solutions, drawing on all levels of human relations and demanding persistence and patience.

R E A D I N G   8 . 1

UN Report on Death Camps*

GENEVA — Iraq has apparently executed hundreds of people from its southern marshes in "death camps" in recent months, a United Nations investigator has said.

In a report to the UN Human Rights commission, Max van der Stoel yesterday cited reports Iraqi agents provoked internal dissent among the marsh residents "that reportedly led to 2000 deaths in the fall of 1992."

Detainees from southern Iraq reportedly were transported in groups of up to 200 to death camps in the north, the report said.

Farmers in nearby Kurdish-controlled areas said they saw busloads of people with southern Iraqi features arrive and heard gunshots on subsequent evenings, van der Stoel said. The former Dutch foreign minister called the allegations "extremely disturbing."

Iraq's marsh Arabs have come increasingly under pressure as President Saddam Hussein battles Shi'ite Muslim rebels holed up in a labyrinth of islands and lagoons since a failed 1991 uprising.

The US and its allies last August banned Iraqi warplanes from below the 32nd parallel to help protect the Shi'ites, who make up 55 per cent of Iraq's 17 million people.

In an interview, Van der Stoel declined to elaborate on his sources but said the mass executions allegedly happened in recent months. He did not offer a total death count.

Van der Stoel's annual report to the commission, the top UN human rights watchdog now meeting in Geneva, also demanded that Iraq end its economic blockade of Kurdish areas in the north and southern Shi'ite regions.

Iraqi Kurds may not survive the next winter because they depend on the government to let through international humanitarian aid and have cut down many fruit trees for firewood this winter, the report said.

Torture by Iraqi security forces, including beatings, burnings and electric shocks, remained widespread in the past year, it said, citing "an all-pervasive order of repression" in which "innumerable violations" of human rights occur.   — AP

*Source: *Waikato* (New Zealand) *Times,* March 3, 1993.

French Flex Muscles in Rwanda*

MARK FRITZ

GOMA, Zaire—French marines and Foreign Legionnaires headed into Rwanda on Thursday to protect civilians from ethnic massacres, ignoring warnings from rebels that they will be treated as an enemy in the civil war.

The commander of the small U.N. peacekeeping force in Rwanda said he hoped the French would stay away from front lines between troops of Rwanda's Hutu-dominated government and the mainly Tutsi rebel movement.

A small group of French soldiers in armored vehicles met no opposition and was welcomed by local residents after advancing several miles into western Rwanda, a military spokesman said in Paris, speaking on condition of anonymity.

The Rwandan army is believed to control the western third of the small Central African nation. The rebels have won control of the eastern two-thirds since the war resumed April 6 after a suspicious plane crash killed Rwanda's Hutu president, who had reached a power-sharing accord with the Tutsi minority.

About 40 Foreign Legion paratroopers protected by helicopter gunships crossed the border from Bukavu, 60 miles south of Goma, the military said. Their goal was to secure a refugee camp near Cyangugu, to protect 8,000 Tutsis from the widespread slaughter being inflicted on Tutsis by Hutu militias.

The United Nations and aid groups estimate more than 200,000 Rwandans have died in the past 2 ½ months, most of them civilians.

A reconnaissance team of French marines also headed from Goma for the northwestern region of Gisenyi, French state radio reported, quoting an unidentified government source.

"The role is only to protect refugees," said Col. Andre Schill, a French spokesman in Goma. He said French troops would use their weapons only if threatened or to protect refugees.

"We are not out here to make a new war, but to protect people. We are not here to shoot," he told reporters.

The French government said it was sending about 2,500 soldiers and marines for the two-month mission that was authorized Wednesday by the U.N. Security Council as a stopgap until a larger, all-African peacekeeping force can deploy.

Schill said 500 French soldiers already were in Goma, including marine infantrymen, supply troops and combat engineers. About 250 paratroopers were in Bukavu, he said. French troops were turning the airport at Kinsangani, Zaire, into an air base to support the mission, dubbed "Operation Turquoise."

In Kigali, Rwanda's capital, Maj. Gen. Romeo Dallaire, the Canadian commander

---

*Source: The Bryan-College Station Eagle, June 24, 1994, pp. A1, A4.

of the 450 U.N. peacekeepers, said he had not been contacted by the French force but expected them to stay away from confrontation zones.

Dallaire cautioned against intervening in a civil war "when you do not have the consent of both sides." He said he took seriously rebel threats to attack French troops.

Although the French government says the operation is a strictly humanitarian mission, the rebel Rwandan Patriotic Front is suspicious because French intervention blocked a rebel offensive in 1990.

"We have no doubt whatsoever that their intentions are far from being humanitarian," Theogene Rudasingwa, secretary-general of the Patriotic Front, told journalists in Paris.

The rebels' representative in Paris, Jacques Bihozagara, said rebel forces would not seek out French troops. But he warned the rebels would "treat them as invaders" if they did make contact.

"Combat is possible" because France "is on the side of the fascists," he said.

French Premier Edouard Baladur said Wednesday that he could not exclude the possibility of fighting, but his conditions for the operation indicated French troops would not deploy near rebel areas.

France sought support Thursday from European and African countries for the virtually solo foray into Rwanda. But many countries have said France's past in Rwanda makes it poorly placed to lead a neutral operation.

R E A D I N G   8 . 3

Internationalism as a Complement to Nationalism*

RONALD STEEL

LOS ANGELES—The unrestricted movement of money and jobs does not benefit all nations equally. There are winners and losers. In relations with its Cold War allies, like Japan, the United States has been a loser. The people of strong nations do not like to be losers, even in the name of internationalism.

Nor does every country that sings the praises of the market play by the rules. The United States sucks in goods from all over the world—even at the cost of throwing Americans out of jobs—on the grounds that Americans have a right to buy whatever they please at the cheapest price.

The Japanese, however, while profiting from America's open doors, are opposed to opening theirs—as is indicated by the current impasse over Japanese barriers to U.S. auto parts. The Japanese believe in production, not consumption; in full employment, not cheap imports. They like America's rules as exporters, but play by their own as importers.

---

*Source: *International Herald Tribune,* June 8, 1995.

Even if economists do not mind the loss of blue-collar jobs, the so-called redundant workers do. Falling incomes and insecurity provoke tension and bitterness. When people feel disenfranchised and disempowered, when there are ever-fewer jobs for blue-collar workers, when factory workers are forced to flip hamburgers to pay the bills, they will make their anger felt. They will do this at the polls, or even violently.

The nation-state, for all the crimes committed in its name, is still the primary source of loyalty for most people. Although there is an international market and the rudiments of what could be called a global culture, there is no such thing as an international loyalty. No one gets a lump in his throat standing before the blue-and-white United Nations flag.

Those who call themselves internationalists have not fully faced the problem of linking domestic needs to presumed foreign policy interests. They seem to assume that the Cold War consensus—which called for the dominance of foreign policy over domestic policy—can be carried over into a totally different era. The most vociferous of the internationalists say that Americans must take sides in a Balkan civil war to show that they are good internationalists. They casually dismiss their critics as "isolationists," hoping that the epithet alone will send them scurrying for cover.

That accusation is not only hyperbolic but ineffectual. There is no serious support for isolationism in America, and has been none for 50 years. There is unlikely to be any unless foreign policy elites succeed, by seeming to sacrifice domestic concerns to foreign policy objectives, in making internationalism appear hostile to U.S. interests.

Economic, political and cultural engagement with the world is not a choice for the United States: It is a simple reality. But it is not the only force at play. While in one sense the world is becoming smaller and more integrated, it is also growing more divided. Traditional cultural and economic barriers, particularly among trained and privileged elites, are being eroded.

Yet there is also a reversion to earlier patterns of international life, regional coalitions, power balances, spheres of influence and conflicts among tribes and faiths. The fragmentation of what recently seemed a politically stable, if divided, world is a hallmark of our times.

If internationalism is to command support it must be not as an alternative to nationalism, but as a supplement to it. Peoples will not switch their loyalties from the nation-states with which they identify to international organizations they cannot control and view as hostile to their interests. Internationalism can marshal respect only if it is seen as a way of achieving, or at least not impeding, national objectives.

Those objectives are not what they were during the Cold War. The American public cannot be expected to continue to permit Cold War allies such as Japan and South Korea, or anti-Soviet partners of convenience such as China, to decimate America's own industrial base in the name of a free trade internationalism that those countries themselves do not practice. A nation that is unwilling or unable to protect its own workers because it is shackled to such intellectual abstractions as open markets and the unrestricted export of money and jobs is a nation doomed to internal strife and second-class status.

An enlightened American nationalism will put a higher priority on the protection of American jobs than on helping corporations move their factories abroad in pursuit of cheap labor. It will not plunge the United States into distant wars it does not understand and cannot resolve, and where its own interests are not involved. It will also stop providing free military protection for its economic rivals in order to maintain the illusion that it thereby preserves its status as "superpower." There is a more accurate description for that role: unpaid security guard.

Internationalism should not be viewed, like charity, as a badge of good intentions. Nor is it, like empathy, an absolute good in itself. It is simply a method to advance the interests of people organized into national societies under particular circumstances. Where it does this it will be embraced. Where it does not, all the pious proclamations in the world will not save it.

CHAPTER 9

THE ENDLESS JOURNEY

Some Concluding Remarks

Aging is an affliction that should be visited only on the young. As I've gotten older, my body has taken to reminding me of each and every excess I indulged in during my younger years. After searching for the perfect point to penetrate my aging fortress, nature has chosen my foot. For reasons unknown to me or medical science, and on a maddeningly unpredictable timetable, pain will flare up in my foot and I will be incapacitated for a while. In our modern age of technology and medical miracles, an injection, a pill, or even an operation that will cure my undeserved and seemingly unprovoked misery seems little to ask. But even though I have visited every medical professional, faith healer, and homeopathic expert, and even a few veterinarians, within a hundred miles of my home, the message I hear is consistent. My treatment must involve both prevention to avoid the flare-ups and treatment when I do suffer a bout of pain. My regimen must include dealing with the problem on a systemic level, such as by changing my diet and getting "into shape" (a prescription for thoroughgoing torture). Other measures must be directed at the exact location of my misery (my foot); these include taking medication, applying magnets, and undergoing acupuncture. And then there is a final insult: these efforts must be sustained, long-term, and continuous. In other words, with effort I can control my problem, but I'll never eliminate it.

You may be wondering why I would subject you to a description of my personal ills. Venting my frustration was not one of the prescribed methods for dealing with my problem, and my aim is not to arouse your sympathy. Rather, my point is to draw an analogy between the advice I received for dealing with my ills and the prescription that must be written for societies attempting to cope with ethnic conflict, hatred, and violence.

A Complex Problem Requires a Complex Prescription

ALL RUNGS OF THE LADDER.   If we seek the factors that contribute to ethnic violence, we must look at all levels of human behavior. As I have pointed out, a spark of ethnic hatred can be found within each of us. We are all endowed with an ethnic heritage that determines which groups we belong to and which groups we are excluded from. Each of us wants to have a unique, positive identity. Each of us faces daily frustrations and hassles that can sometimes enrage us and dispose us to behave aggressively. Like a moth to a flame, we are attracted to others who are similar to us, and we fear those who are different. These conditions lead us to nestle in the bosom of our ethnic group and prepare us to hate those with a different heritage.

But ethnic hatred is not a torch that we bear by ourselves. The groups to which we belong seem only too willing to lend their support. The dynamics of groups often conspire to make extremists out of moderates, activists out of pacifists, and blind conformists out of freethinking independents. Groups themselves struggle for recognition and power, and one group's climb to the top is frequently achieved at the expense of other groups. In-groups often sanction or encourage discrimination against out-groups. Ethnic conflict occurs between individuals and between groups, and its drama unfolds before a world audience.

Because ethnic conflict is nurtured by forces at the individual, group, and intergroup levels, efforts to reduce it must be targeted at each level. Training our children to be open and accepting of others is not enough if our larger social system invites and supports ethnic discrimination. By the same token, there is little to be gained by encouraging groups to adopt policies of ethnic tolerance while individuals continue to segregate themselves from people who are ethnically different. At the broadest level, the collective people must address the issue of human rights directly, not only to define these rights but also to develop ways to protect people whose rights are violated. The strength of even the most effective program will be severely diluted if it is not supported by additional programs aimed at other domains of human experience. We might present the situation as a band in which even the most accomplished musician cannot save the music if other members of the group are playing off-key.

Although a coordinated strategy is necessary for treating our ethnic ills, unfortunately the way our world is constructed makes it difficult to develop systemic approaches. Like the medical profession, our social universe is composed of specialists, each with a specific interest and domain. Our religions cradle our souls, local agencies control the education that shapes our minds, the business world sets the rules for our economic existence, and political organizations provide security and endow us with national identities. Although each agency claims to be the most important, there is no formal coordinator of these various functions. We are part of a social orchestra with no conductor. We have national and regional agendas but no true human agenda that could unite us and enable us to deal effectively with common problems such as ethnic conflict, destruction of the environment, or the safe use of nuclear energy. Quite possibly, earlier limitations on travel and communication saved us. These limits enabled us to deal with social issues using narrow instruments within narrow bounds.

The advances of our modern world have shaken the old structures. We have become global Peeping Toms, instantly aware of events taking place in any corner of our world. We can compare our personal condition with that of someone in the farthest reaches of the world. We can hear the drumbeat of our ethnic brethren in a distant homeland. We are painfully aware that an ethnic storm brewing in a remote cor-

According to many social theories, the path to ethnic harmony must begin by tearing down real and psychological walls between groups. (Reuters/David Brauchli/Archive Photos)

ner of the world can quickly expand and sweep all of us into its eye. Regional and national borders no longer receive the respect they once enjoyed. Ethnic identities compete openly and effectively with national identities. Ethnicity is becoming more, rather than less, central to our personal identity. The increasing pull of ethnic identities can be seen in the frequent use of the term *former* to describe nations: the former Soviet Union, the former Yugoslavia, the former Czechoslovakia, the former East and West Germany. These countries had to step aside to make way for new ones built on an ethnic foundation. People are being drawn back to their native homelands in increasing numbers. Even within national boundaries, ethnic groups are expanding their influence. Every day, newspapers carry stories reflecting this rise in ethnic identity and influence. As the social landscape undergoes dramatic changes, the ability of regional and narrowly focused efforts to address issues is severely tested. Coordinated efforts to prepare societies to develop global policy on the issues raised by the increasing awareness of ethnic identity become more critical if our world is to thrive.

THE IMPORTANCE OF PERSISTENCE.   One of the largest complaints in our modern world is that we don't have enough time. As a result, we seek "quick fixes" for

whatever troubles us. When my foot aches, I demanded a pill or a surgical procedure that will immediately end my pain and cure my ailment. People flock to buy
lottery tickets—with visions of getting rich overnight dancing through their heads.
The seductive lure of drugs is that they will bring us instant happiness. Politicians
know that they can win our hearts with a plan that promises a few quick steps to
end national ills: cut military spending, cut taxes, eliminate welfare or the Internal
Revenue Service. We are a world of quick-fix junkies with little tolerance for the complex or the protracted.

Ethnic identity is woven into the fabric of our society. It touches nearly every aspect of our lives from cradle to grave. There is no social surgical procedure or magic
pill that will instantly set things right. Dealing with ethnic conflict requires strate-
gies both to prevent conflict and to treat it when it occurs. The prescription calls for
constant and continued vigilance and action. New educational programs, a change
in the structure of political representation, or the adoption of a world charter of
human rights may improve the relationship between ethnic groups today. But
today's success offers no guarantee for tomorrow.

As we have seen, there are a multitude of forces within the human psyche that
foster conflict and hatred between ethnic groups, including our basic need for identity and power and our fear of insecurity and dependence. Nature has endowed us
with a willingness to hate others because of the groups to which they belong. There
is no surgical procedure, educational program, or social reengineering that will remove this force. Research in the social sciences, however, has demonstrated that the
force can be controlled. As was noted earlier, in a classic study on intergroup relations Sherif and his colleagues (1961) found that they could reduce hostility between
two groups of campers through *repeated* incidents of cooperation toward a common
goal. A single cooperative endeavor or positive contact did little to mitigate intergroup hostility.

We are too often seduced into believing that we can solve a social ill if we apply
the right solution. We rush into riot-torn areas to build new schools and new housing, create more jobs, and new political organizations. Having made these improvements, we congratulate ourselves and turn our attention toward another issue. We
are shocked when the same area is the scene of a riot again some years later. Similarly,
we can point to numerous places on the world map where ethnic conflict rears its
ugly head time after time, even when social architects believe that sufficient changes
have been made to solve the problem. Germany has no Hitler today, but ethnic tension is once again roiling the waters. Old animosities between Serbs and Croats revisited Yugoslavia after decades of relative harmony and unity. In the United States,
despite the changes instituted during the civil rights movement of the 1960s, there
is rising ethnic tension. A single incident of perceived racially motivated police violence has ignited riots from California to Florida.

We may conclude that the recurrence of violence and hatred proves that the initial plan was flawed. We then scurry into our social laboratories to concoct another
potion; next time we are sure to hit on the "right" formula. But these frantic efforts
distract us from recognizing a fundamental issue. Ethnic conflict is not virus that has
attacked our social system, requiring strong antibodies to destroy it. The propensity
for ethnic conflict is a chronic condition that requires continued treatment and at-

tention. Critical race theory, in fact, argues that racism and ethnic discrimination are so deeply rooted in society that they will never be eliminated (Bell, 1992). But they can be controlled. Efforts to deal with conflict must take a long-term perspective. Indeed, since our social system may develop immunity to programs, a policy that promotes ethnic harmony at one time may not be effective at another time. Those who argue that affirmative action has served its purpose may have a point. The program may be worn out. But to conclude that the only logical option is to declare victory over discrimination and eliminate the program is dangerously shortsighted. The goal of combating discrimination must remain a priority, although different programs or redesigned interventions may be necessary in the future.

We must view efforts to develop ethnic tolerance as an ongoing social experiment with no foreseeable end point. This recognition is bitter medicine for a world accustomed to promises of quick fixes. But to take a short-term perspective is to invite defeat and recurrent disappointment.

OFFERING A CARROT RATHER THAN A STICK.   Raising children is always a challenge, but it is especially daunting when the children are carbon copies of each other. I always felt that twins were especially blessed because they were born with a playmate and would never have to fear being friendless. But my twins have shown

Ethnic harmony is not an end goal but a process that requires constant nurturing and attention. Periodic race riots in the United States stand as a reminder of this message. (Bill Aron/PhotoEdit)

me the other side of the coin. Being a twin also means that one is born with a constant competitor and an ever-present standard of comparison. As a result, the battles between twins are as intense as their bonds of love and friendship. Since I am a concerned parent who craves peace and quiet, the eruption of an energetic duel between my twins once elicited an immediate and equally energetic response from me. I rushed into the fray threatening my battling midgets with punishments ranging from cutting off their allowance to cutting off vital body parts; then I banished them to their rooms. This achieved a few moments of cherished quiet, but soon, from a far corner of the house, the trumpets of war again sounded in the air. I was incapable of devising a punishment severe enough to force harmony. In fact, I felt that my punishment often united my angels to demonstrate that their will to fight was stronger than my resolve to punish. Just when I was ready to put myself up for adoption, I visited a friend, also blessed with twins. During our conversation, her twins played quietly in a corner of the room, cooperating to assemble a jigsaw puzzle. I was about to comment on this unnatural state of affairs when she turned to her children and praised them, promising an afternoon in the park.

When we examine institutional approaches to creating ethnic harmony, we find that most have a common feature; they identify actions that are designated illegal and describe the punishment that will be visited on those who break the rules. In other words, we use coercion to achieve desired behaviors. In a careful analysis of the basis of power, French and Raven (1959) identify the unfortunate consequences of coercion. First, those who are punished resent the enforcer. Second, the effective use of coercion requires surveillance (Shaw & Condelli, 1986). Rarely does anyone come forward to admit violating a rule and request punishment. In the area of ethnic relations, the threat of punishment has often pushed prejudice underground, leading people to develop the increasingly subtle methods of discrimination that social scientists term "symbolic racism" (Sears, 1988). An uneasy truce prevails until surveillance is relaxed, then conflict reignites.

There is, however, an alternative approach to promoting ethnic harmony—the use of rewards to recognize desired behaviors and outcomes. Emphasis could be placed on defining goals in ethnic relations and identifying acts that could achieve those goals. Then, groups that undertake these actions could be rewarded. The advantage of using rewards is that this approach does not require surveillance. Those who perform an appropriate action would come forward to proclaim it. The "enforcer," in this case, becomes a benefactor who is valued and sought out. Imagine a world court whose role was to seek out examples of positive ethnic relations and respect for human rights. Rewards could take a variety of forms, ranging from public recognition to allocating valued resources. The jury would decide the size of a reward rather than the severity of a punishment.

Drawing on the research on power, we could go one step further and use *referent power* to entice people toward ethnic harmony. Referent power rests on our desire to be similar to those we admire, motivating us to imitate them and act as we think they would act (French & Raven, 1959). In a world of few heroes and heroines, a great athlete or brave warrior has a better chance of being singled out as an exemplar than an individual who has healed ethnic wounds. For example, history books devote considerable attention to President Franklin Roosevelt, who guided the United States through World War II, but none give equal attention to Eleanor Roosevelt's staunch support for racial equality or her help in passing the Declaration of Human Rights as her country's delegate to the United Nations.

We need a proactive approach to ethnic relations. Rather than punishing transgressions, we need to reward desirable actions. A reward brings advantage to all parties to an interaction, whereas punishment is administered to one. We gain very little if those who have abused us are themselves abused and punished. But both sides gain if both are rewarded for their cooperative efforts. And if we bestow admiration on those who have worked for ethnic harmony, we set up models for others to follow.

It is unreasonable to assume that we can instantly transform the world's police forces into benevolent benefactors. But it is not unreasonable to consider expanding the scope of our watchful eyes to include identifying and rewarding positive examples, while remaining vigilant for transgressions.

PROACTION RATHER THAN REACTION.   I've referred several times to the value of prevention. I once had a client who observed that people paid attention to him only if he exploded with anger when faced with stress. It often takes a riot, a war, or some other destructive behavior to galvanize efforts to "fix" a problem. A popular television advertisement exhorted automobile owners to perform preventive maintenance on their automobiles by warning, "Pay me [the mechanic] now or pay me much more later." Paying $20 to get an oil change could save us from having to shell out $2,000 to replace an engine in the future.

We can develop programs to promote harmony, cooperation, and understanding now, before a problem manifests itself, or we can wait until a calamity forces us to create such programs. The cost of waiting is obviously much greater. The eruption of ethnic conflict leaves a terrible toll of torn bodies and scarred psyches. Once unleashed, hatred is slow to subside. And solutions to conflict that are developed in the frenzied heat of battle are rarely carefully crafted or well reasoned. The aim of these interventions must be to deal with the crisis at hand, and actions that quell an existing problem may actually foster conflict in the future. The French intervention in Central Africa in 1990 dampened the immediate crisis, but it created a governmental structure that contributed to renewed ethnic violence in 1994.

The time to confront ethnic conflict effectively is before it has reached the point of destructiveness. Obviously, it is beyond the realm of reason to suggest a ghostbuster force that would rush uninvited into areas to rid them of the conditions that spawn ethnic violence. But it is not unreasonable to develop national and international organizations to identify areas in most danger of serious ethnic conflict and to offer help and resources for developing preventive programs. There is no guarantee that any region will accept aid, but we can assume that "benign neglect" will perpetuate a world characterized by intermittent outbreaks of ethnic violence and a con-

Examples of cooperation between ethnic groups deserve as much recognition as do examples of ethnic violence. The public is well schooled in events of destruction but often left ignorant about the rebuilding and cooperation that follows. (David Young-Wolff/PhotoEdit)

stant state of simmering ethnic prejudice. We exist now like firefighters waiting for the alarm to ring and wondering who will answer the call.

Ethnic Conflict: A Silver Lining in a Dark Cloud

It would be quite appropriate to conclude this examination of ethnic identity and conflict on a somber and pessimistic note. We've examined some of the most heinous human behavior. Our trail has been littered with torn bodies and twisted identities. We might well characterize ethnicity as a curse on humanity, one that could lead to its ultimate destruction. But there is another side to the story, one that recognizes the value of ethnic identity and the contributions of conflict between ethnic groups.

Triandis (1994) suggests that one consequence of industrialization is individualism. Traditional societies, especially those based on agriculture, demanded a high level of interdependence between people. Farming required groups of people to work together. Individuals had defined roles to play, and although this structure was confining, it ensured that each person had "a place" within the group structure. Mutual need gave rise to a strong sense of belonging to a greater group. Individuals derived their security, their identity, and their value from the places they held in groups. Industrialization creates profound social change. Self-reliance takes the place of interdependence. There is less need for large interrelated groups. In many cases physical strength does not matter, so men and women can compete for the same jobs.

Possibly the greatest advantages of industrialization are personal freedom and equality. But its greatest cost may be the loss of group identity and the loss of a secure sense of belonging. People join and abandon groups on personal whims and momentary desires. The result is often a sense of personal isolation, fear for one's future, and alienation. We float through industrialized societies like icebergs in a frigid sea. Our ethnic identity has a unique ability to unite us with others, to give us a sense of place and the security of belonging. We cannot be expelled from our ethnic groups. We share a common history and a future destiny with our ethnic kin. These bonds become increasingly important as we adapt to a society increasingly characterized by the temporary. This situation may help explain why individuals are increasingly interested in seeking their ethnic roots and affiliating with their ethnic kin.

In addition to its role in providing personal identity, our ethnicity has adaptive value. The culture of ethnic groups developed as a response to environmental demands. The avoidance of pork and shellfish in the kosher diet did not arise because ancient Jews disliked the taste of these meats or had a special love for these animals. Rather, they recognized diseases commonly found in these foods and the restrictions served as a warning. The modern medical profession has come to recognize the value of many culture-specific remedies and folk medicines. Even the physical characteristics common to an ethnic group represent the result of adaptation to a specific climate or region. The culture associated with specific ethnic groups has served as a vessel for carrying lessons of adaptation. Studying these lessons not only helps us understand a culture but can provide valuable information to aid present-day adaptation.

Although it is rather easy to point to the value of specific ethnic groups, it is harder to see the contributions that have resulted from conflicts between ethnic groups. But there are actually many such positive consequences. The sociologist George Simmel (1955) argues that conflict between groups is a catalyst for social change. The clashes between blacks and whites in the United States led to the adoption of laws and the development of new customs that created greater equality and opportunities for all citizens. South Africa recently adopted a constitution that it boasted granted individuals the greatest personal freedom and individual integrity that have ever existed in the world. The experience of decades of discrimination and ethnic conflict had sharpened the sensitivity of the framers of this constitution.

Simmel also argues that conflict between groups frequently creates greater unity and solidarity within each group. Jesse Jackson, a widely recognized African-American political figure, has suggested that the conflict between blacks and whites in the United States was partially responsible for a renewed desire among African-Americans to learn about their heritage. Heightened conflict between Maori and Pakeha groups prompted an increasing number of Maori people to learn their native language and culture. Discrimination against Arab and Indonesian groups in the Netherlands has heightened ethnic awareness and increased solidarity within these groups. One of the quirks of social behavior is that the desire of one group to depreciate another is often a spark that arouses the targeted group and gives it new life.

Deutsch (1973) states that conflict "prevents stagnation; it stimulates interest and curiosity: it is the medium through which problems can be aired and arrived at" (p. 9). Indeed, an ironic fact of life is that we often know most about those ethnic groups that have come into conflict with our own group. One consequence of the generations of conflict between blacks and whites in the United States is that each group has greater knowledge about the other. Information about black history is now commonly included in school curriculum; February has been designated Black History Month; and a national holiday recognizes Martin Luther King, Jr. Interestingly, there is less instruction in schools and less national recognition regarding other important and long-present ethnic groups, such as Hispanics, Asian-Americans, and Jews. Conflicts involving these groups have been more covert and more regional. In New Zealand, confrontations between Maori and Pakeha have led to renewed interest throughout the country in Maori culture, history, and language. In Canada, ethnic conflicts have raised people's awareness of indigenous groups and French Canadians.

At the global level, atrocities committed against ethnic groups have captured the world's attention and have galvanized efforts to protect these groups. The horror of the Nazi Holocaust was the major catalyst behind the United Nations' efforts to define and protect human rights throughout the world. Ethnic violence in Yugoslavia, South Africa, Mexico, and Africa has sparked debates within the United States, Canada, and many European countries over the responsibility they have to protect people outside their own boundaries. Countries that have been antagonists have cooperated to protect imperiled ethnic groups in the far regions of the world.

The humorist Erma Bombeck once observed that the grass is always greener over the septic tank. Likewise, we might argue that some of the most noble human behavior occurs in the midst of the most terrible human conflict. I recall an evening I spent with the Polish psychologist Janus Reykowski, who recounted stories of unselfish heroism he had uncovered in his interviews with individuals who helped under the most dangerous circumstances. Oliner and Oliner (1988) describe numerous heroic individuals who risked their lives to help Jews during the Nazi persecution. Steven Spielberg's film *Schindler's List*, which captured world attention in 1993, told the story of Oscar Schindler, a German businessman who saved 1,200 Jews from extinction in the Nazi concentration camps. Admittedly, the destruction associated with ethnic conflict is a terrible price to pay for these positive examples of humanity. But these examples offer hope that constructive efforts to deal with ethnic con-

Although conflict has an evil side, it often excites creativity, problem solving, and other positive behaviors. Racial conflict in the United States was a catalyst for the development of courses on Black history. (David Young-Wolff / PhotoEdit)

flict may excite the passion of a silent army and spur united action to build a more humane and harmonious world.

A Closing Note: A New Beginning

Ethnic conflict has been a condition of human existence since people first formed themselves into tribes. Identification with an ethnic group is deeply rooted within us. The intensity of this identification is affected by a host of personal, group, and intergroup factors. Ethnic identity is a foundation for defining personal meaning and place. It is so basic to the human experience that no cleanser can wash it from the human fabric. And the simple act of identifying with certain groups leads to conflict between people across ethnic boundaries.

But identification with ethnic groups and the resultant conflict should not make us despair. Rather, the way we manage conflict and respond to ethnic differences will determine the destiny of humankind. We have no control over ethnicity, but we do control how our ethnicity influences our interactions with others.

My aim in this book has been to explore the steps that can be taken to create harmony while preserving personal uniqueness. Just as there are forces that conspire to separate us, there are also ties that bind us together. One of my daughter's favorite toys is two magnets. She found that if they are turned one way, the two magnets repel each other; no effort on her part can unite them. However, by turning the magnets the other way she found that they come together and resist being separated. Our examination of ways to manage ethnic conflict suggests that we can position human magnets so that they too will bond. What has become clear in developing this work is that we have the knowledge and the means to accomplish this goal. We need not wait for new inventions or new discoveries. We await only the human resolve to undertake the task, the recognition that efforts must be allocated at all levels of human interaction, and the commitment to maintain our vigilance throughout our collective future.

As a closing note, it might be well to remember the Greek myth of Pandora. As legend has it, when the great god Zeus watched over earth, he was bored. Humans had such an easy time; their every need was met, and they had no sicknesses to worry about. People were unwise but happy. There were no differences to separate them and no obstacles to challenge them. Zeus decided the situation had to change. He sent for a young god, Epimetheus, and gave him two boxes to take to earth. The large box, he explained, held differences; these Epimetheus was to pass out among the creatures of earth. The smaller box was not to be opened.

Epimetheus set about his task, giving the mouse timidity, the lion courage, the owl wisdom, and the cat cleanliness. To his horror, he ran out of differences before he got to humans. He was afraid to return to Mount Olympus and admit his mistake, so he stayed on earth. But Epimetheus was terribly lonely. After some time, Zeus was touched by the outcast's loneliness and summoned the gods to create a perfect wife for Epimetheus. When their work was completed, Pandora, the perfect woman, was sent to Earth to be with him. What a wonderful couple they made! Epimetheus told Pandora all about earth, and he gave her one rule that must be followed. Zeus, he told her, had instructed that the small box, now tucked away in the closet, must never be opened.

Over time, the little box occupied more and more of Pandora's thoughts. One day, she decided to take a little peek. Surely one look couldn't hurt. When Pandora opened the lid, troubles flew out. Greed, hunger, fear, and sickness swarmed out the window and descended on the human race. Epimetheus rushed home and found Pandora, crying, on the bed next to the open box. In his shock, he peered into the box. It appeared empty, save for a small movement at the bottom. A cry of joy filled the room, for there, nearly crushed by the escaping troubles, lay hope. Epimetheus proclaimed, "The world may be full of troubles, but things won't be too bad so long as we still have hope" (Potter, 1980, p. 48).

So may it be with ethnic relations. Even in the darkest hours, the human capacity for hope may offer the greatest promise for ethnic harmony. Come to think of it, the search for hope may be one of the forces that still draw me to cemeteries, for the message of hope is inscribed on many tombstones:

> *Yet dear one, we shall meet again*
> *And oh, the thought is bliss.*
> *To meet without mortal pain*
> *In fairer realms than this*
> (Seay, 1997).

Racial Diversity Without Racial Preferences*

MICHAEL L. WILLIAMS

It has been six years since, as Assistant Secretary of Education for Civil Rights, I wrote a letter to the president of the Fiesta Bowl about his proposal for race-based scholarships for the universities that played in the postseason football game. I said that there were legal limits to his proposal if the colleges had no history of past discrimination; I said the legal limitations also applied if the colleges had a history of discrimination but had removed the vestiges of it.

When I waded into the pool of racial preferences back then, it was not without a certain amount of discomfort. I did not want to appear opposed to assistance to minority-group students who want to go to college. I was deeply concerned then—and still am—about the disproportionately small numbers of African-American and Hispanic students attending and graduating from our colleges and universities. But I was concerned that no matter how nobly we intend it, when we rely on proposals that favor some students and not others, we risk violating the words in our Constitution, repeated in Title VI of the Civil Rights Act of 1964, that say "no person" shall be discriminated against because of his race.

Since that time, much has happened to indicate that the public and the courts are ready to dispense with racial preferences. In last week's election, California voters resoundingly passed a referendum designed to eliminate affirmative action in education, public employment, and government contracting.

That vote followed a series of court decisions in recent years that have called racial preferences in education into question. The decisions ruled against preferences in college admissions (the U.S. Court of Appeals for the Fifth Circuit in *Hopwood* v. *State of Texas*); in the hiring and firing of teachers (the Third Circuit in *Taxman* v. *The Board of Education for Piscataway Township*); and in merit-scholarship programs limited to minority students (the Fourth Circuit in *Podberesky* v. *Kirwan*.)

The U.S. Supreme Court refused to review the Fifth Circuit's decision in the *Hopwood* case, barring the use of racial preferences in law-school admissions. In the process, though, it gave no clear indication about the Justices' feelings concerning such preferences in education. Absent some future conflict among the federal appeals courts, the Supreme Court may never address the issue.

Yet despite the three circuits' rulings against aspects of racial preferences in education and no pending case in the Supreme Court, officials in the Clinton Administration characterize their position on affirmative action as: "Don't end it, mend it." That position was set forth in an open letter that the Department of Education sent

*Source: The Chronicle of Higher Education, November 15, 1996, p. A64.

in July to attorneys for the nation's colleges and universities. It advised what amounted to a "wait and see" posture, which also seems to suggest that preferential programs need not be ended.

In the aftermath of the *Hopwood* decision, Dan Morales, the Attorney General of Texas, adopted another approach. He has urged public institutions in the state not to rely on the status quo and said that race-neutral policies, "if crafted properly," should "still allow for significant numbers of minority students to be admitted." Unfortunately, he did not provide any further guidelines for how race-neutral policies in admissions, financial aid, and other areas should be written.

The inconsistent messages of the Department of Education and the Texas Attorney General have left campus administrators confused, asking how they can achieve racial diversity on campuses without using racial preferences. I believe that such preferences are not needed to maintain the racially diverse campuses that we have come to treasure. The doors to colleges can remain open to minority-group students in the absence of preferences.

For one thing, we can fine-tune the college-admissions process. Quite naturally, colleges and universities focus on applicants who they think will succeed, not only on the campus, but in their lives after graduation. Many admissions committees continue to look, sometimes exclusively, to young people who have done well in high-school classes and on standardized tests. But we know that, for a number of socio-economic reasons, this method does not favor many minority-group students, particularly African-Americans and Hispanics.

I believe that admissions officers should save a small percentage of slots for young people whose grades and test scores may not show it, but who for other reasons are believed to be headed for success. Joseph M. Horn, a professor of psychology at the University of Texas at Austin, and Hsin-yi Chen, a graduate student, recently completed a large-scale study of last year's freshman class at the university. It indicates that a personality trait of perseverance can be measured and is related to a student's likelihood of attrition. Colleges could look for evidence of a student's perseverance in various endeavors—in sports, certainly, even in oboe playing. The ability to stick to a task until one is successful may be a good non-academic indicator of success in college.

Another important factor is an individual's persistence in overcoming educational and social obstacles. What about a student who grew up in public housing or whose parents had an annual income lower than $25,000 or who was raised by a single mother on welfare? What about admitting a small number of graduates from high schools that cannot afford to offer a high-quality education, maybe those in inner cities or rural areas?

None of these ideas is race-based. In fact, the Fifth Circuit's decision in *Hopwood* commented favorably on the idea that colleges could rely on factors much like these in admitting a diverse student body. Only the use of race, *per se,* was prohibited.

Still, some argue that these "proxies," because they may net minority-group students more often than not, disproportionately favor certain races and therefore are themselves unconstitutional. It is true that were we to use only proxies that are related to minority students, concern might be warranted. But in cases in which a proxy can be justified on a basis other than race, it is unlikely to be legally problematic. For example, research indicates that there is a relationship between the number of parents in a home and academic achievement.

In the end, whether a proxy is legal is a question to be answered in the context of each college's admissions plan. And there is nothing in the Supreme Court's 1978 decision in *Bakke,* or in any other case, that would proscribe setting aside admission slots or financial-aid dollars on the basis of non-racial criteria.

If we want to continue to have diverse college enrollments, let's also get serious about improving the education of minority-group children from kindergarten through high school. Only improved academic performance will insure that they are well equipped to compete and succeed at the university and postgraduate levels. Through outreach and even their own preparatory programs, higher-education institutions in every state can actively assist the public schools in working toward this goal. Many already are doing so. For example, the University of Notre Dame is part of an alliance of universities that offers improved education to inner-city youngsters. The university's graduates earn a modest stipend for teaching for a year in an inner-city Catholic school.

And, if some elementary schools still fail to accomplish the task of educating their students well, their students must be allowed to escape to schools that will help them succeed, even if those schools happen to be private or parochial.

In planning their admissions and other activities, colleges should remember that no court decision in affirmative action has created a license to discriminate against minority-group students in higher education. Every college administrator must fully understand that. The remedy for current discrimination against minority-group students is not affirmative action, but rather compliance with Title VI of the Civil Rights Act of 1964, which bars any educational institution receiving federal funds (including *student financial assistance*) from discriminating on the basis of race, national origin, or religion. The penalty for violation is loss of federal aid, a penalty that will not be underestimated in any bursar's office.

Further, a college or university in any state may use racial preferences if they are narrowly tailored to remedy the present effects of past discrimination, and in fact they *must* do so. *Hopwood* says that, as do *Podberesky* and *Piscataway.* If vestiges of past bad action persist, then so does the right under the Constitution to use racial preferences in admission and scholarships.

However, the Fifth Circuit, in *Hopwood,* squarely rejected the idea that past segregation in elementary and secondary education in Texas gave the law school the right to use racial preferences today. That decision is particularly noteworthy because Texas is still under a court-ordered consent decree directing it to desegregate its public elementary and secondary schools.

What is the bottom line? It seems clear that creative institutions will be able to maintain racially diverse student bodies. Colleges should not hope for some future change in the makeup of the Supreme Court to help them with the task; nor should they cling to the hope that the U.S. Court of Appeals for the Third or Fourth or Fifth Circuits eventually will recant what they said in their recent decisions.

Waiting for such developments is not a responsible way for educators and lawyers to respond: It will not benefit minority-group students in the long run.

It will be only a matter of time, and the right court case, before race-based affirmative-action programs in all states are affected by decisions such as *Hopwood*. And private colleges and universities that are subject to Title VI also will be affected eventually. The end of racial preferences is here, but the door to a college education is not closed for minority-group students. With some ingenuity and creativity, America's campuses can continue to represent the wide variety that is America. But it's going to take some effort.

Making Sense of East Africa's Wars*

I. WILLIAM ZARTMAN

The current round in the unfolding Central African crisis is the result of three countries' attempts at national consolidation on an ethnic basis—the same type of dynamic that has been driving the civil wars in the former Yugoslavia (especially Bosnia) and the former Soviet Union (especially Tajikistan). The challenge for the U.S., which is sending up to 5,000 troops as part of a multinational force, is to provide relief to a million or more refugees and to ensure their safe repatriation, while not getting involved in the region's civil wars.

Until the early 1990s, Rwanda, Burundi and Zaire lived under stable authoritarian regimes. Burundi was ruled by the minority Tutsis, an extremely tall people who are believed to have migrated from Ethiopia and who had dominated the region's Hutu majority for centuries before colonial days. Rwanda's Tutsi rulers were overthrown by the Hutu majority in 1959. Zaire has been ruled since 1965 by the dictator Mobutu Sese Seko. While it is impossible to assign a "beginning" to events of this kind, the crucial element that changed the equation was the wave of democratization unleashed by the fall of the Soviet Union and of South African apartheid.

1990 Uprising

In Rwanda, the change took the form of a 1990 uprising against the 18-year-old regime of Juvénal Habyarimana, led by Rwandan exiles—mainly Tutsis—in Uganda, who were organized as the Rwandan Patriotic Front. A power-sharing agreement negotiated in Arusha, Tanzania, in August 1993 was seen as a sell-out by extremist leaders of the Hutu majority. When Habyarimana's plane was shot down in April 1994, the extremist organization, the Interahamwe, and the Rwandan armed forces (known as FAR) launched a massacre of Tutsis and sympathizers that took some 800,000 lives as the world looked on. But the RPF completed its takeover of the country, and two million Rwandans, mainly Hutus fled to refugee camps in Zaire and Tanzania. Although most

---

*Source: The Wall Street Journal, November 15, 1996.

are victims rather than perpetrators of the genocide, they fear reprisals if they return and so are controlled by the Interahamwe and ex-FAR organizers among them.

In Tutsi-led Burundi, President Pierre Buyoya handed over power in 1993 to the first president elected by the Hutu majority. The new president's assassination by Tutsi extremists in the army set in motion a spiral of violence between both Hutu and Tutsi extremists, each side fearing reprisals if the government fell into the other's hands. This July Mr. Buyoya returned to power in a Tutsi military coup, replacing a weak government of moderates. Heightened violence followed. Burundian Hutus fled to Zaire's South Kivu province, base of the National Council for the Defense of Democracy, an extremist Burundi Hutu movement backed by Zaire.

In Zaire, Mobutu Sese Seko's 31-year rule has drained the country dry, destroying its productivity and its government capacity. In 1990, in response to the winds of change, Mr. Mobutu encouraged the formation of a national conference to reform the political system, and then undermined it, co-opting many of its leaders and splitting up the rest. To his credit, Mr. Mobutu has managed to instill in Zairians a sense of national pride—but at the cost of encouraging xenophobia. In that spirit, Zaire's parliament passed a resolution in April 1995 preventing Rwandan and Burundian refugees from obtaining Zairian citizenship.

The current refugees were not the first to move west from the heavily populated mountains in Rwanda. Beginning in the 17th and 18th centuries, Tutsi herders moved with their cattle into the neighboring hills of Masisi in today's North Kivu and the mountains of South Kivu; the latter became known as "people of the mountains," or Banyamulenge. Today they number between 300,000 and 400,000. Zairians before there was a Zaire, the Banyamulenge were industrious and aggressive; they annoyed their neighbors.

When the citizenship resolution was passed last year, the Zairian authorities began to apply it not only to the mostly Hutu refugees, but also to the Zairian Tutsis in Masisi and to the Banyamulenge. Harassment began in September 1995 with an inventory of Tutsi property, evictions and expulsions. A United Nations special rapporteur noted in January 1996: "Local tribes were arming in readiness for a struggle against the Banyamulenge, forcing the latter to do the same." In November 1995 Zairian Tutsis in Masis were targeted by Zairian authorities, the army and the locals, and were forced to flee; many were massacred.

This summer the Banyamulenge, seeking recognition of their claim to citizenship, called for international mediation. Their entreaties were ignored. Beginning in September, the Zairian authorities and the local population began attacking the Banyamulenge. But they struck back and beat the Zairian army last month. The Hutu refugee camps were shelled from Rwanda, and Rwandan troops crossed the border to back up the Zairian Tutsis.

The effect has been enormous. The fighting left much of the Kivus under the control of the Banyamulenge, supported by their fellow Tutsis in Rwanda. To avoid the conflict, the Rwandan Hutu refugees broke out of their camps. Fearing persecution at home, they instead fled westward into the jungles of central Zaire. There they now wander, separated from food, water and international assistance.

And the fighting has demonstrated that the Zairian army is not a serious fighting force and that the state support for the vice-royalties that constitute provinces in Mr. Mobutu's Zaire is as vapid as the control of Mr. Mobutu himself. The cancer that has reached Mr. Mobutu's bones has also eaten away the structures of authority in his nation.

The two provinces under the Banyamulenge are unlikely to secede. The sense of Zairian identity Mr. Mobutu's rule has engendered limits provincial separatism. Tutsis throughout Zaire, even in the capital, have been the target of recent persecution, but the notorious reputation of the southern province of Shaba for secessionism has not materialized.

While all this is going on, Zaire is slowly, belatedly pursuing its electoral process, the first chance for free elections since 1960. It's unlikely the nation will be able to hold elections in mid-1997 as planned, but late 1997 is realistic. A new constitution has recently been approved by the parliament and now faces a popular referendum. A census is also called for, but can be replaced by a simpler and cheaper voter registration.

The electoral process is a godsend, for it means that an institutionalized succession procedure is in place, where Mr. Mobutu refused to provide one otherwise. However his last months work out, and even if the vacuum is filled by a military coup, there is now a legitimate mechanism for choosing a successor.

What are the appropriate American responses to this situation? Stopgap humanitarian measures are urgently needed to get food and water to the wandering refugees—but such efforts are not enough. The same scenario will repeat itself again in a few years if relations between and within Rwanda, Burundi and Zaire are not addressed.

Restoring Stability

The Rwandan refugees need to return home; they cannot continue to constitute an autonomous Hutuland in Eastern Zaire, thus encouraging Tutsis to constitute an autonomous Tutsiland and then fight over ownership. The Zairian Tutsis need to be assured of their Zairian citizenship, consistent with the international conventions binding Zaire. The perpetrators of genocide in Rwanda need to be separated from the Hutu masses and brought to trial. And the U.S. and other Western nations need to support the efforts of the East African coalition led by former Tanzanian President Julius Nyerere to force a return of moderation and democracy to Burundi.

All this requires an African policy from Washington—something that has been lacking for years. It requires a response, now woefully belated, to clear early warning signals—including, most simply, taking aerial photos to find the refugees. It requires a clear mission, not only for providing refugees relief, but also for ensuring their safe repatriation to Rwanda and Burundi. It also requires a reaffirmation of the election process in Zaire, to provide for Mr. Mobutu's succession. In the coming months, it will require leadership and support for others' initiatives as well, notably those of U.N. Secretary-General Boutros Boutros-Ghali. Otherwise, we will again have bloody horrors on our conscience, as we did in Rwanda.

References

Abelson, R., Aronson, E., McGuire, W., Newcomb, T., Rosenberg, M., & Tannenbaum, P. (1968). *Theories of cognitive consistency: A sourcebook.* Chicago: Rand McNally.

Abramson, L., Seligman, M., & Teasdale, J. (1978). Learned helplessness in humans: Critique and reformulation. *Journal of Abnormal Psychology, 87,* 49–74.

Adorno, T., Frenkel-Brunswick, E., Levinson, D., & Sanford, R. (1950). *The authoritarian personality.* New York: Harper.

Ainsworth, M. (1979). Infant-mother attachment. *American Psychologist, 34,* 932–937.

Allen, V., & Greenberger, D. (1978). An aesthetic theory of vandalism. *Crime and Delinquency, 24,* 309–321.

Allen, V., & Greenberger, D. (1980). Destruction and perceived control. In A. Baum & J. Singer (Eds.), *Advances in environmental psychology,* Vol 7. Hillsdale, NJ: Erlbaum.

Allport, F. (1924). *Social psychology.* Cambridge, MA: Riverside.

Allport, G. (1954). *The nature of prejudice.* Reading, MA: Addison Wesley.

Amir, Y. (1969). Contact hypothesis in ethnic relations. *Psychological Bulletin, 106,* 319–341.

Argyle, M. (1992). *The social psychology of everyday life.* London: Routledge.

Argyle, M. (1994). *The psychology of social class.* London: Routledge.

Asch, S. (1952). *Social psychology.* New York: Prentice Hall.

Asch, S. (1956). Studies of independence and conformity: I. A minority of one against a unanimous majority. *Psychological Monographs, 70.*

Asher, R., Kotschig, W., Brown, W., Green, J., Sady, E. et al. (1957). *The United Nations and promotion of general welfare.* Washington, DC: The Brookings Institution.

Ashkenasi, A. (1996, June 30). Political issues in the reduction of ethnic conflict. Paper presented at International Society of Political Psychology, Vancouver, Canada.

Austin, W. (1986). Justice in intergroup conflict. In S. Worchel & W. Austin (Eds.), *Psychology of intergroup relations.* Chicago: Nelson Hall.

Avedon, J. (1984). *In exile from the land of snows.* New York: Knopf.

Bandura, A. (1982). Self-efficacy mechanism in human agency. *American Psychologist, 37,* 122–147.

Bandura, A., & Walters, R. (1963). *Social learning and personality development.* New York: Rinehart & Winston.

Banton, M. (1997). *Ethnic and racial consciousness* (2nd ed.). London: Longman.

Bar-Tal, D. (1996). Development of social categories and stereotypes in early childhood: The case of "the Arab" concept formation, stereotype, and attitudes by Jewish children in Israel. *International Journal of Intercultural Relations, 20,* 341–370.

Bar-Tal, D. (1988). Delegitimizing relations between Israeli Jews and Palestinians: A social psychological analysis. In J. Hoffman (Ed.), *Arab-Jewish relations in Israel: A quest for human understanding.* Bristol, IN: Wyndham Hall Press.

Bar-Tal, D. (in press). Formation and change of ethnic and national stereotypes: An integrative model. *International Journal of Intercultural Relations.*

Bar-Tal, D. (1994). Development of social categories and stereotypes in early childhood: The case of "the Arab" concept formation, stereotype, and attitudes by Jewish children in Israel. Paper presented at Second International Congress on Prejudice, Discrimination, and Conflict, Jerusalem, July 4–7.

Bar-Tal, D. (1990). Israeli-Palestinian conflict: A cognitive analysis. *International Journal of Intercultural Relations, 14*, 7–29.

Bar-Tal, D. (1990). Causes and consequences of delegitimization: Models of conflict and ethnocentrism. *Journal of Social Issues, 46*, 65–81.

Bar-Tal, D. (1990). *Group beliefs.* New York: Springer-Verlag.

Bar-Tal, D. (1996). Development of social categories and stereotypes in early childhood: The case of "the Arab" concept formation, stereotype, and attitudes by Jewish children in Israel. *International Journal of Intercultural Relations, 20*, 341–370.

Barth, F. (1969). *Ethnic groups and boundaries: The social organization of cultural difference.* London: George Allen and Unwin.

Bass, B. (1985). *Leadership and performance beyond expectations.* New York: Free Press.

Bauman, Z. (1992). Soil, blood, and identity. *Sociological Review, 40*, 675–701.

Baumeister, R. (1986). *Identity: Cultural change and the struggle for self.* New York: Oxford University Press.

Beal, P. (1996, October 30). "New" Indians give rise to tribal ire. *Wall Street Journal*, p. T1.

Bell, D. (1992). *Faces at the bottom of the well: The permanence of racism.* New York: Basic.

Berman, P. (February 28, 1994). *The other and almost the same.* The New Yorker, pp. 61–71.

Berry, J. (1991). Understanding and managing multiculturalism: Some possible implications of research in Canada. *Psychology and Developing Societies, 3*, 17–49.

Bettelheim, B., & Janowitz, M. (1964). *Social change and prejudice.* London: The Free Press of Glancoe.

Billig, M. (1995). *Banal nationalism.* London: Sage.

Blondel, J. (1987). *Political leadership.* London: Sage.

Bond, M. (1987). Intergroup relations in Hong Kong: The Tao of stability. In J. Boucher, D. Landis, & K. Clark (Eds.), *Ethnic conflict: International perspectives.* Newbury Park, CA: Sage.

Boucher, J., Landis, D., & Clark, K. (1987). *Ethnic conflict: International perspectives.* Newbury Park, CA: Sage.

Boulding, K. (1989). *Three faces of power.* Newbury Park, CA: Sage.

Brehm, J. (1972). *Responses to loss of freedom: A theory of psychological reactance.* Morristown, NJ: General Learning.

Brewer, M. (1986). The role of ethnocentrism in intergroup conflict. In S. Worchel & W. Austin (Eds.), *Psychology of intergroup conflict.* Chicago: Nelson Hall.

Brewer, M. (1991). The social self: On being the same and different at the same time. *Personality and Social Psychology Bulletin, 17*, 475–482.

Brewer, M., & Miller, N. (1984). Beyond the contact hypothesis: Theoretical perspectives on desegregration. In N. Miller & M. Brewer (Eds.), *Groups in contact: The psychology of desegregation.* New York: Academic.

Brown, D. (1971). *Bury my heart at Wounded Knee.* London: Picador.

Brown, R. (1995). *Prejudice: Its social psychology.* London: Blackwell.

Burton, J. (1969). *Conflict and communication: The use of controlled communication in international relations.* London: Macmillan.

Calder, P. (1993, February 11). Identity discovered. *New Zealand Herald*, p. 1 (section 2).

Caldwell, M. (1969). Communication and sex effects in a five-person Prisoner's Dilemma game. *Journal of Personality and Social Psychology, 33*, 273–280.

Campbell, D. (1965). Ethnocentrism and altruistic motives. *Nebraska Symposium on motivation, 13*, 118–147.

Campbell, D. (1958). Common fate, similarity, and other indices of the status of aggregates of persons as social entities. *Behavioral Science, 3,* 14–25.

Campbell, J., Chew, B., & Scratchley, L. (1991). Cognitive and emotional reactivity to daily events: The effects of self-esteem and self-complexity. *Journal of Personality, 59,* 473–505.

Cantor, N., & Mischel, W. (1978). Prototypes in person perception. In L. Berkowitz (Ed.), *Advances in experimental social psychology,* vol 12. New York: Academic Press.

Carnevale, P. (1985). Mediation of international conflict. *Applied Social Psychology Annual, 6,* 87–106.

Chafetz, G. (1996, July 1–3). Interaction, categorization, and international identities: An empirical analysis of social identity theory. Paper presented at International Society of Political Psychology, Vancouver, Canada.

Cialdini, R., Schaller, M., Houlihan, D., Arps, K., Fulz, J., & Beaman, A. (1987). Empathy-based helping: Is it selflessly or selfishly motivated? *Journal of Personality and Social Psychology, 52,* 749–758.

Citrin, J., Green, D., Reingold, B., & Walters, E. (1990). The official English movement and the symbolic politics of language in the United States. *Western Political Quarterly, 43,* 85–108.

Cohen, C. (1981). Person categories and social perception: Testing some boundaries of the processing effects of prior knowledge. *Journal of Personality and Social Psychology, 40,* 441–452.

Cook, S. (1984). Cooperative interaction in multiethnic contexts. In N. Miller & M. Brewer (Eds.). *Groups in contact: The psychology of desegregation.* Orlando: Academic.

Cooley, C. H. (1902). *Human order and social order.* New York: Scribner.

Dalai Lama XIV. (1989). *Freedom from exile: The autobiography of the Dalai Lama.* New York: HarperCollins.

De Vos, G., & Romanucci-Ross, L. (1995). In L. Romanucci-Ross & G. De Vos (Eds.), *Ethnic identity: Creation, conflict, and accommodation.* Walnut Creek, CA: AltaMira.

Deutsch, M. (1973). *The resolution of conflict.* New Haven, CT: Yale University Press.

Deutsch, M., & Krauss, R. (1962). Studies of interpersonal bargaining. *Journal of Conflict Resolution, 6,* 52–76.

Devine, P. (1989). Stereotypes and prejudice: The automatic and controlled components. *Journal of Personality and Social Psychology, 56,* 5–18.

Doob, L., & Foltz, W. (1973). The Belfast workshop: An application of group techniques to a destructive conflict. *Journal of Conflict Resolution, 17,* 489–512.

Dovidio, J., & Gaertner, S. (1986). Prejudice, discrimination, and racism: Historical trends and contemporary approaches. In J. Dovidio & S. Gaertner (Eds.), *Prejudice, discrimination, and racism.* Orlando: Academic Press.

Dr. Seuss (Theodore Geisel). (1984). *The butter battle book.* New York: Random House.

Dress, T. (1994, July 12–15). The resolution of identity-based disputes: The New York experience and its application in the transnational arena. Paper presented at International Society of Political Psychology, Santiago de Composeta, Spain.

Duffy, K. (1991). Introduction to community mediation programs: Past, present and future. In K. Duffy, J. Grosch, & P. Olzak (Eds.), *Issues in community mediation: A handbook for practitioners and researchers.* New York: Guilford.

Duffy, K., Grosch, J., & Olzack, P. (1991). *Community mediation: A handbook for practitioners and researchers.* New York: Guilford.

Duncan, D. (1976). Differential social perception and attribution of intergroup violence: Testing the lower limits of stereotyping of blacks. *Journal of Personality and Social Psychology, 34,* 590–598.

Dunphy, D. (1968). Phases, roles, and myths of self-analytic groups. *Applied Behavioral Science, 4,* 195–224.

Edwards, J. (1985). *Language, society, and identity.* Oxford: Basil Blackwell.

Elias, N. (1987). *Die Gesellschaft der Individuen.* Frankfurt: Suhrkamp.

Ellemers, N. & van Knippenberg, A. (1997). Stereotyping in social context. In R. Spears, P. Oakes, N. Ellemers, & S. A. Haslam (Eds.), *The social psychology of stereotyping and group life.* Oxford: Blackwell.

Ethier, K., & Deaux, K. (1990). Hispanics in Ivy: Assessing identity and perceived threat. *Sex Roles, 22,* 427–440.

Ethier, K., & Deaux, K. (1994). Negotiating social identity when contexts change: Maintaining identification and responding to threat. *Personality and Social Psychology Bulletin, 67,* 243–251.

Farnsworth, D. (1966). Motivation for learning: Community responsibility. In E. Torrance & D. Storm (Eds.), *Mental health and achievement.* New York: Wiley.

Fazio, R. (1986). How do attitudes guide behavior? In R. M. Sorrentino & E. T. Higgins (Eds.), *The handbook of motivation and cognition.* New York: Guilford Press.

Featherstone, M. (1990). Global culture: An introduction. In M. Featherstone (Ed.), *Global culture: Nationalism, globalization, and modernity.* London: Sage.

Fedoseyev, P. N. et al. (1977). *Leninism and the national question.* Institute of Marxism-Leninism, CC CPSU, Moscow: Moscow Progress.

Feldman, J. (1959). Mother-country and fatherland. *The unconscious in history.* New York: Philosophical Library.

Feshbach, S. (1987). Individual aggression, national attachment, and the search for peace. *Aggressive Behavior, 125,* 1243–1248.

Festinger, L. (1954). A theory of social comparison processes. *Human Relations, 7,* 117–140.

Festinger, L. (1957). *A theory of cognitive dissonance.* Palo Alto, CA: Stanford University Press.

Fiedler, F. (1978). Recent developments in research on the contingency model. In L. Berkowitz (Ed.), *Group process.* New York: Academic.

Filley, A. (1975). *Interpersonal conflict resolution.* Glenview, IL: Scott Foresman.

Fisher, J., & Nadler, A. (1974). The effect of similarity between donor and recipient on recipient's reaction to aid. *Journal of Personality and Social Psychology, 4,* 230–243.

Fiske, S., & Taylor, S. (1984). *Social cognition.* New York: McGraw-Hill.

Fiske, S., & Neuberg, S. (1989). Category-based and individuating processes as a function of information and motivation: Evidence from the laboratory. In Dr. Bar-Tal, C. Graumann, A. Kruglanski, & W. Stroebe (Eds.), *Stereotyping and prejudice.* New York: Springer-Verlag.

Flowers, M. (1977). A laboratory test of some implications of Janis' groupthink hypothesis. *Journal of Personality and Social Psychology, 35,* 888–896.

Forsyth, D. (1990). *Group dynamics* (2nd ed). Pacific Grove, CA: Brooks/Cole.

Foster, D. (June 24, 1994). *Black activists: Frenzy over O.J.'s fall feed racial stereotypes.* Bryan-College Station Eagle, p. A5.

French, J., & Raven, B. (1959). The basis of social power. In D. Cartwright (Ed.). *Studies in social power.* Ann Arbor: University of Michigan.

Freud, S. (1933). *New introductory lectures on psycho-analysis.* New York: Norton.

Gaertner, S. (1996, September). Reducing prejudice by inducing a common ingroup identity. Paper presented at EASP Small Group Meeting, Catania, Italy.

Gaertner, S., Dovidio, J., Anastasio, P., Bachman, B., & Rust, M. (1993). The common ingroup identity model: Recategorization and the reduction of ingroup bias. In W. Stroebe & M. Hewstone (Eds.). *The European review of social psychology,* Chichester, England: Wiley.

Gaertner, S., Mann, J., Dovidio, J., & Murrell, A. (1990). How does cooperation reduce intergroup bias? *Journal of Personality and Social Psychology, 59,* 692–704.

Gaertner, S., Mann, J., Murrell, A., & Dovidio, J. (1989). Reducing intergroup bias: The benefits of recategorization. *Journal of Personality and Social Psychology, 57,* 239–249.

Gellner, E. (1983). *Nations and nationalism.* Oxford: Basil Blackwell.

Gergen, K. (1991). *The saturated self.* New York: Basic.

Gilbert, D., & Hixon, J. (1991). The trouble of thinking: Activation and application of stereotypic beliefs. *Journal of Personality and Social Psychology, 60,* 509–517.

Goffman, E. (1959). *The presentation of self in everyday life.* Garden City, NY: Doubleday / Anchor.

Goffman, E. (1967). *Interaction ritual.* New York: Doubleday.

Gomez, L. (1992). Nonviolence and the self in early Buddhism. In K. Kraft (Ed.), *Inner peace, world peace: Essays on Buddhism and nonviolence.* Albany: SUNY Press.

Goodman, M. (1981). Group phases and induced countertransference. *Psychotherapy: Theory, Research, and Practice, 18,* 478–486.

Gralnick, A. (1988). Trust, deterrence, realism, and nuclear omnicide. *Political Psychology, 9,* 175–188.

Greenberg, J., Pyszczynski, T., & Solomon, S. (1986). The causes and consequences of the need for self-esteem: A terror management theory. In R. Baumeister (Ed.), *Public self and private self.* New York: Springer-Verlag.

Greenberg, J., Pyszczynski, T., Solomon, S., Rosenblatt, A., Veeder, M., Kirkland, S., & Lyon, D. (1990). Evidence for terror management theory II: The effects of mortality salience reactions to those who threaten or bolster cultural worldviews. *Journal of Personality and Social Psychology, 58,* 308–318.

Greenwald, A. (1980). The totalitarian ego: Fabrication and revision of personal history. *American Psychologist, 35,* 603–613.

Grezlak, J. (1988). Conflict and cooperation. In M. Hewstone, W. Stroebe, J. Codol, & G. Stephenson (Eds.), *Introduction to social psychology.* Oxford: Basil Blackwell.

Haley, A. (1976). *Roots.* Garden City, NY: Doubleday.

Hamilton, D., & Trolier, T. (1986). Stereotypes and stereotyping: An overview of the cognitive approach. In J. Dovidio & S. Gaertner (Eds.), *Prejudice, discrimination, and racism.* New York: Academic Press.

Harrington, D., Block, J., & Block, J. (1987). Testing aspects of Carl Rogers' theory of creative environments. *Journal of Personality and Social Psychology, 52,* 851–856.

Harris, M. (1983). *Cultural anthropology.* New York: Harper and Row.

Hastorf, A., & Cantril, H. (1954). They saw a game. *Journal of Abnormal and Social Psychology, 49,* 129–134.

Heider, F. (1958). *The psychology of interpersonal relations.* New York: Wiley.

Hewstone, M., & Brown, R. (1986). *Contact and conflict in intergroup encounters.* Oxford: Basil Blackwell.

Higgins, E. (1987). Self discrepancy: A theory relating self and affect. *Psychological Review, 94,* 319–340.

Hilton, J., & von Hipple, W. (1996). Stereotypes. *Annual Review of Psychology, 47,* 237–271.

Hinkle, S., & Schopler, J. (1986). Bias in the evaluation of in-group and out-group performance. In S. Worchel & W. Austin (Eds.), *Psychology of intergroup relations.* Chicago: Nelson Hall.

Hofstede, G. (1991). *Culture and organizations: Software of the mind.* London: McGraw-Hill.

Hollander, E. (1985). Leadership and power. In G. Lindzey & E. Aronson (Eds.), *Handbook of social psychology* (3rd ed). New York: Random House.

Holsti, K. J. (1992). *International politics: A framework for analysis.* Englewood Cliffs, NJ: Prentice Hall.

Holsti, O. (1996, June 30–July 3). Public opinion on human rights in American foreign policy. Paper presented at International Society for Political Psychology, Vancouver.

Hovland, C., & Sears, R. (1940). Minor studies of aggression: Correlation of lynchings with economic data. *Journal of Psychology, 9,* 301–310.

Huo, Y., Smith, H., Tyler, T., & Lind, E. (1996). Superordinate identification, subgroup identification and justice concerns: Is separatism the problem? Is assimilation the answer? *Psychological Science, 7,* 40–45.

Ichheiser, G. (1970). *Appearances and realities.* San Francisco: Jossey Bass.

Ihimaera, W. (1973). *Tangi.* Auckland, New Zealand: Heinemann.

Insko, C., & Schopler, J. (1987). Categorization, competition, and collectivity. In C. Hendrick (Ed.), *Review of personality and social psychology* (vol 8). Beverly Hills: Sage.

Insko, C., Schopler, J., Hoyle, R., Dardis, G., & Graetz, K. (1990). Individual-group discontinuity as a function of fear and greed. *Journal of Personality and Social Psychology, 58,* 68–79.

James, W. (1890). *Psychology.* New York: Holt.

Janis, I. (1972). *Victims of groupthink: A psychological study of foreign policy decisions and fiascoes.* Boston: Houghton Mifflin.

Janis, I. (1982). *Groupthink* (2nd ed). Boston: Houghton Mifflin.

Johnson, C. (1974). *Consistency of reporting ethnic origins in the current population survey.* Bureau of the Census, Technical Paper 31. Washington, DC: Government Printing Office.

Jones, E. E., & Gerard, H. (1967). *Foundations of social psychology.* New York: Wiley.

Jones, E., & Davis, K. (1965). From acts to dispositions: The attribution process in person perception. In L. Berkowitz (Ed.), *Advances in experimental social psychology,* vol. 2. New York: Academic Press.

Jones, E., & Nisbett, R. (1971). *The actor and the observer: Divergent perceptions of the causes of behavior.* Morristown, NJ: General Learning Press.

Jones, J. (1972). *Prejudice and racism.* Reading, MA: Addison Wesley.

Jones, J., & Morris, K. (1993). Individual versus group identification as a factor in intergroup racial contact. In S. Worchel & J. Simpson (Eds.), *Conflict between people and groups.* Chicago: Nelson Hall.

Jones, V. (1948). *The Hatfields and the McCoys.* Chapel Hill, NC: University of North Carolina Press.

Jost, J., & Banaji, M. (1994). The role of stereotyping in system-justification and the production of false consensus. *British Journal of Social Psychology, 33,* 1–27.

Jowett, G., & O'Donnell, V. (1992). *Propaganda and persuasion* (2nd ed.). Newbury Park, CA: Sage.

Judd, C. & Park, B. (1988). Out-group homogeneity: Judgements of variability at the individual and group levels. *Journal of Personality and Social Psychology, 54,* 778–788.

Judd, C., & Park, B. (1993). Definition and assessment of accuracy in social stereotypes. *Psychological Review, 100,* 109–128.

Kalven, H., & Zeisel, H. (1966). *The American jury.* New York: Little, Brown.

Katz, D. & Braly, K. (1933). Racial stereotypes of 100 college students. *Journal of Abnormal and Social Psychology, 28,* 280–290.

Katz, I. (1981). *Stigma: A social psychological analysis.* Hillsdale, NJ: Erlbaum.

Katz, I., Wackenhut, J., & Hass, R. (1986). Racial ambivalence, value duality, and behavior. In J. Dovidio & S. Gaertner (Eds.), *Prejudice, discrimination, and racism.* New York: Academic.

Kelman, H. (1993). Coalitions across conflict lines: The interplay of conflicts within and between the Israeli and Palestinian communities. In S. Worchel & J. Simpson (Eds.), *Conflict between people and groups.* Chicago: Nelson Hall.

Kelman, H., & Cohen, S. (1986). Resolution of international conflict: An international approach. In S. Worchel & W. Austin (Eds.), *Psychology of intergroup conflict.* Chicago: Nelson Hall.

Kelman, H., & Hamilton, L. (1989). *Crimes of obedience.* New Haven, CT: Yale University Press.

Kim, U. (1994). Individualism and collectivism: Conceptual clarification and elaboration. In U. Kim, H. Triandis, C. Kagitcibasi, S. Choi, & G. Yoon (Eds.), *Individualism and collectivism: Theory, methods, and applications.* Thousand Oaks, CA; Sage.

King, C. (1969). *My life with Martin Luther King, Jr.* New York: Holt, Rinehart and Winston.

Kinloch, G. (1974). *The dynamics of race relations.* New York: McGraw-Hill.

Kleiboer, M. (1994, July 12–15). The elusive notion of international mediation. Paper presented at International Society for Political Psychology, Santiago de Compostela, Spain.

Kohn, M. (1976). The interaction of social class and other factors in the etiology of schizophrenia. *American Journal of Psychiatry, 133,* 177–180.

Komorita, S., & Kravitz, D. (1983). Coalition formation: A social psychological approach. In P. Paulus (Ed.), *Basic group process.* New York: Springer-Verlag.

Kraft, K. (1992). Prospects of socially engaged Buddhism. In K. Kraft (Ed.), *Inner peace, world peace: Essays on Buddhism and nonviolence.* Albany: SUNY Press.

Krauss, R., & Deutsch, M. (1966). Communication in interpersonal bargaining. *Journal of Personality and Social Psychology, 4,* 572–577.

Kundera, M. (1984). *The unbearable lightness of being.* New York: Harper and Row.

Kurian, T. (1991). *New World book of rankings* (3rd ed.). New York: Facts on File.

Kuschel, R. (1987). Twenty-four generations of intergroup conflicts on Bellona Island (Solomon Islands). In J. Boucher et al. (Eds.), *Ethnic conflict: International perspectives.* Newbury Park, CA: Sage.

Landis, D., & Bhagat, R. (1996). *Handbook of intercultural training* (2nd ed). Thousand Oaks, CA: Sage.

Landis, D., & Brislin, R. (1993). *Handbook of intercultural training: Issues in theory and design,* Vol. 1. New York: Pergamon Press.

Lazarus, R. (1993). From psychological stress to emotions: A history of changing outlooks. *Annual Review of Psychology, 44,* 1–21.

Lee, Y. (1996). Ichheiserian stereotypes and prejudice: Nothing is false like mainstream "truth." Paper presented at meeting of Society of Experimental Social Psychology, Sturbridge, MA, October 18–20.

Lee, Y., Jussim, L., & McCauley, C. (Eds.) (1995). *Stereotype accuracy: Toward appreciating group differences.* Washington, DC: American Psychological Association.

Lerner, M. (1980). *The belief in a just world: A fundamental decision.* New York: Plenum.

LeVine, R. A. (1984). Properties of culture: An ethnographic view. In R. Shweder & R. LeVine (Eds.), *Culture theory: Essays on mind, self, and emotion.* Cambridge: Cambridge University Press.

Lewin, K. (1947). Frontiers in group dynamics. *Human Relations, 1,* 5–41.

Lindskold, S. (1986). GRIT: Reducing distrust through carefully introduced conciliation. In S. Worchel & W. Austin (Eds.), *Psychology of intergroup relations.* Chicago: Nelson Hall.

Linville, P., Fisher, G., & Salavoy, P. (1989). Perceived distributions of the characteristics of in-groups and out-group members: Empirical evidence and a computer simulation. *Journal of Personality and Social Psychology, 57,* 165–188.

Littlefield, A., Lieberman, L., & Reynolds, L. (1982). Redefining race: The potential demise of a concept in physical anthropology. *Current Anthropology, 23,* 641–655.

Lorenzi-Cioldi, F. (1996, September). Groups' status and perceptions of homogeneity. Paper presented at European Association of Experimental Social Psychology small group meeting, Catania, Italy.

Loretto, R., & Williams, D. (1974). Personality, behavioral, and output variables in a small group task situation: An examination of consenual leader and nonleader differences. *Canadian Journal of Behavioral Science, 6,* 59–74.

Maass, A., & Clark, D. (1984). Hidden input of minorities: Fifteen years of minority influence research. *Psychological Bulletin, 95,* 428–450.

Mann, S. (1977). The use of social indicators in environmental planning. In I. Altman & J. Whowill (Eds.), *Human behavior and environment,* vol. 2. New York: Plemum.

Maslow, A. (1963). The need to know and the fear of knowing. *Journal of General Psychology, 68*, 111–124.

Maslow, A. (1968). *Toward a psychology of being.* New York: Van Nostrand.

Merari, A., & Friedland, N. (1988). Negotiating with terrorists. In W. Stroebe et al. (Eds.), *The social psychology of intergroup conflict.* New York: Academic.

Messe, L., Kerr, N., & Sattler, D. (1992). "But some animals are more equal than others": The supervisor as a privileged status in group contexts. In S. Worchel, W. Wood, & J, Simpson (Eds.), *Group process and productivity.* Newbury Park, CA: Sage.

Metge, J. (1990). *Te Kohao o te Ngira: Culture and learning.* Wellington: Ministry of Education, Learning Media.

Milgram, S. (1963). Behavioral study of obedience. *Journal of Abnormal and Social Psychology, 67*, 371–378.

Milgram, S. (1970). The experience of living in cities. *Science, 167*, 1461–1468.

Miller, M. (1973). *Plain speaking.* New York: Berkeley.

Miller, R. L., Brickman, P., & Bolen, D. (1975). Attribution versus persuasion as a means for modifying behavior. *Journal of Personality and Social Psychology, 31*, 430–441.

Monaghan, P. (1993, July 23). "Critical race theory" questions role of legal doctrine in racial inequality. *Chronicle of Higher Education*, A7-A9.

Morris, W., et al. (1976). Collective coping with stress: Group reactions to fear, anxiety, and ambiguity. *Journal of Personality and Social Psychology, 13*, 131–140.

Moscovici, S. (1980). Toward a theory of conversion behavior. In L. Berkowitz (Ed)., *Advances in experimental social psychology* (vol. 13). New York: Academic Press.

Moscovici, S. (1985). Social influence and conformity. In G. Lindzey & E. Aronson (Eds.), *Handbook of social psychology* (3rd ed). New York: Addison-Wesley.

Moscovici, S., & Mugny, G. (1983). Minority influence. In P. Paulus (Ed.), *Basic group process.* New York: Springer-Verlag.

Mosher, D., & Scodel, A. (1960). A study of the relationship between ethnocentrism in children and the ethnocentrism and authoritarian rearing of practices of their mothers. *Child Development, 31*, 369–376.

Mucchi-Faina, A. (1994). Minority influence effects: Assimilation and differentiation. In S. Moscovici, A. Mucci-Faima, & A. Maass (Eds.), *Minority influence.* Chicago: Nelson Hall.

Murer, J. (1996). Identity and enemies: The formation of nationalism, collective consciousness and national self-identity in Hungary. Paper presented at the International Society of Political Psychology meeting, Vancouver, Canada, June 30.

Myers, D. (1982). Polarizing effects of social interaction. In H. Brandstatter, J. Davis, & G. Stocker-Kreichgauer (Eds.), *Group decision process.* London: Academic.

Nairn, R., & McCreanor, T. (1990). Insensitivity and hypersensitivity: An imbalance in Pakeha accounts of racial conflict. *Journal of Language and Social Psychology, 9*, 293–308.

Nakanishi, M., & Johnson, K. (1993). Implications of self-disclosure on conversational logics, perceived communication competence, and social attraction: A comparison of Japanese and American cultures. In R. Wiseman & J. Koester (Eds.), *Intercultural communication competence.* Newbury Park, CA: Sage.

National Covenant of the Palestine Liberation Movement (1969). In W. Laquwur (Ed.), *The Israel-Arab Reader.* New York: Bantam Press.

Nemeth, C. (1992). Minority dissent as a stimulant to group performance. In S. Worchel, W. Wood, & J. Simpson (Eds.), *Group process and productivity.* Newbury Park, CA: Sage.

Nemeth, C., & Wachtler, J. (1974). Creating perceptions of consistency and confidence: A necessary condition for minority influence. *Sociometry, 37*, 529–540.

Newcomb, T. M. (1943). *Personality and social change.* Hinsdale, IL: Dryden.

Newcomb, T. M. (1947). Autistic hostility and social reality. *Human Relations, 1*, 69–86.

Ng, S., & Bradac, J (1993). *Power in language: Verbal communication and social influence.* Newbury Park, CA: Sage.

Norvell, N., & Worchel, S. (1981). A re-examination of the relationship between equal status contact and intergroup attraction. *Journal of Personality and Social Psychology, 41,* 902–908.

Oakes, P. (1983). *Factors determining the salience of group membership in social perception.* Unpublished Ph.D. dissertation, University of Bristol, England.

Oakes, P., Haslam, S., & Turner, J. (1994). *Stereotyping and social reality.* Oxford: Blackwell.

Oakes, P., & Reynolds, K. (1997). Asking the accuracy question: Is measurement the answer? In R. Spears, P. Oakes, N. Ellemers, & A. A. Haslam (Eds.), *The social psychology of stereotyping and group life.* Oxford: Blackwell.

Oliner, S., & Oliner, P. (1988). *The altruistic personality: Rescuers of Jews in Nazi Europe.* New York: Free Press.

Osgood, C. (1962). *An alternative to war or surrender.* Urbana: University of Illinois Press.

Park, B., Judd, C., & Ryan, C. (1991). Social categorization and the representation of variability information. In W. Stroebe & M. Hewstone (Eds.), *European Review of Social Psychology,* vol. 2. London: Wiley.

Patchen, M. (1991). Conflict and cooperation in U.S.-Soviet relations: What have we learned from quantitative research? *International Interactions, 17,* 127–143.

Patchen, M. (1993). Reciprocity of coercion and cooperation between individuals and nations. In R. Felson & J. Tedeschi (Eds.), *Aggression and violence: Social interactionist perspectives.* Washington, DC: American Psychological Association.

Pettigrew, T. (1997). Generalized intergroup contact effects on prejudice. *Personality and Social Psychology Bulletin, 23,* 173–185.

Phinney, J. (1992). The Multigroup Ethnic Identity measure: A new scale for use with diverse groups. *Journal of Adolescent Research, 7,* 156–176.

Phinney, J. (1996). When we talk about American ethnic groups, what do we mean? *American Psychologist, 51,* 918–927.

Potter, R. (1980). *Myths and folk tales around the world.* New York: Globe.

Provencher, R. (1987). Interethnic conflict in the Malay Peninsula. In J. Boucher et al. (Eds.), *Ethnic conflict: International perspectives.* Newbury Park, CA: Sage.

Pruitt, D. (1971). Indirect communication and the search for agreement in negotiation. *Journal of Personality and Social Psychology, 57,* 239–246.

Pruitt, D., & Johnson, D. (1970). Mediation as an aid to face saving in negotiation. *Journal of Personality and Social Psychology, 57,* 239–246.

Putnam, L., & Holmer, M. (1992). Framing, reframing, and issue development. In L. Putnam & M. Roloff (Eds.), *Communication and negotiation.* Newbury Park, CA: Sage.

Quattrone, G. (1986). On the perception of a group. In S. Worchel & W. Austin (Eds.), *Psychology of intergroup relations.* Chicago: Nelson Hall.

Quattrone, G., & Jones, E. (1980). The perception of variability within in-groups and out-groups: Implications for the law of small numbers. *Journal of Personality and Social Psychology, 38,* 141–152.

Rajecki, D., Halter, C., Everts, A., & Feghall, C. (1991). Documentation of media reflections of patriotic revival in the United States in the 1980s. *Journal of Social Psychology, 3,* 401–411.

Ramcharan, B. G. (1979). *Human rights: Thirty years after the Universal Declaration.* The Hague: Martinus Nijhoff.

Ramirez, J., & Sullivan, B. (1987). The Basque conflict. In J. Boucher, D. Landis, & K. Clark (Eds.), *Ethnic conflict: International perspectives.* Newbury Park, CA: Sage.

Roethlisberger, F., & Dickson, W. (1939). *Management and the worker.* Cambridge, MA: Harvard University Press.

Rogers, C. (1980). *A way of being.* Boston: Houghton Mifflin.

Rosenthal, R., & Jacobson, L. (1968). *Pygmalion in the classroom: Teacher expectation and pupils' intellectual development.* New York: Holt, Rinehart and Winston.

Ross, M. H. (1995). Psychocultural interpretation theory and peacemaking in ethnic conflicts. *Political Psychology, 16,* 523–544.

Rothgerber, H., & Worchel, S. (1997). The view from below: Intergroup relations from the perspective of the disadvantaged group. *Journal of Personality and Social Psychology, 73,* 1191–1205.

Rubin, J. (1980). Experimental research on third-party intervention in conflict: Toward some generalizations. *Psychological Bulletin, 87,* 379–391.

Rubin, J., Pruitt, D., & Kim, S. (1993). *Social conflict: Escalation, stalemate, and settlement.* New York: McGraw-Hill.

Samyutta Nikaya. (1984). Pali Text Society Publications.

Sande, G., Goethals, G., & Radloff, C. (1988). Perceiving one's own traits and others': The multifaceted self. *Journal of Personality and Social Psychology, 54,* 13–20.

Sande, G., Goethals, G., Ferrari, L., & Worth, L. (1989). Value-guided attributions: Maintaining the moral self-image and the diabolical enemy-image. *Journal of Social Issues, 45,* 91–118.

Sartre, J. (1965). *Anti-semite and Jew.* New York: Schocken.

Schachter, S. (1951). Deviation, communication, and rejection. *Journal of Abnormal and Social Psychology, 46,* 190–207.

Schachter, S. (1959). *The psychology of affiliation.* Palo Alto: Stanford University Press.

Schaller, M., & Maass, A. (1989). Illusory correlation and social categorization: Toward an integration of motivational and cognitive factors in stereotype formation. *Journal of Personality and Social Psychology, 56,* 709–721.

Schwartz, S. (1977). Normative influences on altruism. In L. Berkowitz (Ed.), *Advances in experimental social psychology,* Vol. 10. New York: Academic Press.

Sears, D. (1988). Symbolic racism. In P. Katz & D. Taylor (Eds.), *Eliminating racism: Profiles in controversy.* New York: Plenum.

Sears, D. (1993). Symbolic politics: A socio-psychological theory. In S. Iyengar & W. McGuire (Eds.), *Explorations in political psychology.* Durham, NC: Duke University Press.

Sears, D., & Huddy, L. (1993). The symbolic politics of opposition to bilingual education. In S. Worchel & J. Simpson (Eds.), *Conflict between people and groups.* Chicago: Nelson Hall.

Seay, E. (1997, August 15). Graveyard tourism is alive and kicking. *Wall Street Journal,* B1.

Shamir, I. (1982). Israel's role in a changing Middle East. *Foreign Affairs, 60,* 789–801.

Shaw, J., & Condelli, L. (1986). Effects of outcome and basis of power on the powerholder-target relationship. *Personality and Social Psychology Bulletin, 12,* 236–246.

Sherif, M., Harvey, O., White, B., Hood, W., & Sherif, C. (1961). *Intergroup conflict and cooperation: The Robber's Cave experiment.* Norman: University of Oklahoma Press.

Sickels, R. (1972). *Race, marriage and the law.* Albuquerque: University of New Mexico Press.

Sidanius, J. (1993). The psychology of group conflict and dynamics of oppression: A social dominance perspective. In S. Iyengar & W. McGuire (Eds.), *Explorations in political psychology.* Durham, NC: Duke University Press.

Sidanius, J., Feshbach, S., Levin, S., & Pratto, F. (1996). The interface between ethnic and national attachment: Ethnic pluralism or ethnic dominance? Paper presented at Society of Experimental Social Psychology, Sturbridge, MA.

Simmel, G. (1955). *Conflict.* New York: Free Press.

Simon, B., & Brown, R. (1987). Perceived intragroup homogeneity in minority-majority contexts. *Journal of Personality and Social Psychology, 53,* 703–711.

Simonton, D. K. (1986). Presidential personality: Biographical use of the Gough Adjective Checklist. *Journal of Personality and Social Psychology, 51,* 149–160.

Smith, A. (1988). The myth of the modern nation and the myths of nations. *Ethnic and Racial Studies, 11*, 1–26.

Smith, A. (1990). Toward a global culture. In M. Featherstone (Ed.), *Global culture: Nationalism, globalization, and modernity.* London: Sage.

Smith, A. D. (1986). *The ethnic origins of nations.* Oxford: Basil Blackwell.

Smith, E,. & Zarate, M. (1992). Exemplar-based model of social judgement. *Psychological Review, 99*, 3–21.

Smith, T. (1980). Ethnic measurement and identification. *Ethnicity, 7*, 78–95.

Snyder, M., & Swann, W. (1978). Hypothesis-testing process in social interaction. *Journal of Personality and Social Psychology, 36*, 1202–1212.

Spickard, P. (1992). The illogic of American racial categories. In M. Root (Ed.), *Racially mixed people in America.* Newbury Park, CA: Sage.

Sroufe, L. (1985). Attachment classification from the perspective of infant-caregiver relationships and infant temperament. *Child Development, 56*, 1–14.

Stasser, G. (1992). Pooling of unshared information during group discussions. In S. Worchel, W. Wood, & J. Simpson (Eds.), *Group process and productivity.* Newbury Park, CA: Sage.

Stasser, G., & Stewart, J. (1992). Discovery of hidden profiles by decision-making groups: Solving a problem versus making a judgment. *Journal of Personality and Social Psychology, 63*, 426–434.

Stephan, W. (1987). The contact hypothesis in intergroup relations. *Journal of Personality and Social Psychology, 9*, 13–40.

Sumner, W. (1906). *Folkways.* Boston: Ginn.

T'Hart, P., & Kroon, M. (1989, June). Groupthink in context. Paper presented at International Society of Political Psychology, Tel Aviv, Israel.

Tajfel, H. (1970). Experiments in intergroup discrimination. *Science, 223*, 96–102.

Tajfel, H. (1982). *Social identity and intergroup relations.* Cambridge, Eng.: Cambridge University Press.

Tajfel, H., & Turner, J. (1986). The social identity theory of intergroup behavior. In S. Worchel & W. Austin (Eds.), *The psychology of intergroup relations.* Chicago: Nelson Hall.

Taylor, D., & Moghaddam (1987). *Theories of intergroup relations: International social psychological perspectives.* New York: Praeger.

Taylor, S., & Fiske, S. (1975). Point of view and perception of causality. *Journal of Personality and Social Psychology, 32*, 439–445.

Tedeschi, J. (1981). *Impression management theory and social psychological research.* New York: Academic Press.

Thibaut, J. (1968). The development of contractual norms in bargaining replication and variation. *Journal of Conflict Resolution, 12*, 102–112.

Thibaut, J., & Kelley, H. (1959). *The social psychology of groups.* New York: Wiley.

Thigpen, C., & Cleckley, H. (1954). A case of multiple personality. *Journal of Abnormal and Social Psychology, 49*, 135–151.

Thompson, L., Manniz, E., & Bazerman, M. (1988). Group negotiation: Effects of decision role, agenda, and aspiration. *Journal of Personality and Social Psychology, 54*, 86–95.

Thorndike, E. (1913). *The psychology of learning.* New York: Teachers College.

Toland, J. (1993). *Ethnicity and the state.* London: Transaction.

Tonelson, A. (1994). Jettison the policy. *Foreign Policy, 1*, 1–10.

Triandis, H. (1994). Theoretical and methodological approaches to the study of collectivism and individualism. In U. Kim, H. Triandis, C. Kagitcibasi, S. Choi, & G. Yoon (Eds.), *Individualism and collectivism: Theory, methods, and application.* Thousand Oaks, CA: Sage.

Triandis, H. C. (1994). *Culture and social behavior.* New York: McGraw-Hill.

Tuckman, B. (1965). Developmental sequence in small groups. *Psychological Bulletin, 63*, 384–399.

Turner, J. (1975). Social comparison and social identity: Some prospects for intergroup behaviour. *European Journal of Social Psychology, 5*, 5–34.

Turner, J. (1987). *Rediscovering the social group: A self-categorization theory.* London: Blackwell.

Turner, J. (1991). *Social influence.* Milton Keynes: Open University Press.

Van Paag, W. (1986). *The status of Tibet: History, rights, and prospects in international law.* Boulder, CO: Westview.

Von Sturmer, J. (1981, March). Talking with Aborigines. *Australian Institute Aboriginal Studies Newsletter, 15*, 13–30.

Wallach, M., Kogan, N., & Bem, D. (1962). Group influence on individual risk taking. *Journal of Abnormal and Social Psychology, 65*, 75–87.

Wallerstein, I. (1990). Culture as the ideological battleground of the modern world-system. In M. Featherstone (Ed.), *Global culture: Nationalism, globalization, and modernity.* London: Sage.

Waters, M. (1990). *Ethnic options: Choosing identities in America.* Berkeley: University of California Press.

Watson, R. (1973). Investigation into deindividuation using a cross-cultural survey technique. *Journal of Personality and Social Psychology, 25*, 342–345.

Webb, W., & Worchel, P. (1986). Trust and distrust. In S. Worchel & W. Austin (Eds.), *The psychology of intergroup relations.* Chicago: Nelson Hall.

Weber, M. (1947). The sociology of charismatic authority. In H. Gerth & C. Mills (Eds.), *From Max Weber: Essays in sociology.* New York: Oxford University Press.

White, R. (1966). Misperception as a cause of two world wars. *Journal of Social Issues, 22*, 1–9.

Whorf, B. (1956). *Language, thought, and reality: Selected writings of Benjamin Lee Whorf.* New York: Wiley.

Whyte, W. (1956). *The organization man.* New York: Simon and Schuster.

Wilder, D. (1986). Cognitive factors affecting the success of intergroup contact. In S. Worchel & W. Austin (Eds.), *Psychology of intergroup relations.* Chicago: Nelson Hall.

Wilson, E. (1978). *Sociobiology.* Cambridge: Harvard University Press.

Wilson, S. (1992). Face and facework in negotiation. In L. Putnam & M. Roloff (Eds.), *Communication and negotiation.* Newbury Park, CA: Sage.

Winawer-Steiner, H., & Wetzel, H. (1982). German families. In M. McGoldrick et al. (Eds.), *Ethnicity and family therapy.* New York: Guilford.

Wiseman, R., & Koester, J. (1993). *Intercultural communication competence.* Newbury Park, CA; Sage.

Wong, P. (1993, February 24). In search of our roots. *New Zealand Herald*, p. 4 (section 2).

Worchel, S. (1984). The darker side of helping: The social dynamics of helping and cooperation. In D. Bar-Tal, J. Karylowski, & J. Reykowski (Eds.), *The development and maintenance of prosocial behavior.* New York: Plenum.

Worchel, S. (1986). The role of cooperation in reducing intergroup conflict. In S. Worchel & W. Austin (Eds.), *The psychology of intergroup relations.* Chicago: Nelson Hall.

Worchel, S. (1996). Emphasizing the social nature of groups in a developmental framework. In J. Nye & A. Brower (Eds.), *What's social about social cognition?* Thousand Oaks, CA: Sage.

Worchel, S. (1998). A developmental view of the search for group identity. In S. Worchel, J. Morales, D. Paez, & J. Dechamps (Eds.), *Social identity: International perspectives.* London: Sage.

Worchel, S. (1998). The seasons of a group's life. In S. Worchel, J. Morales, D. Paez, & J. Seschamps (Eds.), *Social identity: International perspectives.* London: Sage.

Worchel, S., & Andreoli, V. (1978). Facilitation of social interaction through deindividuation of the target. *Journal of Personality and Social Psychology, 36*, 549–557.

Worchel, S., & Arnold, S. (1973). The effects of censorship and attractiveness of the censor on attitude change. *Journal of Experimental Social Psychology, 9*, 365–377.

Worchel, S., Arnold, S., & Baker, M. (1975). The effect of censorship on attitude change: The influence of censor and communication characteristics. *Journal of Applied Social Psychology, 5*, 227–239.

Worchel, S., Axsom, D., Ferris, F., Samaha, G., & Shwiezer, S. (1978). Factors determining the effect of intergroup cooperation on intergroup attraction. *Journal of Conflict Resolution, 22*, 429–439.

Worchel, S., Cooper, J., & Goethals, G. (1991). *Understanding social psychology*, 5th ed. Pacific Grove, CA: Brooks Cole.

Worchel, S., & Coutant, D. (1997). The tangled web of loyalty: Nationalism, patriotism, and ethnocentrism. In D. Bar-Tal & E. Staub (Eds.), *Patriotism in the lives of individuals and nations*. Chicago: Nelson Hall.

Worchel, S., Coutant-Sassic, D., & Grossman, M. (1992). A developmental approach to group dynamics: A model and illustrative research. In S. Worchel, W. Wood, & J. Simpson (Eds.), *Group process and productivity*. Newbury Park, CA: Sage.

Worchel, S,. Coutant-Sassic, D., & Grossman, M. (1992). A model of group development and independence. In S. Worchel, W. Wood, & J. Simpson (Eds.), *Group process and productivity*. Newbury Park, CA: Sage.

Worchel, S., Coutant-Sassic, D., & Wong, F. (1993). Toward a more balanced view of conflict: There is a positive side. In S. Worchel & J. Simpson (Eds.), *Conflict between people and groups: Causes, processes and resolutions*. Chicago: Nelson Hall.

Worchel, S., Grossman, M., & Coutant, D. (1993). Minority influence in the group context: How group factors affect when the minority will be influential. In S. Moscovici, A. Mucchi-Faina, & A. Maass (Eds.), *Minority Influence*. Chicago: Nelson Hall.

Worchel, S., & Rothgerber, H. (1997). Changing the stereotype of the stereotype. In R. Spears, P. Oakes, N. Ellemers, & S. A. Haslam (Eds.), *The social psychology of stereotyping and group life*. Oxford: Blackwell.

Wright, S., Taylor, D., & Moghaddam, F. (1990). Responding to membership in a disadvantaged group: From acceptance to collective protest. *Journal of Personality and Social Psychology, 58*, 994–1003.

Yzerbyt, V., & Schadron, G. (1994). Stereotypes et jugement social. In R. Bourhis & J. Leyens (Eds.), *Stereotypes, discrimination et relations entre groupes cognition sociale*. Bruxelles: Mardaga.

Zajonc, R. (1968). Attitudinal effects of mere exposure. *Journal of Personality and Social Psychology, 9*, monograph supplement No. 2.

Zimbardo, P. (1970). The human choice: Individuation, reason and order versus deindividuation, impulse and chaos. *Nebraska Symposium on Motivation*. Lincoln: University of Nebraska Press.

Zuckerman, M. (1985). Some dubious premises in research and theory on racial differences. *American Psychologist, 45*, 1297–1303.

Credits

Reading 1.1: Paul Edward Parker, "New England tribes look for identity" from *The Bryan-College Station Eagle* (May 25, 1997). Reprinted with the permission of the Providence Journal-Bulletin .

Reading 1.2: Helen O'Neill, "Descendant digs to flesh out tale of 'first' black family in America" from *Portland Press Herald* (February 9, 1998). Reprinted with the permission of the Associated Press.

Reading 1.3: "In search of our roots" from *The New Zealand Herald)* (February 24, 1993). Copyright © 1993. Reprinted by permission.

Reading 2.1: "Multiracial Americans rally to add new racial category to census" from *The Bryan-College Station Eagle* (July 21, 1996). Reprinted with the permission of the Associated Press.

Reading 2.2: Arlene Levinson, "What kind of American are you?" from *The Bryan-College Station Eagle* (September 28, 1997). Reprinted with the permission of the Associated Press.

Reading 2.3: Pat Beall, " 'New' Indian gives rise to tribal ire" from *The Wall Street Journal* (October 30, 1996). Copyright © 1996 by Dow Jones & Company. Reprinted with the permission of *The Wall Street Journal.*

Reading 3.1: Eduardo Montes, "A Hispanic by any other name would be preferable" from *The Bryan-College Station Eagle* (April 27, 1997). Reprinted with the permission of the Associated Press.

Reading 3.2: Verna Dobnik, "Frenchman fulfills dream of photographing Jewish icons" from *The Bryan-College Station Eagle* (September 22, 1996). Reprinted with the permission of the Associated Press.

Reading 3.3: David Foster, "Black activists: Frenzy over O.J.'s fall feeds racial stereotypes" from *The Bryan-College Station Eagle* (June 24, 1994). Reprinted with the permission of the Associated Press.

Reading 4.1: "Murders stun Solingen" from *Waikato Times* (June 1, 1993). Copyright © 1993. Reprinted with the permission of the Associated Press.

Reading 4.2: "Jewish influence a mystery" from *The New Zealand Herald* (February 25, 1993). Copyright © 1993. Reprinted by permission.

Reading 4.3: "Chinese in Indonesia fear officials won't protect them from attacks" from *Portland Press Herald* (February 9, 1998). Reprinted with the permission of the Associated Press.

Reading 5.1: Roger Thurow, "Can the Balkans heal? A tale from Croatia shows what it'll take" from *The Wall Street Journal* (September 23, 1994). Copyright © 1994 by Dow Jones & Company. Reprinted with the permission of *The Wall Street Journal.*

Reading 5.2: Clarence Page, "Black-Jewish relations still tense" from *The Bryan-College Station Eagle* (June 1, 1996). Reprinted with the permission of Tribune Media Services.

Reading 5.3: Michelle Faul, "Nigerian ethnic divisions widen" from *The Bryan-College Station Eagle* (November 21, 1994). Reprinted with the permission of the Associated Press.

Reading 6.1: Tom Laceky, "A city cries, 'Not in our town!' " from *The Bryan-College Station Eagle* (February 20, 1994). Reprinted with the permission of the Associated Press.

Reading 6.2: "Two workers fired for speaking Spanish" from *The Bryan-College Station Eagle* (August 15, 1997). Reprinted with the permission of the Associated Press.

Reading 6.3: Isabel Wilkerson, "Interracial Marriage Rises, Acceptance Lags" from *The New York Times* (December 2, 1991). Copyright © 1991 by The New York Times Company. Reprinted with the permission of *The New York Times.*

Reading 7.1: Sue Leeman, "World unites in fight against AIDS" from *The Bryan-College Station Eagle* (December 2, 1994). Reprinted with the permission of the Associated Press.

Reading 7.2: Jason L. Riley, "The quota culture's slow demise: Return to self-reliance" from *The Wall Street Journal* (August 13, 1997). Copyright © 1997 by Dow Jones & Company. Reprinted with the permission of *The Wall Street Journal.*

Reading 7.3: Vincent Carroll, "The quota culture's slow demise: We're all 'disadvantaged' now" from *The Wall Street Journal* (August 13, 1997). Copyright © 1997 by Dow Jones & Company. Reprinted with the permission of *The Wall Street Journal.*

Reading 8.1: "UN report on death camps" from *Waikato Times* (March 3, 1993). Copyright © 1993. Reprinted with the permission of the Associated Press.

Reading 8.2: Mark Fritz, "French flex muscles in Rwanda" from *The Bryan-College Station Eagle* (June 24, 1994). Reprinted with the permission of the Associated Press.

Reading 8.3: Ronald Steel, "Internationalism as a complement to nationalism" from *The International Herald Tribune* (June 8, 1995). Copyright © 1995. Reprinted by permission.

Name Index

Abacha, Sani, 146
Abelson, R., 42
Abramson, L., 153
Acton, J. E. E. D., 97
Adorno, L., 47, 74
Ainsworth, M., 151
Akbar, Naim, 177
Alba, Richard D., 175
Alexander the Great, 95
Allen, Richard, 54
Allport, Floyd, 121
Allport, G., 164
Amir, Y., 165
Anastasio, P., 198
Andreoli, V., 92
Argyle, Michael, 135, 152
Arnold, S., 147, 157
Aronson, E., 42, 166
Arps, K., 217
Asch, S., 121
Asch, Solomon, 91
Ashkenasi, Abraham, 149, 151
Austin, W., 154
Axsom, D., 132

Bacall, Lauren, 83
Bachman, B., 198
Baker, M., 147
Baladur, Edouard, 239
Banaji, M., 64
Bandura, A., 75, 151
Banijska, Stara, 143
Banton, M., 8, 14, 20, 230
Bar-Tal, Daniel, 67, 68, 69, 73, 79, 180
Barth, F., 16
Bass, Bernard, 94
Bauman, Z., 43
Baumeister, R., 3, 119
Bazerman, M., 218
Beal, P., 23
Beaman, A., 217

Bean, Clive, 112, 113
Bem, D., 100, 215, 246
Beresford, John, 52
Berman, Paul, 69, 77, 129
Berry, John, 202
Bettelheim, B., 73
Bhagat, R., 188
Bihozzagara, Jacques, 239
Billig, Michael, 11
Block, J., 150
Blondel, J., 95
Bombeck, Erma, 251
Bomell, Anne, 29–30
Bond, M., 50
Botula, Mike, 84
Boulding, K., 109
Boutros Boutros-Ghali, 259
Braly, K., 66
Brehm, J., 157
Brewer, M., 124, 164
Brewer, Marilyn, 48
Brezhnev, Leonid, 185
Bridgman, 166
Brislin, R., 188
Bronfman, Edgar, Jr., 83
Bronfman, Edgar, M., 84, 145
Brown, D., 11, 178, 181, 187, 211
Brown, R., 63, 189
Burton, J., 192
Bush, G., 95, 107, 138, 170
Buyoya, Pierre, 258

Calder, P., 23
Caldwell, M., 187
Campbell, D., 62, 135
Campbell, J., 75
Cantor, N., 66
Cantril, Hadley, 120
Cardenas, Blandino, 81
Carnevale, P., 218
Carroll, Vincent, 208

Subject Index